W9-APC-851

Why Do You Need this New Edition?

We have always believed in the centrality of ethics to the study of media. And now, more than ever, we are bombarded with cases that force us to question the decisions of individuals and organizations. The real decisions these individuals and organizations have made both impact and reflect the values of our society. We believe that ethical decision making matters, and that it is possible in almost every situation you are likely to encounter. With over 35 new high-profile and highly relevant cases, the eighth edition of *Media Ethics* gives you the tools necessary to think critically about the issues our society faces and to make sound ethical decisions of your own. What follows are just some of the new features you will find only in the eighth edition:

- The **Introduction** includes a new section on Islamic ethics, offering another philosophy with which to evaluate ethical decision making.
- **Part 1** *(News)* features new cases on the obesity epidemic, the humanitarian tragedy in Darfur, and the Danish Muhammad cartoon controversy. This section also introduces a discussion of online journalism and a code of ethics for blogging.
- **Part 2** *(Advertising)* has been restructured to better address the issues confronting the advertising industry today. This section includes new cases on cause-related marketing and social responsibility, the Dove-Axe-Unilever controversies, and advertising aimed at particular ethnic groups. These new cases join updated cases on Channel One, direct-to-consumer pharmaceutical advertising, and guerilla advertising.

- **Part 3** *(Public Relations)* provides new cases on the American Red Cross and Hurricane Katrina relief; the Abramoff lobbying scandal; and the Sago mine disaster. This section also includes updated discussions of digital tools such as corporate blogs, video news releases, and websites.
- **Part 4** *(Entertainment)* presents new cases on comics, docudrama, video games, disability programming and stereotyping, and the depiction of sexual violence on cable television.
- The one-of-a-kind **media ethics website** for students and instructors (www.ablongman.com/christians8e) has been thoroughly updated and includes:
  - An extensive collection of annotated streaming video clips related to each part of the book
  - A media ethics film library for instructors that includes annotations and downloadable scenes from your favorite motion pictures
  - Video and audio podcasts from the authors that include section overviews, commentary on cases in the book, and emerging issues
  - New supplemental material for each case in the book
  - New and expanded online quizzes, in-class exercises, annotated websites, glossary terms, sample syllabi, recommended readings, annotated bibliography, PPTs, cartoons, and other original illustrations
  - Cases from previous editions of the book

MEDIA ETHICS

CASES AND MORAL REASONING

EIGHTH EDITION

Clifford G. Christians
University of Illinois

Mark Fackler
Calvin College

Kathy Brittain McKee
Berry College

Peggy J. Kreshel
University of Georgia

Robert H. Woods, Jr.
Spring Arbor University

PEARSON

Boston   New York   San Francisco
Mexico City   Montreal   Toronto   London   Madrid   Munich   Paris
Hong Kong   Singapore   Tokyo   Cape Town   Sydney

Dedicated to the memory of our co-author through seven editions,
our colleague and friend, Dr. Kim Brewer Rotzoll,
August 21, 1935–November 4, 2003

Acquisitions Editor: Jeanne Zalesky
Project Manager: Lisa Sussman
Marketing Manager: Suzan Czajkowski
Production Editor: Pat Torelli
Editorial Production Service: Modern Graphics, Inc.

Manufacturing Buyer: JoAnne Sweeney
Electronic Composition: Modern Graphics, Inc.
Interior Design: Modern Graphics, Inc.
Cover Designer: Joel Gendron

For related titles and support materials, visit our online catalog at www.ablongman.com.

Copyright © 2009, 2005, 2001 Pearson Education, Inc.

All rights reserved. No part of the material protected by this copyright notice may be reproduced or utilized in any form or by any means, electronic or mechanical, including photocopying, recording, or by any information storage and retrieval system, without written permission from the copyright owner.

To obtain permission(s) to use material from this work, please submit a written request to Allyn and Bacon, Permissions Department, 501 Boylston Street, Suite 900, Boston, MA 02116 or fax your request to 617-671-2290.

Between the time website information is gathered and then published, it is not unusual for some sites to have closed. Also, the transcription of URLs can result in typographical errors. The publisher would appreciate notification where these errors occur so that they may be corrected in subsequent editions.

ISBN-13: 978-0-205-57970-9   ISBN-10: 0-205-57970-1

Library of Congress Cataloging-in-Publication Data

Media ethics : cases and moral reasoning / Clifford G. Christians ... [et al.].-- 8th ed.
    p. cm.
Includes bibliographical references and index.
ISBN-13: 978-0-205-57970-9
ISBN-10: 0-205-57970-1
1. Mass media--Moral and ethical aspects. I. Christians, Clifford G.
P94.M36 2009
170--dc22

2008015150

Printed in the United States of America

10 9 8 7 6 5 4 3 2   RRD-VA   12   11   10   09   08

Contents

v

Preface

Media ethics has been traveling a rough road at the junction of theory and practice. Occasionally, textbooks will include an ethics chapter but will not integrate it with the workaday problems that follow. Principle and practice do not merge well in such endeavors, nor in our daily actions. The rush of events forces us to make ethical decisions by reflex more than by reflection, like drivers wheeling around potholes, mindful that a blowout sends them into a courtroom at one ditch and into public scorn at the other. Some books that focus on journalism ethics will be entirely case-driven for lack of theoretical substance. Some few others, clearly, are books we respect and learn from. We hope this one sits on shelves next to them.

Two different mind-sets are involved in press ethics; thus, fusion becomes difficult. Whereas the study of ethics requires deliberation, careful distinctions, and extended discussion, the newsroom tends to emphasize toughness and the ability to make quick decisions in the face of daily crises. Similarly, advertising and public relations professionals are expected to be competitive and enterprising, entertainment writers and producers to value skepticism, confident independence, and hot blood. Therefore, for the teaching of ethics to be worthwhile, the critical capacity must emerge in which reasoning processes remain paramount. Yet executives of media firms value people of action, those who produce volumes of work in a high-pressure environment. If media ethics is to gain recognition, the gap between daily media practice and the serious consideration of ethics must be bridged creatively.

Like the previous editions, this revision attempts to integrate ethics and media situations through case studies and commentaries. Communication is a practice-oriented field: Reporters for daily newspapers tend to work with episodes, typically pursuing one story after another as it happens; advertisers ordinarily deal with accounts and design campaigns for specific products; public relations professionals advocate a specific cause; and actors and writers move from program to program. Because communication is case-oriented, media ethics would be uninteresting and abstract unless it addressed practical experiences. However, media ethics ought to be more than a description of professional challenges. Therefore, in this book we analyze cases and connect them with the ethical guidelines set forth in the Introduction. The reader will be prodded and stimulated to think ethically. Considering situations from a systematic framework advances our problem-solving capacity. That, in turn, prevents us from treating each case independently or having to reinvent the wheel. The commentaries pinpoint some critical issues and introduce enough salient material to aid in resolving the case responsibly. Much of this project's inspiration came from Robert Veatch's award-winning *Case Studies in Medical Ethics*, published in 1977 by the Harvard University Press. Veatch mixed his commentaries, and we have followed suit—raising questions for further reflection in some, introducing relevant ethical theories in others, and pushing toward closure where doing so seems appropriate.

All the cases are taken from actual experiences or have been created to illustrate the actual ethical pressures faced by professionals. In order to protect anonymity and increase clarity, names and places have been changed in many of them. Though our adjustments do not make these cases timeless, they help to prevent them from becoming prematurely dated and shopworn. We attempted to find ongoing issues that occur often in ordinary media practice and did not select only exotic, once-in-a-lifetime encounters. In situations based on court records or in instances of historic significance where real names aid in the analysis, the cases have not been modified.

As the integration of theory and practice in ethics is important, so is the integration of news with other aspects of the information system. The four sections of this book reflect the four major media functions: reporting, persuading, representing, and entertaining. Because we want readers to do ethics rather than puzzle over their immediate experience, we have chosen a broad range of media situations. Many times when similar issues are encountered in several phases of the communication process, new insights can be gained and sharper perspectives result. Issues such as deception, economic temptation, and sensationalism, for example, are common in reporting, advertising, public relations, and entertainment. The issue of how violence is handled can be explored in reporting as well as in entertainment. Stereotyping is deep seated and pervasive in every form of public communication; cases dealing with this issue occur in all four sections. Moreover, the wider spectrum of this book allows specialists in one medium—television, newspapers, or magazines, for example—to investigate that medium across all its uses. Often practitioners of journalism, advertising, public relations, and entertainment are part of the same corporation and encounter other media areas indirectly in their work. The distinctions among them will blur as convergent technologies and integration of the industry accelerate.

The Potter Box is included in the Introduction as a technique for uncovering the important steps in moral reasoning. It is a model of social ethics, in harmony with our overall concern in this volume for social responsibility. It can be used for analyzing each case and reaching responsible conclusions. (Instructors who wish to use a video lecture to explain the Potter Box will find it on the book's website at www.ablongman.com/christians8e.) This book is intended for use as a classroom text or in workshops for professionals. We are especially eager to have communication educators and practitioners read and think their way through this textbook on their own. Whether using this volume as a text or for personal reading, the Introduction can be employed flexibly. Under normal circumstances, we recommend that the Potter Box be studied first and the theoretical foundations given in the Introduction be considered thoroughly before readers proceed to the cases. However, readers can fruitfully start elsewhere in the book with a chapter of their own choosing and return later to the Introduction for the theoretical perspective.

Whether used in an instructional setting or not, the book has two primary goals. First, it seeks to develop analytical skills. Ethical appraisals are often disputed; further training and study can improve the debate and help weaken rationalizations. Advancement in media ethics requires more attention to evidence, more skill in valid argument, and more patience with complexity. Without explicit procedures, as Edward R. Murrow reportedly complained, "What is called thinking is often merely a rearranging of our prejudices."

Second, this book aims to improve ethical awareness. Often the ethical dimension goes unrecognized. The authors are not content merely to exercise the intellect; they believe that the moral imagination must be stimulated until real human beings and their welfare become central. Surprising as it may seem, improving ethical awareness is in many ways more elusive than honing analytical skills. In stark cases, such as the Janet Cooke affair, we realize instantly the cheating and deception involved.[1] Cleverly fabricating the story of an 8-year-old heroin addict for *The Washington Post* is outrageous and unacceptable by everyone's standards. But often the ethical issues escape our notice. What about the stolen voice mail in Case 13? The legal questions about taping are relatively clear, but what is explicitly unethical about using this undercover strategy to report on immoral behavior? Or naming a shoplifter, printing photographs of grieving parents whose children just died in a fire, writing about the sexual escapades of a senator, exposing a prominent right-to-lifer concealing an abortion, or revealing secret information about government policy that contradicts public statements? The ethical issues here are not always self-evident; thus, actual and hypothetical cases become a primary tool for firing up the moral imagination.

Improving analytical skills and raising moral sensitivity are lifelong endeavors that involve many facets of human behavior. Studied conscientiously, the terms, arguments, and principles introduced in these chapters also may improve the quality of discourse in the larger area of applied ethics. We trust that using the Potter Box model for the seventy-seven cases in this volume will aid in building a conceptual apparatus that facilitates the growth of media ethics over time.

We are fully aware of the criticism from various areas of radical social science that ethics is a euphemism for playing mental games while the status quo remains intact. That criticism warrants more discussion than this Preface permits, but it should be noted that we find this charge too indiscriminate. Much of the current work in professional ethics is largely a matter of semantics and isolated incidents, but this volume does not belong to that class. The social ethics we advocate challenges the organizational structures. Many of the commentaries—and even entire chapters—probe directly into significant institutional issues. Certainly, that is the cumulative effect also. Reading the volume through in its entirety brings into focus substantive questions about economics, management and bureaucracy, allocation of resources, the press's raison d'être, and distributive justice. We have employed the case-and-commentary format for its instructional benefits. It allows us to separate issues into their understandable dimensions without slipping into small problems of no consequence on the one hand, yet not encouraging a complete dissolution of the democratic order on the other.

We recognize also that today's crusading relativism is a formidable challenge to such efforts. Moral commitments are crumbling beneath our feet. Cultural diversity has hoodwinked us into ethical relativity. Divine-command theories and metaphysical foundations for norms are problematic in a secular age on the far side of Darwin, Freud, and Einstein. Many academics believe truth claims are impossible after Jacques Derrida and Michel Foucault. In a world of sliding signifiers and normlessness, ethical principles seem to carry little resonance. Though this textbook is not an appropriate place for coming to grips with the complexities of relativism, we believe that the idea of normative principles can be successfully defended in contemporary terms. For example, Chapter 6 of *Good News: Social Ethics and the Press*, by Clifford Christians, John Ferré, and Mark Fackler (Oxford University Press, 1993) develops such a defense. Two other books construct normative models also: Edmund Lambeth's *Committed Journalism: An Ethic for the Profession* (Indiana University Press, 2d ed., 1992) and John C. Merrill's *Journalism Ethics: Philosophical Foundations for News Media* (New York: St. Martin's Press, 1997). Deni Elliott has demonstrated in empirical terms that, without shared values, the practice of everyday journalism is impossible. In other words, although reporters and editors are pluralists, they are not relativists.[2]

Serious students will recognize that we maintain the traditional distinction between ethics and morality. Ethics we understand as the liberal arts discipline that appraises voluntary human conduct insofar as it can be judged right or wrong in reference to determinative principles. The original meaning of *ethos* (Greek) was "sent," "haunt," "abode," "accustomed dwelling place," that is, the place from which we start out, the "home base." From *ethos* is derived *ethikos*, meaning "of or for morals." In the Greek philosophical tradition, this word came to stand for the systematic study of the principles that ought to underlie behavior.

On the other hand, *morality* is of Latin origin. The Latin noun *mos* (pl. *mores*) and the adjective *moralis* signify a way, manner, or customary behavior. The Romans had no word that is the exact equivalent of Greek ethos. Unlike the Greeks, they paid more attention to the inner disposition, the hidden roots of the conduct, the basic principles of behavior, than they did to its external pattern. This perspective is in accord with the Roman genius for order, arrangement, and organization and with its generally unphilosophical bent of mind. The Romans looked to the outside more than to the inside. The Latin *mores* has come into the English language without modification (meaning "folkways, how people behave"). However, in English usage, the ethics of a people are not the same as their morality. Morality refers to practice and ethics to a basic system of principles.

We incurred many debts while preparing this volume. The McCormick Foundation generously supported our original research into ethical dilemmas among media professionals; many of the cases and the questions surrounding them emerged from this research. Ralph Potter encouraged our adaptation of his social ethics model. Louis Hodges wrote the initial draft for the commentary in Case 21. Eve Munson wrote the initial draft for Case 5 and gathered material for several more. Paul and Stephanie Christians and Kevin Healey wrote cases and updated them; their research was invaluable. Mary Hulst wrote Case 15. Jackie Ayrault gathered information for many of the advertising cases. Enbar Toledano gathered information and was the primary author of Cases 27, 28, 29 and 34. Their contributions are very much appreciated. Our thanks to Eric Beach for Case 65, Christopher Smit and Lisa Kosinski for Case 69, Peggy Goetz for Case 72, and Ted Fackler for Case 77. Carol Pardun thoughtfully responded to many cases in Part 3. Jay Van Hook and John Ferré edited the Introduction along with other chapters. Diane Weddington recommended the Potter Box as the organizing idea and wrote the original draft applying it to communications. Several teachers, students, and professionals who used the earlier editions provided worthwhile suggestions which we have incorporated. The following individuals reviewed the manuscript and provided helpful suggestions: John J. Breslin, Iona College; Lyombe Eko, University of Iowa; Karen C. Pitcher, Eckerd College; and Michael P. Savoie, Valdosta State University. The authors also thank the following Spring Arbor University students enrolled in the Masters of Communication program who worked as research assistants on the companion website: Christy Mesaros-Winckles, Tanja N. Morgan, Constance A. Britner, Linda A. Libert, Jillian W. Moller, and Timothy W. Ross.

We absolve these friends of all responsibility for the weaknesses that remain.

Clifford G. Christians
Mark Fackler
Kathy Brittain McKee
Peggy J. Kreshel
Robert H. Woods, Jr.

NOTES

1. For a thoughtful analysis of this historic case, see Lewis H. Lapham, "Gilding the News," *Harper's*, July 1981, pp. 31–39.
2. Deni Elliott, "All Is Not Relative: Essential Shared Values and the Press," *Journal of Mass Media Ethics* 3:1 (1988): pp. 28–32.

About the Authors

Clifford G. Christians is Director of the Institute of Communications Research, a Charles H. Sandage Distinguished Professor, Research Professor of Communications at the University of Illinois, Urbana–Champaign, and also a Professor of Journalism and a Professor of Media Studies. He has a B.A. in classics, a B.D. and Th.M. in theology, an M.A. in sociolinguistics from the University of Southern California, and a Ph.D. in communications from the University of Illinois. He has been a visiting scholar in philosophical ethics at Princeton University and in social ethics at the University of Chicago and a PEW scholar at Oxford University. He is a co-author of *Responsibility in Mass Communication; Jacques Ellul: Interpretive Essays; Good News: Social Ethics and the Press; Communication; Ethics and Universal Values; Moral Engagement in Public Life: Theorists for Contemporary Ethics;* and *The Handbook of Mass Media Ethics.*

Mark Fackler is Professor of Communications at Calvin College, Grand Rapids, Michigan. He holds an A.B. in philosophy, an M.A. in communications, an M.A. in theology, and a Ph.D. in communications from the University of Illinois. He has been a Hoover Fellow at the European Center for Ethics in Leuven, Belgium, and a guest lecturer in press ethics at Makerere University, Kampala. He teaches regularly in Nairobi, Kenya. He is co-author of *Good News: Social Ethics and the Press.*

Kathy Brittain McKee is Associate Provost and Professor of Communication at Berry College, Rome, Georgia. She has a B.A. in communication and religion/philosophy from Shorter College and an M.A. in journalism and a Ph.D. in mass communication from the Grady College of Journalism and Mass Communication at the University of Georgia. She is co-author of *Applied Public Relations* and has published journal articles and book chapters in media ethics, visual imagery, communication pedagogy, and student-press regulation.

Peggy J. Kreshel is an Associate Professor of Advertising at the Grady College of Journalism and Mass Communication at the University of Georgia. She is an active affiliate faculty member of the Institute for Women's Studies and a member of the Teaching Academy at the university. She earned an undergraduate degree in advertising and psychology and a master's degree in mass communication at the University of Nebraska–Lincoln. Her Ph.D. is from the Institute of Communication Research at the University of Illinois at Urbana–Champaign. Her research areas are focused on feminist media studies, the professional culture of advertising, and advertising history.

Robert H. Woods, Jr., is Associate Professor of Communication at Spring Arbor University, Spring Arbor, Michigan, where he teaches media ethics and research at the undergraduate and graduate levels. He has a B.A. in communication from the University of New Mexico and an M.A in communication and a Ph.D. in communication from Regent University, Virginia. He also holds a J.D. (Juris Doctor) from Regent University and is licensed to practice law in the Commonwealth of Virginia. He has published journal articles on law, computer-mediated communication, research, and mass media.

Ethical Foundations and Perspectives

The true story out of Liverpool, England, was beyond belief. Two ten-year-old boys skipped school on February 12, went to a shopping mall, and spent the day stealing candy and soft drinks. They hung around a video store and shoplifted cans of modeling paint. In the autumn term, Robert Thompson had missed forty-nine days of school and Jon Venables forty days. February 12 was routine for them, until they carved out their diabolical plan. They lured a two-year-old child away from his mother, dragged and kicked him along a two-and-one-half-mile journey, stoned him with bricks, and smashed his head with a twenty-two-pound iron bar. Police found James Bulger's half-naked body two days later. Thompson and Venables had tied the battered corpse to a railroad track, and a passing train had cut it in two. Forty-two injuries were identified; one of the accused's shoes had left a sole print on James's cheek.

At age ten children can face criminal charges in Britain. But under British law, reporting on the family background and revealing the children's names are prohibited until their trial is completed. Jon and Robert were eleven as their trial began before a twelve-member jury in Preston.[1]

Imagine a British television station honoring British law and reporting on the court proceedings only by reference to Child A and Child B. In contrast, imagine a U.S. newspaper revealing the defendants' names and providing detailed information on their personal histories. As the trial progressed, the question of motive was most troubling. What could drive ten-year-old boys to commit a vicious murder? Are there telltale signs other parents might recognize in their children? As it turned out, both boys were from broken homes, lived in poverty, and were prone to stealing and outbursts of anger. Jon Venables was easily led. A neighbor testified that if anyone told Jon to throw stones at someone, he would do it. When Robert was six, his father ran off with another woman, leaving his twenty-nine-year-old mother to raise seven sons on her own.

Both the British and the U.S. news teams had a rationale for their decisions—the British broadcaster feeling constrained by the law and a foreign newspaper responding to intense reader interest. Is the legal standard the only possible one here? If so, is Britain's domestic standard compelling on the international scene? What if the news directors wanted to act in a morally appropriate manner?

In June 2001, as both turned eighteen, a parole board granted their release from prison, and the same issue emerged once again. To protect the killers against vengeance, both were given new names and passports. The British government forbade the media from disclosing their new names and residences or publishing their photographs. But there were widespread doubts that their anonymity could be preserved. Publishers outside Britain have no legal restrictions against publishing the offenders' photographs and new names.

When a case such as this is presented to a media ethics seminar for discussion, the students usually argue passionately without making much headway. Analysis degenerates into inchoate pleas that eleven-year-old boys deserve mercy or into grandiose appeals to the privilege of the press. Judgments are made on what Henry Aiken calls the evocative, expressive level—that is, with no justifying reasons.[2]

Too often communication ethics follows such a pattern, retreating finally to the law as the only reliable guide. Students and practitioners argue about individual sensational incidents, make case-by-case decisions, and never stop to examine their method of moral reasoning. Instead, a pattern of ethical deliberation should be explicitly outlined in which the relevant considerations can be isolated and given appropriate weight. Those who care about ethics in the media can learn to analyze the stages of decision making, focus on the real levels of conflict, and make defensible ethical decisions. This test case can illustrate how competent moral justification takes place. Moral thinking is a systematic process: A judgment is made and action taken. The British television station concludes that the juvenile defendants ought to be protected and withholds names. What steps are used to reach this decision? How does a paper decide that an action should be taken because it is right or should be avoided because it is wrong? The newspaper in the United States considers it inappropriate to withhold news from its readers and prints the names.

Any single decision involves a host of values that must be sorted out. These values reflect our presuppositions about social life and human nature. To value something means to consider it desirable. Expressions such as "her value system" and "American values" refer to what a woman and a majority of Americans, respectively, estimate or evaluate as worthwhile. We may judge something according to aesthetic values (harmonious, pleasing), professional values (innovative, prompt), logical values (consistent, competent), sociocultural values (thrift, hard work), and moral values (honesty, nonviolence). We often find both positive and negative values underlying our choices, pervading all areas of our behavior and motivating us to react in certain directions.[3]

Newspeople hold several values regarding professional reporting; for example, they prize immediacy, skepticism, and their own independence. In the case of the Liverpool murder, readers, family members, and reporters all value juvenile rights in varying ways. Taken in combination with ethical principles, these values yield a guideline for the television news desk, such as, in the case of the juveniles, to protect their privacy at all costs. The good end, in this instance, is deemed to be guarding a person's right to a fair trial. The means for accomplishing this end is withholding information about the defendants.

Likewise, the U.S. newspaper came to a conclusion rooted in values and based an action on that conclusion. The public has a right to know public news, the newspaper decided; we will print the names and background details. What values prompted this decision? This paper strongly values the professional rule that important information should be distributed without hesitation, that everyone ought to be told the truth. But professional values may be stated in positive or negative terms. In fact, in debates about values, an ethical principle might be invoked to help determine which values are preferable. In the newspaper's case, the moral rule "tell the truth under all conditions" is particularly relevant.

If we do this kind of analysis, we can begin to see how moral reasoning works. We understand better why there can be disagreement over whether to publicize personal details in this case. Is it more important to tell the truth, we ask ourselves, or to preserve privacy? Is there some universal goal that we can all appreciate, such as truthtelling, or do we choose to protect some persons, suppressing the truth in the process? We do ethical analysis by looking for guidelines, and we quickly learn to create an interconnected model: We size up the circumstances, we ask what values motivated the decision, we appeal to a principle, and we choose loyalty to one social group instead of to another. Soon we can engage in conflicts over the crucial junctures of the moral reasoning process rather than argue personal differences over the merits of actual decisions. One disagreement that appears to be at stake here is a conflict between the norm of truthtelling and the norm of protecting the privacy of juvenile defendants. But differing values and loyalties can be identified too.

THE POTTER BOX MODEL OF REASONING

Creative ethical analysis involves several explicit steps. Dr. Ralph Potter of the Harvard Divinity School formulated the model of moral reasoning introduced in our analysis of the Liverpool murder. By using a diagram adapted from Professor Potter (the "Potter Box"), we can dissect this case further (see Figure I.1). The Potter Box introduces four dimensions of moral analysis to aid us in locating those places where most misunderstandings occur.[4] Along these lines we can construct action guides.

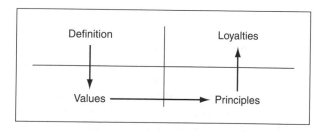

Figure I.1

Note how this box has been used in our analysis: (1) We gave a definition of the situation, citing legal constraints, details of the abduction and murder, and events from the trial. One news outlet printed the names and biographical material only after the court case was completed; the newspaper waited until the trial began, but then decided it was free to make news available to its readers that was already available to it. In this case, they chose differently. (2) We then asked: Why? We have described the values that might have been the most important. The British broadcaster valued legal orderliness. For the U.S. newspaper, the operating professional value was not to suppress news. Its London correspondent had received anonymous information on the assailants shortly after James Bulger was killed. Presumably, the victim's family and supporters wanted it known that Thompson and Venables were conniving, mean-spirited, and ruthless—not mentally deranged. The newspaper completed its investigation by the time the trial began and followed the newsroom value of publishing without delay. But these overriding values may not exhaust all the possibilities. We could have stressed that public persons—in this case, the juvenile defendants—must be reported consistently in news dissemination or readers and viewers will not trust the media's integrity in other situations. American newspaper readers may not make fair trials a supreme value or see any relevance in the fact the murderers were ten years old. A professional value regarding the news flow may be interpreted as less than humane. Each value influences our discourse and reasoning on moral questions. (3) We named at least two ethical principles, and we could have listed more. The television station concluded that the principle of other-regarding care meant protecting the victim's right to privacy. The newspaper invoked truthtelling as an ethical imperative. But other principles could have been summoned: Do the greatest good for the greatest number, even if innocent people such as the murderers' families might be harmed. The television station did not broadcast the names, even at the risk of losing some credibility. The news-hungry may conclude that the station is not competent enough to obtain these details. (4) From the outset, a conflict of loyalties is evident. The station claimed to act sympathetically toward the juvenile offenders; the newspaper insisted it was acting out of sympathy to its readership in general.

Moving from one quadrant to the next, we finally construct our action guides. But the problems can be examined in more depth: Conceive of the box as a circle and go one step further. This time, concentrate on the ethical principles. Next time in the cycle, focus on the definition of loyalties. If the major source of disagreement is over professional values, for example, concentrate on that area the second time around. Often we value certain things without thinking about them; debating them with those who are not easily convinced will make us more critical of ourselves in the positive sense. The newspaper valued release of information, and properly so. But was that an absolute, overriding all other considerations? Our professional values are often honestly held, but having them periodically challenged leads to maturity. In such a process of clarification and redefinition, each element can be addressed in greater detail, and then the deeper insight can be connected to the other quadrants.

The matter of choosing loyalties usually needs the closest scrutiny. The Potter Box is a model for social ethics and consequently forces us to articulate precisely where our loyalties lie as we make a final judgment or adopt a particular policy. And in this domain we tend to beguile ourselves very quickly.

Examine the station's decision once again: Protect juveniles in court; publish no names or background data. Who was the staff thinking about when they made that decision? Perhaps they were considering only themselves. They say they did not wish to increase the suffering of the accused and the grief of their families. They claim they did not want to inflict pain. They contend they did not want to lead people to label the defendants or to become overly involved in the motivations for their behavior. They seem to be saying that they could not live with their conscience if they were to broadcast the news. But, on additional reflection, their loyalties actually may be different. Is the news team really protecting the juveniles or protecting themselves? Certainly, not reporting names is a means to an end, but the end could be their private comfort. The staff members appear to be interested in a gain for society. They appear to protect the trial process, maximizing the defendants' privacy and minimizing scandalous gossip. The crucial question, however, must be faced once more: For whom did they do all this? If we do not return to the top right-hand quadrant of the diagram and inquire more deeply where their allegiances lie—for whom they did it—we have not used the Potter Box adequately.

Consider the newspaper's decision in the same manner: Tell the truth; print the names. If the paper does not withhold juvenile names in a domestic trial, why should it make an exception for one overseas? Will exceptions be necessary again and again until the paper's credibility is ended? The newspaper's readers have certain expectations; the staff seems to be asking if such expectations should be met. But, in responding to a short-term expectation, could its decision undermine the paper's overall credibility? Has the newspaper's long-range ability to contribute to society been damaged? What is more important: the welfare of the readers or the welfare of those involved in the crime?

In the initial analysis, the newspaper did not seem to be concerned for the juvenile offenders. Its imperative was to tell the truth or lose the trust of advertisers, readers, and employees. But maybe this newspaper's loyalties to its readers actually can benefit both the victim's and criminals' families. With accurate details, those directly involved in the tragedy could become more than objects of curiosity. The truth of this devastating event finally may outweigh idle speculation about Venables and Thompson and cool the gossip about a mother not watching her two-year-old closely enough or mall security guards inattentive to detail. Important issues such as these are encountered and clarified when the loyalty quadrant is considered thoroughly, either in the first round of decision making or later in more intensive analysis.

Choosing loyalties is an extremely significant step in the process of making moral decisions. As the preceding paragraphs indicate, taking this quadrant seriously does not in itself eliminate disagreements. In this arena, honest disputes may occur over who should benefit from a decision. For media personnel who are sincere about serving society, choices must be made among various segments of that society: subscribers and viewers, sources of information, politicians, ethnic minorities, children, law enforcement personnel, judges and lawyers, and so forth. Our calculations need to consider that flesh-and-blood people known by name ought not be sacrificed for euphemisms and abstractions such as the public, clients, audience, or market. In any case, the Potter Box is an exercise in social ethics that does not permit the luxury of merely playing mental games. Conclusions must be worked out in the rough and tumble of social realities. As developed in the following section, ethical principles are crucial in the overall process of reaching a justified conclusion. However, in the pursuit of socially responsible media, clarity regarding ultimate loyalties is of paramount importance.

In addition to considering each step carefully, the Potter Box must be seen as a circle, an organic whole (see Figure I.2). It is not merely a random set of isolated questions, but a linked system. We have moved from first impressions to explaining various aspects of what happened in this case. Each news outlet declared its loyalties. The Potter Box gives us a mechanism to further assess the values and principles in this case. But the Potter Box also can be used to adopt policy guidelines that will govern future behavior in similar circumstances. On the basis of this episode, the station or the newspaper might decide to alter its policy regarding names and background data. At least the editorial staffs could be made aware that there is a system for reaching a comprehensive policy regarding similar events. Through the four steps, media institutions can establish or strengthen their policy regarding anonymous sources, suicide coverage, confidentiality, trial coverage, deception in advertising, and so forth.

But we are still left with the initial question: Which news team made the right decision? This returns us to a central inquiry raised by this exercise: Is there a universal ground for making ethical decisions, an overarching theory from

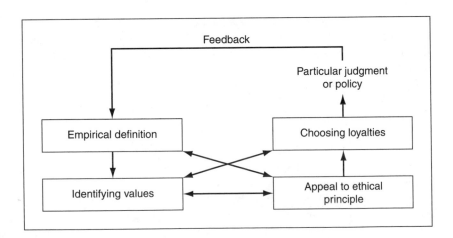

Figure I.2

which we can choose among competing alternatives? Or is ethical decision making a process of adjusting to the mores and commitments of a given community? Potter's circular model, with its potential for continual expansion, takes both aspects seriously (see Figure I.3). Community mores are accounted for when we elaborate in step two on the values people hold and when we identify our loyalties before making a final choice. But these sociological matters are tempered in the Potter Box by an appeal to an explicit ethical principle. Without such an appeal, a conclusion is not considered morally justified. Unfortunately, under the press of circumstances, the media tend to move directly into action from quadrant two, ignoring three and four.

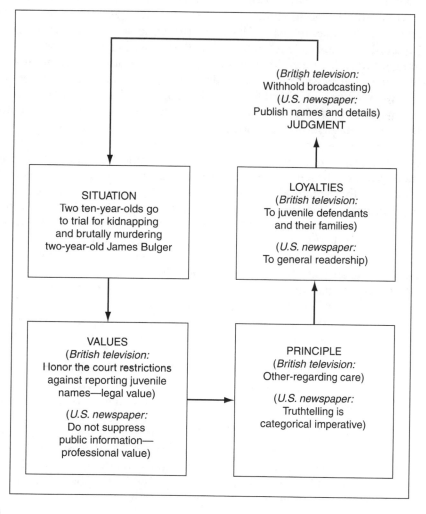

Figure I.3

In this situation, both the station and the newspaper make a defensible decision in terms of their newsroom values. In this particular case, both values can be defended; neither is outrageous. Both news staffs aim toward a social value that is widely held in Western society. Often one media company will adopt a morally enlightened option, and the other will choose to break promises, cheat, and deceive. Such immoral behavior cannot be justified through the Potter Box cycle. Fortunately, there are situations in which different values are themselves credible. In such instances, one professional value can compete legitimately with another using the Potter Box process. Then the values can be resolved in quadrant three or four.

When competing values all seem appropriate in quadrant two, resolution usually occurs in step three while working on ethical theory. Typically, one news operation appeals to an explicit ethical principle and the other has made a decision based on a professional value after step two. But in this case, two different ethical theories are relevant. The agape principle of other-regarding care insists on protecting the juvenile offenders by withholding personal information until they are convicted by a jury. Telling the truth is a categorical imperative with Kant. In this case, the newspaper has made every reasonable effort to verify the facts. When two different ethical theories both appear to be relevant, as in this situation, conflicts can be addressed in terms of the adequacy of the theories themselves and through metaphysics or theology.[5]

In resolving this case, the appropriate ethical choice does not appear until quadrant four. A news bureau seeking an ethically sound conclusion cannot merely appeal to a professional value and argue for an ethical theory that corresponds to that value. Although most cases come to a head over ethical principles in step three, the loyalty issue is the deciding factor here. Loyalty to the innocent victims of tragedy is paramount in this instance. How can the news bureaus demonstrate their total commitment to the Bulger family? The newspaper appears to be taking advantage of this family's tragic circumstances for its own gain—it busily publishes all the gory details. Should one be loyal to oneself—that is, to a newspaper's credibility or competence or inquisitive readership—at the expense of the suffering few? Under conditions of innocence, should the suffering family be able to control information about itself through publicly certified legal procedures rather than surrender those prerogatives to others ruled by their own agenda?

For our purposes, the process by which choices are made is of the greatest importance. Media professions are demanding, filled with ambiguous situations and conflicting loyalties. The practitioner must make decisions quickly and without much time for reflection. Knowing the elements in moral analysis sharpens our vocabulary and thereby enhances our debates in media ethics. By understanding the logic of social ethics, we improve the quality of our conceptual work and thereby the validity of the choices actually made in media practice over the long term. The four dimensions introduced with the Potter Box instruct media practitioners and students in developing normative ethics rather than leaving situations trapped in a crisis or confusion.

USING ETHICAL PRINCIPLES

The Potter Box can help to guide us through the various cases presented in this book. In the Liverpool murder case, the relevant empirical matters are complicated but not impossible to sort out. There may be some dispute over the circumstances in the mall and which of the two ten-year-olds was the most vicious, but not over the essential details: The body was found in two days and the suspects arrested twenty-four hours later. Thus the Potter Box insists that we always treat the specifics very carefully.

Our disagreements often result from our seeing the actual events differently. For example, when a newspaper purchases a building secretly, sets up a bar, and records city officials on camera, a host of details must be clear before a conclusion can be reached, before we can decide whether the paper is guilty of entrapment, invasion of privacy, or deception. Or, when debating a television station's responsibility to children, much of the disagreement involves the station's profits and how much free programming of high quality it can contribute without going broke. The question of controlling advertising is usually divided over the effect we consider advertising to have on buyer behavior. Often we debate whether we must overthrow the present media system or work within it. Actually, these quarrels are usually not genuine moral disagreements. Regarding the need to destroy the system or work within it, for example, both sides may appeal to a utilitarian principle that institutions must promote the greatest amount of good possible. The debate might simply be over facts and details, over conflicting assessments of which strategy is more effective, and so forth.[6]

Also, our values need to be isolated and accounted for. Several values usually enter and shape the decision-making process. No exhaustive list of the values held by participants is ever possible, but attention to values helps to prevent us from basing our decisions on personal biases or unexamined prejudices.

Our values constitute the frame of reference in which theories, decisions, and situations make sense to us. Sometimes our moral values correspond favorably to carefully articulated ethical theories. We may value gentleness and compassion so highly, for example, that our attitudes and language mesh with a stringently systematic ethics of pacifism. It is more likely, however, that stepping into quadrant three to examine principles will critique the values that may cloud our judgment. For example, journalists sometimes defend the "smoking out" process—making public an accusation about a politician under the assumption that guilt or innocence will emerge once the story gets played out fully in public. This professional value is usually contradicted by ethical principles regarding truth and protecting privacy.

Values motivate human action. Values are a distinctive mark of the human species. But our values are never pure. We tend to become defensive about them and typically rationalize our behavior when we violate them. Professional values are inscribed in power.[7] Professions such as journalism or law or engineering are very influential; generally, they operate in their own interests. Often our professional values are high-minded. Film producers may be strongly committed to aesthetic values and advertisers to hard work, for example. But no values are in-nocent. In institutions, values are a complicated mixture of ideas that often need to be checked, questioned, or corrected. Steps three and four in the Potter Box (naming the principles and loyalties) help us to think critically about the conflict-ing or inappropriate signals we receive from quadrant two (naming the values).

The format in this book of first describing cases and then giving commen-taries attempts to clarify the first two quadrants in the Potter Box. Case studies, by design, give the relevant details and suggest the alternatives that were considered in each situation. The cases themselves, and the commentaries particularly, expli-cate the values held by the principal figures in the decision-making process. Usu-ally in conversations, speeches, memos, and animated defenses of one's behavior, a person's important values become clear. Ethicists examine rhetoric very care-fully in order to determine what material is relevant for quadrant two. The man-ager of an advertising agency, for example, may value innovation so highly that other dimensions of the creative process are ignored; efficiency may be so prized in a film company that only subordinate values survive; and a reporter's commit-ment to the adversary relationship may distort her interpretation of a politician's behavior.

Occasionally, the commentaries extend even further and offer ethical princi-ples by which the decision can be defended—yet, on the whole, these norms, or principles, must be introduced by readers themselves. To aid this process, the fol-lowing pages summarize five major options. As the Potter Box demonstrates, ap-pealing to ethical principles that illuminate the issues is a significant phase of the moral reasoning process. Often one observes newspapers and broadcasters short-circuiting the Potter Box procedures. They typically act on the basis of profes-sional values, in effect deciding in quadrant two what their action will be. For example, in the Pentagon Papers dispute, *The New York Times* decided to publish the story because it valued First Amendment privileges so strongly that no other considerations seemed important. In this classic case, the Pentagon's review of Vietnam policy in secret documents were stolen by Daniel Ellsberg in early 1971 and leaked to *The New York Times*. Though they were under National Security pro-tection, the *Times* saw duplicity and abuse of the Constitution by the U.S. govern-ment, and concluded the American people had a right to know. However, on the basis of the Potter Box, we insist that no conclusion can be morally justified with-out a clear demonstration that an ethical principle shaped the final decision. The two quadrants on the left side, including values, explicate what actually happens. The two on the right side, including ethical principles, concern what ought to hap-pen. The left half of the box is descriptive and the right half normative.

We will follow the standard definitions that locate the act of valuing deep within the human will and emotions, whereas ethics involves critical reasoning about moral questions. As Sigmund Freud argued in *Totem and Taboo*, all societies, as far as we know, raise up certain ideals to emulate—but they also separate them-selves from other cultures by establishing boundaries or taboos. A totem pole may indicate that a tribe supremely values the strength of a lion or the craftiness of a weasel. Similarly, rituals are maintained to pronounce a curse on behaviors con-sidered totally unacceptable. In other words, valuing occurs as an aspect of our human condition as moral beings; it automatically comes to expression in every-day circumstances.[8] Values pervade all dimensions of human experience; even scientific experiments are saturated with value components. On the other hand, ethics involves an understanding of theology and philosophy as well as debates in the history of ideas over justice, virtue, the good, and so forth. Ethics also emphasizes reasoning ability and adequate justification.

Sometimes a working journalist will ask: "Why worry about principles? We know what we should do!" Such a comment often reflects a professional impatience with the idea of a moral dilemma, but it sounds a note that many moral philosophers are also asking: "Why principles? What principles? Whose principles?" The philosophical mind and social critics today tend to challenge the practice of searching for moral norms.[9] Yet norms rightly understood are foundational for moral commitment. Along those lines, Charles Taylor writes: "A framework is that in which we make sense of our lives spiritually. Not to have a framework is to fall into a life which is spiritually senseless."[10]

However, while the morally appropriate options can be outlined, the imposing of ethical principles by teachers and authors is normally counterproductive in that it undercuts the analytical process. The purpose of sound ethical reasoning is to draw responsible conclusions that yield justifiable actions. For this purpose, several ethical norms are introduced below. In analyzing the cases, these principles can be incorporated wherever appropriate and beneficial to given situations. Theories arise in specific historical circumstances and address specific issues. Therefore, no one theory can satisfactorily resolve all the questions and dilemmas in media ethics. One of the important tasks for instructors and students is learning which theory is the most powerful under what conditions. While other texts may focus on one approach across the board—utilitarianism or virtue ethics, for instance—identifying the right theory is a significant step in the decision-making process with the Potter Box. In coming to grips with privacy, for example, agape and caring are more penetrating than utility.

Historically, ethicists have established many ethical principles.[11] However, ethicist Louis Hodges is correct in organizing all the various options into five categories—ethical theories based on virtue, duty, utility, rights, and love. For four of them, we provide the most influential time-tested representative of each of these traditions. Within the contractarian tradition of John Locke emphasizing rights, Rawls has been selected as the dominant contemporary theorist in that category. Judeo-Christian agape is included as the historic and pervasive ethical theory based on love, with Nel Noddings' "ethics of care" included also as a contemporary example of this approach. By working with these theories, students learn how they apply in situations close to their own experience. Readers acquainted with other theories from across the globe and with moral issues in other cultures are encouraged to substitute them instead. Thus Confucius and Islamic ethics are included in the following discussion to stimulate work in other traditions and to illustrate how such theories enrich the Potter Box model for teaching ethics.

These master theories are not canonical; that is, they are not a body of self-evident truths without contradiction. Such a celebration is too glib and ignores the cultural power that dominant theories represent. The Greek *Kanon* means measuring stick, a taxation table, or a blueprint. Canons do grant privilege to certain texts on the grounds that without boundaries, there is only chaos, dissipated energies, "a babble of . . . complaints rather than a settled critique." Diversity arises out of unity; without a buffer zone, struggle is impossible. The canon "depends on who is teaching it how; . . . living in the same place does not mean living with the same history." The French philosopher Maurice Merleau-Ponty once wrote: "What is original about Machiavelli is that having laid down the source of struggle, he goes beyond it without ever forgetting it." Socrates makes the same point in the *Crito*—recognizing that the fact that he criticizes, what he criticizes, and how he criticizes is made possible by the very city he is criticizing. Throughout this text, theorists provide a common language not as abstract authority, but in order that we can think on our own—rebelliously or amiably, as circumstances demand it.[12]

FIVE ETHICAL GUIDELINES

1. *Aristotle's Mean: "Moral virtue is a middle state determined by practical wisdom."*
From Aristotle's predecessor, Plato, the Greeks inherited the four cardinal virtues: temperance, justice, courage, and wisdom. Of these virtues, temperance was the capstone, the virtue through which the others flowed. When doing his ethics, Aristotle emphasized moderation, or temperance, and sharpened it. Just as intellectual life is reasoning well, moderation is living well. In Aristotle's philosophy, justice is a mean lying between indifference and the selfish indulgence of insisting on personal interests. Courage is a mean between cowardice and temerity. Wisdom is a middle state between stultifying caution and unreflective spontaneity.

Propriety is stressed rather than sheer duty or love. As a biologist, Aristotle notes that both too much food and too little spoil health. Whereas many ethical theories focus on behavior, Aristotle emphasizes character rather than conduct per se. Outer behavior, in his view, reflects our inner disposition. Virtuous persons have developed habits in terms of temperance; in order for them to flourish as human beings, the path they walk is that of equilibrium and harmony.[13]

In Aristotle's own words, the principle is this: "Moral virtue is a fixed quality of the will, consisting essentially in a middle state, as determined by the standard that a person of practical wisdom would apply."[14] Practical wisdom (*phronesis*) is moral discernment, a knowledge of the proper ends of conduct and the means of attaining them. Practical wisdom is distinguished in Aristotle's teaching from both theoretical knowledge and technical skill. Humans who are not fanatics or eccentrics, but of harmonious character, develop their proportion and balance through everyday habit, guided by reason. "Over a career of moral growth. . . . [we develop] acuity in our perceptions and a disposition to reason wisely. . . . [We acquire] states of emotional maturity and character traits that dispose us toward the virtuous mark in our choices. . . . The wise person within whom there are well-integrated traits of character is the ultimate arbiter of right and wrong."[15]

Aristotle challenges those of practical wisdom to apply this discernment "to individual facts" by locating "the mean between two vices, that which depends on excess and that which depends on defect."[16] And the basic principle of the middle state applies to several diverse areas. In journalism, the sensational is derided, and the virtues of balance, fairness, and equal time are recognized. When faced with a decision of whether to prohibit all raising of tobacco or to allow unregulated promotion, the Federal Trade Commission operated in a middle state—they banned cigarette ads from television and placed warning labels on cigarette packages. Recommendations about liquor advertising fall between the extremes of not advertising at all and no restrictions on it whatsoever. A classic political example is nuclear arms reduction. Those who favor an arms buildup without restrictions, on the one hand, and those who favor total dismantling of nuclear weapons, on the other, both stymie a summit meeting. The legitimate claims of two legally appropriate entities must be negotiated, Aristotle would contend. The middle state mean is the most fair and reasonable option for honorably resolving disputes between labor and management, between school board and striking teachers, and between Palestinian and Israeli politicians. Generally speaking, in extremely complicated situations with layers of ambiguity and uncertainty, Aristotle's principle has the most intelligent appeal. This is the path recommended, for example, in the CNN in Baghdad case (Case 2).

However, some issues are not amenable to a center. A balanced diet positioned between famine and gluttony is undoubtedly wise, but occasionally our health requires drastic surgery also. There were slaves in Greece; Aristotle opted for treating them well and fairly but not for the radical change of releasing them altogether. In considering action regarding a hostile editor, a reporter cannot say, "The two extremes are to murder him or burn down his house, so I will take the middle state and merely pummel him senseless in a back alley." In the same way, bank robbers cannot justify themselves by operating at night so that customers will not be hurt and by taking only $10,000 instead of $100,000.

Not every action or every emotion admits of a middle state. The very names of some of them suggest wickedness. For instance, spite, shamelessness, envy, and, among actions, adultery, theft, and murder; all these and similar emotions and actions are blamed as being intrinsically wicked and not merely when practiced to excess or insufficiently. Consequently, it is not possible ever to feel or commit them rightly; they are always wrong.[17]

Extreme oppression demands extreme resistance. Fascism needs opposition. Richard Nixon's middling strategy ("Vietnamization" as it was called) requires protest.

It bears repeating that Aristotle was not advocating a bland, weak-minded consensus or the proverbial middle-of-the-road compromise. The mean is not isolated action reduced to political wheeling-and-dealing or bureaucratic fixing. We say of an artistic masterpiece, "Nothing can be added or subtracted without spoiling it." This is Aristotle's intent with the middle state as well. Although the word *mean* has a mathematical flavor and a sense of average, a precise equal distance from two extremes is not intended. Aristotle speaks of the "mean relative to us," that is, to the individual's status, particular situation, and strong and weak points.[18] Thus, if we are generally prone to one extreme, we ought to lean toward another this time. Affirmative action programs can be justified as appropriate in that they help correct a prior imbalance in hiring. The mean is not only the right quantity, but as Aristotle puts it, "the middle course occurs at the right time, toward the right people, for the right motives, and in the right manner."[19] This is the best course and is the mark of goodness. The distance depends on the nature of the agents as determined by the weight of the moral case before them. Consider the Greek love of aesthetic proportion in sculpture. The mean in throwing a javelin is four-fifths of the distance to the end, in hammering a nail, nine-tenths from the end.

1A. Confucius' Golden Mean: "Moral virtue is the appropriate location between two extremes."

Virtue ethics rooted in temperance emerged at the earliest beginnings of Western philosophy in fourth-century B.C.E. Greece. But the theory of the mean—more exactly rendered as "Equilibrium and Harmony"—was developed before Aristotle by the grandson of Confucius in fifth-century B.C.E. China.[20]

Confucius (551–479 B.C.E.) worked as a professional teacher in the states of Qi and Chou. In his fifties, he became a magistrate, then minister of justice in Chou. At age fifty-six, however, he fell out of favor and spent the next thirteen years traveling and teaching. Finding the rulers of other states uninterested in his ideas, he returned to Lu (the small state where he was born) at sixty-eight and taught there until his death eight years later. He is reported to have had over 3000 students.[21]

A century and a half before Aristotle, Confucius rooted his ethical theory in virtue. Confucius turned on its head the traditional idea of a superior person as born into an aristocratic family. Human excellence is seen as depending on character rather than on social position. "The virtuous person, according to Confucius . . . is benevolent, kind, generous, and above all balanced, observing the mean in all things. . . . Confucius thinks of virtue as a mean between extremes."[22]

From one of his four major books, *The Doctrine of the Mean*, representative sayings describe his teaching on virtue:

> Equilibrium (*chung*) is the great root from which grow all human actings in the world. And . . . harmony (*yung*) is the universal path all should pursue. Let the states of equilibrium and harmony exist in perfection, and happy order will prevail throughout heaven and earth, and all things will be nourished and flourish [*Four Books*, vol. I, I.4, I.5].
>
> The superior man embodies the course of the mean; the mean man acts contrary to the course of the mean. . . . The superior man's embodying the course of the mean is because he is a superior man, and so always maintains the mean [*Four Books*, vol. I, II.1, II.2].
>
> The master said, "Perfect is the virtue which is according to the mean" [*Four Books*, vol. I, III].

The superior man cultivates friendly harmony without being weak. . . .
He stands erect in the middle, without inclining to either side. How firm is he
in his energy [*Four Books*, vol. I, X.5].

One begins operating with this principle by identifying extremes—doing
nothing versus exposing everything, for example, in a question of how to report
some event. In cases where there are two competing obligations, they often can be
resolved through the golden mean. Should newspaper staffs be actively involved
in community affairs, for example? The journalist's role as practitioner may at
times contradict the journalist's role as citizen. In terms of Confucius' mean, the
newspaper rejects both extremes: the defect of excluding all outside involvements
and the excess of paying no attention to external affiliations. In this situation, the
application of Confucius' principle would recommend that the newspaper publish a financial disclosure of the publisher's holdings, withdraw from potential
conflicts of interest such as local industry boards, report all staff connections, and
so forth but allow other civic involvements.[23]

*2A. Kant's Categorical Imperative: "Act on that maxim which you will to become a
universal law."*
Immanuel Kant, born in 1724 in Königsberg, Germany, influenced eighteenth-century philosophy more than any other Western thinker. His writings
established a permanent contribution to epistemology and ethics. Kant's
Groundwork of the Metaphysic of Morals (1785) and *Critique of Practical Reason* (1788)
are important books for every serious student of ethics.
Kant gave intellectual substance to the golden rule by his categorical imperative, which implies that what is right for one is right for all. As a guide for measuring the morality of our action, Kant declared: "Act only on that maxim
whereby you can at the same time will that it should become a universal law."[24] In
other words, check the underlying principle of your decision, and see whether
you want it applied universally. The test of a genuine moral obligation is that it
can be universalized. The decision to perform an act must be based on a moral law
no less binding than such laws of nature as gravity. *Categorical* here means unconditional, without any question of extenuating circumstances, without any exceptions. Right is right and must be done even under the most extreme conditions.
What is morally right we ought to do even if the sky should fall, that is, despite
whatever consequences may follow.
Kant believed there were higher truths (which he called *noumena*) superior
to our limited reason and transcending the physical universe. Conscience is in-
born in every person, and it must be obeyed. The categorical imperatives, inherent in human beings, are apprehended not by reason but through conscience. By
the conscience one comes under moral obligation; it informs us when we ought to
choose right and shun evil. To violate one's conscience—no matter how feeble and
uninformed—brings about feelings of guilt. Through the conscience, moral law is
embedded in the texture of human nature.
The moral law is unconditionally binding on all rational beings. Someone
breaks a promise, for example, because it seems to be in his or her own interest,

but if all people broke their promises when it suited them, promises would cease to have meaning, and societies would deteriorate into terror. Certain actions, therefore, are always wrong: cheating, stealing, and dishonesty, for example. Benevolence and truthtelling are always and universally right.[25] These moral duties are not abrogated by the passage of time nor superseded by such achievements as the Bill of Rights. Even if one could save another's life by telling a lie, it would still be wrong. Deception by the press to get a good story or by advertisers to sell products cannot be excused or overlooked in the Kantian view. Dishonesty in public relations is unacceptable. Violent pornography in entertainment is not just one variable among many; it is too fundamental an issue to be explained away by an appeal to the First Amendment.

Kant's contribution is called *deontological ethics* (*deon* from the Greek word for duty). The good will "shines like a jewel," he wrote, and the obligation of the good conscience is to do its duty for the sake of duty.[26] Ethics for Kant was largely reducible to reverence for duty, visible in his work as a hymn on its behalf. For Kant, categorical imperatives must be obeyed even to the sacrifice of all natural inclinations and socially accepted standards. Kant's ethics have an austere quality, but they are generally regarded as having greater motivating power than subjective approaches that are easily rationalized on the basis of temporary moods. His categorical imperative encourages obedience and faithful practice.

Sir David Ross, a twentieth-century Oxford philosopher, developed a different version of duty ethics in his books *The Right and the Good* (1930) and *The Foundation of Ethics* (1939). Moral duties such as keeping your promises were compelling to him as they were for Kant. But rather than constructing such principles rationally, he argued that "objective moral truths are intuitively known, self-evident facts about the world."[27] Obligations not to lie and duties of justice, gratitude, and noninjury have inherent value, and Ross called them "prima-facie duties"—prima facie meaning upon first view or self-evident. Since it is immediately obvious to human beings that they should not kill, Kant's universalizability construction was unnecessary, and accepting a universe of formal laws was not required. Telling the truth is a self-evident obligation to media professionals, and attempting to justify it further in Ross's view only divides and deters potential adherents. While *Media Ethics: Cases and Moral Reasoning* emphasizes the classic deontological ethics of Kant, Ross's prima facie duties will be helpful at various points as an alternative.

2B. Islam's Divine Commands: "Justice, Human Dignity and Truth are Unconditional Duties."

Islamic morality is known through the original sources of Islam, that is, the *Qur'an* and the revelations to successive prophets and messengers, the last of whom was Muhammad of Arabia (572–632 A.D.)

In Islamic ethics, justice, human dignity, and truth are divine commands. This is a duty ethics based on unconditional imperatives. Rather than a system of formal laws as in Kant, ethical principles are commanded by Allah. Islam is based on the oneness (*Tawhid*) of God. Whatever denies a belief in God is unacceptable: "Do not make another an object of worship" (*Qur'an* 51:51).[28] No God exists but

Allah. All Islamic virtues specifically and human responsibility generally are grounded in monotheism (the belief in one God).

From *Tawhid* is the overarching duty to command the right and prohibit the wrong. All Muslims have the responsibility to follow Islamic principles and to encourage others to adopt them (Mowlana, 142). "Let there arise out of you a band of people inviting all that is good, and forbidding what is wrong" (*Qur'an* 3:104). "Commanding to the right and prohibiting from the wrong" is one of Islam's best known precepts.

This system of ethics, commanded by Allah and revealed in the holy *Qur'an*, is comprehensive for all of life. The teachings of Islam cover all fields of human existence. As Muhammad Ayish and Haydar Badawi Sadig (1997) observe, "This ethical system is broad enough to tackle general issues confronting the Islamic community and specific enough to take care of the slightest manifestations of human behavior."[29] Muhammad the prophet is described in the *Qur'an* as "a perfect model" (33:21) and "the exemplar of virtues" (68:4). Patience, moderation, trust, and love are all included in the Islamic life of virtue, and prudence is a core virtue among all the others. It is well known that moral decadence portrayed in the media is unacceptable, regardless of political guarantees of free expression. But three principles are basic and of special importance to communication: justice, human dignity, and truth.[30]

Islam emphasizes justice ('*adl*), considering justice, in fact, the essence of Islam itself. The goal of the Prophet Muhammad and the purpose of the *Qur'an* was "to establish justice among the people" (*Qur'an* 57:25). "Justice is God's supreme attribute; its denial constitutes a denial of God Himself."[31] The injunctions are clear: "O believers. Stand firmly for justice as witnesses of God, even if it be against yourself, your parents and relatives, and whether it be against the rich or poor" (*Qur'an* 4:135). "When you judge among people, judge with justice" (*Qur'an* 4:58). As Ali Mohamed observes, this umbrella concept "balances between rights and obligations without discrimination, without an emphasis on one at the expense of the other." Islam gives priority to justice as "the supreme value that underpins other values such as freedom and equality."[32]

Respecting human dignity is the second major principle revealed in the *Qur'an* as commanded by Allah. God honors humans above all His creatures, and therefore, the human species is to honor its members to the maximum. Allah "created man in the best of molds" (*Qur'an* 95:4). In secular ethics, the concept of dignity is individualistic and horizontal, but in Islamic ethics, it is rooted in the sacredness of human nature: "Humans are not just one element in the vast expense of God's creation but are the *raison d'etre* for all that exists."[33]

To safeguard the individual's dignity, the *Qur'an* warns against defamation, backbiting, and derision. Respecting others as human beings is a wide-ranging theme, including the smallest details: "Let not some men among you laugh at others. It may be that the latter are better than the former. Nor let some women laugh at others. It may be that the latter are better than the former. Nor defame nor be sarcastic to each other, nor call each other by offensive nicknames" (*Qur'an* 49:11). Many of the virtues on Islam's extensive list are rooted in the honor owed to the human species. As Malaysian scholar Zulkiple Abdullah Ghani puts it: "Islam provides universal values and ethics in designating communication functions and verifying its end products, with the main objective of enhancing the dignity of mankind."[34] Kant uses different language, but for him, human dignity is an unconditional imperative also. In his language: "Act so that you use humanity, as much in your own person as in the person of every other, always at the same time as an end and never merely as means."[35]

And truth is a pillar of Islamic ethics also. The Prophet speaks the truth, and Allah's word in the *Qur'an* is true. Therefore, truthfulness is likewise at the center of human affairs and fundamental to Islamic communication. "Telling lies is as evil as worshipping idols, which is the worst offence Muslims can commit."[36] As it says in the *Qur'an*, "Shun the abomination of idols, and shun the word that is false" (22:30). There is no other pathway to Paradise than telling the truth, as the Prophet said: "Truthfulness leads to righteousness and righteousness leads to Paradise."[37] Muslims are able to uphold the truth when they follow the Islamic way of life: "They are steadfast, truthful, obedient, charitable, and they pray for forgiveness at dawn" (*Qur'an* 3:17).

In Islam, the principles provided by the *Qur'an* and the Prophetic examples are the framework for believers. The First International Conference of Muslim Journalists held in Jakarta in 1981 recommended that all Muslims in the media should follow the Islamic rules of conduct. But Islamic ethics also testifies to the human race as a whole that following these principles brings fulfillment and well-being to societies everywhere. These three principles are directly relevant to media ethics. In those situations where unconditional imperatives are the most appropriate, justice, human dignity, and truth recommend themselves as enduring standards.

3. Mill's Principle of Utility: "Seek the greatest happiness for the aggregate whole."[38]

Utilitarianism is an ethical view widespread in North American society and a notion well developed in philosophy. There are many different varieties, but they all hold in one way or another that we are to determine what is right or wrong by considering what will yield the best consequences for the welfare of human beings. The morally right alternative produces the greatest balance of good over evil. All that matters ultimately in determining the right and wrong choice is the amount of good promoted and evil restrained.

Modern utilitarianism originated with the British philosophers Jeremy Bentham (1748–1832) and John Stuart Mill (1806–1873). Their traditional version was hedonistic, holding that the good end is happiness or pleasure. The quantity of pleasure depends on each situation; it can be equal, Bentham would say, for a child's game of kickball as for writing poetry.[39] Mill contended that happiness was the sole end of human action and the test by which all conduct ought to be judged.[40] Preventing pain and promoting pleasure were for Bentham and Mill the only desirable ends.

Later utilitarians, however, have expanded on the notion of happiness. They have noted that if pleasure is upheld as the one object of desire (in the sense of "wine, women, and song"), then all people do not desire it (Puritans did not), and therefore, it cannot be the only desired goal. Thus these utilitarians argue that other values besides pure happiness possess intrinsic worth—values such as friendship, knowledge, health, and symmetry. For these pluralistic utilitarians, rightness or wrongness is to be assessed in terms of the total amount of value ultimately produced. For example, after burglars broke into the Democratic Party's National Committee offices in the Watergate Hotel in 1972, the press's aggressive coverage did not yield a high amount of pleasure for anyone except enemies of Richard Nixon. Yet, for utilitarians, the overall consequences were valuable enough so that most people considered the actions of the press proper, even though pain was inflicted on a few.

Worked out along these lines, utilitarianism provides a definite guideline for aiding our ethical choices. It suggests that we first calculate in the most conscientious manner possible the consequences of the various options open to us. We would ask how much benefit and how much harm would result in the lives of everyone affected, including ourselves. Once we have completed these computations for all relevant courses of action, we are morally obligated to choose the alternative that maximizes value or minimizes loss. The norm of utility instructs us to produce the greatest possible balance of good over evil. Actors should focus on "the greatest amount of happiness altogether."[41] To perform any other action knowingly would result in our taking an unethical course.

Two kinds of utility are typically distinguished: act and rule utilitarianism. For act utilitarians, the basic question always involves the greatest good in a specific case. One must ask whether a particular action in a particular situation will result in a balance of good over evil. Rule utilitarians, also attributing their view to Mill, construct moral rules on the basis of promoting the greatest general welfare. The question is not which action yields the greatest utility, but which general rule does. The principle of utility is still the standard, but at the level of rules rather than specific judgments. The act utilitarian may conclude that in one specific situation civil disobedience obtains a balance of good over evil, whereas rule utility would seek to generate a broadly applicable moral rule such as "civil disobedience is permitted except when physically violent."[42]

Although happiness is an end few would wish to contradict, utilitarianism does present difficulties. It depends on our making accurate measurements of the consequences, when in everyday affairs the result of our choices is often blurred vision, at least in the long term. For instance, who can possibly calculate the social changes that we will face in future decades in the wake of converging media technologies? Moreover, the principle of the greatest public benefit applies only to societies in which certain nonutilitarian standards of decency prevail. In addition, utilitarians view society as a collection of individuals, each with his or her own desires and goals; the public good is erroneously considered the sum total of private goods.[43]

These ambiguities, although troublesome and objectionable, do not by themselves destroy the utilitarian perspective, at least for those who are intellectually sophisticated. For our purposes in examining media ethics, no moral norms can be considered free of all uncertainties. However, the obvious difficulties with utilitarianism usually can be addressed in round two or three when circulating through the Potter Box for specificity and clarification.[44] Occasionally, in resolving the cases considered in the following pages, utility is the most productive principle to include in the lower right-hand quadrant. In the classic case of Robin Hood accosting the rich in order to provide for the poor, act utilitarianism appropriately condones his behavior as morally justified.

   4. *Rawls's Veil of Ignorance: "Justice emerges when negotiating without social differentiations."*
   John Rawls's book, *A Theory of Justice* (1971), has been widely quoted in contemporary work on ethics. From Rawls's perspective, fairness is the fundamental idea in the concept of justice.[45] He represents a return to an older tradition of substantive moral philosophy and thereby establishes an alternative to utilitarianism. He articulates an egalitarian perspective that carries the familiar social contract theory of Hobbes, Locke, and Rousseau to a more fundamental level.
   In easy cases, fairness means quantity: Everyone in the same union doing similar work would all fairly receive a 10 percent raise; teachers should give the same letter grade to everyone who had three wrong on a particular test; and at a birthday party, each child should get two cookies. Eliminating arbitrary distinctions expresses fairness in its basic sense. However, Rawls struggles more with inherent inequalities. For example, players in a baseball game do not protest the fact that pitchers handle the ball more times than outfielders do. We sense that graduated income taxes are just, though teachers pay only 22 percent and editors, advertisers, public relations staff, and film producers perhaps find themselves in the 50 percent bracket.
   When situations necessitating social contracts are inherently unequal, blind averages are unfair and intuitional judgments are too prone to error. Therefore, Rawls recommends his now classic "veil of ignorance," asking that all parties step back from real circumstances into an "original position" behind a barrier where roles and social differentiations are eliminated.[46] Participants are abstracted from individual features such as race, class, gender, group interests, and other real conditions and are considered equal members of society as a whole. They are men and women with ordinary tastes and ambitions, but each suspends these personality features and regains them only after a contract is in place. Behind the veil, no one knows how he or she will fare when stepping out into real life. The participants may be male or female, ten years old or ninety, Russian or Polish, rookie or veteran, black or white, advertising vice president or sales representative for a weekly. As we negotiate social agreements in the situation of imagined equality behind the veil of ignorance, Rawls argues, we inevitably seek to protect the weaker party and to minimize risks. In the event that I emerge from the veil as a beginning reporter rather than a big-time publisher, I will opt for fair treatment for the former. The most vulnerable party receives priority in these cases. Therefore, the result, Rawls would contend, is a just resolution.
   Because negotiation and discussion occur, the veil of ignorance does not rely merely on intuition. Such individual decisions too easily become self-serving and morally blind. Nor is the veil another name for utility, with decisions based on what is best for the majority. Again, the issue is morally appropriate action, not

simply action that benefits the most people. In fact, Rawls's strategy stands against the tendency in democratic societies to rally around the interests of the majority and give only lip service to the minority.

Two principles emerge from the hypothetical social contract formulated behind the veil. These, Rawls declares, will be the inevitable and prudent choices of rational women and men acting in their own self-interest. The first principle calls for a maximal system of equal basic liberty. Every person must have the largest political liberty compatible with a like liberty for all. Liberty has priority in that it can never be traded away for economic and social advantages. Thus the first principle permanently conditions the second. The second principle involves all social goods other than liberty and allows inequalities in the distribution of these goods only if they act to benefit the least advantaged party. The inequalities in power, wealth, and income on which we agree must benefit the members of society who are worse off.[47]

Consider the press coverage in the well-known case of William Kennedy Smith for the alleged rape of a woman at the Kennedy Palm Beach compound in 1991. The extensive media coverage was justified on the basis of Senator Edward Kennedy's role at the bar earlier in the evening and public interest in the Kennedy family. Given conventional news values, the public's right to know supersedes the Kennedy family's right to privacy. But what if we go beyond values to ethical theory? Put Ted Kennedy and a newsperson behind the veil of ignorance, not knowing who will be who when they emerge. Undoubtedly they would agree that reporting on the public acts of public officials is permissible but that publicizing the alleged rape incident itself, now several years later, would be undue harassment in the absence of any new material. Rawls's principle precludes reporters from using their power to pester without end those who are caught in a news story.

On a broader level, place politicians and journalists behind the veil and attempt to establish a working relationship agreeable to all after the veil is parted and space/time resumes. All stark adversary notions would disappear. There would be no agreement that elected officials as a class should be called the enemy or liars because those who emerge as politicians would resent such labels. Independence, some toughness, and persistence seem reasonable for media professionals, but a basic respect for all humans would replace an unmitigated and cynical abrasiveness among those wielding instruments of power.

5A. Judeo-Christian Persons as Ends: "Love your neighbor as yourself."[48]

Ethical norms of nearly all kinds emerge from various religious traditions. The highest good in the *Bhagavad Gita,* for example, is enlightenment. Of all the options, however, the Judeo-Christian tradition has dominated American culture to the greatest extent, and its theological ethics have been the most influential. By studying a prominent religious perspective in terms of the issues and cases in this textbook, students should be inspired to take other religious ethics seriously as well. The intention here is pedagogical—to learn a system of ethical reasoning and ethical concepts within a familiar context. On that foundation, other frameworks can be added, and dilemmas in different cultural contexts can be addressed responsibly. Islam and Confucianism, for example, have developed sophisticated ethical traditions.[49]

The ethics of love is not exclusively a Judeo-Christian notion. Already in the fourth century B.C.E., the Chinese thinker Mo Tzu spoke in similar terms: "What is the Will of Heaven like? The answer is—To love all men everywhere alike."[50] Nor are all Judeo-Christian ethics a pure morality of love; some ethicists in that tradition make obedience or justice or peace supreme.[51] But the classic contribution of this religious perspective, in its mainline form, contends that ultimately humans stand under only one moral command or virtue: to love God and humankind. All other obligations, though connected to this central one, are considered derivative.

"Love your neighbor" is normative, and uniquely so in this tradition, because love characterizes the very heart of the universe. Augustine is typical in declaring that divine love is the supreme good.[52] The inexhaustible, self-generating nature of God Himself is love. Therefore, human love has its inspiration, motive, and ground in the highest reaches of eternity. Humans are made in the image of God; the more loving they are, the more like God they are. At this very point the Judeo-Christian norm differs from other ethical formulations. Love is not only a raw principle, stern and unconditional, as in Kant's categorical imperative. Regard for others is not simply based on just a contract motivated by self-interest, as in John Rawls's theory. It remains personal at its very roots, and although rigorously dutiful, it is never purely legalistic. As Heinrich Emil Brunner noted in summarizing the biblical exhortations:

> "Live in love." Or, still more plainly: "Remain in love." . . . It is the summons to remain in the giving of God, to return to Him again and again as the origin of all power to be good and to do good. There are not "other virtues" alongside the life of love. . . . Each virtue, one might say, is a particular way in which the person who lives in love takes the other into account, and "realizes" him as "Thou."[53]

The Old Testament already spoke of loving kindness, but the Christian tradition introduced the more dramatic term *agape*—unselfishness; other-regarding care and other-directed love; distinct from friendship, charity, benevolence, and other weaker notions. In the tradition of agape, to love a human being is to accept that person's existence as it is given; to love him or her as is.[54] Thus human beings have unconditional value apart from shifting circumstances. The commitment is unalterable; loyalty to others is permanent, indefectible, in sickness and in health. It is unloving, in this view, to give others only instrumental value and to use them merely as a means to our own ends. Especially in those areas that do not coincide with a person's own desires, love is not contradicted. In this perspective, we ought to love our neighbors with the same zeal and consistency with which we love ourselves.

Agape as the center of meaning in Judeo-Christian ethics raises significant issues that ethicists in this tradition continue to examine: the regular failure of its adherents to practice this principle; the relationship of love and justice, of the personal and institutional; the role of reason as distinguished from discernment; and whether agape is a universal claim or, if not, what its continuity is with other alternatives.[55]

However, all agree that loving one's neighbor in this tradition is far from sentimental utopianism. In fact, agape is strong enough to serve as the most appropriate norm in Chapters 4, 5, and 14. Moreover, it is thoroughly practical, issuing specific help to those who need it. (*Neighbor* was a term for the weak, poor, orphans, widows, aliens, and disenfranchised in the Old Testament.) Even enemies are included. This love is not discriminatory: no black or white, no learned or simple, no friend or foe. Although agape does not deny the distinctions that characterize creaturely existence, it stays uniquely blind to them. Love does not first estimate rights or claims and then determine whether the person merits attention. The norm here is giving and forgiving with uncalculating spontaneity and spending oneself to fulfill a neighbor's well-being. Because of its long attention to understanding the character of humanness, the agape principle has been especially powerful in its treatment of social injustice, invasion of privacy, violence, and pornography.

5B. Noddings' Relational Ethics: "The 'one-caring' attends to the 'cared-for' in thought and deeds."

Feminist scholarship in the past decade has given more precise development and higher status to the central terms in love-based ethics: nurturing, caring, affection, empathy, and inclusiveness.[56] For Carol Gilligan, the female moral voice roots ethics in the primacy of relationships. Rather than the basic standard of avoiding harm to others, she insists on compassion and nurturance for resolving conflicts among people.[57] Nel Noddings' *Caring* rejects outright the "ethics of principle as ambiguous and unstable," insisting that human care should play the central role in moral decision making.[58] For Julia Wood (1994), "an interdependent sense of self" undergirds the ethic of care, wherein we are comfortable acting independently while "acting cooperatively . . . in relationship with others."[59] In Linda Steiner's work, feminists' ethical self-consciousness also identifies subtle forms of oppression and imbalance and teaches us to "address questions about whose interests are regarded as worthy of debate."[60]

For Noddings, ethics begins with particular relations, and there are two parties in any relation. The first member she calls the "one-caring," and the second, the "cared-for." The one-caring is "motivationally engrossed in the cared-for," attending to the cared-for in deeds as well as thoughts. "Caring is not simply a matter of feeling favorably disposed toward humankind in general. . . . Real care requires actual encounters with specific individuals; it cannot be accomplished through good intentions alone." And, "when all goes well, the cared-for actively receives the caring deeds of the one-caring."[61]

Noddings does not explicitly define a care ethics, but she emphasizes three central dimensions: engrossment, motivational displacement, and reciprocity. The one-caring is engrossed in the needs of the other. "The one-caring is fully disposed and attentive toward the cared-for, has regard for the other, desires the other's well-being, and is responsive and receptive to the other." Through motivational displacement, those caring retain but move beyond their "own interests to an empathy for or 'feeling with' the experiences and views of the cared-for." The cared-for must reciprocate in order to complete the caring relationship. "Reciprocity may be a direct response or it simply may be the delight or the personal growth of the cared-for witnessed by the one caring."[62]

TO WHOM IS MORAL DUTY OWED?

The Potter Box forces us to get the empirical data straight, investigate our values, and articulate an appropriate principle. Once these steps are accomplished, we face the question of our ultimate loyalties. Many times, in the consideration of ethics, direct conflicts arise between the rights of one person or group and those of others. Policies and actions inevitably must favor some to the exclusion of others. Often our most agonizing dilemmas revolve around our primary obligation to a person or social group. Or we ask ourselves, Is my first loyalty to my company or to a particular client?

To reach a responsible decision, we must clarify which parties will be influenced by our decision and which ones we feel especially obligated to support. When analyzing the cases in this book, we will usually investigate five categories of obligation:

1. *Duty to ourselves.* Maintaining our integrity and following our conscience may be the best alternative in many situations. However, careerism is a serious professional problem and often tempts us to act out of our own self-interest while we claim to be following our conscience.
2. *Duty to clients/subscribers/supporters.* If they pay the bills, and if we sign contracts to work for them, do we not carry a special obligation to them? Even in the matter of a viewing audience that pays no service fee for a broadcast signal, our duty to them must be addressed when we are deciding which course of action is the most appropriate.
3. *Duty to our organization or firm.* Often company policy is followed much too blindly, yet loyalty to an employer can be a moral good. Whistle blowing, that is, exposing procedures or persons who are harming the company's reputation, is also morally relevant here. Reporters might even defy court orders and refuse to relinquish records in whistle-blowing cases, under the thesis that ultimately the sources on which media companies depend will dry up. Thus duty to one's firm might conceivably take priority over duty to an individual or to a court.
4. *Duty to professional colleagues.* A practitioner's strongest obligation is often to colleagues doing similar work. Understandably, reporters tend to prize,

most of all, their commitments to fellow reporters and their mutual standards of good reporting. Some even maintain an adversarial posture against editors and publishers, just short of violating the standards of accepted etiquette. Film artists presume a primary obligation to their professional counterparts, and account executives to theirs. However, these professional loyalties, almost intuitively held, also must be examined when we are determining what action is most appropriate.

5. *Duty to society.* This is an increasingly important dimension of applied ethics and has been highlighted for the media under the term *social responsibility.* Questions of privacy and confidentiality, for example, nearly always encounter claims about society's welfare over that of a particular person. The "public's right to know" has become a journalistic slogan. Advertising agencies cannot resolve questions of tobacco ads, political commercials, and nutritionless products without taking the public good fully into the equation. When some Tylenol bottles were laced with cyanide, the public relations staff of Johnson and Johnson had its foremost obligation to the public. Violence and pornography in media entertainment are clearly social issues. In such cases, to benefit the company or oneself primarily is not morally defensible. In these situations, our loyalty to society warrants preeminence.

Throughout this volume, the media practitioner's moral obligation to society is stressed as critically important. Admittedly, the meaning of that responsibility is often ill-defined and subject to debate. For example, when justifying one's decision, particular social segments must be specified: the welfare of children, the rights of a minority, or the needs of senior citizens. We have emphasized that, in spite of the difficulties, precisely such debate must be at the forefront when we are considering the loyalty quadrant in the Potter Box. No longer do the media operate with a crass "public be damned" philosophy. Increasingly, the customer is king, whereas belligerent appeals to owner privilege have been lessened. However, these gains are only the beginning. They need to be propelled forward so that a sincere sense of social responsibility and a genuine concern for the citizenry become characteristic marks of all contemporary media operations in news, advertising, public relations, and entertainment.

The version of the Potter Box described in this introduction furthers this textbook's overall preoccupation with social responsibility. Consider the upper tier of the Potter Box (empirical definition and ultimate loyalties), which stresses the social context. As was noted earlier, the Potter Box as a schematic design is not just an eclectic, random gathering of several elements for justifying a decision or policy. Although the lower half (values and ethical principles) deals more with analytical matters than it does with sociological ones in everyday experience, it also feeds into the higher half. Additionally, the two levels are integrated at crucial junctures so that social situations initiate the process and the choice of cultural loyalties forces one toward the final decision. Thus the loyalty component especially provides a pivotal juncture in moral discourse and indicates that conceptual analysis can hardly be appraised until one sees the implications for institutional arrangements and the relevant social groups. Along those lines, Nel Noddings strongly urges that caring—a notion of relatedness between people—take a central role in decision making. From her perspective, mere subscription to principle without concentrating on the people involved has caused much needless wrong.[63]

The line of decision making that we follow, then, has its final meaning in the social order. Certainly, precision is necessary when we are dealing with ethical principles, just as their relation must always be drawn to the values held and empirical definition described. But the meaning becomes clear when the choice is made for a particular social context or a specific set of institutional arrangements. Considered judgments, in this view, do not derive directly from normative principles but are woven into a set of obligations one assumes toward certain segments of society. In this scheme, debate over institutional questions is fundamental, and ethical thinking is not completed until social applications and implications have been designated. In social ethics of this kind, the task is not just one of definition but also an elaboration of the perplexities regarding social justice, power, bureaucracies, and cultural forms. Social theory is central to the task, not peripheral.[64]

WHO OUGHT TO DECIDE?

During each phase of ethical reasoning, some actor or group of actors is directly involved in deciding, determining values, selecting moral norms, and choosing loyalties. The cases in this book cannot be read or discussed fruitfully without constant attention to the question of who is making the decision. At every step, applied ethics always considers seriously the issue of who should be held accountable.

Usually numerous decision makers are involved. In simple cases, it is an organizational matter where an editor or executive decides rather than a reporter or sales representative. In more complicated areas, can producers of entertainment dismiss their responsibility for quality programming by arguing that they merely give the public what it wants? Are parents to be held solely accountable for the television programs that children watch, or do advertisers and networks carry responsibility also? If advertisers and networks have responsibility, in what proportions? Does the person with the greatest technical expertise have the greatest moral obligation? We must be wary of paternalism, in which consumers and informal social networks are removed from the decision-making process. When is the state, through the courts, the final decision maker? Giving absolute authority or responsibility to any person or group can be morally disastrous. Requiring accountability across the board helps to curb the human penchant for evading one's own liability.

For all the emphasis in this textbook on social ethics, individual practitioners ought not become lost. The individual is the authentic moral agent. A firm or institution, when infused and animated by a single spirit and organized into a single institution, is more than a mere sum of discrete entities—it has a personality of its own. It is also true that such institutions can, in a sense, be held accountable for their deeds and become the object of moral approval or disapproval. But only in a limited sense. Such institutions are real enough, but they lack concreteness. It is the individual who reasons morally that we consider the responsible agent. These individuals alone can be praised or blamed.[65]

Certainly, corporate obligation is a meaningful notion. When individuals join an organization, and for as long as they remain members, they are coresponsible for the actions taken by that organization. What is most important, however, is that ultimate responsibility finally rests on individuals. It should be obvious that this is not a plea for a heavy-handed individualism; that would stand directly at odds with the social ethics of the Potter Box model. The point is that responsibility, to be meaningfully assigned and focused, must be distributed among the individuals constituting the corporation. Individuals are not wholly discrete, unrelated, atomistic entities; they always stand in a social context with which they are morally involved. But individuals they nevertheless remain. And it is with each person that ethics is fundamentally concerned. Gross attacks and broad generalizations about entire media systems usually obscure more than they enlighten. On most occasions, such assessments are not normative ethics but hot-tempered moralism. The cases and commentaries that follow, filtered through the Potter Box model, steer media practitioners toward socially responsible decisions that are justified ethically.

NOTES

1. For details, see AP wire copy, 12 February and 26 November 1993, and Ray Moseley, "What Made Toddler's Killers Tick?" *Chicago Tribune*, 26 November 1993, sec. 1, 1. See also David Lynch, "Killers Released into a Maelstrom in England," *USA Today*, 27 June 2001, 102.
2. Henry D. Aiken, *Reason and Conduct* (New York: Alfred A. Knopf, 1962), 65–87.
3. For helpful background, see Richard L. Morrill, "Values as Standards of Action," in his *Teaching Values in College* (San Francisco: Jossey-Bass Publishers, 1980); David Boeyink, "What Do We Mean by Newspaper Values," unpublished paper, 8 February 1988, Southern Newspaper Publishers Association, St. Petersburg, Florida; Everette E. Dennis, "Values and Value-Added for the New Electronic Journalism," The Freedom Forum Media Studies Center, 15 March 1995; and *Journalism Values Handbook*, The Harwood Group, American Society of Newspaper Editors, 11690B Sunshine Valley Dr., Reston, VA 20195. For values among artists, see Horace Newcomb and Robert Alley, *The Producer's Medium: Conversations with Creators of American TV* (New York: Oxford University Press, 1983).

   Below are examples of the values that are often important in media practice.

   Professional values: proximity, firstness, impact, recency, conflict, human interest, entertainment, novelty, toughness, thoroughness, immediacy, independence, watchdog, public's right to know, no prior restraint, independence.

   Moral values: truthtelling, humanness, fairness, honesty, stewardship, nonviolence, commitment, self-control.

Sociocultural values: thrift, hard work, energy, restraint, heterosexuality.
Logical values: consistency, competence, knowledge.
Aesthetic values: harmonious, pleasing, imaginative.

4. Dr. Karen Lebacqz of the Pacific School of Religion named the model "Potter Box" after the original version described in Ralph B. Potter, "The Structure of Certain American Christian Responses to the Nuclear Dilemma, 1958–63" (Ph.D. diss., Harvard University, 1965). See also Ralph B. Potter, "The Logic of Moral Argument," in *Toward a Discipline of Social Ethics,* ed. Paul Deats (Boston: Boston University Press, 1972), 93–114.

5. Potter himself labeled it the "ground of meaning" level. As he describes it in his dissertation, "Even when ethical categories have been explicated with philosophical exactitude it is possible for one to ask, 'Why ought I to be moral?' or 'Why ought I to consider your expressions of ethical judgment and your pattern of ethical reasoning to be convincing?' " Further inquiry "drives men ultimately to reflect on their more fundamental ideas concerning God, man, history, and whatever is behind and beyond history." Potter, "The Structure of Certain American Christian Responses," 404–405.

6. Taking the empirical dimension seriously does not necessarily imply a commitment to neutral facts and what is called "abstracted empiricism" in C. Wright Mills, *The Sociological Imagination* (New York: Oxford University Press, 1959), 50–75. W. I. Thomas's "definition of the situation" is actually a more sophisticated way of explicating the empirical dimension of moral questions; see W. I. Thomas, *Primitive Behavior: An Introduction to the Social Sciences* (New York: McGraw-Hill, 1937), 8. For a comprehensive introduction to this strategy, see *Handbook of Qualitative Research,* 2d ed. eds. Norman K. Denzin and Yvonna S. Lincoln (Newbury Park, CA: Sage Publications, 2000).

7. See Karen Lebacqz, *Professional Ethics: Power and Paradox* (Nashville, TN: Abingdon Press, 1985).

8. Obviously, the anatomy of values and their relation to beliefs and attitudes is a complex question both in psychology and in axiology. In terms of the Potter Box model, our concern is to identify the values invoked in various cases and to ensure that they are understood as only one phase of the decision-making process. In that sense, instead of the values-clarification approach of Louis Rath, Sidney Simon, and Merrill Harmin, we insist on the critical normative reflection represented in quadrant three.

9. Richard Rorty, *Contingency, Irony, Solidarity* (New York: Cambridge University Press, 1989).

10. Charles Taylor, *Sources of the Self* (Cambridge, MA: Harvard University Press, 1989), 18; see also his *Ethics of Authenticity* (Cambridge, MA: Harvard University Press, 1991), and his *Multiculturalism and the Politics of Recognition* (Princeton, NJ: Princeton University Press, 1992).

11. Ethical egoism has not been included in the list despite its immense popularity. The authors stand with those who doubt its adequacy and coherence as an ethical theory. Furthermore, the view that everyone ought to promote his or her own self-interests does not agree with the emphasis on social responsibility in the Potter Box model. There are several formulations of ethical egoism, however. Students interested in pursuing this option should see Edward Regis's significant attempt to present a conception that overcomes the standard objections. Edward Regis, "What Is Ethical Egoism?" *Ethics* 91 (October 1980): 50–62. For a history of the debates in this area, see Tibor R. Machan, "Recent Work in Ethical Egoism," *American Philosophical Quarterly* 16 (1979): 1–15.

12. Peter Euben, "The Debate Over the Canon," *The Civic Acts Review* 7:1 (Winter 1994): 4–15. Euben gives a comprehensive overview of the canonicity issue in this article. The ideas in this paragraph and the cited material are taken from Euben's essay.

13. For example, see *Nicomachean Ethics*, in *Introduction to Aristotle*, ed. Richard McKeon (New York: Modern Library, 1947); (1104a), 333; (1106a), 340; (1107a), 341; (1138b), 423.

14. *Nicomachean Ethics*, Bk. II, ch. 6. This is H. Rackham's translation in William Alston and R. B. Brandt, *The Problems of Philosophy* (New York: Allyn and Bacon), 1978, 187. In J. A. Stewart's version: "Moral Virtue may then be defined, as a habit involving choice, lying in a relative mean fixed by reason, that is, as the prudent man would fix it."

15. Stanley B. Cunningham, "Getting It Right: Aristotle's 'Golden Mean' as theory Deterioration," *Journal of Mass Media Ethics* 14:1, 10. Cunningham correctly insists that "congruent behavior within a career of character and emotional development, rather than isolated answers to textbook-style conflicts, defines the Aristotelian moral enterprise" (11).

16. *Nicomachean Ethics*, ed. McKeon (1107A), 340. For practical wisdom in Aristotle, see Christopher L. Johnstone, "Aristotle's Ethical Theory in the Contemporary World: Logos, Phronesis, and the Moral Life," in S. Bracci and C. Christians, eds., *Moral Engagement in Public Life: Theorists for Contemporary Ethics* (New York: Peter Lang, 2002), 16–34.

17. Ibid. (1107A), 340–341.

18. Ibid. (1107a), 340.

19. Ibid. (1106b), 340.

20. For "The Doctrine of the Mean" by Confucius, selected from *The Four Books*, see Daniel Bonevac, William Boon, and Stephen Phillips, eds., *Beyond the Western Tradition: Readings in Moral and Political Philosophy* (Mountain View, CA: Mayfield Publishing Co., 1992), 264–269. See also James Legge, ed., *Four Books of the Chinese Classics: Confucian Analects, the Great Learning, Doctrine of the Mean, Works of Mencius*, 4 vols. (Corona, CA: Oriental Book Store, 1991).

21. Bonevac et al., "The Doctrine of the Mean," 252.

22. Ibid., 252–253.

23. For an application of Confucius to business, see Stefan Rudnicki, ed., *Confucius in the Boardroom: Ancient Wisdom, Modern Lessons for Business*, 1998. See also Tom R. Reid, *Confucius Lives Next Door: What Living in the East Teaches Us About Living* in the West (New York: Random, 1999). For Confucius as the basis of human rights, see Dong-Hyun Byung and Keehyeung Lee, "Confucian Values, Ethics and Legacies in History," in S. Bracci and C. Christians, eds., *Moral Engagement in Public Life: Theorists for Contemporary Ethics* (New York: Peter Lang, 2002), 73–96.

24. Immanuel Kant, *Groundwork of the Metaphysic of Morals*, trans. H. J. Paton (New York: Harper Torchbooks, 1964), 69–71, 82–89.

25. Patrick Plaisance elaborates on the truthtelling imperative in Kant based not only on Kant's *Groundwork* but also his *Metaphysic of Morals* published twelve years later in 1797. He demonstrates that Kant's deontological system should not be grounded first of all in the universalist maxim but in the philosophical basis for his categorical imperatives—human dignity. Kant's claim regarding the distinctive rational agency and free will of the human species expands our understanding of truthtelling as an imperative so that transparency in communication may be considered Kant's "greatest gift to media ethics today" (191). Patrick Plaisance, "Transparency: An Assessment of the Kantian Roots of a Key Element in Media Ethics Practice," *Journal of Mass Media Ethics* 22:2–3 (2007): 187–207.

26. *Groundwork of the Metaphysic of Morals*, 62.

27. Christopher Meyers, "Appreciating W. D. Ross: On Duties and Consequences," *Journal of Mass Media Ethics* 18:2 (2003): 81–97.

28. The translation is from A. Yusuf Ali, *The Holy Qur'an*, 10th ed., (Beltsville, MD: Amana Corp., 2001). The description of Islamic ethics in this section relies principally on Ali Mohamed, "Journalistic Ethics and Responsibility in Relation to Freedom of Expression: An Islamic Perspective," unpublished paper, McGill University, March 2007. See also Muhammad A. Siddiqi, "New Media of the Information Age and Islamic Ethics," *Islam and the Modern Age* 31:4 (2000): 1–5.

29. Muhammad Ayish and Haydar Badawi Sadig, "The Arab-Islamic Heritage in Communication Ethics," in C. Christians and M. Trabers, eds., *Communication Ethics and Universal Values* (Thousand Oaks, CA: Sage Publications, 1997), 108.

30. Hamid Mowlana explains some of the different emphases in Islamic ethics over history, among varied schools of thought, and in different geographic regions (137–141). For applications to media issues and practices, see Hamid Mowlana, "Communication Ethics and the Islamic Tradition," in Thomas Cooper, ed., *Communication Ethics and Global Change* (New York: Longman, 1989), 137–146.

31. Ayish and Sadig, "Arab-Islamic Heritage in Communication Ethics," 115.

32. Mohamed, "Journalistic Ethics and Responsibility in Relation to Freedom of Expression," 8–9.

33. Ayish and Sadig, "Arab-Islamic Heritage in Communication Ethics," 109.

34. Zulkiple Abdullah Ghani, "Islamic Ethics and Values in the Life of a Communication Scholar," *Journal of Communication and Religion* 27 (March 2004): 58.

35. Kant, *Groundwork of the Metaphysic of Morals*, 429. For elaboration of the principle of human dignity and application to communications, see Plaisance, "Transparency," 187–207; and Lee Anne Peck, "Foolproof or Foolhardy? Ethical Theory in Beginning Reporting Texts," *Journalism and Mass Communication Educator* 58:4 (2004): 343–362.

36. Ayish and Sadig, "The Arab-Islamic Heritage in Communication Ethics," 113.

37. Quoted in Mohamed, "Journalistic Ethics and Responsibility in Relation to Freedom of Expression," 13; from *The Translation of the Meanings of Sahih al-Bukhari* (Chicago: Kazi Publication, 1979), 75.

38. When utilitarianism is linked to both Jeremy Bentham and John Stuart Mill, the principle of utility is ordinarily stated as "seek the greatest happiness for the greatest number." Deni Elliott argues that when speaking of Mill's theory, "the greatest good for the greatest number" is misleading. Mill's principles of justice come before the utility calculus, and throughout his work, Mill seeks to protect individuals who may be sacrificed for the good of the whole. "The greatest number" is an arithmetic statement, implying that the majority wins. Elliott suggests that "the aggregate good" is more accurate to Mill—those actions are right that produce the most overall good for the community as a whole or "for all the people who can be identified as being affected by a particular action" [Deni Elliott, "Getting Mill Right," *Journal of Mass Media Ethics* 22:2–3 (2007): 100]. In order to indicate the importance in Mill of valuing all people involved, the term *aggregate whole* is used here.

39. Bentham suggested a scheme for measuring the quantity of pleasure in human acts in Jeremy Bentham, *An Introduction to the Principles of Morals and Legislation* (New York: Hafner, 1948), chs. 3–7.

40. John Stuart Mill reached this conclusion in the last chapter of *A System of Logic* (London: J. W. Parker, 1843). He attempted eighteen years later to expand and defend this conviction. See John Stuart Mill, *Utilitarianism* (London: J. M. Dent & Sons, 1861), esp. ch. 2.

41. Mill, *Utilitarianism* (1863), in *Utilitarianism: Text and Critical Essays*, ed. Samuel Gorovitz (Indianapolis: Bobbs Merrill, 1971), 59–401.

42. The Potter Box can function without this distinction, but a working knowledge of act and rule utility increases the Potter Box's sophistication. Students are therefore encouraged to read additional descriptions of these two forms of utilitarianism, such as William Frankena, *Ethics* (Englewood Cliffs, NJ: Prentice-Hall, 1962), 29–35; C. E. Harris, Jr., *Applying Moral Theories*, 2d ed. (Belmont, CA: Wadsworth, 1992), 123–154; and Robert L. Holmes, *Basic Moral Philosophy* (Belmont, CA: Wadsworth, 1993), 154–174. A twentieth-century act utility is presented in George E. Moore, *Principia Ethica* (Cambridge, UK: Cambridge University Press, 1954), ch. 5. Richard Brandt and J. O. Urmson are prominent rule utilitarians. See Richard Brandt, "Toward a Credible Form of Utilitarianism," in *Morality and the Language of Conduct*, ed. H. N. Castaneda and G. Nakhnikian (Detroit: Wayne State University Press, 1963), 107–143; and J. O. Urmson, "The Interpretation of the Moral Philosophy of J. S. Mill," *The Philosophical Quarterly* 3 (1953): 33–39.

43. For a detailed critique of utilitarian ethics, see Clifford G. Christians, "Utilitarianism in Media Ethics and Its Discontents," *Journal of Mass Media Ethics* 22:2–3 (2007): 113–131.

44. For an exceptional analysis of utilitarianism for beginners, see Arthur J. Dyck, *On Human Care: An Introduction to Ethics* (Nashville, TN: Abingdon Press, 1977), 57–71.

45. John Rawls, *A Theory of Justice* (Cambridge, MA: Harvard University Belknap Press, 1971), 3–53.

46. Ibid., 118–192.

47. For a critique and elaboration of the two principles, see *Reading Rawls: Critical Studies of a Theory of Justice*, ed. Norman Daniels (New York: Basic Books, 1976), 169–281. For an effective classroom strategy to teach Rawls's theory, see Ronald M. Green, "The Rawls' Game: An Introduction to Ethical Theory," *Teaching Philosophy* 9:1 (March 1986): 51–60.

48. A secularized account of this principle was developed by Kant, who contended that we ought to treat all rational beings as ends in themselves and never as means only. The Judeo-Christian version is included here because of its vast influence on the popular level. William Frankena judged Judeo-Christian ethics to be even more important to Western society than utilitarianism.

49. For an introduction to the central concepts and relevant literature, see Part IV, "East Asia," in Bonevac, *Beyond the Western Tradition*; and Hamid Mowlana, "Communication Ethics and the Islamic Tradition," in *Communication Ethics and Global Change*, eds. Thomas W. Cooper et al. (New York: Longman, 1990), 137–146. The best historical background for Confucianism is Kai-wing Chow, *Ethics, Classics, and Lineage Discourse: The Rise of Confucian Ritualism in Late Imperial China, 1600–1830* (Stanford, CA: Stanford University Press, 1993). A comprehensive list of the relevant material is included in *Bibliography of Comparative Religious Ethics*, eds. John Carmen and Mark Jürgensmeyer (New York: Cambridge University Press, 1991). For a theoretical attempt to integrate diversity and universality, see Clifford G. Christians and Michael Traber, *Communication Ethics and Universal Values* (Thousand Oaks, CA: Sage Publications, 1997). Important essays on intercultural studies and moral norms are included in Ellen F. Paul et al., eds., *Cultural Pluralism and Moral Knowledge* (Cambridge, UK: Cambridge University Press, 1994).

50. See E. R. Hughes, *Chinese Philosophy in Classical Times* (London: J. M. Dent and Sons, 1942), 48.

51. Pedro Gilberto Gomes, *Direto de ser: A ética da Comunicácáo na Americana Latina* (*The Right to Be: An Ethics of Communication in Latin America*) (São Paulo, Brazil: Ediciones Paulinas, 1989).

52. Augustine, *The Confessions*, trans. J. G. Pilkington (New York: Liveright Publishing Corp., 1943); (2.2), 40; (4.10–4.13), 71–75; (7.12), 150; (9.1), 188; (10.1), 218; (10.29), 249;

(13.1–13.4), 340–343. God's love is a basic theme throughout Augustine's writings. For a summary, see Frederick Copleston, "St. Augustine: Moral Theory," in his *A History of Philosophy*, vol. 2 (Westminster, MD: Newman Press, 1960), 81–86.

53. Heinrich Emil Brunner, *The Divine Imperative*, trans. Olive Wyon (Philadelphia: Westminster Press, 1947), 165, 167.

54. For a comprehensive review of this concept, see Gene Outka, *Agape: An Ethical Analysis* (New Haven, CT: Yale University Press, 1972); 7–16 are particularly helpful in understanding the meaning of agape.

55. For the best available introduction to the historical and contemporary issues in Christian ethics, see Edward LeRoy Long, Jr., *A Survey of Christian Ethics* (New York: Oxford University Press, 1967); and his *A Survey of Recent Christian Ethics* (New York: Oxford University Press, 1982). See also E. Clinton Gardner, *Justice and Christian Ethics* (Cambridge, UK: Cambridge University Press, 1995). James M. Gustafson develops a systematic approach to theological ethics in his *Ethics from a Theocentric Perspective* (Chicago: University of Chicago Press, 1981 and 1984). As an alternative to both rationalist and narrative ethics, see Oliver O'Donovan, *Resurrection and the Moral Order*, 2d ed. (Grand Rapids, MI: William B. Eerdmans, 1994).

56. For an evaluation of the role of gender in contemporary theoretical ethics, see Seyla Benhabib, *Situating the Self: Gender, Community and Postmodernism in Contemporary Ethics* (Cambridge, UK: Polity Press, 1992). Of particular interest to students of communication is Charlene Siegfried's *Pragmatism and Feminism: Reweaving the Social Fabric* (Chicago: University of Chicago Press, 1996); Virginia Held's *Feminist Morality: Transforming Culture, Society, and Politics* (Chicago: University of Chicago Press, 1993); Lea P. Stewart's "Facilitating Connections: Issues of Gender, Culture, and Diversity," in Josina M. Makau and Ronald C. Arnett, eds., *Communication Ethics in an Age of Diversity* (Urbana: University of Illinois Press, 1997), 110–125; Julia T. Wood, "Gender and Moral Voice: Moving from Woman's Nature to Standpoint Epistemology," *Women's Studies in Communication* 15 (1992): 1–24; and Virginia Held, *The Ethics of Care: Personal, Political, and Global* (New York: Oxford University Press, 2006). For a general overview of the current theorists and issues, see Rosemarie Tong, *Feminine and Feminist Ethics* (Belmont, CA: Wadsworth, 1993); C. Card, ed., *Feminist Ethics* (Lawrence: University of Kansas Press, 1991); Maurice Hamington and Dorothy C. Mille, eds., *Socializing Care: Feminist Ethics and Public Issues* (Oxford, UK: Rowan and Littlefield, 2000). Paul Martin Lester and Susan Dente Ross's *Images That Injure*, 2d ed., (Westport, CT: Praeger, 2003) includes a section of eight chapters on "Gender Stereotypes."

57. Cf. Carol Gilligan, *In a Different Voice: Psychological Theory and Women's Development* (Cambridge, MA: Harvard University Press, 1982); Carol Gilligan et al., *Mapping the Moral Domain* (Cambridge, MA: Harvard University Graduate School of Education, 1988).

58. Nel Noddings, *Caring: A Feminine Approach to Ethics and Moral Education* (Berkeley: University of California Press, 1984), 5. Cf. Nel Noddings, *Starting at Home: Caring and Social Policy* (Berkeley: University of California Press, 2002).

59. Julia T. Wood, *Who Cares? Women, Care and Culture* (Carbondale: Southern Illinois University Press, 1994), 108–110. Cf. also her *Relational Communication*, 2d ed. (Belmont, CA: Wadsworth, 2000).

60. Linda Steiner, "Feminist Theorizing and Communication Ethics," *Communication* 12:3 (1991): 158; cf. Linda Steiner, "A Feminist Schema for Analysis of Ethical Dilemmas," in Fred L. Casmir, ed., *Ethics in Intercultural and International Communication* (Mahwah, NJ: Lawrence Erlbaum, 1997), 59–88; and Linda Steiner and C. M. Okrusch, "Care as a

Virtue for Journalists," *Journal of Mass Media Ethics* 21:2–3 (2006): 102–122. Daryl Koehn, *Rethinking Feminist Ethics: Care, Trust, and Empathy* (New York: Routledge, 1998) supports the turn away from an abstract rationalistic ethics and likewise emphasizes a relational rather than individualistic understanding of persons. She insists on an empathic rather than legalistic approach to community life. However, in her view, the Gilligan–Noddings tradition tends to favor caregivers over those on the receiving end. She calls for a dialogic ethics that is shaped by feminist ethics but is broader in scope.

61. Tong, "Nel Noddings's Relational Ethics," in her *Feminine and Feminist Ethics*, 109.

62. Quotations from Richard Johannesen's summary of Noddings' *Caring* (12–19, 69–75, 176–177, 182–197), "Ned Noddings' Uses of Martin Buber's Philosophy of Dialogue," unpublished paper, 4.

63. Noddings goes further than urging that human loyalty mitigates stern application of principles; she rejects outright the "ethics of principle as ambiguous and unstable," *Caring* (5). As further background to Noddings's work, refer to Nel Noddings, "Ethics from the Standpoint of Women," in D. L. Rhode, ed., *Theoretical Perspectives on Sexual Difference* (New Haven, CT: Yale University Press, 1990), 160–173; also helpful is Nel Noddings, *Women and Evil* (Berkeley: University of California Press, 1989), and Noddings et al., eds., *Justice and Caring: The Search for Common Ground in Education* (New York: Teachers College Press, 1999).

64. The precise role of philosophical analysis and social theory has been debated even among those who generally follow this decision-making paradigm. Potter himself emphasized philosophical analysis as the primary element in moral deliberation, highlighting, in effect, the third quadrant as the key to a tough-minded social ethics. James Childress follows the spirit of Potter's apparent focus on philosophical ethics in the analytical tradition. See James Childress, "The Identification of Ethical Principles," *Journal of Religious Ethics* 5 (Spring 1977): 39–66.

   The desire for precision threatens the power of a comprehensive method. But the issue is not over the desirability of philosophical rigor versus the benefit of social theory. Both are indispensable forms of knowledge for ethical reflection. The question is which domain galvanizes the total process of reaching a justifiable moral decision. Which particular emphasis achieves a superior disciplinary coherence for applied ethics? Stassen argues for a "focus upon social theory which includes philosophical analysis but extends beyond it" [Glen H. Stassen, "A Social Theory Model for Religious Social Ethics," *The Journal of Religious Ethics* 5 (Spring 1977): 9]. In this volume, we provide a streamlined version of Stassen's adaptation of Potter, a schematic model that seeks to be both useful and rigorous.

65. Henry Stob, *Ethical Reflections: Essays on Moral Themes* (Grand Rapids, MI: Eerdmans, 1978), 3–6. For a distinction between task and collective responsibility, see Clifford G. Christians, "Can the Public Be Held Accountable?" *Journal of Mass Media Ethics* 3:1 (1988): 50–58.

News

Democratic theory gives the press a crucial role. In traditional democracies, education and information are the pillars on which a free society rests. Informed public opinion is typically believed to be a weapon of enormous power—indeed, the cornerstone of legislative government. Therefore, a free press is also central to Jefferson's understanding of politics, for example; Jefferson characteristically referred to an independent information system as "that liberty which guards our other liberties."[1]

Because of the press's privileged position (commonly termed the *enlightenment function*), outside critics and inside leaders have persistently urged it toward responsible behavior. Thomas Jefferson himself lamented how such a noble enterprise could degrade itself by publishing slander and error. Joseph Pulitzer worried that without high ethical ideals, newspapers would fail to serve the public and could even become dangerous. Early in the seventeenth century, the French moralist La Bruyère chided newswriters for reporting trivia and demeaning their high obligation: "They lie down at night in great tranquility upon a piece of news . . . which they are obliged to throw away when they awake." A few years earlier, John Cleveland cautioned against respecting diurnal makers, "for that would be knighting a Mandrake . . . and giving an engineer's reputation to the maker of mousetraps."[2]

Modern criticisms of journalism seem merely to echo complaints that are centuries old. However, the number of today's cavilers and the bitterness of their attacks set the present decade apart. A free press remains our national glory in a complicated world where expectations of journalistic performance are higher than ever before. Actually, the intense and widespread criticism may have yielded a modest dividend: Never before have the media been so aware of the need for responsible behavior.

A self-conscious quality hangs heavily over newsrooms and professional conventions. Aside from the bandits and the pompous who remain untouched by any attacks, some movement is evident. How can journalists fulfill their mission credibly? Should Pulitzer Prizes be given to reporters who use deception to get a story? Why not form an ethics committee? Are codes of ethics helpful? Should journalism schools teach ethics courses or not? Such well-intentioned questions crop up more and more. The cases in Part 1 present the primary issues and problems that are currently being debated among those with a heightened awareness of journalism's ethical responsibility.

The fresh interest in ethics and the profit to be gained from working through these cases may be threatened by the Western press's commitment to independence. There is a rhetoric from as far back as Jefferson, who called for a nation "where the press is *free*." Others have argued: "You cannot chain the watchdog"; "The First Amendment guarantees the news media's independence"; "Allowing controls by anyone makes us a mockery." And in countries where freedom is valued above all, accountability is not often understood clearly. Accountability, properly requested and unreservedly given, is alien territory. Although the belief in a free press is sincere and of critical importance, it often plays tricks on the press's thinking about ethics. Ethical principles concerning obligation and reckoning do not find a natural home within a journalism hewn from the rock of negative freedom. Part 1 advocates freedom of the press, but it promotes an accountable news system and attempts to provide content for that notion.

Ethical questions concerning conflict of interest, truthfulness, privacy, social justice, confidentiality, and the other issues we address here must be considered in an environment of stress. The latest Gallup polls reveal press credibility at 16 percent in the United States, the lowest figure in decades and an alarming one by anyone's measure. For some, it represents kicking the chair on which you stubbed your toe. The anxieties experienced in a nation uncertain of its world leadership role often provoke outbursts against the messenger. Nonetheless, we must continue working on media ethics, even in these hard times. Restrictions tend to make newspersons feel stifled, yet the contemporary cultural climate demands that journalism employ restraint and sobriety.[3] Although all the problems cannot be solved in the five chapters in this section, the analysis and resolution of the moral dilemmas presented here address matters of high priority on the journalist's agenda.

NOTES

1. Thomas Jefferson, "Address to Philadelphia Delegates," 25 May 1808, in *The Writings of Thomas Jefferson*, ed. Andrew J. Lipscomb (Washington, D.C.: The Thomas Jefferson Memorial Association, 1903), vol. 16, 304. For similar highly quoted passages, see his "Letter to Marquis De Lafayette," 4 November 1823, and his "Letter to Dr. James Currie," 18 January 1786, in *The Writings of Thomas Jefferson*, ed. Paul L. Ford (New York: G.P. Putnam's Sons, 1894), vol. 4, 132.

2. La Bruyère and Cleveland are quoted in William Rivers, Wilbur Schramm, and Clifford Christians, *Responsibility in Mass Communication*, 3d ed. (New York: Harper and Row, 1980), 2.

3. An important line of scholarship accounts for some of these shifts and stresses by understanding news as social narrative. See Gertrude J. Robinson, "Making News and Manufacturing Consent: The Journalistic Narrative and Its Audience," in Theodore L. Glasser and Charles T. Salmon, eds., *Public Opinion and the Communication of Consent* (New York: Guilford Press, 1995), Ch. 14, 348–369; James A. Ettema and Theodore L. Glasser, *Custodians of Conscience: Investigative Journalism and Public Virtue* (New York: Columbia University Press, 1998); Stuart Allan, *News Culture* (Buckingham, UK: Open University Press, 1999); and Michael Schudson, *The Sociology of News* (New York: W.W. Norton, 2003).

CHAPTER ONE

Institutional Pressures

William Peter Hamilton of *The Wall Street Journal* once argued that "A newspaper is private enterprise owing nothing whatever to the public, which grants it no franchise. It is emphatically the property of the owner, who is selling a manufactured product at his own risk."[1] This is an extreme statement, yet over the past two centuries many American publishers and broadcasters have shared this attitude. Based on the principles of classical democracy and traditional capitalism, the individual's right to publish has been a strongly held convention.

This mood may be shifting somewhat, at least in theory. Increasingly, enlightened newspaper owners and executives realize their special obligation precisely because news—and not widgets—is their business. In First Amendment perspective, journalism is in fact a business, but of a particular kind.

Nothing is more difficult in the mass media enterprise than promoting the public good even though the rewards—professionally and financially—are not commensurate with such altruism. In actual practice, it becomes extraordinarily difficult to separate the media's financial interests from the public's legitimate news interests. The Constitution protects the media from government constraint, but the news is under the perpetual risk of corporate control. Granted, a conflict between the public's need for unpolluted information and the stockholders' need for profit is not inevitable. Needing to earn a respectable income and deciding to stop a dead-ended investigation could both be appropriate; moral questions emerge when the two are connected as cause and effect. Without a press pool to help pay expenses for a charter, a minor party candidate could not conduct a modern political campaign. One person serving in two potentially conflicting capacities—for example, as executive for Columbia Broadcasting and board member for Columbia University—may indeed be working ethically.[2] Not every owner or executive is automatically suspect.

Nonetheless, ever since mass communications took on the character of big business at the turn of the twentieth century, there have been built-in commercial pressures. The angry critic Upton Sinclair said accusingly in 1920: "The Brass

Check is found in your pay envelope each week . . . the price of your shame—
you who take the fair body of truth and sell it in the market-place, who betray
the virgin hopes of mankind into the loathsome brothel of Big Business."[3] As
the ominous trend continues toward concentrated ownership of media properties,
cost-conscious publishers threaten to overwhelm the press's noble mission.[4] The
five cases that follow demonstrate how media practitioners are often caught in
conflicting duties to their employers, to their readers or viewers, and to their
own professional conscience. Examples in Parts 2 and 3 regarding persuasion
(advertising and public relations) and in Part 4 involving media ownership illustrate some of the conundrums that occur regularly in today's news business.
It is no wonder the public remains enormously concerned whether media en-
terprises spend money honorably.

The first case, "*The New York Times* Fires Jayson Blair," is a sensational story
of Blair's wild antics of plagiarism and fake stories. It raises old ghosts from
Dante's lower levels that are reserved for fabricators. However, institutional
failures to supervise his work and ensure his accountability are the heart of the
problem.

The second case, "CNN in Baghdad," examines the enormous pressure on the
news enterprise to maintain credibility in dictatorships and war zones.

The third case, "The Time Warner Colossus," illustrates a disturbing trend in
cross-media ownership. The pattern toward concentration has been occurring for
decades, but it is reaching dangerous levels of integration. Although it was financially beneficial in this case to combine the strengths of print and visual communications, the integration of Time, Warner, Turner, and AOL raises ethical questions
about independent artists and cultural imperialism.

The fourth case, "NBC and GM's Pickup," concerns the blurred lines between
news and entertainment. Given the profitability of television news magazines, the
pressures toward big audiences and cheap production have become virtually un-
stoppable.

The fifth case, "The Wichita Experiment," deals with *The Wichita Eagle*'s twin
commitment to society and to subscribers/investors. The *Eagle* attempts to combine this traditional dichotomy in innovative ways. Out of its creative struggles,
public journalism emerges.

Since biblical times, sages have warned against serving two masters. Nearly
all professions—politics most notably—confront the same problem. Yet the issues
cut especially deep in reporting. The highly publicized conviction of former *Wall
Street Journal* reporter R. Foster Winans has become a classic reminder that easy
cash is always a temptation—for individuals as well as for companies. Leaking
advance information from his "Heard on the Street" column to stockbroker Peter
Bryant yielded a $30,000 under-the-table payment. Apparently even small
amounts of money are occasionally worth more than our integrity as journalists.
As some observers have noted, the issues of handling profit responsibly and
spurning fattened pockets are not just a chapter in a book; they are the cornerstone
of media ethics.

1 The New York Times *Fires Jayson Blair*

On 11 May 2003, the following headline dominated the front page of *The New York Times*: "*Times* Reporter Who Resigned Leaves Long Trail of Deception." Jayson Blair, a twenty-seven-year-old reporter for one of the United States' oldest and most venerated newspapers, had resigned on the first of May amid strong evidence of plagiarism and gross inaccuracy. The *Times* summarized:

> The reporter . . . misled readers and *Times* colleagues with dispatches that purported to be from Maryland, Texas, and other states, when often he was far away, in New York. He fabricated comments. He lifted material from other newspapers and wire services. He selected details from photographs to create the impression he had been somewhere or seen someone when he had not.
>
> And he used these techniques to write falsely about emotionally charged moments in recent history. . . . [5]

An internal investigation involving no less than five reporters, three editors, and two researchers uncovered problems in at least thirty-six of seventy-three national articles by Blair since October 2002; prior compositions contained progressively increasing levels of fabrication, fake sources, and inaccuracy.[6] Clearly, the reporter's long-term output contradicted several of the most basic tenets of professional morality.

But how did Blair come to "represent a profound betrayal of trust and a low point in the 152-year history of the newspaper"?[7] Various facets of the man should be considered. To begin, several colleagues and bosses had repeatedly emphasized his gifts as a reporter and corporate worker. After a successful undergraduate internship at the paper in the summer of 1998, Jayson Blair returned the following summer and dived in. Coworkers noticed his interest in their work, charismatic personality, strong writing ability, and long hours spent at the office. Yet inaccuracy characterized his compositions from the beginning.

As time progressed, he made consistent errors in reporting and seemed increasingly careless to supervisors. Even so, he moved up through the ranks—gaining full-time status in 2001. Though editors were sometimes openly critical, most still believed him a gifted young reporter just learning the ropes. They made adjustments, giving Blair both time away to refocus his attention and assignments in different departments. But it didn't help. In April 2002, Jonathan Landman, the *Times*' metropolitan editor, e-mailed that "we have to stop Jayson from writing for the *Times*. Right now."[8]

The combination of his personal skills and carelessness allowed larger and larger fabrications, and by April 2003, the jig was up. The *San Antonio Express-News* officially asked *The New York Times* to investigate a Blair story extremely similar to one of theirs. When the reporter was asked to authenticate his on-assignment travel using billing receipts, he officially resigned on May 1. The internal investigation followed and continued beyond the May 11 article.

Externally, Jayson Blair caused varying amounts of damage to the parties and sources his stories involved. For instance, when Blair wrote of Private Jessica Lynch—a young soldier wounded in the Iraqi invasion and a national media sensation—he detailed the hilltop view of tobacco fields and pastures from the family's front porch. Her family was highly surprised to read his description because no such view exists from their valley home; amused, they didn't bother calling the *Times*, although they wondered what caused the falsehood.[9] However, others' reputations were irrevocably damaged. Pete Mahoney, associate athletic director of Kent State University, was told by his boss one morning that

continued

the *Times* quoted him as agreeing that his school would bend NCAA attendance require-ments for their Division I football team. Blair, author of the story on Division I athletics, never even spoke with Mahoney. Laing Kennedy, the school's athletic director, commented that the "story was corrected in a local newspaper, but that's 100,000 readers. The *Times* has over 1 million readers. The *Times* is a world-class, national newspaper, and the article questioned our credibility. It hurt us. Of course it hurt us."[10]

But the internal disruption was even greater. The scandal not only decreased the paper's longstanding integrity as a credible news source but also illuminated deeper prob-lems among its elite and staff. It became clear that a strong lack of communication be-tween supervisors and colleagues contributed to the overall lack of action against Jayson Blair. Linda Greenhouse, veteran *Times* staff member, argued that "There is an endemic cultural issue at the *Times* . . . which is a top-down hierarchical structure."[11] That Blair per-sisted for so long testified to a lack of cohesiveness among the paper's reporters, editors, and management. Moreover, Howell Raines and Gerald Boyd—the publication's executive and managing editors, respectively—eventually resigned due to the managerial questions their reporter's actions exposed.[12] In retrospect, the *Times* published a fifty-eight-page re-port ("Safeguarding the Integrity of Our Journalism") prepared by a committee headed by Assistant Managing Editor Allan Siegal and that included twenty-one other *Times* journal-ists and three outsiders. The report focused on personnel policies, called for a healthy bal-ance between work and personal commitments, and recommended the appointment of a senior-level Editor for Career Development.

Three months after being fired, Blair signed a book contract for his memoirs, with a mid-six-figure advance. "It's a marvelous story. I think (Blair) is one of the best writers in the country today," said New Millennium publisher Michael Viner. *Times* columnist Clyde Haberman took the opposite view: "I hope they have a great fact checker. We're living in a society that rewards inexcusable behavior. We seem to have lost our capacity for shame."[13] "I lied and I lied, and then I lied some more, "Blair writes on page one of the book. "And these were no everyday little white lies—they were complete fantasies, embellished down to the tiniest detail" (1). Whether the result of an increased capacity for shame or de-creased desire for more ink on Blair is up for debate, *Burning Down My Master's House* (2004) sold fewer than 5000 copies, despite an initial printing of 250,000.   ■

Some have raised questions about the role of race in Jayson Blair's career, whether in his hiring, promotion, or resignation. Many reporters acknowledge that as an African-American, the young reporter differed from the white majority at the *Times* and indeed more generally from the journalism profession as a whole. Some question, a few even wonder, if his rapid progress to national reporter was due in part to his race—almost an affirmative action promotion.[14] However, others con-tend that "it would be a huge mistake to forget that black, white, or green, he also was cut some slack because he could *write*."[15] While it is always possible that race played some role in the events, Blair was in obvious ways a talented journalist.

In the end, the Jayson Blair affair is more than just an isolated, though shock-ing, occurrence of irresponsible journalism. Blair's bizarre pranks, plagiarism, and deception are indefensible and unethical. However, while all newspapers refuse to condone fabricated stories such as Blair's, some in the journalism enterprise believe that newspaper leadership also must be watched more carefully and made accountable. A study by the Readership Institute at the Media Management Center of Northwestern University found that top-down management in journalism hurts readership and promotes an atmosphere of silence in the workroom.[16] And that lack of communication provides an environment where unethical behavior becomes much easier. While staff are responsible for their actions, and leadership for theirs as well, ethical media practice also requires that both groups communicate with each other and work hard to promote good journalism together.

The Potter Box helps us clarify the issues and pinpoint the problem. Blair is to blame for violating the ethical principles of quadrant three, and doing so without contrition. Step one reveals practices and decisions by *Times* management that are likewise unacceptable, but in this case for being unprofessional. These managerial mistakes need to be corrected, byline and date policies changed, and structural improvements made in the news operation itself to prevent them from happening again.

2 CNN in Baghdad

On 11 April 2003, CNN's chief news executive, Eason Jordan, published the following op-ed piece in *The New York Times*, "The News We Kept to Ourselves":

> Over the last dozen years I made 13 trips to Baghdad to lobby the government to keep CNN's Baghdad bureau open and to arrange interviews with Iraqi leaders. Each time I visited, I became more distressed by what I saw and heard—awful things that could not be reported because doing so would have jeopardized the lives of Iraqis, particularly those on our Baghdad staff.
>
> For example, in the mid-1990s one of our Iraqi cameramen was abducted. For weeks he was beaten and subjected to electroshock torture in the basement of a secret police headquarters because he refused to confirm the government's ludicrous suspicion that I was the Central Intelligence Agency's Iraqi station chief. CNN had been in Baghdad long enough to know that telling the world about the torture of one of its employees would almost certainly have gotten him killed and put his family and co-workers at grave risk.
>
> Working for a foreign news organization provided Iraqi citizens with no protection. The secret police terrorized Iraqis working for international press services who were courageous enough to try to provide accurate reporting. Some vanish, never to be heard from again. Others disappeared and then surfaced later with whispered tales of being hauled off and tortured in unimaginable ways. Obviously, other news organizations were in the same bind we were when it came to reporting on their own workers.
>
> We also had to worry that our reporting might endanger Iraqis not on our payroll. I know that CNN could not report that Saddam Hussein's eldest son, Uday, told me in 1995 that he intended to assassinate two of his brothers-in-law who had defected, and also the man giving them asylum, King Hussein of Jordan. If we had gone with that story, I was sure he would have responded by killing the Iraqi translator who was the only other participant in the meeting. After all, secret police thugs brutalized even senior officials of the Information Ministry, just to keep them in line (one such official has long been missing all his fingernails).

continued

Still, I felt I had a moral obligation to warn Jordan's monarch, and I did so the next day. King Hussein dismissed the threat as a madman's rant. A few months later Uday lured his brothers-in-law back to Baghdad; they were soon killed.

I came to know several Iraqi officials well enough that they confided in me that Saddam Hussein was a maniac who had to be removed. One Foreign Ministry officer told me of a colleague who, finding out his brother had been executed by the regime, was forced, as a test of loyalty, to write a letter of congratulations on the act to Saddam Hussein. An aide to Uday once told me why he had no front teeth: henchmen had ripped them out with pliers and told him never to wear dentures, so he would always remember the price to be paid for upsetting his boss. Again, we could not broadcast anything these men said to us.

Last December, when I told Information Minister Muhammad Said al-Sahhaf that we intended to send reporters to Kurdish-controlled northern Iraq, he warned me they would "suffer the severest possible consequences." CNN went ahead, and in March, Kurdish officials presented us with evidence that they had thwarted an armed attack on our quarters in Erbil. This included videotaped confessions of two men identifying themselves as Iraqi intelligence agents who said their bosses in Baghdad told them the hotel actually housed CIA and Israeli agents. The Kurds offered to let us interview the suspects on camera, but we refused, for fear of endangering our staff in Baghdad.

Then there were the events that were not unreported but that nonetheless still haunt me. A thirty-one-year-old Kuwaiti woman, Asrar Qabandi, was captured by Iraqi secret police occupying her country in 1990 for "crimes," one of which included speaking with CNN on the phone. They beat her daily for two months, forcing her father to watch. In January 1991, on the eve of the American-led offensive, they smashed her skull and tore her body apart limb by limb. A plastic bag containing her body parts was left on the doorstep of her family's home.

I felt awful having these stories bottled up inside me. Now that Saddam Hussein's regime is gone, I suspect we will hear many, many more gut-wrenching tales from Iraqis about the decades of torment. At last, these stories can be told freely.

In 2005, Eason Jordan resigned from his position as CNN's news chief after making remarks in a World Economic Forum at Davos, Switzerland, to the effect that the U.S. military killed several journalists in Iraq. (Some consider his resignation the result of pressure from conservative bloggers because the story went largely unreported in the media until his resignation, two weeks after the remarks.) Since then, he has founded Praedict, a news and journalist safety organization. His biography states that Praedict was in response to the killing of two of his colleagues in Iraq in 2004 (http://00578ea.netsolhost.com/bio2.html).   ■

Covering the news in countries where the press is not free raises hard questions. During its twelve years in Baghdad, CNN's reporters and producers were expelled five times, an employee was abducted and tortured, crews were threatened, and sources disappeared. Meanwhile, Eason Jordan in his thirteen visits to keep the Baghdad bureau open heard of horrendous brutality by Hussein's regime that CNN did not dare to report, fearing further torture-harassment.[17] However, despite CNN's troubles, Jordan's disclosure received little sympathy from his peers. To most critics, withholding critical information about the regime to avoid being ousted sacrificed CNN's credibility. "It's reasonable for the public to question whether CNN or other news organizations have held back or watered down their reports to avoid offending leaders in tyrannies they are covering."[18]

Instead of gathering and publishing the news, the Baghdad bureau was sitting on it. By default, the argument goes, CNN served as a mouthpiece for Hussein's regime and lost its value as a news organization. "From now on discriminating viewers cannot be blamed for wondering whether CNN reporters in Cuba, China, Sudan, and Syria and other international hotspots are pulling their punches, not telling all they know, or even covering up critically important information. That is about the worst thing that can happen to a news organization."[19] From this perspective, it is better not to report at all than to report misleading information. CNN's ads call it "the most trusted name" in cable news, but for its critics, the compromises of the twelve years contradict that claim.

When there are conflicting duties, Aristotle's temperance is ordinarily the best alternative. In this case, the commitment of CNN executives to the safety of their employees and sources conflicts with their obligations to their viewers for credible news. Bob Steele, director of the ethics program at the Poynter Institute, basically follows this path. For Steele, CNN's decisions were "morally complex and pragmatically complicated. There were many factors in the calculus Jordan faced, including competing principles and conflicting loyalties."[20] In negotiating with Hussein's regime so that CNN could continue reporting from Iraq, "Jordan was trying to balance not only CNN's best interests in a competitive market, but also human lives."[21] According to Steele, critics who accuse CNN of being soft on Hussein "fail to embrace the moral complexity within this issue." The outrage of such critics "might deter other news organizations from coming forward to discuss the compromises they had made in Iraq."[22]

Besides staying in Baghdad and working through the conflicts, another option is consistent with Aristotelian and Confucian thinking. On being expelled the first time, rather than negotiating reentry, CNN could have found other ways to get the truth out. When reporting the truth through an inside presence is compromised, courageous coverage from outside the country is both mandatory and possible.

3 The Time Warner Colossus

In June 1989, Time, Inc., acquired Warner Communications for $13 billion in cash and securities, following a ferocious struggle against Paramount's takeover attempt. Over four months, the dramatic story filled 12,000 pages of sworn depositions about the legal entanglements that accompanied the clashes in the corporate boardrooms. The result was a business deal made in heaven: Time Warner had assets of $25 billion. "The first stretch of the information highway was laid."[23]

On 12 September 1996, the term *big media* was redefined once again. The Federal Trade Commission (FTC) approved Time Warner's $7.5 billion merger with Turner Broadcasting System, creating the world's largest media and entertainment company. On the same day as the FTC established "a new standard for media heavyweight,"[24] Rupert Murdoch announced that his worldwide communications empire, News Corporation, would purchase

continued

the New World Communications Group—making News Corporation, the parent of the Fox television network, the biggest owner of television stations in the United States. Twelve months earlier, Walt Disney had purchased Capital Cities/ABC, Inc., for $19 billion, and a month earlier, Westinghouse Electric had bought the Infinity Broadcasting Corporation for $4.9 billion. Viacom bought out CBS for $32 billion in September 1999. And in January 2000, America Online agreed to buy out Time Warner for $165 billion, making AOL Time Warner the biggest corporate merger in history. AOL Time Warner's stock market value equaled the gross national product of Mexico. By the merger, Time Warner acknowledged that the Internet was central to its music, TV, and publishing businesses and that its own efforts in online and high-capacity networks were ineffective.[25]

One set of ethical issues that pervades these megamergers was established already in 1989 when Time acquired Warner. During its days as a separate corporation, Time, Inc.'s magazines included *Time*, *Southern Living*, *Sports Illustrated*, *Fortune*, *Life*, *Money*, and *People*. The magazine division had long been wonderfully profitable, controlling nearly one-fourth of all U.S. magazine advertising revenue. However, during the late 1980s, Time's investment bankers could no longer project more than 6 percent revenue growth annually for the future. The corporate strategy began to focus investment on video programming. But in spite of increasing involvement in video, the company considered itself underdeveloped here, given today's explosion in visual technologies. Since the early 1960s, Time, Inc., had diversified into cable and book publishing in order to expand its growth potential. Most of these ventures had become household words: Book of the Month Club, HBO Video, Home Box Office, Time-Life Books, and Scott-Foresman. However, Warner's wildly successful records-and-music division, its film production capabilities, and extensive overseas marketing made the merger an attractive way to prevent an unwelcome buyout from a hostile company such as Paramount. Warner Bros. had long been one of the movie industry's top studios, scoring number one in the box office four of the past five years. It owned 2200 films—including *Batman* and *Lethal Weapon*—1500 popular cartoons, and 23,000 television programs. Management predicted that combining the revenues and sales of Time and Warner would jump-start the new corporation into a growth cycle neither one would experience separately.

Critics have charged that executives from both companies were more interested in padding their own income and stock holdings than in serving either stockholders or the public. According to *Fortune*, Steve Ross of Warner orchestrated a compensation package for himself with the new corporation "so abundant in dollars that, should the oilman fail to show this winter, Ross can shovel money into his furnace and have plenty left over in the spring." In addition to a multimillion-dollar salary and pension packages, on completion of the deal, Ross received $193 million in cash and stock-based compensation. In fact, these early warning signals about Ross dogged his career until he died of cancer in December 1992, when the company was in a positive cash flow but still staggering "under $15 billion in debt, and $1.2 billion in annual debt service."[26] As a matter of fact, the legacy of soft profits and warring leadership continued unabated under Ross's successor, Gerald Levin. Levin engineered the $7.5 billion deal with Turner, but, as Johnnie Roberts puts it:

> Whew! Levin needed that victory. Since the 1989 transaction that created Time Warner, the company's stock has languished. And the fate of Levin, who succeeded the late chairman Steve Ross in 1993, has often been in doubt. Under his watch, the company has been distinguished for its corporate coups, feuds and flavor-of-the-month approach to corporate strategy.[27]

continued

The acquisition by AOL actually worsened the company's finances. AOL in 2000 was riding the Internet stock boom and purchased Time Warner at overvalued shares. As the stock bubble burst, AOL Time Warner became one of the biggest sinkholes in America, with $200 billion in stock vaporizing by 18 July 2002, when Robert Pittman from AOL was fired as CEO. On 16 January 2003, Robert Parsons from the Time Warner side became the new CEO, and two weeks later Ted Turner stepped down as vice chairman. On 21 September 2003, AOL became a subunit, and the corporate name was changed back to Time Warner, Inc.

Henry Luce III of Time, Inc.'s Board of Directors and former Editor-in-Chief Hedley Donovan objected to the 1989 merger on the grounds that Time had been primarily a journalistic enterprise in contrast to Warner's entertainment structure. As a matter of fact, the management staff responsible for the acquisition turned the independence of the news-editorial component into one of Time's problems. Video and print had never been integrated, they said; putting *Sports Illustrated*'s swimsuit issue into video format had been one of Time's few meager attempts to exploit the company's resources. Warner's electronic and visual expertise was seen to overcome that "deficiency" forever. And the acquisition of Turner strengthened this strategy further. As Time Warner wanted to have even more entertainment content, Turner Broadcasting fit the bill with its empire, including the Cartoon Network, TNT, Turner Pictures, the MGM film library, Hanna-Barbera cartoon stars, Castle Rock Entertainment, World Championship Wrestling, New Line Cinema, along with CNN and its affiliates.

The rationale for the AOL–Time Warner merger was the same. America Online had 22 million paying subscribers, and each of them, in principle, was an outlet for Time Warner products. In addition, the merger presumed advertising synergy. Ad space in magazines and airtime on cable networks could be synchronized with spots on American Online and licensing opportunities with the Warner film studio. Due to a soft advertising market, dissension, and mismanagement, the advertising promise has not been fulfilled. Ad revenue actually fell 17 percent in 2002. During 2003, CNN lost its ratings preeminence to Fox News Channel, and the gap between the two continues to widen as CNN is left fighting for "table scraps" with MSNBC. More recently, Time Warner sold some of the very assets that had been part of its initial merger strategy, including Warner Music Group, Time Life, Inc., and the Time Warner Book Group. Meanwhile, Time, Inc., has laid off hundreds of workers every year since 2005, a clear reflection of Time Warner's steadily decreasing market capitalization.[28] With regard to programming and advertising, the biggest merger in history has produced only misery. ∎

The problem of Time's journalistic integrity that concerned Luce and Donovan has not been resolved. Stanley Kubrick's film, *Eyes Wide Shut*, stars Tom Cruise and Nicole Kidman in a daring tale of sexual exploration. The film's opening was delayed until the summer of 1999 because the director and his two attractive stars took fifty-two long weeks, instead of the originally scheduled eighteen, to ensure that all the important nuances of fear, jealousy, and despair were done right.

Lest audiences grow weary waiting for this sizzler, *Time* magazine devoted its cover to the film two weeks before opening. During a week when news from Kosovo and Sierra Leone was capturing headlines elsewhere, *Time*'s cover read like advertising copy: "Cruise and Kidman like you've never seen them," leading readers to wonder if peeking inside this issue would show more of both actors, or if one must rather wait for the movie itself. Either way, Time Warner wins. Owning both the magazine and the studio, the corporation preferred that readers buy both. Indeed, there is more inside. More photos, a rare preview by *Time* critic Richard Schickel, an intimate interview of the stars by a reporter in Sydney, and a thinly disguised invitation to squeamish viewers by Richard Corliss that this hot movie is a "must see."[29]

Time has enjoyed a long reputation as a leader in American journalism. Its reporting has helped shape a national conscience, and its covers have helped set a national agenda. *Time* intended to be the best when it was born, and the corporate merger was supposed to enhance and not undermine this commitment. Why, then, does this successful and profitable voice of journalism devote a cover to promoting a film? Perhaps because it is the last film of a notable director. Stanley Kubrick died four days after the film was finished. But if noting this swan song was *Time*'s reason, it should have featured Kubrick himself, perhaps because *Eyes Wide Shut* may be an important film about the convoluted human passions associated with sexual attraction, a film so serious that it becomes a cultural marker and milestone. If such was *Time*'s sense, it might have placed *Eyes* in the context of film history and explored its semiotic possibilities and aesthetic merit.

Perhaps *Time* went to its cover because *Eyes* was an expensive film that, because of its artistry or its reserve, could suffer the worst possible fate of a Hollywood product and bomb at the box office. For all the hyped sex in the trailers, the ads, and *Time*'s cover, some critics have complained that too little actually happens. Audiences might expect more. In this case, *Time*'s spread is pure publicity designed to ring up an outstanding opening weekend. And that's precisely what happened. On *Eyes*' first weekend, it topped the charts at $22 million. No one assigned *Time* a social duty to report the news. But over nearly seventy-five years, that's what *Time* has done. If now it intends to exercise its considerable influence for the promotion of corporate projects, it should say so explicitly, letting readers know that its pages may now be bought, but only if the buyer is also the owner.

Kant requires that each person or institution contribute its morally right thing to the common good. *Time* has no more reason to hype a film than it does to become a supporter of only one political party. Duty rightly understood focuses a magazine on its mission and eliminates distractions and subversions. *Time*'s duty articulated over three generations was sacrificed in this case to the interests of the parent corporation. It became something other than it had previously purported to be and injured its credibility for the sake of profits that do not benefit its news capability. On a deeper and broader level, the Time Warner merger illustrates a disturbing trend of the last decade toward media conglomeration.

> In 1983 there were fifty dominant media corporations; today there are five. These five conglomerates are Time Warner, by 2003 the largest media firm in the world; The Walt Disney Company; Murdoch's News Corporation, based in Australia; Viacom; and Bertelsmann, based in Germany. Today, none of the

dominant media companies bother with dominance merely in a single medium. Their strategy has been to have major holdings in all the media, from newspapers to movie studios. This gives each of the five corporations and their leaders more communications power than was exercised by any despot or dictatorship in history. . . . The media conglomerates are not the only industry whose owners have become monopolistic in the American economy. But media products are unique in one vital respect. They do not manufacture nuts and bolts: they manufacture a social and political world.[30]

It is almost impossible to believe that in two decades those corporations largely controlling the mass media would shrink to only five. The public learns about this monopolization through gargantuan stock market transactions, the glamorous personalities of executives, and its fascination with empire building. The social consequences of a few companies regulating what citizens know are submerged. The unsettling political and economic results are obvious for a nation that prizes diversity of opinion and access to the marketplace. Obviously, the independent decision making of practitioners becomes increasingly difficult as corporations expand into impersonal behemoths.

In terms of the agape principle in ethics, two issues have become evident from the AOL Time Warner mergers in 1989, 1996, and 2002: (1) the rights of independent producers and (2) the problem of cultural imperialism. The takeover by AOL did not solve these problems but only made them worse.

In spite of the profitability of Time, Inc., and its general corporate luster, its top executives were complaining in the late 1980s that it did not own any important copyrights in the video sector of its business. Time's cable operations gave the company a distribution system, but software had to be purchased in the open market, where prices continued to climb. Time concluded that "in the media and entertainment business of the future, the winners will own the copyrights to creative products, as well as avenues of distribution. We intend to increase our ownership of both."[31]

In order to own copyrights without violating the law, Time needed to own more creative talent. Thus, by merging with Warner, it expanded its copyright capabilities a hundredfold. In the process, Time Warner was no longer motivated to draw on the resources of independent writers and producers. Time Warner solved its copyright problem by cutting itself off from the world's pool of ideas in favor of a creative staff, which generally conformed to the values of the mainstream media. This "repression by the bottom line," although enhancing the corporation's business position, ironically diminished the quality, flexibility, independence, and variety of the very programming it was designed to market.[32]

In addition to putting a squeeze on the creative sector, Time Warner in its formation viewed the international audience in an ethically inappropriate manner according to the agape principle. At a time when so-called foreign markets offered the greatest growth opportunities, only 10 percent of Time, Inc.'s revenues were from overseas. Warner Communications, however, was a stunning financial success worldwide, with 40 percent of its profits coming from outside the United States.

In the media business, Warner's concept is called "synergy"; that is, an article can be spun off as a book, movie, or television show domestically and then sold abroad through an international distribution network. Warner's prowess in spinning off *Batman*, *Superman*, and *Wonder Woman* set the standard by which the merged corporation would now compete with Sony of Japan, Viacom, Rupert Murdoch's empire, Bertelsmann of West Germany, Pearson PLC of England, and the handful of communications companies that control the world's media. Whenever the merger talks were threatened in 1989, acquiring Turner debated in 1996, and the acquisition by America Online in 2000, global international media competition became the trump card to move negotiations forward.

The ethical problem is that throughout the planning and execution of one of today's biggest media and entertainment companies, the international audience has been seen exclusively as a paying market, as an exploitable resource. No attention has been given to indigenous programming and enhancing local talent. It is this notion of a one-way information flow that carries over the colonial and paternalistic spirit no longer acceptable in politics or even in international economics. Since World War II, seeking to dominate another's culture is becoming increasingly as reprehensible as dominating another's government or business out of exploitative self-interest.

4 NBC and GM's Pickup

On 17 November 1992, *Dateline NBC* ran a fifteen-minute segment, "Waiting to Explode." Its focus was the safety of General Motors' full-size pickup trucks in model years 1973–1987. These trucks were designed with gas tanks mounted outside the frame.

The *Dateline* report began with the story of Shannon Moseley, a teenager killed in a pickup given to him by his parents. A law officer described Shannon's screams as he died in the fire. Another segment showed a tearful twenty-two-year-old mother whose two infant daughters died in a similar crash. She could hear their screams as fire engulfed the cab. In this episode, *Dateline* also showed an empty pickup being hit from the side and bursting into flames. NBC called it "an unscientific demonstration" of how the gas would ignite if the tank were punctured on impact or fuel was forced out of the cap.

NBC did not tell viewers that the tank had been filled to the brim and an improper gas cap had been used to seal it. *Dateline NBC* did not inform viewers that toy rocket engines had been taped under the truck to ensure a fire even if the tank did not explode or gas did not leak out during the crash test. The incendiary devices were connected to a remote control and activated just before impact. NBC claimed a faulty headlight wire on the old car sent crashing into the pickup had actually sparked the fire, in effect making the flares unnecessary; therefore, they were not mentioned in the program.

And NBC did not tell viewers that its estimates of crash speeds were underplayed for both crashes. All these facts would come to light through the careful investigative work of—not the media—but the corporation whose reputation *Dateline* had impugned.

In a 19 November memo, GM blasted the program as "grossly unfair, misleading and irresponsible, . . . vicious and unjust," and charged that it was filled with "inaccurate statements, distortions, and facts wrenched out of context." It asked NBC why viewers were not told that the original crash giving rise to the lawsuit "was caused by a speeding, drunken driver who was convicted and spent time in jail for his crime." It complained that the audience was not informed that GM pickups during this period "actually had the lowest incidence of fatal injury in side collisions."[33]

Dateline producer Robert Read responded on November 20, claiming a fair and balanced report. "As to our crash demonstration," Read wrote, "we did show the public that at about 40 mph there was no leakage, and we feel our use of these demonstrations was accurate and responsible."[34] Now the battle heated up. In early December, GM demanded to inspect the demonstration vehicles firsthand. NBC dodged and avoided GM's request. GM insisted on seeing the test vehicles. NBC replied that the vehicles "have been junked and therefore are no longer available for inspection by anyone."[35]

Perhaps the matter would have died slowly in corporate memos but for an anonymous call to the editor of *Hot Rod* magazine, informing the trade journal of the real cause of the fire at the crash test site. The caller was probably associated with the Brownsburg (Indiana) Fire Department and was present at the crash simulation; clearly this person did not like what she or he saw.

Immediately, *Hot Rod* called GM for comment. The new information gave GM the break it needed. Within two hours, company representatives had located the demonstrator in a junkyard near Indianapolis. The videotape taken by firemen who were standing by suggested that only a brief burst of flame had occurred from the rockets and around the cap. The tank had not exploded. GM's examination of the truck's gas tank revealed no puncture at all.

GM outlined the facts about the "unscientific demonstration" in a scalding letter to NBC producer Robert Read, with copies to NBC CEO Robert Wright and NBC News President Michael Gartner.[36] It was a journalist's worst nightmare: The investigators had done their own investigation. Consequently, GM's evidence would show NBC's economical unscientific test (conducted for only $8000) to be ludicrous and deceptive.

On 8 February 1993, Gartner replied to GM's letter (on the same day GM initiated a suit against NBC), stating NBC's belief that the *Dateline* report "accurately detailed widespread concerns" and was neither "false" nor "misleading." Gartner explained that the sparking device fixed to the crash truck "was intended to simulate sparks which could occur in a collision."[37] NBC was defending itself by admitting to shoddy journalism.

The next day, the network apologized. On Tuesday, February 9, the cohosts of *Dateline NBC* admitted point by point how the crash had been staged. "Within the past couple of hours," Jane Pauley told viewers, "the people at General Motors and our bosses at NBC have agreed to settle GM's lawsuit." "NBC has concluded," said cohost Stone Philips, "that unscientific demonstrations should have no place in hard news stories at NBC. That's our new policy."[38]

NBC News President Michael Gartner announced his resignation in March. It was not to take effect until August 1 so that he could be ensured maximum pension benefits. ■

Gartner had at first defended the broadcast; he ordered an apology only when GM exposed the fraud and threatened NBC through a lawsuit. Thus Gartner's critics were unimpressed.

> In his belated statement of resignation, Gartner did not seem fully cognizant of the enormity of his role in the near self-destruction of his once trusted and respected news organization. He said only that he hoped his leaving would

"take the spotlight off all of us and enable us to concentrate fully on our business. . . ." His handling of the GM fiasco only confirmed the notion that news standards were not high on his list of journalistic imperatives.[39]

Subsequent public opinion polls indicated that CNN had emerged as the most trusted news organization. NBC, which had previously held the top slot, slid to fourth place, behind CBS and ABC. And Hugh Breslin of WHAG-TV in Hagerstown, Maryland, an NBC affiliate, pointed to another disastrous consequence.

> What NBC did with that piece is inexcusable. . . . The affiliates as a body of people are outraged. It was a terrible thing, and they certainly have heard from me, as well as all the other affiliates who are involved in disseminating the NBC news product.[40]

NBC violated the conventional standards and values of a professional news operation. In the initial stages, it relied too heavily on parties with an axe to grind. NBC cut corners by hiring a testing company on a bare-bones budget. The story's producer was aware that the crash was rigged. Nevertheless, *Dateline NBC* proceeded even though its own written guidelines do not permit staging news. The best in the news business do not tolerate shoddy information-gathering practices or inaccurate stories—especially not outright fabrication. The guidelines in ABC's "News Standards" book are typical of broadcast news practices generally:

> Everything seen or heard on ABC News must be what it purports to be. We are in the business of reporting what has happened, and we are not in the business of making things happen. Consequently, ABC News has strict rules that prohibit various techniques and devices intended to stage, simulate, or recreate what actually happened. ABC News will not tolerate any practice which misleads the viewer.

There is a fine line between professionalism and ethics. If NBC had strictly followed standard news practices, it would not have acted immorally in this case. In order to prevent another fiasco, on 26 May 1993, NBC's David McCormick added a detailed section on testing procedures and expert credentials to its "News Policies and Guidelines" handbook.

Two trends in corporate thinking set the stage for the mess at NBC. For one thing, it has been assumed in the broadcast business that news operations lose money, but now all units of the media enterprise are expected to be profitable. It is no longer compelling to maintain quality news as a loss leader to enhance a network's credibility. And second, CBS's *60 Minutes* proved that there is big money in prime-time news shows. They cost about 50 percent less to produce than entertainment programming. NBC news was just turning a profit—hoping to compete with *20/20*, *60 Minutes*, *48 Hours*, and the other network magazines. As Everette Dennis, then senior vice president of the Freedom Forum, concluded:

> There's enormous pressure on the TV magazines for pictures and hype. Once they become profit centers for the networks, they become susceptible to all of

the same pressures that the entertainment divisions always had in keeping the audience and in keeping the ratings up.[41]

In terms of the Potter Box, the problem centers on the first quadrant. Demanding profitability for news operations tends to create a leadership style in which sound professionalism and solid ethics are not paramount: the heart of the issue and its resolution concentrated in step one.

If dramatized news is done in a *cinéma vérité*, eye-of-the-storm way, then it is not surprising that since the GM debacle the ratings for *Dateline NBC* have gone up. As Douglas Gomery of the University of Maryland says: "In the end, I don't think it hurts NBC. The model is Hollywood. . . . 'All publicity is good publicity.' At least more people know about the show. Journalistically it's a disaster. Everybody is up in arms about it. But surprise, surprise, it's making more money."[42] Gartner was the cost-cutter par excellence at NBC News and turned it into an efficient machine. Television news magazines are now netting $1 billion annually. And *Dateline NBC* is one of those cashing in on the profits.

5 The Wichita Experiment

In Kansas, journalists at the *Wichita Eagle*, a Knight-Ridder paper and the biggest newspaper in the state, decided they needed to look more closely at the newspaper's relationship with the community it purported to cover. In the 1990 gubernatorial primary, Democrat Joan Finney, a former state treasurer, won the office despite the perception at the newspaper that she did not have a chance. "Obviously, she knew more about what people were thinking than we did," said the paper's editor, Davis "Buzz" Merritt, Jr.[43]

Caught off guard by this development, and then frustrated with the vague rhetoric of the general election, Merritt changed the newspaper's approach to campaign coverage. The new tactics would be aimed at forcing the candidates to reveal their platforms and ventilating issues in such a way that the will of the electorate would not come as a surprise. Reporters were to press for answers aggressively when candidates dodged questions, especially on ten issues that the newspaper had targeted as being of special interest. The ten issues were selected on the basis of 500 interviews (conducted by the newspaper's research department) with local residents. The *Eagle* featured each of the ten issues in an extended background piece but also reported on them in brief every week, updating the positions of the candidates and taking note when candidates declined to state a position. The *Eagle* encouraged residents to vote and even arranged for people to register to vote at the newspaper office. The newspaper distributed a simplified election guide to more than 100,000 nonsubscribers and at adult literacy classes. It also cooperated with the local ABC affiliate, KAKE-TV, in encouraging people to register and vote.

These efforts dovetailed with a push for "customer obsession" undertaken chainwide by Knight-Ridder, a push borne out of concerns for the future of an industry with sluggish circulation statistics. At a lecture at the University of Kansas, the state's largest university, James K. Batten, Knight-Ridder's chief executive, said that people who feel "a real sense of connection to the place they live" are more likely to read newspapers. He asked, "If

continued

communities continue to erode, how can we expect communities to prosper over the long term?"[44] The *Eagle*'s new style of election coverage was aimed directly at strengthening that sense of connection to community and attacking head-on declining voter turnout rates.

The next year, residents surprised journalists at the *Eagle* in a new way—with their passion over an issue. Operation Rescue, a huge, well-orchestrated anti-abortion protest, came to Wichita. Over the summer, almost 1800 people were arrested in a month and a half as abortion protesters and counterprotesters turned the city upside down. Merritt said, "I don't think we knew enough about our community to know that that many people would invest that much time and energy."[45] This tumultuous "Summer of Mercy" reminded the newspaper of another aspect of "community connectedness"—the need for journalists to have sufficient knowledge of their community to know what issues would stir local emotions.

The *Eagle* extended its efforts at community connectedness with its "People Project." The newspaper published an extensive series of in-depth articles on issues it had already identified as important to its readers. This time, though, the articles were framed in a way intended to encourage responses from readers. Additionally, three times during the course of the series, the newspaper rented a hall where those interested in sharing their views could gather to discuss the issues without a leader of any kind directing things. In short, the newspaper (again cooperating with a local television station and a radio station) was attempting literally to create a public sphere.   ■

In its efforts at community connectedness, the *Wichita Eagle* is taking two professional values usually seen as being mutually exclusive and assuming, instead, that they can overlap. The *Eagle* staff looked for creative ways to practice them both at the same time. One value is called "spinach journalism": The newspaper's role is to tell people what they *need* to know in order to be well-informed citizens. The other value is that newspapers must tell readers what they *want* to know, or else readers will spend their information budget (of both time and money) elsewhere, and newspapers will perish. Often it is assumed that readers are not very interested in what they need to know—the confusing details of a state budget, for instance. However, what they want to know—celebrity gossip or school lunch menus, for example—is not very important or likely to give them the information they need to act as a responsible electorate. Ordinarily, making readers the source of the newshole results in pandering or "dumbing down."

Under the first commitment (i.e., to give information readers need to be well informed), a newspaper's duty is to society. In a democratic system that gives voters the responsibility to pick their leaders and to decide on assorted ballot initiatives, it is crucial that voters have access to sufficient facts to make an informed decision. Under the second commitment (i.e., to tell readers what they want to know), the newspaper's duty is to subscribers and investors, those who provide the revenue that allows the newspaper to stay in business.

It is often noted that this dichotomy naively overlooks the inescapable economic fact that newspapers cannot give readers what they need unless they also give them what they want. That is, a newspaper has to remain profitable if it is to have the resources to tackle unpopular issues and causes. What often goes unremarked is the paternalism implicit in this dichotomy, the assumption that readers have to be force-fed the information they need. Editors at the *Eagle* seem to be confronting the second assumption as well as the first in their efforts to improve "community connectedness."

Aristotle's golden mean is helpful in sorting out this dichotomy. At one extreme is the greedy newspaper motivated only by the potential for profit, and thereby giving its readers nothing but titillating, entertaining news that is cheap and easy to gather. At the other extreme is the serious, socially responsible newspaper that is willfully oblivious to its readers' desires on the premise that "we know what's best for you."

The *Wichita Eagle* is trying to find the ideal ground between these extremes. It is looking for ways to decide with, rather than for, its readers what the content of the newspaper needs to be. In this process, employees at the newspaper will have to look carefully at how they are assigning their loyalties. "The motivation behind the activist model is not without risk. . . . In their efforts to turn the news agenda over to readers, editors must guard against freezing the agenda."[46] In striving to do right by society, journalists might be glossing over their own obvious responsibilities. Investigative pieces about some political or economic scandal are more important to work on than a story about who made the local high school honor roll.

Editors, in formulating editorial policy by community referenda, risk losing control over news decisions. Editors often seem alone in believing an issue is important, and their unpopular stands have helped change society for the better. Speaking out against racism was a noble but dangerous tactic, yet the progressive writings of these editors eventually helped bring about change.[47]

Wichita Eagle Executive Editor Sheri Dill involved reporters in a study of area residents who "ought to be readers" but aren't—people who have strong ties to the community but no connection with the local newspaper. They found that these people were looking for "good news" about their local churches, schools, and charities. One reporter commented that "Some of these people are pretty self-involved; they are not curious about the rest of the world."[48] Certainly, journalism driven by markets is always tempted to appeal to them on their own terms. But to the extent that reporters dismiss as "self-involved" those interests of readers that do not happen to intersect with their professional interests, efforts at expanding community connectedness probably will stall. On the other hand, to the extent that the staff at the *Wichita Eagle* vigorously involves readers in debates about the community's long-term problems, both the paper and citizens are likely to benefit.

Out of these efforts at reform, public journalism is born.[49] According to Buzz Merritt, this new kind of journalism is a shift away from conventional journalism by moving "beyond the limited mission of telling the news to the broader mission of helping public life to go well." Instead of detachment, it means "becoming a fair-minded participant in public life." Instead of thinking of people as consumers, public journalism sees them "as a public, as potential actors in arriving at democratic solutions to public problems."[50] In Jay Rosen's terms, journalism is "democracy's cultivator as well as its chronicler."[51]

In the United States, the *Akron Beacon Journal* applied public journalism strategies to deal with race in a way that mobilized the community rather than just reporting on crimes one by one.[52] "We the People Wisconsin" is a combined effort of television, newspapers, radio, town hall meetings, hearings, debates, and citizen juries to involve the community on policy issues and elections (www .wtpeople.com). Sam Chege Mwangi identifies similar "experiments carried out by media houses around the world" to engage citizens in healthy democracy. In Latin America, more public journalism projects have been carried out than in any other continent. Social issues are not reduced to financial and administrative problems for politicians to solve, but the press enables the public to come to terms with the problems and solutions themselves.[53]

NOTES

1. Fred S. Siebert, Theodore Peterson, and Wilbur Schramm, *Four Theories of the Press* (Urbana: University of Illinois Press, 1956), 72.
2. The question is whether one's dual obligation in this instance prevents the fulfilling of both contracts. See Joseph Margolis, "Conflict of Interest and Conflicting Interests," in *Ethical Theory and Business*, eds. Tom L. Beauchamp and Norman E. Bowie (Upper Saddle River, NJ: Prentice Hall, 1979), 361–372.
3. Upton Sinclair, *The Brass Check: A Study of American Journalism* (Pasadena, CA: published by author, 1920), 436. New edition, with Introduction (9–33) by Robert McChesney and Ben Scott (Urbana: University of Illinois Press, 2003).
4. For a comprehensive account of concentration in various media, see Robert McChesney, *Rich Media, Poor Democracy: Communication Politics in Dubious Times* (New York: The New Press, 2000); cf. also Robert McChesney, *The Problem of the Media: U.S. Communication Politics in the 21st Century* (New York: Monthly Review Press, 2004).
5. Dan Barry, David Barstow, Jonathon Glater, Adam Liptak, and Jacques Steinberg, "Correcting the Record," *New York Times*, 11 May 2003, 1, sec. 1. Article also available online at www.nytimes.com/qst/abstract.html.
6. Seth Mnookin, "A Journalist's Hard Fall," *Newsweek*, 19 May 2003, 40.
7. *New York Times*, 11 May 2003.
8. Ibid.
9. Ibid.
10. Quoted in Adeel Hassan, "Blair's Victims: That Helpless Feeling," *Columbia Journalism Review* (July/August 2003): 19, 21.
11. Quoted in Evan Jenkins, "Fixing the System," *Columbia Journalism Review* (July/August 2003): 14.
12. Joe Strupp, "Raines Falls, But Other Editors Face Own Issues," *Page One*, 9 June 2003, 4.
13. Cesar Soriano, "Jayson Blair Lands a Book Deal," *USA Today*, 10 September 2003. www .usatoday.com/life/books/news/2003-09-10-blair-book_x.htm.
14. Lucia Moses, "Jayson Blair Returns to School," *Page One*, 9 June 2003, 5.
15. Seth Mnookin, "A Journalist's Hard Fall," 41.
16. Evan Jenkins, "Fixing the System," 16.
17. CNN's Web site explains that its policy "is not to report information that puts operational security at risk." See www.cnn.com/privacy.html.
18. *Chicago Tribune*, Editorial, "Did CNN Compromise Coverage," 19 April 2003, sec. 1, 20.

19. *News Gazette*, Editorial, "We Can't Tell You the Truth, CNN Admits," 20 April 2003, B-2.
20. Steele interviewed Eason Jordan and wrote "The Secrets He Kept," which is posted on the Poynter Institute's Web site at www.poynter.org/column.asp?id.
21. Elaine Hargrove-Simon, "Journalists Face the Challenge of Wartime Ethics," *Silha Center Bulletin* 8:3 (Spring 2003): 4.
22. Steele, "The Secrets He Kept."
23. E. E. Dennis and E. C. Pease, "The Race of Content," *Media Studies Journal* (8:1): xi–xxiii. For the other quotations and the background negotiations summarized in this case, see Bill Saporito, "The Inside Story of Time Warner," *Fortune*, 20 November 1989, 164–210.
24. Tim Jones, "Big, Big Media Deals Roll On," *Chicago Tribune*, 18 July 1996, sec. 3, 1.
25. "America Online Agrees to Buy Time Warner for $165 Billion," *New York Times*, 11 January 2000.
26. Sharon Moshavi, "Fire Sale," *Forbes*, 8 November 1993, 96–98; and "Time and Warner May Now Become Time Warner," *BusinessWeek*, 9 March 1992, 31–32.
27. Johnnie L. Roberts, "Main Men," *Newsweek*, 29 July 1996, 43.
28. Bob Garfield, "The Post Advertising Age," *Advertising Age*, March 26, 2007.
29. *Time*, 5 July 1999, 66–74.
30. Ben H. Bagdikian, *The New Media Monopoly*, 7th ed. (Boston: Beacon Press, 2004), 3, 16.
31. Charles Thiesen and Barbara Beckwith, "Marketplace of Creative Ideas May Now Go to Highest Bidder," *Los Angeles Times*, 20 November 1989, B7.
32. For a description of this problem and the international audience issue that follows, see "Business: The Counterattack," *Newsweek*, 26 June 1989, 48–54.
33. For a copy of this memo written by William J. O'Neill, write the authors at the College of Communications, 119 Gregory Hall, University of Illinois, Urbana, Illinois 61801. Copies of all the correspondence between NBC News and General Motors between 5 November 1992 and 9 February 1993 are also available from the authors.
34. Letter from Robert Read to William O'Neill, 20 November 1992.
35. Letter from Robert Read to William O'Neill, 4 January 1993.
36. Letter from William O'Neill to Robert Read, 2 February 1993.
37. Letter from Michael Gartner to William O'Neill, 8 February 1993.
38. "No Scandal, No Story," *Newsweek*, 22 February 1993, 42–43.
39. Bob Sunde, "Fake News: A Passing Scandal or Here to Stay?" *Quill* (April 1993): 10; Walter Olson details similar incidents at other networks since the late 1970s, "It Didn't Start with *Dateline NBC*," *National Review*, 21 June 1993.
40. W. Dale Nelson, "Competition Casualty," *Quill* (May 1993): 38.
41. David Zurawik and Christina Stoehr, "Money Changes Everything," *American Journalism Review* (April 1933): 27–28.
42. Ibid., 30. For financial details regarding network news magazines, see 27–30.
43. As quoted in Michael Hoyt, "The Wichita Experiment," *Columbia Journalism Review* (July/August 1992): 44. For background and reflections by the *Wichita Eagle* editor, see Davis Merritt, *Public Journalism and Public Life: Why Telling the News Is Not Enough* (Hillsdale, NJ: Erlbaum, 1995).
44. James K. Batten, "Newspapers and Communities: The Vital Link," Forty-first Annual William Allen White Speech, University of Kansas, 8 February 1990, as quoted by Jay Rosen, in "Community Connectedness Passwords for Public Journalism," *The Poynter Institute for Media Studies*, St. Petersburg, FL, 1993, 4.
45. Hoyt, "The Wichita Experiment," 44.
46. John Bare, "Case Study—Wichita and Charlotte: The Leap of a Passive Press to Activism," *Media Studies Journal* 6:4 (Fall 1992): 156.

47. Ibid., 157.

48. Hoyt, "The Wichita Experiment," 46–47.

49. For details on practicing public journalism competently, see Arthur Charity, *Doing Public Journalism* (New York: Guilford Press, 1995). For the history and theory of public journalism, see Jay Rosen, *What Are Journalists For?* (New Haven, CT: Yale University Press, 1999). See also Edmund Lambeth et al., eds., *Assessing Public Journalism* (Columbia: University of Missouri Press, 1998) and Theodore Glasser, ed., *The Idea of Public Journalism* (New York: Guilford Books, 1999).

50. Merritt, *Public Journalism and Public Life*, 113–114.

51. Rosen, *What Are Journalists For*, 8.

52. Ibid., 92–101.

53. Sam Chege Mwangi, "International Public Journalism," *Kettering Foundation Connections* 12:1 (2001): 23–27; Sam Chege Mwangi, "The International Media and Democracy Project," available online at www.centralstate.edu/imdp/survey/c_studies.html, 5/26/2007.

Truthtelling

T he press's obligation to print the truth is a standard part of its rhetoric. Virtually every code of ethics begins with the newsperson's duty to tell the truth under all conditions. High-minded editors typically etch the word on cornerstones and on their tombstones. Credible language is pivotal to the communication enterprise.

When Pontius Pilate asked, "What is truth?" he posed the question people of every kind have struggled to answer. And as ideas and worldviews shift, so does the definition of truthfulness. Newspeople must live within the larger ambiguities about truth in Western scholarship and culture today. Their situation is further complicated by budget constraints, deadlines, reader expectations, editorial conventions, and self-serving sources. Journalism is often referred to as "history in a hurry"; providing a precise, representative account can rarely occur under such conditions. At the same time, sophisticated technology generates unceasing news copy so that the journalistic gatekeeper must choose from a mountain of options, often without the time to sift through the moral intricacies.

The cases that follow introduce several dimensions of the truthtelling issue. Although not every conceivable aspect is offered, truth is enlarged beyond a simple facts-only definition.[1] One way to broaden our scope, for example, is to consider the antonym of truthfulness and to account for newsgathering as well as newswriting. The opposite of truthtelling is deception, that is, a deliberate intention to mislead. Outright deceit occurs infrequently in the newswriting phase; only rarely, if ever, does a reporter or editor specifically and consciously give the wrong story. But deception in newsgathering is a persistent temptation because it often facilitates the process of securing information.

The first case in this chapter, on the obesity epidemic in the United States and elsewhere, centers on the Institute of Medicine's report of 2004 authorized by the U.S. Congress. The issue is the press' ability to communicate scientific findings to the many parties involved.

The second case introduces Al Jazeera, the independent news organization based in Qatar, which is in a region where state-owned media dominate the airwaves. As an Arab news network, it reflects Arab culture. Is Al Jazeera a truthful news source, or does it slant its broadcasts against the West?

The third case, "The Unabomber's Manifesto," struggles with the ethical issues of violence and technology. Does someone advocating and engaged in violent attacks against an evil technological order deserve a hearing?

The fourth case, "Fabrication at the *Globe*," struggles with the ethical issue of plagiarizing. Making up quotations and fabricating people and events are uniformly unacceptable in news. The challenge is getting beyond lip service and written guidelines to prevent it from happening in the first place.

The fifth case introduces the worldwide controversy over the publication of the Muhammad cartoons, a complicated story involving religion, politics, and press freedom. The challenge for the news media is to present a truthful account of highly emotional issues in a multicultural context.

6 Obesity Epidemic

Over the past two decades, the diet and health of millions of people across the world have changed. For most developing nations, obesity has become a more serious health threat than hunger. In Mexico, Egypt, and South Africa, more than half the adults are either overweight or obese. In virtually all of Latin America and much of the Middle East and North Africa, one of four adults is overweight. Malnutrition and hunger are significant problems in sub-Saharan Africa and South Asia, but even poor countries such as Nigeria and Uganda face the dilemma of obesity. Worldwide, more than 1.3 billion people, are overweight, whereas about 800 million are underweight, and this difference continues to diverge.[2] "The problem is especially acute in the larger cities, where the population has a more sedentary lifestyle and greater access to soft drinks, caloric sweeteners, vegetable oils, and animal foods. In Mexico, in 1989 fewer than 10 percent were overweight. In 2006, 71 percent of Mexican women and 66 percent of Mexican men were overweight or obese—statistics that approximate those of the United States."[3]

Over the past several decades, the number of overweight Americans has grown dramatically. In 1996, the National Center for Health Statistics reported that obese or overweight people outnumbered other Americans for the first time. In 2007, about 65 percent of adults over age 20 were overweight, and the rates of obesity (body mass index of 30 or higher) have doubled from 15 percent in 1980 to over 30 percent today. The prevalence of type 2 diabetes among children and youth (adult-onset diabetes) has more than doubled in the past decade. Diets that are high in calories and saturated fats and low in certain nutrients are putting American children and youth at risk later in life for heart disease, stroke, circulatory problems, diabetes, some cancers, and osteoporosis. In 2001, the surgeon general reported for the first time that obesity might soon overtake cigarette smoking as the leading cause of preventable death.

In 2004, Congress through its Health, Labor, and Education Committee directed the Centers for Disease Control and Prevention (CDC) to undertake a study of the role that the marketing of food and beverages may play in determining the nutritional status of children and youth and what marketing approaches might be used as a remedy. The CDC turned to the Institute of Medicine (IOM) of the National Academies to conduct this study, and its report is the most comprehensive review to date of the scientific studies available (*Food Marketing to Children and Youth: Threat or Opportunity*; available at http://books.nap.edu/catalog/1514.html). Among IOM'S findings are these:

- The preponderance of television food and beverage advertising promotes high-calorie and low-nutrient products and influences children and youth to prefer and request high-calorie and low-nutrient foods and beverages.
- Exposure to television advertising is associated with adiposity (body fatness) in children 2 to 11 years of age and teens 12 to 18 years of age.
- Food and beverage companies, restaurants, and marketers have underutilized resources for supporting healthy diets for children and youth.
- Achieving healthy diets for children and youth will require sustained and integrated efforts across society, including industry leadership.

The IOM's ten recommendations for dealing with obesity in America cover a broad spectrum of society—education, homes, government, industry, and the media. These are illustrative of the ways obesity can become a public health priority of the highest order:

Recommendation 1: Food and beverage companies should use their creativity, resources, and full range of marketing practices to promote and support healthful diets for children and youth.

Recommendation 3: Food, beverage, restaurant, retail, and marketing industry trade associations should assume transforming leadership roles in harnessing industry creativity, resources, and marketing on behalf of healthful diets for children and youth.

Recommendation 6: Government, in partnership with the private sector, should create a long-term, multifaceted, and financially sustained social-marketing program supporting parents, caregivers, and families in promoting healthful diets for children and youth.

Recommendation 7: State and local educational authorities, with support from parents, health authorities, and other stakeholders, should educate about and promote healthful diets for children and youth in all aspects of the school environment (e.g., commercial sponsorships, meals and snacks, curriculum).

Recommendation 8: Government at all levels should marshal the full range of public policy levers to foster the development and promotion of healthful diets for children and youth.

Recommendation 10: The secretary of the U.S. Department of Health and Human Services should designate a responsible agency, with adequate and appropriate resources, to formally monitor and report regularly on the progress of the various entities and activities related to the recommendations included in this report. ■

When the source of news is a scientific report on a complicated social issue, how should the press handle it? What is necessary to tell the truth? On a basic level, statistical data will be presented accurately and in readable fashion. But describing the problem and the conclusions involves interpretation. Winners and losers are identified. The importance of the issue itself and whether it can be solved at all are central to reporting this kind of material, and the choices made influence the quality of the public discussion about it. And is the tone correct, that is, no more pessimistic or optimistic than the report itself? The report genre is inherently boring, with the tendency to sensationalize the content or even initiate a moral panic when reporting on it as news. One study of news coverage of obesity concluded that "journalists tended to exaggerate the risks of obesity by reporting disproportionately on the most alarmist scientific studies."[4]

A ten-year study of newspaper articles and television news centered on the question of news framing—who is considered responsible for causing the obesity problem and who must fix it. The research presumed that the media tell the audience which crises to think about and also how to think about them. Therefore, the way responsibility is framed is an important moral issue in news.

A content analysis showed these results: An *unhealthy diet* is cited most often as the cause of obesity (23 percent of the new stories). Following next was a *sedentary lifestyle*, principally a lack of exercise (18.2 percent). *Food industry practices*, including heavy advertising of its junk food products, was the chief institutional cause, mentioned 12.4 percent of the time. *Genetic conditions* and body chemistry appeared less often (11.8 percent); reports did include medical research identifying genes that contribute to obesity. *Schools* (i.e., unhealthy cafeteria food and lack of physical education) only appeared in 4.2 percent of the news as a major cause. And *socioeconomic factors* (i.e., eating patterns and education among low-income families) was cited least in 3.4 percent.[5]

Consistent with the same results, personal-level solutions were mentioned most often: healthy diet, physical activity, and medical treatment (i.e., surgeries and weight-loss medications). Together, personal solutions were included as the best alternative in 90 percent of the news stories. Regulation of the food industry and changes in schools and education together accounted for 18.2 percent of the articles and transcripts. Socioeconomic changes were mentioned in only three newspaper articles as an important solution and never appeared in television news.[6] None advocated drastic societal solutions, such as regulation of the food industry and its aggressive marketing. On the policy level, taxing junk food or sugar-rich drinks (the so-called Twinkie tax) was noted but not seriously developed. Lawsuits filed against fast-food restaurants appeared intermittently, but without the presumption that fast-food restaurants are responsible for making Americans obese and sick.[7]

Meanwhile, the sobering fact is that despite surging news coverage over the past decade, large-scale changes in the public's eating habits, and growth in exercise gym membership and diet programs, obesity continues to increase at a faster rate than before.[8]

An ethics of other-regarding care is sympathetic in its outlook. News that follows this principle does not condemn unfairly. It is cautious about generalizations, recognizing that medical conditions explain obesity for some. However, it is also important to report the truth that people are accountable for their decisions, although how to do so without being judgmental and alienating is difficult. Truthtelling in the context of other-regarding care is one of the greatest challenges an ethical journalist can face.

7 Al Jazeera

Mention Al Jazeera to the average American, and the response is likely to be less than positive. Al Jazeera is the Qatar-based Arab network that has become a household name in the United States primarily because it chooses to air audio and videotapes received from the elusive Osama bin Laden, as it did from Saddam Hussein when he was in power. Due to what he considered this unseemly connection, Vice President Dick Cheney has accused Al Jazeera of providing "a platform for terrorists." But what North Americans may find interesting is that Al Jazeera isn't uniformly embraced by Arab leaders either.

After he seized ruling power from his father, Sheikh Hamad bin Khalifa Al Thani of Qatar established Al Jazeera (which means "The Peninsula") to promote modernization and democracy. Al Thani set aside $137 million for Al Jazeera, hoping that it would be self-sustaining within five years of its 1 November 1996 debut.

Before Al Jazeera went on the air, state-owned media dominated the airways in most Arab countries, and government leaders were accustomed to controlling the message. Citizens of Arab countries expected the media to serve as a voice for the government.

The creation of Al Jazeera changed that. Suddenly there was an Arabic news channel unconcerned with the promotion of any government's agenda. Al Jazeera sought to present the news in an unbiased and objective way, which often meant unflattering portrayals of existing Arab leaders.

Because of Al Jazeera's insistence on independent reporting, the agency has been the recipient of various punishments doled out by Arab leaders. The government in Algiers once cut its signal. Egypt's state media ran a campaign against Al Jazeera, stating that they aired a "sinister salad of sex, religion, and politics" topped with "sensationalist seasoning."[9] The station's repeated interviews of Hamas' spiritual leader Sheikh Ahmed Yassin angered Yasir Arafat. The religiously conservative government of Saudi Arabia bars Al Jazeera from its territory. And on it goes.

If it were not for the events of 11 September 2001 and the conflicts that followed in Afghanistan and Iraq, Al Jazeera would have remained a Middle Eastern station known primarily to Arabs. Its focus would have remained on the leadership of the Arab states and on the ongoing conflict between Israel and Palestine, and Al Jazeera would have remained relatively unknown and uncontroversial to citizens of the West. However, as the world's attention turned to Afghanistan, and then to Iraq, the world's journalists had to rely on this relatively small media outlet based in Qatar.[10]

Following September 11, the Taliban evicted Western journalists from Kabul. Al Jazeera, which had a history of covering Afghanistan, was allowed to stay. When the air strikes against Iraq began on October 7, Al Jazeera had exclusive access to the sights and sounds of the bombing campaign. They then sold the images to the other news agencies. It became the hit station of the war. Al Jazeera was transformed the way CNN was by the Gulf War a decade earlier.

This access has been financially profitable for Al Jazeera. Exclusive footage from places no one else can get to but that everyone wants to see has allowed them to rise in international prominence as a news leader. While Western journalists struggle to understand the language and culture of the Middle East, Al Jazeera's reporters are on the ground and among the people, speaking the language and knowing the customs.

continued

In 2003, Imad Musa, a news producer at the Washington bureau of Al Jazeera, wondered how "this tiny station"—with a worldwide staff of less than 650 and short lifespan of seven years—has become a household name in the United States, where many people cannot name any media outlet in France, Germany, Mexico, or even Canada. The news outlet has continually expanded its reach, launching an English-language Website in 2003 and an English-language satellite channel in 2006. Al Jazeera English has its headquarters in Doha, with studios in Kuala Lumpur, London, and Washington, D.C. It reaches some 80 million households worldwide,[11] and it recently has begun to offer segments of its broadcast on YouTube in order to overcome its limited availability in the United States.[12]   ■

Many Western governments remain unconvinced of Al Jazeera's neutrality. Their special status in Afghanistan made them suspect to the forces trying to root out the Taliban. Because of their airing of his tapes, their link to Osama bin Laden was questioned. Two months after 9/11 and six weeks after Colin Powell expressed his concerns about Al Jazeera to the Qatari emir, their agency in Kabul was bombed.

American officials claim it was accidental. But Al Jazeera's leadership knows that the location of their building was common knowledge among other news agencies and among the military forces invading Afghanistan. When asked about the loss, Al Jazeera's Managing Director Mohamed Jasem al Ali said, "Whether it was targeted or not, I can't answer. But I can say for 100 percent that the United States knew about the office. Everyone knew we had an office in Kabul. It was very easy to find."[13] The site in Kabul was not the only one hit. Al Jazeera's Iraq station also was leveled in the bombing run that hit Baghdad on 8 April 2003, and speculation about the intentional nature of the bombings was further fueled when *The Daily Mirror* obtained a leaked memo from a 2004 meeting between then Prime Minister Tony Blair and President Bush in which the U.S. president allegedly revealed a plan to bomb the Qatar headquarters of Al Jazeera.[14] Two British government employees were jailed in 2006 for leaking the memo, but as of 2007, Al Jazeera's efforts to obtain its contents had not yielded any results.[15]

Some wonder if the hits were intended to send a message to Al Jazeera to cease airing the tapes of bin Laden and Hussein. Some say that when Al Jazeera airs such speeches in their entirety, they are serving as a mouthpiece for terrorists. The leaders of Al Jazeera object. They point out that they air the complete speeches of all world leaders, lest the station be accused of editing out words they didn't think people should hear. "Are we a mouthpiece for bin Laden?" asks Dana Suyyagh, an Al Jazeera new producer who was educated in Canada. "Maybe, but that would make us Bush's mouthpiece as well. He gets more airtime, actually."[16]

While talking heads make up a significant part of their coverage, what really sets Al Jazeera apart from other media outlets is its use of images. Unlike agencies that seek moderation in the airing of objectionable scenes, Al Jazeera is unapologetic in showing images that disturb.

The images that Al Jazeera beamed from inside Iraq displayed the horrors of war. Unlike on CNN, no anchor prepares viewers for what is to come. Without warning, gory images of dead bodies or wounded children fill the screen. On Al Jazeera, the blood is part of the story:

> It's pretty hard to adequately describe the level of bloodiness during an average Al Jazeera newscast. It's mesmerizing bloodiness. It's not just red but gooey. There's no cutaway. They hold the shot for the full vicious effect. It's vastly grislier than anything that's ever been shown on television before. It's snuff-film caliber.[17]

While Western journalists may focus on the humanitarian aid extended to the citizens of Afghanistan or Iraq, Al Jazeera's inside look at bombed out houses and wounded people communicates a different message to the world. "We don't show the faces of the dead. We don't show the faces of the wounded, especially in this time of satellite television. We don't want to be in a position where we on television are notifying the next of kin."[18]

The message Al Jazeera communicated in airing pictures of American and British war dead and POWs was not warmly welcomed. U.S. Secretary of Defense Donald Rumsfeld claimed that the footage was a violation of the Geneva Convention rulings on the rights of prisoners of war. Following this, Al Jazeera economic correspondents on Wall Street, Ramsey Shibar and Ammar al Sankari, had their press credentials revoked by the New York Stock Exchange—the first time NYSE had ever withdrawn them. The next day, Nasdaq followed suit. "The corpses, the sea of blood, the faces of the wounded—yes, and 'since when is a television network governed by the Geneva Conventions,' retorted the Al Jazeera staff, turning the free-press argument on the free press itself."[19]

The turmoil reveals the crux of the issue: Is Al Jazeera a neutral news source, or does it slant its broadcasts against the West and for Arabs, even such Arabs as bin Laden or Hussein? In November of 2001, *The New York Times Magazine* ran a cover story by Fouad Ajami, a professor of Middle East studies at Johns Hopkins, who accused Al Jazeera of exactly that:

> One clip juxtaposes a scowling George Bush with a poised, almost dreamy bin Laden. Between them is an image of the World Trade Center engulfed in flames. . . . [I]n its rough outlines, the message of Al Jazeera is similar to that of the Taliban: there is a huge technological imbalance between the antagonists, but the foreign power will nonetheless come to grief.[20]

Ajami went on to accuse the station of "mimicking Western norms of journalistic fairness while pandering to pan-Arabic sentiments." The Canadian Jewish Congress and B'nai Brith Canada have labeled Al Jazeera "virulently anti-Semitic." The Canadian Arab Federation counters with the assertion that "the views of the people who make the news should not be confused as the views of the station that airs it."[21]

Imad Musa points out that Al Jazeera is an Arab news medium and therefore reflects Arab culture. In referring to their choice to air images of POWs, Musa states:

> To Al Jazeera, war is ugly, and these were the images of war. . . . [W]e realize that the time to air bad news will never come, so it is preferable not to play politics with the news and air whatever is timely, relevant, accurate, and of interest to our viewers. . . . Al Jazeera's preference is to give its viewers unfiltered information as soon as possible before political pressures begin to flood in from all over the globe and despite accusations of hurting morale.[22]

8 The Unabomber's Manifesto

On 19 September 1995, the *Washington Post* and *The New York Times* jointly published a 35,000-word manifesto from an unknown person identified as the Unabomber.[23] The Justice Department had been trailing him for more than seventeen years, during which time he mailed bombs that injured twenty-three people and killed three. In late June, the document arrived with a cover letter that gave the newspapers three months to publish it, upon which time he promised to "desist from terrorism." He warned that if they refused, he would "start building [his] next bomb" when the deadline expired on September 29. The Unabomber also demanded that he be allowed to publish 3000-word rebuttals for the next three years directed to any critics who attacked his manifesto.

New York Times publisher Arthur O. Sulzberger, Jr., and *Washington Post* publisher Donald E. Graham issued this joint statement:

> For three months the *Washington Post* and the *New York Times* have jointly faced the demand of a person known as the Unabomber that we publish a manuscript of about 35,000 words. If we failed to do so, the author of this document threatened to send a bomb to an unspecified destination "with intent to kill."
>
> From the beginning, the two newspapers have consulted closely on the issue of whether to publish under the threat of violence. We have also consulted law enforcement officials. Both the Attorney General and the director of the Federal Bureau of Investigation have now recommended that we print this document for public safety reasons, and we have agreed to do so.

In a statement to his staff, Sulzberger insisted that the case was unique and not likely to become a journalistic precedent. "Newsrooms regularly receive messages from people threatening dire action unless their demands are met. Our traditional response will continue to serve us well—we notify law enforcement officials, when appropriate, and print nothing." Sulzberger explained: "You print and he doesn't kill anybody else, that's a pretty good deal. You print it and he continues to kill people, what have you lost? The cost of newsprint?"

The Unabomber's central point in the manifesto is that the industrial-technological system in which we live is a disaster for the human race. Therefore, he seeks to "propagate anti-industrial ideas" and to encourage "those who hate the industrial system." The task of those who oppose the industrial system is to advance its breakdown by promoting "social stress and instability," which presumably includes bombing. For lasting change, "reform is insufficient" and "revolution is necessary." Revolution, in the Unabomber's terms, involves destroying and wrecking "the system" and seeing "its remnants . . . smashed beyond repair."[24]

When he saw the text, the Unabomber's brother informed the FBI that his sibling was the likely author of the manifesto. On April 1, FBI agents surrounded the cabin of Theodore Kaczynski in the mountains of Montana and arrested him. In June, Kaczynski was indicted in Sacramento, California, on federal charges that he mailed two fatal bombs from that city, as well as two other bombs that injured their targets. On 1 October 1996, a federal grand jury in Newark, New Jersey, indicted him on charges that one of his mail bomb attacks killed a North Caldwell, New Jersey, advertising executive, Thomas J. Mosser. The Newark indictment charged Kaczynski with mailing a bomb that arrived at Mosser's home on 9 December 1994. Mosser was killed when he opened the package the next day.

In a letter published in *The New York Times* in April 1995, the Unabomber said that Mosser had been killed because his company, Burson-Marsteller, had "helped Exxon clean up its public image after the *Exxon Valdez* incident" in Alaska in 1989. Burson-Marsteller has denied working with Exxon in connection with the oil spill.

The Justice Department ruled that Theodore Kaczynski would be tried first in California. A prison psychiatrist, Sally Johnson, declared him competent to stand trial, and after often dramatic proceedings, Kaczynski was sentenced to four consecutive life terms in return for a guilty plea. He is now detained in solitary confinement in a federal prison in Colorado.

In October 1993, federal authorities had announced a $1 million award for helping them find the elusive terrorist. On 21 August 1998, the government paid the award to David Kaczynski. Some of the money has been used to pay off the family's legal bills. For months prior to Theodore Kaczynski's guilty plea, the family had lobbied the government not to seek the death penalty. The rest of the award is set up in a trust fund for the victims' families.[25] In February 1999, Theodore Kaczynski signed a book deal to tell his story, with the proceeds also designated for the victims' families.[26]   ∎

For two reasons, several journalists objected strongly to the *Times* and *Post* decision to publish the manifesto. First, that "these two champions of a free press" would publish on "recommendation of federal law enforcement authorities" was reprehensible to Jane Kirtley of the Reporters Committee for Freedom of the Press: "It signaled a dangerous erosion of the line between the media and government, a line that should be fixed and immutable."[27] Second, objections also centered on conceding to the demands of an anonymous terrorist. As Rem Rieder, editor of the *American Journalism Review*, put it:

> It is analogous to negotiating with those who take hostages. Law enforcement experts have long advised against doing so, because it only encourages the taking of yet more hostages. It says that if you are desperate enough and irresponsible enough and violent enough, we will turn our news columns over to you.
>
> Ours is a society filled with rage: against women, against minorities, against government. And many of those angry people possess the anger of

righteousness. Their cause is so right, their opponents so wickedly misguided, that violence to advance the former and hurt the latter is justified in their minds.

Publishing the Unabomber's manifesto says to the true believer: Do enough damage, wreak enough havoc, take enough innocent lives, injure enough people, and the printing press is yours.[28]

Paul McMasters, First Amendment ombudsman of the Freedom Forum in Arlington, Virginia, wondered whether publication in the name of public safety would expose "other newspapers and television and radio stations to a higher risk of being hijacked for similar purposes."[29]

Thus the issues can be understood in terms of quadrant two of the Potter Box. Important professional values are at stake here—the independence of newspapers from government and their independence from hostile groups who make threats. From this perspective, the *Times* and *Post* violated two basic journalistic values that will hurt the press's integrity and effectiveness over the long term.

However, there are ambiguities in quadrant two. Richard Harwood of the *Post* called the criticism a "species of poppycock."

> The government had no . . . power to dictate the papers' decision. . . . Newspapers on many occasions have consulted with government officials on matters of national security that might put lives at risk. Choices were made freely . . . [as editors and publishers] defined for themselves the obligations of citizenship and conscience.[30]

And appearing to cave into the Unabomber's remarks is at least understandable if the decision to publish could save lives and help generate leads to the Unabomber's identity.

Regarding the debate over professional values, the issue of newsworthiness is also involved. Sulzberger and Graham did not use newsworthiness as a rationale for publication. However, they could have justified "publishing the manuscript on the grounds that it was a matter of public interest and that the media are not in the business of depriving their readers of information."[31] Different aspects of the Unabomber story had been developing for months, the newspapers had published excerpts already, and executives from the papers had met with public officials. Some of the Unabomber's concerns about technology were relevant. Defending publication as a journalistic decision connected to an ongoing story is at least plausible and keeps editors and reporters in control rather than following the dictates of outside interests.

An analysis of professional values in quadrant two leaves ambiguity over appropriate action. What about step three? Are ethical theories helpful?

Aristotle's mean is not applicable because the two parties are not both legitimate. A position of ideal balance is not possible when one party is engaged in criminal activity. Agape specializes in justice and privacy, but not as explicitly regarding sources and truthtelling. Because the Unabomber's response is unpredictable, utilitarianism is unhelpful; refusal to publish may create intolerable risk and harm. The categorical imperative typically is most decisive when a short list of moral questions is at stake—promise keeping, deception, theft, and so forth.

But, clearly, the first principle in Rawls's theory of justice is relevant—the largest amount of political liberty for all. The Unabomber's practice of violence and threat of violence does not pass this first principle. Violence against technological growth is not a credible alternative. It need not demand the journalist's attention. Several broadcasters and newspapers refuse to publish or air blatantly racist material. Similarly, terrorist propaganda advocating violence ought not be published either. According to Rawls's first principle, actions or messages that deprive equal liberty for everyone are immoral.

9 Fabrication at The Globe

In June 1998, award-winning columnist Patricia Smith of *The Boston Globe* confessed to making up quotes and people in her columns and was dismissed. In August, star columnist Mike Barnicle resigned on charges first of plagiarizing George Carlin's *Brain Droppings* and then of lifting quotes from media critic A. J. Liebling.

Patricia Smith joined the *Globe* staff in 1990 and began writing her twice-weekly metro column in 1994. In the Spring of 1998, she won the Distinguished Writing Award for commentary from the American Society of Newspaper Editors and in April 1998 was named a Pulitzer Prize finalist in the commentary category.

In May, however, editors at the *Globe* "became concerned by what the Managing Editor, Greg Moore, 'called an almost too perfect a fit' of quotations in some of her recent columns. A spot check of columns over the past four months by Assistant Managing Editor Walter Robinson turned up a number of named people who did not seem to exist."[32] In a confrontation with Moore, Patricia Smith admitted to making up four of them. This is how she put it in her final column, "A Note of Apology," on 16 June 1998:

> From time to time in my metro column, to create the desired impact or slam home a salient point, I attributed quotes to people who didn't exist. I would give them names, even occupations, but I couldn't give them what they needed most—a heartbeat. As anyone who's ever touched a newspaper knows, that's one of the cardinal sins of journalism: Thou shalt not fabricate. No exceptions. No excuses. . . . It may ring hollow—after the fact, excuses always do—but I always believed that I needed to do it all. Instead of popping out of J-school with a nice, neat, byline-ready package, I was fueled by a heady mixture of naivete, ambition, and an almost insane love for the powers of language. To make up for the fact that I didn't get that "correct" start in journalism, I set out to be 10 times as good by doing 10 times more. . . . And sometimes, as a result of trying to do too much at once and cutting corners, they didn't. So I tweaked them to make sure they did. It didn't happen often, but it did happen. And if it had happened once, that was one time too many.[33]

One of Smith's columns to which she admitted fabrication happened on 11 May 1998. It quotes a fictitious cancer patient named Claire, reacting to news of cancer therapies that showed promise in mice. Claire was quoted as saying, "I'm not proud. Right away, I said, 'Rub it on my skin, pop it to me in a pill, shoot me up with it.' If I could find a way to steal it, I would. Hell, if I could get my hands on it, I'd swallow the whole mouse."[34] According to *Globe* editor Matthew Storin, Smith also admitted to other fabricated characters, including a worker named Jim Burke, who was erecting barricades for the Boston Marathon, a woman named Dorothy Gibson whose young daughter was getting a painful hair

continued

makeover for Easter Sunday, and a South End cosmetologist named Janine Byrne, who was commenting on the case involving kidnapping defendant Stephen Fagan.[35] The *Globe* asked for Patricia Smith's resignation, and she resigned without protest.

Mike Barnicle's resignation was more contorted. In his 2 August 1998 column, "I Was Just Thinking, . . ." Barnicle used jokes that paralleled the writings of George Carlin. When confronted with the similarities in his list of ten, he told his editors that he had not read Carlin's book and these were ten funny things he had heard from a friend, without checking their origin. They suspended him for one month.

"Within hours, a local television station, WCVB-TV, broadcast a videotape of a 22 June program showing Mr. Barnicle recommending the book as summer reading."[36] While acknowledging he had recommended the book, Barnicle insisted to the editors that he had not actually read it himself. *Globe* editor Matthew Storin asked for Barnicle's resignation, but he refused. In addition to his suspension, he agreed to reduce his television appearances on MSNBC and on PBS' *News Hour with Jim Lehrer.*

With Barnicle defiant and a deluge of support from readers and professional colleagues over five days, Storin began a series of conversations with his top staff. He concluded, with their endorsement, that Mr. Barnicle's actions were not "reasons for termination or in hindsight, asking for his resignation."[37]

Allegations emerged the next week, on Wednesday, August 19, that facts in a 1995 column could not be verified by the *Reader's Digest,* which wanted to reprint it. Barnicle resigned. On Thursday, the weekly *Boston Phoenix* reported that he had plagiarized critic A. J. Liebling in a 1986 article on Governor Earl Long of Louisiana, even using colloquialisms and spellings without attribution to Liebling. " 'A four-hundred-dollar suit on old Uncle Earl,' he used to say, 'would look like socks on a rooster,' Barnicle quoted Long as saying. Liebling wrote: 'A four-hundred-dollar suit on old Uncle Earl would look like socks on a rooster,' the *Phoenix* article reported."[38] Purportedly this material was sent to the *Globe* ombudsman at the time by Northeastern University Professor Bill Kirtz, though Robert Keirstead denies ever seeing it.

According to Matthew Storin, after hearing complaints about his metro columnists in 1995, the *Globe* began monitoring their columns for accuracy. In late 1995, Storin met with them and laid out the "Rules of the Road" for each of them. "The main rule was that they were to provide to their editors details about the identity of any significant figure mentioned in a column, whether by name or not. At a minimum, . . . this information should contain the name of the individual and at least one other item by which this person can be identified."[39] Less than three years later, both star-studded professionals could not meet these tests and resigned in disgrace.   ∎

Plagiarism is unacceptable in news. It is a convention of reporters personally and the policy of newspapers and news magazines and of radio and television news as well. Guidelines similar to those of the *Globe's* "Rules of the Road" are widely used or endorsed. The question raised by Howell Raines of *The New York Times* is whether we maintain and enforce these professional rules "with doctrinal ferocity."[40] As he put it, "Life is full of gray areas, but the intellectual contract that makes mainstream newspapering possible is stark and clear. Editors have to be able to trust what reporters and columnists write and say. Journalists do not make things up or present others' writing and thought as their own."[41] But all members "of this profession know the rules when we sign up." The issue is whether we "believe in strict enforcement of rules about borrowing, lifting and leveling with colleagues," so strict, in fact, that we believe that if we "have to choose between a worthy but errant colleague and the newspaper itself," we choose for the paper.[42]

The *Globe*'s waffling on the immensely popular Barnicle appeared to indicate that he was more important than the veracity of the *Globe* or the journalism enterprise itself. His middle-aged white colleagues, who defended him until the evidence became too overwhelming to ignore, and Barnicle's own defiance and evasion with his supervisors led the *Globe* to a double standard racially in implementing its rules against fabrication. Granted, there is no painless or unequivocal way to deal administratively with failure, and gender and racial biases are not easily overcome. But, if the principle of truthtelling is the cornerstone of news, the issue is how we can get beyond formal agreement to an organizational culture of total commitment to it.

10 Muhammad Cartoon Controversy

On 30 September 2005, the *Jyllands-Posten*, Denmark's largest newspaper, published a series of twelve cartoons depicting the Prophet Muhammad. Fleming Rose, *Jyllands-Posten*'s culture editor, commissioned the cartoons in response to the incidents of self-censorship and intimidation within Islam he observed in Denmark and across Europe. He wanted moderate Muslims to speak out in favor of healthy criticism. He insisted that the paper had a tradition of satire with the royal family and public figures and that the cartoonists were treating Islam in the same way they treat Christianity, Hinduism, Buddhism, and other religions.

Although there have been irreverent portrayals of the Prophet by Europeans since the Middle Ages, the right-of-center *Jyllands-Posten* was known for its anti-immigrationist stance, and publication of the cartoons appeared to many Muslims as racial hatred toward a besieged community. The act of even creating an image of Muhammad is blasphemous according to a tradition in Islam, so not surprisingly, many Muslims were outraged for that reason alone. To a neutral observer, some of the cartoons were mild and innocuous. A few were aimed at the editor's call for cartoons, not at Muhammad directly. One showed Muhammad as a Bedouin flanked by two women in burqas. But others were more explosive. One depicted Muhammad wielding a cutlass, and another had him saying that paradise was running short of virgins for suicide bombers. In the most offensive cartoon, the Prophet is wearing a bomb-shaped turban, complete with burning fuse—a reference to the Aladdin story where an orange falling into his turban brought him great fortune. Those who took offense at the cartoons viewed their publication as yet another instance of Western religious intolerance and prejudice.

In mid-November, some Danish fundamentalist imams set off on a journey through the Middle East. They took with them the twelve cartoons, ten others from a November publication of the Danish *Weekend Avisen*, and three more of unknown origin (one showing Muhammad with a pig's nose). The violence that occurred in the beginning of 2006 as a result of this dossier of cartoons outweighed the attention the *Jyllands-Posten* set received immediately after their publication. As such, some view the imams' visit and inclusion of additional incendiary cartoons as the major cause of the worldwide turmoil that

continued

ensued. A baseless rumor that Danes planned to burn copies of the *Qur'an* in Copenhagen's City Square fanned the protests even more. In late January, the imam of the Grand Mosque of Mecca issued an ultimatum, "He who vilifies the Prophet should be killed."[43]

On 30 January 2006, gunmen raided the European Union's offices in Gaza, demanding an apology for allowing the paper to publish the cartoons. While the Danish paper apologized, Danish Prime Minister Anders Fogh Rasmussen defended freedom of speech as essential to democracy. In a show of support for freedom of the press, papers in Spain, Germany, Italy, and France reprinted the cartoons the following day.

A battle of wills ensued in a cycle of publication and subsequent protests. On 4 February 2006, Syrians retaliated by attacking the Norwegian and Danish embassies in Damascus. Protesters also stormed Danish embassies in Beirut, Damascus, and Tehran. Protests in Afghanistan and Somalia turned deadly, and in Libya, ten people were killed in riots. Pakistan's Jamaat-e-Islamic party placed a bounty of 50,000 Danish kroner on the cartoonists.[44] Editors in Jordan who dared to reprint the cartoons were arrested. The prime minister of Malaysia called for calm but described the cartoons as an act of provocation, and editors in Malaysia considering publication were threatened with injunctions.[45] The newspaper *France Soir* published the cartoons, along with Buddhist, Jewish, and Christian caricatures, and declared defiantly: "No religious dogma can impose its view on a democratic and secular society. We have a right to caricature God." Its managing editor was sacked.[46] Several days later, the French magazine *Charlie Hebdo* also published the cartoons. Muslim groups filed charges of racism against Philippe Val, the magazine's editor, but lost their case in 2007.

Western newspapers continued to champion freedom of the press by printing the cartoons, whereas many Muslims likewise have defended their freedom of religion by protesting the publications. Some have referred to this situation as the most contentious one since the events surrounding the 1988 publication of the novel *The Satanic Verses*, when Iran's then leader, Ayatollah Ruhollah Khomeini, declared a Fatwa death sentence on the book's author, Salman Rushdie. "The broader issues raised by the furor are certain to persist. To some, the dispute over the cartoons is a bellweather of a deepening divide between Western societies and Islam, a civilizational clash on issues as basic as the role of religion in society, and the limits of liberty."[47]   ■

Publication of the twelve cartoons brought to the surface a number of competing values. The debate and actions around the world were driven by contending political, religious, and social values. These deeply rooted beliefs produced both moderate and extreme reactions, depending typically on the group's leadership.

Those who valued free expression in democratic societies wanted the cartoons published. For many in Europe, defending the cartoons was a defense of the superior core values of Western democracy. One dimension of this social value is the public's right to know, prompting several papers to publish in order to inform their constituencies of the source of the furor. The Danish prime minister refused to meet with ambassadors of eleven Muslim countries on the grounds that governments in democracies do not control the press, although it appeared to be inflexibility and political ineptitude.

For Muslims, an assault on the Prophet cuts across all political issues and unites Muslims everywhere. In fact, all religions in various ways respect their leaders and forbid blasphemy of the sacred. Religion is the core of Islamic identity and needs to be taken seriously, beyond a right to worship freely. Given the religious values, as might be expected, at a meeting in the Muslim Holy City of Mecca in early 2006, leaders of the world's fifty-seven Islamic countries issued a joint statement that condemned "the desecration of the image of Muhammad."

Economic values surfaced also. Some newspapers declined publication out of fear of the consequences. They decided not to risk offending their readership on this issue. The *Daily Illini* at the University of Illinois was the only student newspaper to publish all twelve cartoons (on 9 February 2006). As the editor saw it: "All across this nation, editors are gripped in fear of printing. As a journalist, this flies in the face of everything I hold dear. If anything, journalists all over this country should be letting the public decide for themselves what to think of these cartoons."[48]

In addition, aesthetic values complicated the debates. Cartoons are an important genre in newspaper publishing. By character, they are provocative and often unflattering, but not necessarily inspired by hatred. Their purpose is to stimulate further reading and thinking, not preclude them. For a large segment of Islam, with any drawings of the Prophet forbidden, this genre cannot be appreciated on its own terms. Satirical depictions of leadership figures are taken for granted in Western democratic nations, clashing in this instance with those who regard the sanctity of a religious icon to be untouchable.

Following the Potter Box strategy, step three is crucial after the values are clarified in quadrant two. When values conflict, as they often do, an ethical principle is needed to move forward toward resolution. If action is taken already after step two based on one's values, those actions typically lead to inadequate decisions and continuing disputes. While the two major values in this case are social—freedom of the press and freedom of religion—economic and aesthetic values complicate mutual understanding and motivations. Step three is necessary for justified conclusions and unified action.

When cultures clash and religious beliefs are in dispute, the ethics of other-regarding care is ordinarily the strongest ethical principle for quadrant three. The imperative to love our neighbors as ourselves means that we begin with the other. The other's needs, desires, and aspirations establish our attitudes and actions. Others are treated with dignity and respect because they are human beings, regardless of their status or achievements. Granting others their right to the freedom of religion also means religious toleration.

Editors and publishers following the ethical principle of other-regarding care would decline publication. The democratic political value of free expression is suspended in this case by editors who want to act ethically, believing that in the long run ethics produces the best journalism. The right to take action does not mandate the action.

For Muslims adhering to Islamic ethics, the *Qur'an*'s principle of human dignity leads to the same conclusion against publication. It also supports the moderates in Islam who reject violence to others based on the same principle. Muslims living by human dignity can find satisfaction in the overall statistics: Of the billion Muslims in the world, fewer than 0.01 percent were involved in protests or violence over the cartoons. The *Qur'an*'s principle of human dignity agrees with other-regarding care that condemnation of entire groups (Danes, Muslims, Europeans, Western democracies) is unacceptable rhetoric.[49]

NOTES

1. For a classic statement of truthfulness in context, see Dietrich Bonhoeffer, *Ethics* (New York: Macmillan, 1955), pp. 363–372.
2. On worldwide poverty, see Per Pinstrup-Anderson and Cheng Fuzhi, "Still Hungry," *Scientific American*, September 2007, pp. 88–95.
3. Much of the data in this paragraph are from Barry M. Popkin, "The World Is Fat," *Scientific American*, September 2007, pp. 96–103.
4. T. Boyce, "The Media and Obesity," *Obesity Reviews* 8:suppl. 1 (November 2006): 201–205.
5. Sei-Hill Kim and L. Anne Willis, "Talking About Obesity: News Framing of Who Is Responsible for Causing and Fixing the Problem," *Journal of Health Communication* 12:4 (June 2007): 359–376.
6. Ibid., p. 367.
7. Ibid., p. 374.
8. Ibid., p. 374.
9. Quoted in Rick Zednik, "Inside Al Jazeera," *Columbia Journalism Review* (March/April 2002): 47.
10. Imad Musa, "Al Jazeera TV: When the Medium Becomes the Story," *IPI Global Journalist*, second quarter 2003, p. 20. For more details on the history and sociology of Al Jazeera, see Mohammed el-Nawawy and Adel Iskandar, *Al Jazeera: The Story of the Network That Is Rattling Governments and Redefining Modern Journalism* (Cambridge, MA: Westview Books, 2003).
11. Jonathon Curiel, "Al-Jazeera Speaks English," *The San Francisco Chronicle*, November 16, 2006.
12. Sara Ivry, "Now on YouTube: The Latest News from Al Jazeera in English," *The New York Times*, April 16, 2007.
13. Neil Hickey, "Perspectives on War: Different Cultures, Different Coverage," *Columbia Journalism Review* (March/April 2002): 45.
14. Kevin Maguire and Andy Lines, "Bush Plan to Bomb His Arab Ally," *The Daily Mirror*, November 22, 2005.
15. "Al Jazeera Pursues Bush Bomb Claim as Civil Servant Jailed," *Brand Republic News* May 11, 2007. Available at www.brandrepublic.com/News/656892.
16. Ibid., p. 46.
17. "Al Jazeera's Edge," www.newyorkmetro.com/nymetro/news/media, 08/21/2003.
18. Ted Koppel, "Deciding What Images to Show," *Nieman Reports*, Summer 2003, p. 95.
19. "Al Jazeera's Edge."
20. Fouad Ajami, "What the Muslim World Is Watching," *The New York Times Magazine*, 18 November 2001, p. 48.
21. Norman Spector, *Globe and Mail*, www.theglobeandmail.com/servlet/story, 08/21/2003.

22. Musa, "Al-Jazeera TV," p. 21.
23. For elaboration of this case and four responses from journalists, see Louis Hodges, "Cases and Commentaries," *Journal of Mass Media Ethics* 10:4 (1995): 248–256. For a book-length treatment, see Alston Chase, *Harvard and the Unabomber: The Education of an American Terrorist* (New York: Norton, 2003).
24. Cf. Kirkpatrick Sale, "Unabomber's Secret Treatise: Is There Method in His Madness?" *The Nation*, 25 September 1995, pp. 305–311.
25. Karen Brandon, "$1 Million Paid to Unabomber Kin," *Chicago Tribune*, 26 August 1998, sec. 1, p. 3.
26. "Unabomber Gets Book Deal to Tell His Story," *Los Angeles Times*, 12 February 1999, p. A 1.
27. Hodges, ibid., p. 249.
28. Ibid., p. 253. For editors' reactions on publication, see www.naa.org/Presstime/96/PTIME/actsurv.html. A *Presstime* online survey on September 21 showed ninety-nine answering "yes" and ninety-six checking "no" to the question whether these editors would have published or not.
29. Ibid., p. 256.
30. Richard Harwood, *The Washington Post*, 23 September 1995.
31. Hodges, ibid., p. 250.
32. Ellen Warren, "The Poetic Columnist Who Fell From Grace," *Chicago Tribune*, 12 August 1998, sec. 5, p. 7.
33. Patricia Smith, "A Note of Apology," *Boston Globe*, 19 June 1998, p. B6.
34. Mark Jurkowitz, "Admitting Fabrications, *Globe* Columnist Resigns," *Boston Globe*, 19 June 1998, p. A1.
35. Ibid.
36. Felicity Barringer, "Lobbying Blitz Saves Job of *Globe* Newspaperman," *The New York Times*, 12 August 1998, p. A 10.
37. Ibid.
38. Tim Jones, "Report Questions Barnicle Column," *The Chicago Tribune*, 21 August 1998, sec. 3, p. 3.
39. *Globe*, 19 June 1998, p. A1.
40. Howell Raines, "The High Price of Reprieving Mike Barnicle," *The New York Times*, 13 August 1998, p. A 22.
41. Ibid.
42. Ibid. Also note that Barnicle now works for the *Boston Herald* and is a regular contributor on conservative shows such as "Hannity." Smith's firing, however, ended her decade-long career in journalism. She continues writing as a poet.
43. Romesh Ratnesar, "Fanning the Flames," *Time*, vol. 167, February 20, 2006.
44. Paul Marshall, "The Mohammed Cartoons," *The Weekly Standard*, February 13, 2006, pp. 14–15.
45. For these and other details on reactions around the world, see Maha Azzam, "Cartoons, Confrontation and a Cry for Respect," *The World Today* 62:4 (April 2006), pp. 7–8.
46. Marshall, "The Mohammed Cartoons," p. 14.
47. Ratnesar, "Fanning the Flames."
48. Acton H. Gordon, "Editor's Note," *The Daily Illini*, February 9, 2006, p. 5a.
49. For a thoughtful application of Islamic ethics to this controversy, see Ali Mohamed, "Journalistic Ethics and Responsibility in Relation to Freedom of Expression: An Islamic Perspective," unpublished paper, McGill University, March 2007, pp. 18–28.

CHAPTER THREE

Reporters and Sources

Well-informed sources are a reporter's bread and butter, and dependence on them creates some genuine complexities. A news medium's pledge to divulge its sources of information would be welcomed by the public; however, printing names usually results in the sources thereafter speaking guardedly or even drying up. Several tactics are used in confronting this dilemma so that audiences are served and sources remain content. As Hugh Culbertson wrote, "The unnamed news source has been called a safety valve for democracy and a refuge for conscience, but also a crutch for lazy, careless reporters."[1] A classic *Washington Post* editorial captured some of the struggle in its description of "Source's" family tree:

> Walter and Ann Source (nee Rumor) had four daughters (Highly Placed, Authoritative, Unimpeachable, and Well-Informed). The first married a diplomat named Reliable Informant. (The Informant brothers are widely known and quoted here; among the best known are White House, State Department, and Congressional.) Walter Speculation's brother-in-law, Ian Rumor, married Alexandre Conjecture, from which there were two sons, It Was Understood and It Was Learned. It Was Learned just went to work in the Justice Department, where he will be gainfully employed for four long years.[2]

The complications here are not easily resolved. Walter Lippmann noted this journalistic bind more than fifty years ago in *Public Opinion*, where he distinguished news from truth. News he saw as fragments of information that come to a reporter's attention; the pursuit of truth, according to him, followed explicit and established standards.[3] In this sense, the judicial process, for example, adheres to rigorous procedures for gathering evidence. Academics footnote and attribute sources so that knowledgeable people can verify or dispute the conclusions. Medical doctors rely on technical precision and expertise. Reporters, however, cannot compete with these other professions. They have found no authoritative way of examining, testing, and evaluating their information, at least not in a public arena and not under risky, hostile conditions.

The difficulties result primarily because a multitude of practical considerations need to be jockeyed under deadline pressures. On occasion, reporters must be adversarial, at least skeptical; at other times, friendliness and cooperation work better. If newspeople become too intimate with important men and women, they lose their professional distance or develop unhealthy biases protecting them. However, to the degree that powerful sources are not cultivated and reporters establish no personal connections, the inside nuance and perspective may be lost. At times, written documents supplemented by public briefings are superior to information painfully dug out by a conscientious reporter. On most other occasions, the official source is blinded by self-interest. But who can predict? Regarding sources, the American Society of Newspaper Editors' (ASNE) Statement of Principles correctly warns: "Journalists must be vigilant against all who would exploit the press for selfish purposes."[4] Little wonder that as information came to light about the burglary of the headquarters of the Democratic National Committee at the Watergate hotel, several "scoops" proved to be stories leaked originally by Mr. Nixon's staff.

Most news operations have developed specific procedures to help prevent chaos and abuse. Certain conventions also hold together journalistic practice. It is typically assumed that all information must be verified by two or three sources before it can be printed. Most codes of ethics and company policies insist on attribution and specific identification whenever possible. A few news operations allow reporters to keep sources totally secret, but a majority openly involve editors as judges of the data's validity. The rules also require accurate quotation marks, correction of errors, and an account of the context. However, even with these safeguards, a responsible press must continually agonize over its treatment of sources in order to prevent lapses.

This chapter chooses four entangled aspects of the reporter–source relationship, all of them actual occurrences of some notoriety. The first case, on the crisis in Darfur, illustrates the enormous difficulties in getting reliable information in high-tension circumstances. The second case, on the Israeli–Palestinian conflict, concerns the question of reliable and balanced sources amid ongoing conflict. In the third case, the debate revolves around the use of stolen materials. The *Cincinnati Enquirer*'s investigation of Chiquita Brands provides an opportunity to examine Kant's restrictions against theft and lying. The last case involves the increasingly complex issues of chemicals in foods, asking whether reliable and unbiased sources are possible. Cheap answers are not forthcoming, but at every point the ethical issues ought to form a prominent part of the resolution.

11 Crisis in Darfur

After the Rwandan genocide that occurred during the 1990s, many people vowed never to allow such atrocities to go unnoticed again. Yet ethnic cleansing has ravaged the Darfur region of Sudan, and once again, the international community has been slow to act. While accounts vary, an estimated 200,000 people have died as a result of the violence. More than two million people have been displaced, with many fleeing to neighboring Chad and the Central African Republic.

continued

Darfur for several hundred years was an independent Islamic sultanate with a population of both Arabs and black African tribes—both of them Muslim. Darfur was annexed to Sudan by the British in 1916, but it was neglected by the colonial power. When Sudan became independent in 1956, the new government continued to overlook Darfur. The core area around Khartoum and inhabited by riverine Arabs has largely ignored all the rural territory in the country, although it covers the largest geography and has the largest population.[5]

Sudan is no stranger to conflict. In 1962, just six years after achieving its independence, a decade-long civil war broke out between the Arabs residing in the north and the Africans living in the south. After eleven years of peace, another civil war erupted, this time raging on for two decades. Things appeared to be calming down when, in February of 2003, a rebellion occurred in the Darfur region of Sudan—an area plagued not only by drought and desertification but also by continued tensions between the farmers and nomads who inhabit the area. The rebels began attacking government targets, claiming that the Sudanese government was discriminating against them because of their black African identity. The Sudanese government retaliated by employing local Arab militias to quash the uprising—nicknamed the *Janjaweed* (translated as "the evil horsemen"). Because the insurgents were mostly blacks, choosing the Darfuri Arab tribes was a brilliant strategy for terrorizing them.

While the Sudanese government is reluctant to admit its complicity in this tragedy, the events that have transpired in Darfur are nothing less than genocide. (The December 1948 International Convention on the Prevention and Punishment of Crimes of Genocide defines *genocide* as "deliberately inflicting on the group, conditions of life calculated to bring about its physical destruction in whole or in part.") After the government conducts air strikes on targeted villages, the Janjaweed descend on the area, murdering and raping anyone left alive. To ensure that no one returns, the militias burn any remaining structures and poison the water supply. By backing the militias, the Sudanese government is able to engage in ethnic cleansing and at the same time deny responsibility for the human rights violations, claiming the violence is due to "tribal conflicts."[6]

Attempts by the international community to bring an end to this crisis have been slow and ineffective. The United States and the European Union have contributed to humanitarian efforts but show no resolve to do anything meaningful in terms of policy. Furthermore, Sudan has been reluctant to keep its word when negotiations have led to cease-fire or peace agreements. In July 2007, the U.N. Security Council passed a resolution authorizing a peacekeeping force made up entirely of African troops, but without authorization to act. The Western countries were let off the hook easily, and Khartoum got an impotent and probably mute presence with no clear mandate to intervene.[7]

As Sudan continues to hemorrhage citizens to neighboring countries, the region has become increasingly unstable. This instability has had a negative impact on humanitarian efforts in the area and has caused many to scale back or abandon their efforts entirely. ■

What is known as the "greatest humanitarian crisis of the twenty-first century" requires the best possible international reporting. The ethical principle is truth. The world deserves to know the truth about Darfur, and the news media have a major responsibility to help provide it.

But standard definitions of truth are not adequate. Fairness and balance are important but not sufficient. Accuracy is required on the details, but the complications are enormous, and being accurate is not strong enough either. Hard news coverage that is sensational and crisis-oriented is obviously inadequate.

To meet the ethical principle of truth in this case means comprehensiveness. The term *interpretive sufficiency* is one way to define it. A sufficient interpretation opens up public life in all its dynamic dimensions. A truthful account is grounded historically and represents complex cultures and religions adequately. The people involved at all levels are portrayed authentically without stereotype or simplistic judgments.[8]

In this deeper understanding of truth in international news, truth means authentic disclosure. Truth is disclosing the essence of the events or, in other words, getting to the heart of the matter. And on this level, the truth about Darfur is still debated, even though the crisis has been unfolding since early 2003. According to Gerard Prunier, director of the French Center for Ethiopian Studies and author of *Darfur: The Ambiguous Genocide* (2005), four different explanations are being disputed yet today: (1) the Sudan government claims that it is an explosion of tribal conflicts exacerbated by drought; (2) some leading specialists and governments see it as a counterinsurgency gone wrong with the Janjaweed militias brutal and out of control; (3) a few call it "ethnic cleansing," with the African tribes being replaced by Arabs who are more supportive of Arab rule in Khartoum, and (4) a stronger version of number three is genocide, with genocide meaning the violent annihilation of one race by another.[9]

Meeting the standard of truth as authentic disclosure is complicated by unending difficulties with sources. Visas to Sudan are difficult to get for journalists and typically mean months of waiting. Reporting in Darfur itself is expensive and dangerous. The news networks presume a lack of interest in Africa, and several have exhausted their budgets and personnel covering Iraq and Afghanistan. The government assigns "minders" to accompany correspondents, and local sources who speak honestly to the media have to be protected for their own safety. Compassion fatigue is often noted too—editors and the public are weary of a complex conflict with no end in sight and meanwhile difficult to sort out. In addition to knowing events on the ground—gang rape, bombings, murder, burned-out villages, children slaughtered in daylight—reporters need to interview government administrators and rebel commanders. Aid workers and United Nations workers are accessible, but leaders typically are evasive or deceptive.

Some serious reporting does overcome the hurdles and meets the truth principle. Nicholas Krist of *The New York Times* and Emily Wax of *The Washington Post* are distinguished in the United States, and the BBC covers Darfur at length and regularly. According to the Tyndall Report, however, the failures of U.S. television are inexcusable. In 2004, for the entire year, ABC News had eighteen minutes on Darfur, NBC five minutes for the year, and CBS three minutes. In contrast, Martha Stewart received 130 minutes of coverage by the three networks. CNN, Fox News, NBC, MSNBC, ABC, and CBS together ran fifty-five times as many stories about Michael Jackson as they did about Darfur.[10]

In this case on the Darfur region, there is general agreement about which ethical principle is most relevant. And, this principle, truth as authentic disclosure, is readily understandable. The challenge is overcoming the failure to act on this principle. There are examples of overcoming the problems with sources and reporting comprehensively. How can they be disseminated and used effectively by journalism educators and professionals?

12 Covering the Middle East

In 1947, the United Nations established the State of Israel and the Palestinian settlements from the former British mandate of Palestine. Three regional wars have followed, that is, two Palestinian intifadas, and Israeli incursions into Arab-populated territories.

During each war, Israel expanded its boundaries. In 1948, it extended the Jewish areas in the original partition plan to its current internationally recognized borders. In 1967, it took the West Bank from Jordan and the Gaza strip from Egypt—what remained of British-administered Palestine.

> Significantly these were areas that large numbers of Palestinian refugees were forced to flee to when the Jewish state was created in 1948. So while the 1967 war had defended Israel against combined Arab armies massed on its borders, it had also put a significant Arab population under Israeli rule. It was in the following years that Israel began an illegal programme of settlement building in the now occupied territories, which it successfully defended in the 1973 Yom Kippur war.[11]

The 1980s intifada took place in a decade when Israel made peace with Egypt and pursued Yasser Arafat's Palestinian Liberation Organization (PLO) into Lebanon. The intifada demonstrated the rage the Palestinians felt toward the Israeli occupation, which resurfaced again in September 2000 with the beginning of the al-Aqsa intifada.

A major peace initiative—the Oslo process—began in 1992 with secret negotiations between Yasser Arafat, the exiled head of the PLO, and the then Israeli prime minister, Yitzhak Rabin, who was later assassinated by a Jewish fanatic. The Oslo process continued through the 1990s and into January 2001, despite suicide bombings in Jerusalem and Tel Aviv, the continued building of Israeli settlements in the occupied territories, and the beginning of the al-Aqsa intifada.

> Ehud Barak, then the Israeli prime minister, made a series of offers to Yasser Arafat on what Israel would concede to a Palestinian state, but none of them was accepted. The final offer, made in January 2001 at Taba in Egypt, was the best of the lot but whether it was the best Mr. Arafat could reasonably expect remains controversial.[12]

Early in 2003, President George W. Bush unveiled a new "road map to peace." It was drawn up by the United States, the United Nations, the European Union, and Russia, with Israeli and Palestinian consultation. It seeks an independent Palestinian state in the West Bank and Gaza strip alongside Israel. The plan proposed a three-stage plan to achieve this by 2005. The first stage demands an immediate cessation of Palestinian violence, reform of Palestinian political institutions, the dismantling of Israeli settlement outposts built since March 2001, and a progressive Israeli withdrawal from the occupied territories. In the second phase, an independent Palestinian state would be created. The third stage seeks a permanent end to the conflict by agreeing on the final borders, the status of Jerusalem, the fate of Palestinian refugees, and peace deals between Arab states and Israel.

Like the Oslo peace process, the plan leaves the difficult issues until last—borders, the status of Jerusalem, Israeli settlements, and four million Palestinian refugees. Its early advocates pointed to the backing of the United Nations, the European Union, and Russia and hoped that after three years of fighting and civilian deaths, the militant group Hamas and the Israeli army might consider a truce. However, the road map's status among the principal parties was controversial from the outset. Skeptics suggested that then Prime Minister Sharon might have accepted it only to ride out U.S. pressure or in the expectation that it had no chance to succeed. Internal Palestinian politics, Mr. Arafat's objections to governmental restructuring, and his longstanding animosity with Sharon were likely to sidetrack the process as well. In fact, six months after its introduction, with the resignation of Palestinian Prime Minister Abu Mazen, Israel's building of a security fence in the West Bank, and unrelenting violence, pundits from around the world had already declared the Bush initiative dead.

By the summer of 2004, President Bush conceded that the 2005 goal was unrealistic.[13] That winter, Arafat died, and the following year, Abu Mazen was elected president of the Palestinian Authority. Shortly thereafter, Sharon and Abu Mazen convened a summit with the Eqyptian and Jordanian presidents at which the leaders restated their support for the road map.[14] When Sharon suffered an incapacitating stroke in 2006, his successor, Ehud Olmert, continued discussions with Abu Mazen. The victory of Hamas in the 2006 Palestinian elections raised alarm among Israeli and U.S. officials and caused conflicts within the Palestinian government itself. Throughout 2006, Israel engaged in violent conflicts with Hamas in the Gaza strip and with Hezbollah in Lebanon. These conflicts once again caused pundits to declare the road map dead. While President Bush is trying, in the last year of his Administration, to revive negotiations for peace, no tangible results are evident.   ■

American newsrooms feel constant heat from their coverage of the Middle East conflict. Attacks come from both sides. The Committee for Accuracy in Middle East Reporting condemns NPR's coverage as "false" and "skewed" against Israel. At the same time, Fairness and Accuracy in Reporting attacks what it sees as NPR's pro-Israeli bias. As the *Columbia Journalism Review* observes, "No news subject generates more complaints about media objectivity than the Middle East in general and the Israeli–Palestinian conflict in particular."[15] "As a hard news subject, [Middle East coverage] is probably the no. 1 issue that consistently comes up across the country," says Mike Clark, reader advocate of the Florida *Times-Union* and Web editor for the Organization of News Ombudsmen.[16] Allegations of pro-Israeli bias include more prominent attention to Israeli deaths than Palestinian casualties and the use of words such as *retaliation* for Israeli attacks and *terrorists* or *gunmen* for Palestinians. Pro-Palestinian bias is indicated by more attention to Palestinian children and violence being softened to *protests*.

But complaints that come from both sides are no indication that the press is doing its job correctly:

> The media do indeed love to point out that they are getting it from both sides.
> The fact that both sides attack them and accuse them of bias comes in quite

handy for them during heated meetings with media activists. . . . But that is almost always used as an end-all argument and a way to avoid dealing with specific concerns that are raised.[17]

Charges of unfair coverage are not new; they have persisted since 1948.
But criticism has intensified with Israeli military incursions and Palestinian suicide bombings. David Demers of the Center for Global Media Studies accounts
for the dual response in this way: "The two sides in a conflict will always see
the mainstream media as biased on the other side. When the conflict flares up,
and especially when violence increases, both sides become more vociferous in
their criticism."[18]

Aristotle's mean is the most appropriate principle in complicated, multilay-
ered cases where two legitimate entities are at odds with each other. The
Israeli–Palestinian conflict fits that guideline explicitly, and news reporters typically seek the appropriate location between two extremes. The ethical challenge is
implementing Aristotle's principle effectively.

Executing the right balance is complicated by several factors, such as a "lack
of understanding of the underlying historical and political background."[19] Ira Stoll
identifies a "structural imbalance" as the greatest impediment to fairness, one that
comes "from journalists being able to work mostly free and uninhibited in Israel
but being subject to severe restrictions in countries like Syria or Iran."[20] David Demers draws a slightly different conclusion: "Content analyses by scholars generally conclude that media coverage tends to favor Israel over Palestine. It's not a
conspiracy by any means, but what it boils down to is they depend on government officials. And these government officials represent the administration, which
tends to be pro-Israel."[21] Ahmed Bouzid adds another perspective:

> The media have very easy access to Israeli spokespersons, who are always
> on the ready with a statement, a TV appearance, who actively promote their
> point of view. Access to the Palestinians, meanwhile, is made extremely dif-
> ficult by the realities of the occupation, the curfews, the town closures, the
> checkpoints, and of course, by deliberate harassment from the Israeli army
> against journalists.[22]

In this case, being virtuous in Aristotle's sense requires a keenly developed
moral discernment and an especially sophisticated professional practice.

13 Stolen Voice Mail

On 3 May 1998, the *Cincinnati Enquirer* published an eighteen-page special section of ten
stories on Chiquita Brands International, Inc.

The *Enquirer* had spent hundreds of thousands of dollars investigating one of Cincinnati's most prominent businesses, controlled since the 1970s by the city's most powerful
corporate executive, Carl Lindner. "Chiquita Secrets Revealed: Power, Money and Control"
charged the company with environmental recklessness, bribery, and constructing secret

trusts to evade land and labor regulations. *Enquirer* reporters had been working on the story since May 1997 and had traveled from the Caribbean, Honduras, and Panama to Brussels and Antwerp in Belgium, plus Vancouver, New York, and Washington.

Mike Gallagher, a decorated and highly respected reporter, led the investigation, and the editor, Lawrence Beaupre, praised its "thorough reporting." Beaupre had upgraded the *Enquirer* substantially since becoming editor in 1995, with Gannett honoring him as one of its top ten editors in 1996. The *Enquirer* expected the Chiquita stories "to complete the paper's metamorphosis from middling corporate protector to purveyor of a journalism worthy of the ultimate accolade, the Pulitzer Prize."[23]

Less than two months later, on June 28, the *Enquirer* withdrew its story, with "An Apology to Chiquita" spread across the entire front page. The apology was reprinted on two later occasions, admitting that the report created "a false and misleading impression of Chiquita's business practices." While the May 3 story had promoted some 3000 internal Chiquita voice mail messages as documentation, apparently the paper now believed Gallagher had illegally taped some of them. As the apology stated, "Despite [Gallagher's] assurances to his editors prior to publication that he had obtained his information in an ethical and lawful manner, we can no longer trust his word." The apology was part of a $10 million settlement from Gannett in which Chiquita removed the threat of litigation against the paper and its corporate sponsor. Instead of repudiating Gallagher's conduct but defending the contents of the report, the *Enquirer* guaranteed that the allegations would be lost to history.

Mike Gallagher was fired, and on July 2, Chiquita filed suit against him in federal district court for "deformation, trespass, conversion, violations of state and federal wiretapping laws and other intentional misconduct." Editor Lawrence Beaupre was removed and given a responsibility in Gannett's corporate headquarters for conducting ethics seminars. Gallagher's assistant in the investigation, Cameron McWhirter, was reassigned to the *Detroit News*. In September, Michael Gallagher pleaded guilty to two felony counts. But he likely kept himself from jail by signing a cooperation agreement with law authorities to provide "a full, truthful and complete disclosure as to all sources and their activities." Former Chiquita lawyer George Ventura has now been indicted—after Gallagher turned over to authorities "his notes, thirty-nine computer disks, a series of e-mails, his hard drive, and at least seven taped telephone conversations between Ventura and reporters."[24] Ventura's lawyer, Marc D. Mezibov, believes "it could be the first time a source has been prosecuted criminally as a result of a reporter refusing to live up to his promises of anonymity. . . . He's Judas. He committed the ultimate sin in journalism. He's Benedict Arnold or any other scoundrel you can think of."[25]

In January 1999, Gannett brought in Ward H. Bushee III from its Reno *Gazette-Journal* as the *Enquirer*'s new executive editor, with the task of repairing its damaged reputation and rescuing a news operation in shambles.   ∎

From a Kantian perspective, lying, theft, and breaking promises are always wrong. The full details of the case are constrained within the judicial process—the editor's agreement not to discuss it publicly, for example. But the *Enquirer* declared in its apology that the staff believes Mike Gallagher lied to them. Precisely how Gallagher obtained the voice mail information is unclear, but Gannett's willingness to settle means that its lawyers have concluded Gallagher stole at least some of them by recording the voice mail himself.

The categorical imperative suggests that we do not permit for ourselves what we do not wish to make a universal law. From this viewpoint, societies cannot exist—and the institutions within them have no integrity—if stealing, lying, and breaking one's promises are allowed. When these basic moral duties are violated, the tragic circumstances are understandable.

The investigation followed the standards of traditional reporting—interviews, extensive travel for onsite observation, examining court records and company documents obtained legally, financial resources for veteran reporters, and the courage to examine a powerful local company.[26] But from Kant's perspective, unless we tell the truth, keep our promises, and honor property that's not ours, the entire well-intentioned enterprise will fail. Instead of fulfilling its purpose of informing the public on matters of vital importance to it, the *Enquirer*'s public role for the foreseeable future has been seriously jeopardized.

This case has a number of complications, and other analyses of the debacle are possible. The cause of the breakdown could center on Gallagher's alleged criminal behavior; "he almost certainly violated federal wiretapping law, according to several experts . . . we can do these stories without breaking laws."[27] Gallagher's zealous and self-righteous style could explain the excesses also. Colleen Gallagher gave the judge another explanation of her brother's role in the Chiquita story:

> . . . With his trip to South America, when he saw firsthand the suffering of the people he perceived to be victims of Chiquita, he became emotionally involved, incensed and believed that he needed to do what he could to right what he saw as a grievous wrong. I believe that in his quest to do this, he will acknowledge that he made an error in judgment as to how he accessed information. He is responsible for that choice. . . . But I do not believe he made this choice for personal gain or with criminal intent.[28]

The *Enquirer*'s management, reporting, and editing policy and procedures may need to be corrected or strengthened. But Kant's deontological ethics appears to provide the most persuasive framework for analysis.

14 Risky Foods

Food safety is an issue of serious concern in the United States and the rest of the world, and food-contamination problems are increasingly important to the media.[29]

Food-borne illness is one such public issue, and in one study it topped the list of food and safety issues covered by U.S. news magazines between 1990 and 2000.[30] The U.S. Food and Drug Administration (FDA) estimates that economic losses from food-borne illness are nearly $17 billion annually. Food-borne illnesses are caused by bacteria and viruses and occur largely because consumers and food service workers do not handle food properly. Lance Gay, writing for the Scripps Howard News Service, illustrates how food-borne illness is typically treated in the press:

> In the last half-century, Americans have become accustomed to periodic food scares, even though food scientists say simple advances like cellophane wrapping, tamper-proof packaging, and stable refrigeration have served to make the food supply more sanitary and safer than it has ever been.
>
> Food scientists say that doesn't mean the food supply is as safe as it could be. The Centers for Disease Control and Prevention estimate that each year there are 76 million cases of food-borne illness in the United States resulting in 325,000 hospitalizations and 5000 deaths.
>
> Resources for the Future, a Washington think tank, says the annual loss from major food-borne illnesses range from $3 billion to $9 billion, and more than half of the illnesses are unidentified.
>
> Michael Taylor, a senior fellow at the think tank and a former administrator of the Agriculture Department's Food Inspection and Safety Service, said the lack of knowledge about food-borne pathogens and the strategies to counter them contrasts with the vast data banks for research compiled in the twentieth century on chemical contaminants.
>
> "We've got a lot more to do on the microbial side," said Taylor, who contends public health would be better protected if the government concentrated its resources on dealing with pathogens that cause the most problems. Many of the serious pathogens like *E. coli* in hamburger and *Vibrio vulnificus* in raw oysters have been identified as the cause of food-borne illnesses and deaths in the last 30 years.
>
> The Centers for Disease Control and Prevention in Atlanta estimate that 90 percent of the illnesses are caused by three pathogens—Norwalk-like viruses that were linked most recently to outbreaks of diarrhea on cruise ships, *Campylobacter* commonly found in raw chicken that causes stomach disorders, and *Salmonella* in eggs and raw meat that causes nausea and is linked to arthritis.
>
> About 75 percent of the deaths are linked to three pathogens: *Salmonella*; *Listeria*, a refrigerator-tolerant bacteria on hot dogs, prepared meats, and cheeses; and *Toxoplasma* caused by a protozoa that lives primarily in uncooked pork.
>
> Although the government has launched campaigns noting that cooking is the most effective way to kill food-borne pathogens, surveys document that the public isn't listening.
>
> Agriculture Department surveys show that only half of the American kitchens have thermometers, and a 1998 survey concluded that only 3 percent of cooks regularly used thermometers to determine if hamburgers were cooked to the recommended 160 degrees Fahrenheit needed to kill pathogens.
>
> Barry Swanson, a food scientist at Washington State University in Pullman, said many consumers are turned off by false food scares and are skeptical about warnings they read or hear.
>
> Swanson said consumers need to be more alert and cautious because America's food supply network is now global; outbreaks are no longer just local affairs. A decade ago, the typical outbreak of food disease involved contaminated potato salad at a church picnic. Today, contaminated hamburgers made in Nebraska can be distributed at fast-food stores on both East and West coasts by the time the contamination is discovered.

continued

"We used to feel isolated from one another, but we aren't there anymore," Swanson said. "Because of our distribution system and the fact that goods move from coast to coast overnight, if we've got a problem, it's a big problem rather than a small problem that it once was. . . ."

Ruth Kava, director of nutrition at the American Council on Science and Health in New York, an industry-supported group, . . . points out that normal foods contain chemicals that could be classed as poisons if used in excess: Lima beans contain hydrogen cyanide, a classic poison, while potatoes contain solanine, arsenic, and chaconine. Carrots contain carototoxin, a nerve poison. And nutmeg, black pepper, and carrots all contain myristicin, a hallucinogenic.

"There's something in every plant that can be toxic," Kava said. She urged people with compromised immune systems to take special caution handling or eating raw foods. "But if it's handled properly, not spoiled and not contaminated, it's OK."[31]

Gay includes in a side box ("A Dozen Rules to Keep You Healthy") safety suggestions from food scientists that minimize the risks of contamination.

A host of other food-safety issues is also on the public agenda, for example, genetically modified foods. Nearly three-quarters of U.S. grocery shelves are stocked with genetically modified products, with debates across the country over their health and environmental dangers. The European Union explicitly bars genetically modified food from international trade. The use of growth hormones in dairy cattle to boost milk production is controversial, too, even though their negative impact on the healthfulness of dairy products has not been proven. And mad cow disease (bovine spongiform encephalopathy), infecting 100,000 animals in Europe, has been a major media event, throwing the public into turmoil over sensationalism on the one hand and the possible linkage between mad cow disease and the deadly Creutzfeldt-Jacob brain cell disease in humans on the other.[32]

Food irradiation is a spin-off issue of food-borne disease, but it now has a life of its own. The radiation process used in food preservation destroys microorganisms that contaminate food or cause spoilage. Although irradiation processing has been approved by the FDA for many products, anti-irradiation advocates have built resistance by comparing the radiation treatment of food to exposing the human body to radiation. Opposition groups "allude to dangers from nuclear bombs, raise fears of leaks from nuclear power facilities, and explicitly state that eating irradiated food causes cancer."[33] The emotional controversy over food irradiation has not permitted sufficient scientific information to shape public discussion. ■

To keep modern society from becoming terrified and immobile, one body of opinion insists that strong government surveillance and more detailed consumer information in the supermarket are essential. Based on this view, the press should not consider itself the guarantor of public health but should play an adjunct role to those social units that can treat issues in a more discriminating way—in this case, the local retailer—without creating a social crisis. At the other extreme, some media advocates insist that media warnings about potential dangers are essential in a fast-paced and complex age, even though they often lead to societal dysfunction. From this perspective, if the media give too much deference to economic and legal interests, the public will be lulled into a self-destructive complacency. In these terms, the "watchdog function" is never so important as when powerful industries stand to save millions of dollars by equivocating on the safety of their products.

John E. Cox, Jr., founder of the Foundation for American Communications in Los Angeles, has proposed a set of guidelines, based on Aristotle's middle state, that he believes place risk reporting in an appropriate context.[34]

1. Journalists should delay the presentation of a story until all the facts are in.

The most famous food scare in American history did not meet this standard. In February 1989, the television show *60 Minutes* aired a story that apples treated with the chemical Alar were dangerous to small children. It was initiated by a report from the Natural Resources Defense Council (NRDC), a nonprofit environmental group, stating that Alar could raise the level of daminozide dangerously high in children. The NRDC, through its public relations counsel, negotiated an "exclusive coverage" agreement with *60 Minutes* and did so without scientific evidence or presenting its charges to experts for evaluation.

An apple scare followed. School cafeterias in Los Angeles, Chicago, and New York City ordered apples removed from their menus and storerooms. Signs were posted above bins in grocery stores stating that the apples therein were Alar-free. Washington State, which grows 50 percent of the nation's apples, faced crippling economic losses. Said one school official, "It was overreaction and silliness carried to the point of stupidity."[35] Kenneth W. Kizer, director of the California Department of Health Services, said the panic created a "toxic bogeyman."[36]

Since 1968, Alar had been important to the apple industry for making the apples redder and slowing the ripening process to keep them from falling prematurely. But when scientists in 1985 reported that Alar could cause lung and kidney tumors in mice, many growers stopped using it. The fact that only 5 percent of all apples grown are sprayed with Alar wasn't included in the report, nor that humans would have to drink gallons of juice from those apples to ingest even miniscule levels of daminozide. The story was staged by *60 Minutes* as a confrontation between a money-hungry commercial industry and inept government agencies. Critics considered the news media part of the problem in this case because they were presenting this complicated issue prematurely and therefore haphazardly. Saying a chemical was toxic without clarifying the meaning of that phrase, for example, led the public into thinking that by eating an apple one could get cancer.[37]

2. Journalists must put risk into perspective, not by simply reporting two points of view, but through presenting careful analysis.

Figures from the National Safety Council, for example, show that fewer than one dozen people per year die in the United States directly from food poisoning— though approximately 1500 perish annually from diseases connected to food contamination. With 46,000 dying each year in motor vehicle accidents, 12,000 in falls, 5000 in fires, 5000 in drownings, and so forth, the public needs a broader picture of risk and safety, not one centered predominately on warring companies and agencies or confrontational politics.

3. Reporters must have the training and education to deal with complex data and ask tough questions, particularly in such areas as toxicology, radiation, chemistry, and medicine.

As a former broadcast journalist in California, Mr. Cox has developed educational programs to improve the news coverage of science, economics, and business. For example, the Internet-based information service FACSNET, created by FACS and the San Diego Supercomputer Center in 1996 is designed to educate journalists on issues of food and science.

The NRDC has developed into a strong and well-informed watchdog on government policy and enforcement, making information publicly available through its magazine, *The Amicus Journal*, news releases, and its website (www. nrdc.org/default.asp). The Consumers Union and the American Council on Science and Health (www.acsh.org/factsfears/) also are valuable resources. But journalists must develop additional sources of information other than industry and public interest groups. At least to some observers, if the news media had shown adequate sophistication, the issues regarding Alar could have been focused on the Environmental Protection Agency (EPA), giving it an opportunity to act. As a matter of fact, the EPA later did ban Alar as a potentially dangerous pesticide, although available scientific evidence as to Alar's danger still has not been conclusive. Accepting data blindly is irresponsible, but the public is entitled to know of tests systematically conducted in a nonindustry laboratory.

NOTES

1. Hugh M. Culbertson, "Leaks a Dilemma for Editors as Well as Officials," *Journalism Quarterly* 57 (Autumn 1980): 402–408.
2. Editorial in the *Washington Post*, 12 February 1969. Quoted in John L. Hulteng, *The Messenger's Motives*, 2d ed. (Englewood Cliffs, NJ: Prentice-Hall, 1985), p. 79.
3. Walter Lippmann, *Public Opinion* (New York: The Free Press, [1922] 1949), Part 7, pp. 201–230.
4. John L. Hulteng, *Playing It Straight* (Chester, CT: Globe Pequot Press, 1981), p. 15.
5. Gerard Prunier, "The Politics of Death in Darfur," *Current History* (May 2006): 195–196. For further details, see his book, *Darfur: The Ambiguous Genocide* (Ithaca, NY: Cornell University Press, 2005).
6. Matthew Lippman, "Darfur: The Politics of Genocide Denial Syndrome," *Journal of Genocide Research* 9:2 (2007): 192–213.
7. Prunier, "Politics of Death in Darfur," p. 199.
8. For an authoritative study of eight daily newspapers from around the world on the question of interpretive sufficiency, see Bella Mody, "Uncovering Darfur Sudan 2003–2005: Which News Organization Offered the Most Comprehensive Coverage?" unpublished paper, University of Colorado–Boulder, (7 July 2006).
9. Prunier, "Politics of Death in Darfur," p. 200.

10. Sherry Ricchiardi, "Déjà Vu," *American Journalism Review* (February/March 2005).
11. Simon Jeffrey, "The Road Map to Peace," *The Guardian Review*, 4 June 2003, p. 2. For further details on this history, see www.guardian.co.uk. Accessed on 1 October 2003.
12. Jeffrey, *The Guardian Review*, p. 3.
13. "Newspaper Interview with George W. Bush," Federal News Service, 9 May 2004.
14. Steven Erlangen, "Urging New Path, Sharon and Abbas Declare Truce," *The New York Times*, February 9, 2005.
15. "Questions of Balance in the Middle East," *Columbia Journalism Review* (May/June 2003): 54.
16. Charles Burress, "U.S. Newspapers Catch Flak for Mideast Coverage," *The News-Gazette*, 21 April 2002, p. B4.
17. Ahmed Bouzid, "The Other War: A Debate," *Columbia Journalism Review* (May/June 2003): 55.
18. Quoted in Burress, *News-Gazette*, 21 April 2002, p. B4.
19. Ira Stoll, "The Other War: A Debate," *Columbia Journalism Review* (May/June 2003): 54.
20. Ibid.
21. Quoted in Burress, *News-Gazette*, p. B4.
22. Bouzid, *Columbia Journalism Review*, pp. 54–55.
23. For quotations and details, see Nicholas Stein, "Banana Peel," *Columbia Journalism Review* (September/October 1998): 46–51. For the case and three commentaries, see "The *Enquirer* and Chiquita," *Journal of Mass Media Ethics* 16:4 (2001): 313–321.
24. Alicia C. Shepard, "The Chiquita Aftermath," *American Journalism Review* (May 1999): 48.
25. Stein, "Banana Peel," p. 46.
26. For a thoughtful analysis, see Mike Hoyt, "Essay: Just How Far Is Too Far?" *Columbia Journalism Review* (September/October 1998): 48–49. Bruce Shapiro expands: "A 'false and misleading' picture? The *Enquirer*'s lawyers may have found it necessary to bend over fast and far. But in fact the 'Chiquita Secrets Revealed' series presents a damning, carefully documented array of charges, most of them 'untainted' by those stolen executive voice mails. Gallagher's and McWhirter's allegations are largely based on old-fashioned reportorial legwork: land records in Central America, interviews with environmental scientists and trade unions, lawsuit records, leaked corporate memoranda and the reporters' own visits to workers' villages and campuses." ("Rotten Banana," *Salon*, July 8, 1998).
27. Hoyt, "Just How Far Is Too Far," p. 49.
28. Shephard, "The Chiquita Aftermath," p. 48. For a detailed account of the aftermath, see Donald Challenger and Cecilia Friend, " 'Fruit of the Poisonous Tree': Journalistic Ethics and Voice-Mail Surveillance," *Journal of Mass Media Ethics* 16:4 (2001): 255–272.
29. For a review of the issues and role of the media, see Sherrie R. Whaley and Mark Tucker, "The Influence of Perceived Food Risk and Source Trust on Media System Dependency," paper presented at the Association for Education in Journalism and Mass Communication conference, Kansas City, Missouri, 31 July 2003.
30. S. R. Whaley and D. L. Doerfert, "Is Your Food Safe or Scary? How U.S. News Magazines Communicated Food Safety Issues, 1990–2000," paper presented at the Agricultural Communications in Education conference, Kansas City, Missouri, June 2003.
31. Lance Gay, "Dealing with Food Scares," *The News Gazette*, 3 September 2003, pp. D1–D2. Used by permission of the author. See also www.acsh.org and http://www.rff.org/fsrc.

32. For elaboration see, Whaley and Tucker, "Influence of Perceived Food Risk . . . ," pp. 2–4.
33. Hong-Lin Choi, "The Framing of an Agricultural Controversy: Constructing News About Food Irradiation," paper presented at the Association for Education in Journalism and Mass Communication conference, Kansas City, Missouri, 31 July 2003, p. 5.
34. "Inquiry: Reporting on Risks," *USA Today*, 15 May 1989, p. 9A.
35. "Apples without Alar," *Newsweek*, 30 October 1989, p. 86.
36. Details of this event and the quotations are from Margaret Carlson, "Do You Dare to Eat a Peach?" *Time*, 27 March 1989, pp. 24–30; cf. also "Alar as a Media Event," *Columbia Journalism Review* (March/April 1990): 44–45.
37. "Inquiry: Reporting on Risks," p. 9A.

Social Justice

Historian Charles Beard once wrote that freedom of the press means "the right to be just or unjust, partisan or nonpartisan, true or false, in news columns and editorial columns."[1] Very few people still have confidence in such belligerent libertarianism. There is now substantial doubt whether the truth will emerge from a marketplace filled with falsehood. The contemporary mood among media practitioners and communication scholars is for a more reflective press, one conscious of its significant social obligations. But servicing the public competently is an elusive goal, wherein no aspect of this mission is more complicated than the issue of social justice. The Hutchins Commission mandated the press to articulate "a representative picture of the constituent groups of society." The commission insisted that minorities deserved the most conscientious treatment possible and chided the media of their day for tragic weaknesses in this area.[2]

Often a conflict is perceived between minority interest on the one hand and unfettered freedom of expression on the other. The liberty of the press is established in the First Amendment. Thus this freedom continues to be essential to a free society. Practitioners thereby tend to favor an independent posture on all levels. Whenever one obligates the press—in this case, to various social causes—one restrains its independence in some manner. Obviously, the primary concern is government intervention, but all clamoring for special attention from the press ought to be suspect.

In spite of debate over the precise extent of the media's obligation to social justice, there have been notable achievements. Abolitionist editors of the nineteenth century crusaded for justice even though the personal risks were so high that printing presses were thrown into rivers and printing shops burned down by irate readers. A symbiosis between television and the black movement aided the struggle for civil rights in the 1960s.

This chapter introduces four problems of social justice on a lesser scale but involving typical issues of justice nonetheless. In all cases, a responsive press is seen to play a critical role. All four situations assume that genuine social concerns are at stake and not just high-powered special-interest groups seeking their own ends. Each of the four examples pertains to the disenfranchised: the racially disadvantaged in the first case, the information-poor in the second, women in the third, and Native Americans who had run out of options in the fourth example. In all cases, the reporters felt some measure of obligation. Although press response is sometimes extremely weak, no cause is dismissed out of hand by journalists in these situations.

Social ethicists typically show a strong commitment to justice. We assume this principle here and try to apply it in complicated situations. The heaviest battles in this chapter usually occur over questions in the middle range, issues that media personnel confront along with the larger society. For example, do the media carry a particular mandate from subscribers and audiences, in the same way politicians may sense a special obligation to represent the people who voted for them—or who at least live in their district? And further, does the press have a legitimate advocacy function, or does it best serve democratic life as an intermediary, a conduit of information and varying opinions? In a similar vein, should the press just mirror events or provide a map that leads its audience to a destination? The kind of responsibility for justice that a particular medium is seen to possess often depends on how we answer these intermediate questions about the press's proper role and function.[3]

15 Affirmative Action in Michigan

Jennifer Gratz, a student at a suburban Detroit high school, believed she had what she needed to gain admittance to the University of Michigan. Her transcript boasted a strong GPA earned in honors courses, and it was accompanied by a varied list of extracurricular and volunteer activities. Together her academic and personal credentials formed a strong application. There was only one problem: Jennifer was white.

In its points-based admission system, the University of Michigan awarded an extra twenty points to an applicant from an underrepresented minority group. Without the extra twenty points, Jennifer didn't make the cut. In a system that gave twelve points for a perfect SAT score, the bonus for being a person of color seemed out of line. When she was denied admission, Gratz chose to sue. Her suit was taken up by the Center for Individual Rights, which paired Gratz's suit with one from Barbara Grutter. Grutter, also white, was denied admission to the University of Michigan law school while racial minority applicants whose test scores and GPAs were lower than hers were admitted.

The two suits, *Gratz v. Bollinger* and *Grutter v. Bollinger*, raised the issue of affirmative action in college admissions before the Supreme Court for the first time in twenty-five years. In 1978, the Court had ruled in *Regents of California v. Bakke* that holding open a certain number of slots to be filled with minority applicants was illegal. However, the Court said that universities may use race as a factor in admissions.

While the technical question before the justices was whether either Michigan school used a quota-based system to ensure a certain number of racial minorities in their programs, the larger question centered on the role of affirmative action in university admission policies in the twenty-first century. Is a university best served by intentionally creating a diverse student population or by selecting the best possible applicants regardless of race? What role should affirmative action play when selecting students? Are white students sacrificed for the sake of diversity?

Lee Bollinger, the former president of the University of Michigan, was named as the defendant in the suit. Now serving as president of Columbia University, he spoke in favor of Michigan's system:

> The majority of students who each year arrive on a campus like Michigan's graduated from virtually all-white or all-black high schools. The campus is their first experience living in an integrated environment. This is vital. Diversity is not merely a desirable addition to a well-rounded education. It is as essential as the study of the Middle Ages, or international politics, and of Shakespeare. For our students to better understand the diverse country and world they inhabit, they must be immersed in a campus culture that allows them to study with, argue with, and become friends with students who may be different from them. It broadens the mind, and the intellect—essential goals of education.[4]

Syndicated columnist Armstrong Williams rejects the use of race as a factor in admissions. Williams was offered scholarships to prestigious schools on the basis of his race, but he turned them down, choosing instead to attend historically black South Carolina State:

> My father wouldn't let me take any of the enticements. His reasoning was straightforward: scholarship money should go to the economically deprived. . . . If the goal of affirmative action is to create a more equitable society, it should be need-based. Instead, affirmative action is defined by its tendency to reduce people to fixed categories: at many universities, it seems, admissions officers look less at who you are than what you are. As a result, affirmative action programs rarely help the least among us. Instead, they often benefit the children of middle- and upper-class black Americans who have been conditioned to feel they are owed something.[5]

On 23 June 2003, the Court ruled six to three in favor of Jennifer Gratz. In writing for the majority, Chief Justice Rehnquist wrote that the point-based system used in the University of Michigan's undergraduate admission was unconstitutional and had to be modified: "The university's use of race in its current freshman admission policy is not narrowly tailored to achieve respondents' asserted compelling interest in diversity."[6]

Grutter's suit, however, was not upheld. The Supreme Court ruled five to four that the law school's policy, which used race as a factor but did not assign point values, does not violate the equal protection clause of the Fourteenth Amendment. In writing for the majority, Justice O'Connor said the Constitution "does not prohibit the law school's narrowly tailored use of race in admissions decisions to further a compelling interest in obtaining the educational benefits that flow from a diverse student body."[6]

For Ted Shaw, associate director-counsel for the NAACP Legal Defense and Educational Fund, the ongoing use of affirmative action was approved: "I think today's opinions, taken together, constitute a strong endorsement of the constitutionality of affirmative action with the proviso that institutions have to make sure that they structure these programs the right way."[6] The Court upheld race as a factor in shaping admissions programs, concluding that a broad social value may be gained from diversity in the classroom.

University of Michigan President Mary Sue Coleman hailed the decisions: "This is a wonderful, wonderful day—a victory for all of higher education, because it means at its core that affirmative action may still be used, and the court's given us a road map to get there."[7]

continued

While the immediate result of the Court's action is the revision of one school's admission process, the long-term effects are less certain. Cases like *Gratz* and *Grutter* are bound to come before the Court again. Certainly there will be action on the state level and perhaps through Congress. The clearest result of these recent rulings may be that future plaintiffs and their attorneys now have a better plan for how to fight.

Reporting on discrimination in public life is an extraordinary challenge. Since affirmative action was introduced as a policy in 1965 by President Lyndon Johnson and applied to higher education twenty-five years ago in the *Bakke* case, it has been an unending battleground. The public pathway for affirmative action has been tumultuous, and reporting the newsworthy dimensions of complicated and entangled social issues such as affirmative action is wearisome and demanding. Accurate, comprehensive, fair, and balanced news of race and education has long been difficult and will be a supreme challenge once again as the Court's rulings work their way through university life and policies.   ∎

Although University of Michigan and affirmative action supporters cheered the decisions, others warn that these suits are just the beginning of the challenges that will come. Curt Levey serves as director of legal and public affairs at the Center of Individual Rights, which represented Gratz and Grutter in their suits. Levey notes that the Court's ruling was not intended to stand for all time. He points to the "sunset provisions" called for by the justices and a twenty-five-year time limit on the use of racial preferences to achieve diversity. Writing shortly after the rulings were issued, Levey suggests that colleges and universities "would do well to cut the celebration short and begin planning now for the eventual phaseout of race-based admissions. Public opinion will demand it, voters and legislators may compel it, and continued litigation will necessitate it, long before the court's respite ends."[8]

Levey's predictions were correct. Three years later, in 2006, Michigan voters passed the Michigan Civil Rights Initiative, which amended Michigan's constitution to "ban public institutions from discriminating against or giving preferential treatment to groups or individuals based on their race, gender, color, ethnicity or national origin." Jennifer Gratz served as the executive director of the coalition that initiated the amendment. Barbara Grutter and Ward Connerly also lent their support to the effort. (Connerly was a prominent figure in the passage of California's Proposition 209 in 1996 where public institutions were prohibited from considering race, ethnicity, or gender.)

Other court watchers note that the five-to-four decision in favor of the law school was far from a strong majority, and this lack of uniformity is consistent with previous affirmative-action decisions. Attorney Martin Michaelson, who filed a brief in the Michigan cases on behalf of fifty-four higher-education associations, points out that "Not since 1954, when Chief Justice Earl Warren wove together a unanimous bench in *Brown v. Board of Education,* has the court spoken with one voice in a major ruling that affected race and education. It has found about as many affirmative-action programs that it has reviewed unlawful as lawful, and has done so fractiously, as in *Bakke*, where it issued six opinions."[9]

Popular myths and common misunderstandings about affirmative action complicate public communication and discussion.[10] One widely held myth, for example, is that affirmative action has not succeeded in increasing female and minority representation. The fact is that several studies have documented important gains in racial and gender equality through affirmative-action policies. Another myth is that affirmative action undermines the self-esteem of racial minorities. Statistical evidence does not support this claim. In addition to overcoming errors in fact and judgment, labels and biased language distort the communication process: "quotas," "preferential selection," "social engineering," "victims," "reverse discrimination," and "liberal jurists," for example. All the while, a host of competing values must be accounted for, though they are often at odds with one another—the needs of promising students for a quality education, private versus public institutions, the wide range in high school preparation, financial aid guidelines, which minorities are targeted, and more.

In addition to the duty to report public affairs with clarity and in context, print and broadcast news have editorial responsibilities regarding affirmative action. In opinion pieces, editorials, commentary, and documentaries that deal with the underlying arguments and present the broader picture, Rawls' ethics serve as the most appropriate framework. The legal dimensions need to be clarified and critiqued, but articulating the ethical foundations of affirmative action are of long-term importance as well. In *Gratz v. Bollinger* and *Grutter v. Bollinger*, the Court focused on narrow aspects of policy rather than grappling with the whole. In fact, most affirmative-action cases have been approached legally in a piecemeal fashion. The ethics of John Rawls provides the rationale for affirmative action and guidelines for editorials and commentary.

16 Distributing the Internet

A global information order is coming into its own. Massive multimedia conglomerates are at war for the 3.5 trillion dollars annually at stake—Pearson PLC in England, Bertlesmann in Germany, Microsoft and Disney in the United States, Rupert Murdoch's empire, and Sony of Japan. An interactive industry of giant companies is emerging from television, telecommunications, electronics, recording, financial service, computer, and book-publishing firms. Today's business tycoons do not specialize in steel, but in images, data, software, and ideas.

Clusters of high-tech electronic firms are remapping what they call the "virtual planet." Silicon Valley, California, and Silicon Alley, New York, are home to more than 5000 communication companies. Israel's "Silicon Wadi" is coming on strong as a cybersuperpower. Bangalore, India, is a magnet for multinational chip and computer firms. Singapore is transforming itself into an Internet island in which every office, home, and school will be

continued

linked to an ultrafast multimedia network. South Korea's Seoul is the world's most connected city electronically. Zhongguancum is Beijing's international home for computer outlets, high-tech start-ups, and Internet cafés. Previous geographic alignments organized by political power are being reordered in terms of electronic megasytems.

Convergence is the critical concept—the storage capacity of digital data banks integrated with the unlimited transmission capabilities of fiberoptics and satellites, video imaging, and the switching capabilities of cellular telephones. Thanks to services such as iTunes and TiVo, we no longer need to settle for whatever happens to be on at a particular time. We can select any item from an encyclopedic menu of offerings and have it routed directly to our television or computer screen. Tomorrow's newspaper or yesterday's episode of *The Office*? The latest gag on YouTube? Type in what you want, and it appears just when you need it. Welcome to the information superhighway.[11]

Electronics are rapidly engulfing our family life, schools, professions, and religious institutions. Cell phones, iPods, PCs, video games, the World Wide Web, and virtual reality—the electronic world is increasing our native habitat. This megaindustry is by all odds the most important and lucrative marketplace of the twenty-first century.   ■

As global media empires take shape, several ethical issues become obvious. Privacy: How can users protect themselves from the intrusion of unnecessary and unwarranted messages? Surveillance: Will government agencies misuse confidential data? Commercialism: Will nonprofit uses and information services be central or marginalized? Offensive speech: Will hate speech, pornography, and violence have free rein in cyberspace?

Although these problems are important, the overriding issue in this chapter on social justice is distribution. Will there be universal, affordable access? With the global media almost exclusively in the private sector, there is little incentive to include the information-poor. Business firms do not consider themselves charitable organizations. From the perspective of private ownership, we can best admit from the beginning that some people will be left behind. Universal diffusion driven by profits alone is unlikely. The history of the communications media indicates that they follow existing political and economic patterns; inequalities in society lead to inequalities in technology. Therefore, the important ethical question is whether one can justify allocation of electronic resources to all parties without discrimination.[12] On what basis can one argue that it is morally desirable to ensure comprehensive information for every person regardless of income or geographic location?

Marketplace economies, to be sure, do not accede to this concern. Private enterprise represents a view of social justice based on merit. There are several variants of this approach, but all of them judge on the basis of conduct or achievement and not solely on the inherent value of human beings. Thus, the argument goes, those who have expended the most energy or taken the greatest risk or suffered the most pain deserve the highest reward. Though not all differences in people result from varying amounts of their own effort or accomplishment, in this view, ability to pay is considered a reasonable basis for determining who obtains this service. A prominent canon is whether consumers are at liberty to express preferences, to fulfill their desires, and to receive a fair return on their expenditures. The information structure would be unjust only to the degree that supply and demand or honest dealings are ended.

However, another notion of social justice, "to each according to one's essential needs," does validate a concern for universal, affordable access. The contention here is not that all felt needs or frivolous wants ought to be met, but that basic human requirements must be satisfied equally. The basis for judging is not activity or achievement, but our being human. Whereas there is legitimate argument over which needs qualify, agreement is rather uniform on most fundamental issues such as food, housing, safety, and medical care. People as persons share generic endowments that define them as human. Thus we are entitled—without regard for individual success—to those things in life that permit our existence to continue in a humane fashion. Whenever a society allocates the necessities of life, the distribution ought to be impartial. Free competition among goods and services has been the historically influential rationale for media practice, but in the case of a total national structure performing a vital function, the need-based criterion appears to be the more fitting ethical standard.

In the Tenth Report on the Internet and Computer Technology issued by the United Nations Development Program, the gap between rich and poor nations is seen as intensifying. The report concludes that the rules of globalization should be rewritten to save the sixty countries that are worse off than they were in 1980 when the reports were first written. The report notes that the United States has more computers than the rest of the world combined, with English the language of choice for 80 percent of websites: "26 percent of Americans use the World Wide Web—as opposed to 3 percent of Russians, 4 one-hundredths of 1 percent of the population of South Asia, and 2 tenths of 1 percent for Arab states."[13] And given the explosion in Internet technology, the gap between globally well-connected and unconnected people is likely to grow. Finland has more Internet hosts, for example, than all of Latin America, and such disparities undoubtedly will increase rather than diminish.

The need principle of social justice challenges us to consider as one possibility the Tenth Report's recommendation of a 1 cent tax "on lengthy e-mails to raise $70 billion a year that could be used to connect the world's Internetless."[14] Even in wired societies, the existence of Internet technology does not guarantee that it will reach its potential as a democratic medium. There is a direct correlation between per capita gross national product and Internet distribution. In the United States, for example, 80 percent of those households with annual incomes of $75,000 have computers; only 6 percent of those with incomes of $15,000 or less do. Thus the Rand Corporation has called for $1 billion per year in government subsidies to provide universal access to e-mail through libraries or public access stations.[15]

However, through the principle of justice, we ought to be concerned not just with physical access but also with a deeper divide over social practices. What is most important about Internet technology is not so much the availability of the computing device or the Internet line but rather people's ability to make use of the device as a conduit for meaningful social practices. People who cannot read, who have never learned to use a computer, and who do not know the major languages of software and Internet content will have difficulty even getting online, much less using the Internet productively.[16]

17 Sexism and World Cup Soccer

On 10 July 1999, the American soccer team defeated China in two overtimes for the Women's World Cup. Following a grueling 0–0 tie, the United States beat China 5–4 in one of the most intense experiences in sports—the best of five shootout to decide a championship. As U.S. Coach Tony DiCicco put it, "there are two champions here today, and only one is taking a trophy home."

The sold-out game in Pasadena's Rose Bowl was attended by 90,185 fans, the largest number ever for a women's sporting event. Over 650,000 tickets had been purchased for the tournament of thirty-two soccer matches. ABC estimated that 43 million viewers tuned in, nearly double the previous year's Men's World Cup final between Brazil and France. President Clinton, who was in the stands, called it "in some ways, the biggest sporting event of the last decade."[17]

For *Newsweek*, World Cup fever seemed to signal that twenty-seven years after Title IX legislation mandated equal financing for girls' athletics, women's team sports had truly arrived.[18] From the genteel world of women's tennis, golf, and gymnastics and individual gold medalists such as Jackie Joyner-Kersee at the Seoul Olympics in 1988, the decade of the 1990s saw rapid growth in women's sports, including 100,000 more girls and women playing soccer now than in 1989. *Newsweek* observed that this World Cup team of "charismatic female athletes—young muscular women of surpassing skill—had become a new kind of national hero . . .and [they] taught the rest of us lessons too . . .The World Cup women, minimum wagers by pro-sports standards, reminded the country that sports superstars can be gracious and grateful. On the field, the team showed us leadership and teamwork—and they kicked butt."[19]

China and the United States entered the final game as clearly the two best teams in the tournament. China had outscored opponents 19–2, and the United States had won eighteen games and lost only three. In fact, these teams had developed a monumental rivalry since the United States had won the first women's World Cup in China in 1991. The Americans beat the Chinese 2–1 for the 1996 Olympic Gold Medal and 2–0 for the 1998 Goodwill Games Championship. But China had won two of three matches already in 1999, including the prestigious Algarve Cup.

The longstanding rivalry, remarkable tournament victories along the way for both teams, and their world stage produced a host of heroes on July 10. U.S. goalkeeper Briana Scurry deflected the third kick off her fingertips.

In the one-hundredth minute, Kristine Lilly was positioned perfectly and blocked Fan Yunjie's possible game-winning shot at the goal line. Michelle Akers, the game's oldest player at thirty-three, dominated the midfield on defense but needed intravenous fluids after the game because of heat exhaustion and a slight concussion on a late-game collision. Yan Jin of China showed once again that she is generally considered the most brilliant athlete in the game.

But Brandi Chastain was the hero of the finale. She stepped up with the shoot-out score 4–4 and without hesitating kicked the ball into the net for the win. She exploded, with the crowd and her teammates, and celebrated by throwing her shirt into the air. And that's where the Associated Press wire story focused its first four paragraphs, returning to it in paragraph ten: The ball flew into the corner of the net. The World Cup was theirs—and Brandi Chastain dropped to her knees and stripped.

Well, not completely. After all, there were 90,185 fans at the Rose Bowl and millions elsewhere watching on television. But, after scoring the championship-winning goal against China on a penalty kick, she ripped off her jersey, swinging it over her head and waited to be mobbed by her jubilant U.S. teammates. "Momentary insanity," Chastain said after the Americans beat China 5–4 in the shootout following a 0–0 tie Saturday. "I just lost my mind. I thought, my God, this is the greatest moment of my life on the soccer field."

Chastain, who was cut from the national squad in 1994 and had to work her way back onto it, posed for *Gear Magazine* in June with nothing but a placed soccer ball hiding her naked body. This time, she revealed a black sports bra as she and her teammates leapt on one another in celebration.[20]

Newsweek's opening paragraph also described how the "flamboyant, ponytailed blonde known as Holly Wood . . .whipped off her shirt . . .strip[ping] down to her black sports bra."[21]

The Associated Press reported the same details in its Monday release on the team's rally in Los Angeles and Disneyland. It included a reference to them from cocaptain Julie Foudy when talking to a crowd of fans: "Brandi says 'temporary insanity,' but who believes that?"[22] Tuesday's AP story about the team's New York visit referred to the shirt as well.[23] Wednesday's wire copy included a feature on Nike's attempt "to convert that moment of marketing magic into sales" for its Inner Actives sports bra.[24]

In June 2003, the Federation Internationale de Football Association (FIFA) banned players—men and women—from removing shirts during celebrations after goals. Its objective was "maintaining discipline and order on the field of play." But the ruling didn't intimidate Brandi Chastain:

If I am in the same situation when we play the World Cup as I was in '99, that shirt's coming off. Soccer's always been free flowing, very rhythmic, very creative. Scoring a goal doesn't happen very often. So, in my eyes and in my own opinion, taking off your shirt has nothing to do with discipline. It shows emotion, it shows spontaneity, it shows you could be hot.[25] ∎

Is the Associated Press sexist in its coverage of Brandi Chastain? Can one argue that removing her shirt only duplicated what male athletes have long done to celebrate triumph?

Is she being treated as a sex object, or is the AP only following in its stories what the soccer players themselves have made available? Michelle Akers said the team was "full of cool chicks." Teammate Julie Foudy described Brandi Chastain as "a woman who has the uncanny knack for taking her clothes off" and called the team "hot-blooded babes with a lot of physical energy." Goalie Briana Scurry had promised to run naked through the streets of Athens, Georgia, if the United States won the gold medal at the 1996 Olympics and kept her word. Chastain posed voluntarily for *Gear*'s story, "She's Got Game." Mia Hamm created a gender difference with her advice to Tony DiCicco: "Coach us like men, but treat us like women." Perhaps Team U.S.A. is secure enough about itself to express healthy attitudes toward its athleticism and sexuality.

Contrasting reactions to "the babe factor" are expressed by *Chicago Tribune* sports columnist Skip Bayless and by Bonnie Erbe, host of the PBS program *To The Contrary* and a weekly columnist for Scripps Howard News Service.

Writing on the eve of the final game, Bayless challenged his male readers to view the team as spectacular athletes:

> You, there . . . John Wayne Jr. Mr. Macho. So you're going to check out the "hot-blooded babes" on Saturday, eh? You're tuning in to the Women's World Cup for the first time because everyone from Letterman to your favorite sports-talk host to your buddies down at the Boys Will Be Boys sports bar is buzzing about the "booters with hooters" as co-captain Julie Foudy calls Team U.S.A.
>
> If you're as tough as you look, you'll take my dare. I dare you to view these athletes as, well, simply athletes.[26]

For Bayless, the issue is the game of outdoor soccer, period: the players' speed, teamwork, coaching, dribbling, kicking left foot and right foot, head play, attacking offense, defense-defense-defense. And the same for Milka Duno, Sarah Fisher, and Danica Patrick—the Indy 500's female race car drivers in a pool of thirty three. Their women's bodies should not matter in sports reporting, but racing tactics and talent on the Indianapolis Motor Speedway certainly do.

Bonnie Erbe addresses her column to feminists who may "be offended by the 'babe' factor":

> In trying to explain the phenomenal popularity of Team U.S.A. . . . television news magazine *Dateline NBC* suggested the "babe" factor may, among other reasons, account for some of the team's following.
>
> Now, I don't pretend to speak for feminists, never having embraced that or any other mantel myself (labels make me nervous). But that doesn't stop me from offering them advice nonetheless. If the perfect physiques of team members such as Mia Hamm, Brandi Chastain, and Lorrie Fair are part of the attraction, then let feminists now praise beautiful women. . . .
>
> If beauty and sex appeal are simply two items on a long list of reasons why people may tune in to watch women's sports, then women should be thankful for and not resentful of that.
>
> Why? First of all, to be honest, women have been watching men's sports for years to get a sneak peak at perfect bodies in scant clothing. . . . "to watch the meat fly by". . . . And what's sauce for the gander is sauce for the goose. . . .
>
> What is so offensive to . . . most women about men ogling women on the beach, or putting up old Snap Tools calenders at work (featuring over-done beauties in skimpy bikinis) is that such behavior negates women's other talents. But even if male supporters of male athletics come to women's soccer at the first instance to admire the sex appeal of women players, they cannot help

but be impressed by the prowess of these same women as world class athletes. It hardly matters what brings them to the sport initially if they become, as most inevitably will, followers of women's athletic achievements. . . .

So should feminists put down, upbraid or scorn the babe factor? No, they should applaud support and promote it for all it's worth. Because it may be (among many others) one of the key factors in finding advertising and financial support for a professional women's soccer league.[27]

Rather than choosing sides, one might argue that we should welcome these disagreements in sports reporting when radical shifts are under way in society and the guidelines are not always clear. The ethical challenge is to eliminate sexist language in news reporting as a whole, acting aggressively on the basic guidelines that are already obvious.

Women have been stereotyped regularly by the press. The problem has long, historical roots. During the women's suffrage movement, for example, news accounts often distorted the issues. Editorials regularly denounced women's "petty whims," spoke of "appalling consequences," and even used labels such as "insurrection." Sample twentieth-century writing of any kind (including journalism) and the failures become obvious: overemphasis on clothes and physical appearance, the glorification of domesticity, the portrayal of women as empty-headed or at least nonintellectual.

Evidence abounds that such problems persist. Pay scales are still not equitable across genders. Joann Byrd and Geneva Overholser have been ombudspersons for *The Washington Post*, and some women are high-ranking executives now, but women are still underrepresented in influential positions. Jane O'Reilly assails the "pale male" pundits (in skin color and perspective) who dominate editorials and commentary.[28] In fact, the existence of sexism in the media has been proven so repeatedly, and with so little change over time, that one scholar has concluded we should quit doing studies that prove what we already know about media sexism and start teaching "readers to talk back to their newspapers in ways that make clear their dissatisfaction with how women are represented and portrayed."[29]

Where does sexist language creep into reporting? Where are women missing as sources, and how could they be incorporated? How can we bring more women on staff and into management positions so that their points of view are more likely to be represented?

In order to help promote change, readers and viewers ought to monitor closely the media's gender sophistication. The Global Media Monitoring Project is an example of a volunteer organization working to eliminate sexism in the media. It has done worldwide surveys every five years since 1995, in 2005 covering roughly 57 percent of the world's surface. This latest involved men and women in 102 countries who monitored the day's news on TV, radio, and in newspapers, and 16,000 news items and 70,000 people in the news were coded. The results indicated that women were included in 18 percent of the news stories and men in 82 percent. The idea of the study is to compile data that can be used to deal with station managers and as background for training journalists (www.globalmediamonitoring.org). The Global Media Monitoring project has been principally concerned over these three studies in 1995, 2000, and 2005 that old ideas of authority with diminished voices for women get in the way of new ideas of community and leadership.[30]

Sexual harassment is one entangled issue that demands precise, non-sensational reporting. Educational institutions, government agencies, health organizations, and religious bodies over the last decade all have adopted some form of harassment policies based on gender and sexual orientation. They vary in detail, but all such policies are no-tolerance in character and insist on mandatory action against offenders. Elaborate procedures for implementation are required so that violators are prosecuted, the innocent protected, and retaliation does not result later. Overall the aim is preventative rather than focusing on violations themselves. The news media play a crucial role in ensuring that policies are implemented actively and fairly, but to do so without creating a public trial of spectacle is nearly impossible.

Sexism is embedded in our culture and social order. It will take the persistent, thoughtful attention of editors everywhere to identify and expunge it. We could fairly conclude that the best professionals are not sexist, but instead, they are aggressive reporters or sometimes uncertain in their judgment as social mores shift. However, the broader agenda remains. Even if press behavior is improving rapidly in particular cases, there is an urgent need for institutional and structural reform. Otherwise, a long and entrenched history will not be permanently changed.[31]

18 Ten Weeks at Wounded Knee

One of this century's leading civil libertarians, Zechariah Chafee, Jr., once wrote: "Much of our [national] expansion has been accomplished without attacking our neighbors. . . . There were regrettable phases of our history, such as breaches of faith with the Indians, but these are so far in the past that they have left no running sores to bother us now. . . . We have not acted the bully."[32]

If a distinguished Harvard law professor, a man considered a champion of oppressed minorities, could write so casually about the plight of American Indians, little wonder a tight circle of American Indian Movement (AIM) leaders thought they needed a major event to publicize their concerns. And what better event than an old-fashioned "uprising" complete with teepees, horses, rifles, war paint, and television cameras.

On 27 February 1973, some 200 Indians seized the hamlet of Wounded Knee on the Pine Ridge Sioux Indian Reservation in southwest South Dakota. Tension had been growing steadily for three weeks, ever since a group of Indians clashed with police in Custer, South Dakota, protesting the light charge (second-degree manslaughter) returned against a white man accused of stabbing and killing an Indian there. Thirty-six Indians were arrested in that melee, eight policemen were injured, and a Chamber of Commerce building was burned.

But the problem at Wounded Knee was of a different magnitude. Indians had taken hostages (eleven townspeople who later declared they were not being held against their will and who refused to be released to federal authorities) and were prepared to hold their ground by violence if necessary. They gathered considerable public support, trading on sympathy for Chief Big Foot's band slaughtered there in 1890 by the U.S. Seventh Cavalry—the last open hostility between American Indians and the U.S. government until February 1973.

As the siege began, news crews rushed to cover the developing story. On February 28, Indians demanded that the Senate Foreign Relations Committee hold hearings on treaties made with Indians and that the Senate begin a full investigation of the government's treatment of Indians. George McGovern, a liberal Democrat and South Dakota senator at the time, flew home to negotiate, but to no avail. Meanwhile, FBI agents, federal marshals, and Bureau of Indian Affairs (BIA) police surrounded Wounded Knee, hoping to seal off supplies and force a peaceful surrender.

But the siege turned violent. On March 11, an FBI agent was shot and an Indian injured as gunfire erupted at a roadblock outside town. On the same day, AIM leader Russell Means announced that Wounded Knee had seceded from the United States and that federal officials would be treated as agents of a warring foreign power. A marshal was seriously wounded on March 26, and two Indians were killed in gunfire as the siege wore into April. Finally, on May 6, with supplies and morale nearly expended, the Indians negotiated an armistice and ended the war.

An incredible 93 percent of the population claimed to follow the story through television, but Indian attorney Roman Roubideaux did not think they were seeing the real story:

> The TV correspondents who were on the scene filmed many serious interviews and tried to get at the essence of the story, but that stuff never got on the air. Only the sensational stuff got on the air. The facts never really emerged that this was an uprising against the Bureau of Indian Affairs and its puppet tribal government.[33]

Television critic Neil Hickey summarized the feelings of many:

> In all the contentiousness surrounding the seizure of Wounded Knee last winter, a thread of agreement unites the disputants: namely, the press, especially television, performed its task over a quality spectrum ranging from "barely adequate" to "misguided" to "atrocious." For varying reasons, no party to the fray felt that his views were getting a decent airing.[34]

The lack of compelling evidence foiled prosecutors at the subsequent trial of AIM leaders Russell Means and Dennis Banks. Defense attorneys Mark Lane and William Kunstler argued that the Indians were not guilty because they were merely reclaiming land taken from them by treaty violations. But the real defense was an inept offense. In September 1974, U.S. District Judge Fred Nichol accused the FBI of arrogance and misconduct and the chief U.S. prosecutor of deceiving the court. After an hour's lecture to the government, he dismissed the case.   ∎

The occupation at Wounded Knee was deliberately staged for television. AIM leaders knew that the legends of Chief Big Foot and the recent popularity of Dee Brown's *Bury My Heart at Wounded Knee* would virtually guarantee good press. And it was a newsworthy event. The Indians at Pine Ridge had just witnessed what they perceived to be a breakdown in the judicial system at Custer.

The American Indian Movement had tried other forums for airing their argument that 371 treaties had been violated by the U.S. government, including failed grievance procedures through the Bureau of Indian Affairs.

The moral issue concerns the degree to which the conflicting voices were fairly represented. In fact, the ten-week siege produced so many aggrieved parties that fairness to all became impossible. How accurately did reporters cover the law officials ordered to the scene, for example? After the event, FBI agents and marshals were hissed by hostile crowds near Wounded Knee and ordered to leave lest another outbreak occur. And how could the press treat the Bureau of Indian Affairs fairly? Its policies became the lightning rod of attack, catching all the fury born from 200 years of alleged broken promises. An inept Justice Department, abuses from ranchers and storekeepers, racism from area whites, and inadequate congressional leadership also contributed to the situation but received only a minor part of the blame. How does one evaluate where accusations are appropriate and yet recognize legitimate achievements in a volatile setting? The BIA contended, for example, that it was not responsible for every abuse and that it had sponsored nearly all the vocational training and employment on the reservation.

But the hardest questions concern treatment of the Sioux grievances. According to the ethical principle that human beings should be respected as ends in themselves, the moral ideal entails an account that clearly reflects the viewpoint of these aggrieved. And even minimum fairness requires avoidance of stereotypes. A young Ogalala Sioux bitterly criticized the press for stories that cast the standoff as a "Wild West gunfight between the marshals and Indians." On 30 December 1890, *The New York Times* warped its account of the original Pine Ridge battle with biased phrases about "hostiles" and "reds." The story concluded: "It is doubted if by night either a buck or squaw out of all Big Foot's band is left to tell the tale of this day's treachery. The members of the Seventh Cavalry have once more shown themselves to be heroes of deeds of daring."[35] After eighty-five years, many newspapers and broadcasters had still not eliminated clichés, prejudices, and insensitive language.[36]

Russell Means complicated the press's task with his quotable but stinging discourse. Years later, in fact, Means was working to erect a monument at the site of the 1876 Battle of the Little Big Horn. In the process, he called for razing the statue of the "mass murderer" George Custer. "Can you imagine a monument to Hitler in Israel?" he demanded in a news conference. "This country has monuments to the Hitlers of America in Indian country everywhere you go."[37] Means called for a fitting memorial to a battle that "continues to epitomize the indigenous will to resist oppression, suppression, and repression at the hands of European parasites."[38]

Fairness, at a minimum, requires that news coverage reflect the degree of complexity inherent in the events themselves. Admittedly, when events are refracted through the mirrors of history, separating fact from fiction becomes impossible. Moreover, the Pine Ridge Indians themselves disagreed fundamentally about the problems and the cure. Richard Wilson, president of the tribal council, despised the upstarts of AIM: "They're just bums trying to get their braids and mugs in the press." He feared a declaration of martial law on the reservation and considered Means and Banks to be city-bred leaders acting like a "street gang," who could destroy the tribe in the name of saving it.

"No more red tape. No more promises," said Means in response. "The federal government hasn't changed from Wounded Knee to My Lai and back to Wounded Knee." Raymond Yellow Thunder, after all, had been beaten to death earlier by whites and the charges limited to manslaughter by an all-white jury in Custer. The average annual wage at Pine Ridge was $1800, with alcoholism and suicide at epidemic rates. Why were the AIM occupiers, speaking for thousands of Indians, unable to get a hearing for themselves? Where is the truth in all the highly charged rhetoric?

Some reporters did break through the fog with substantive accounts. NBC's Fred Briggs used charts and photos to describe the trail of broken treaties that reduced the vast Indian territory to a few small tracts. CBS's Richard Threlkeld understood that AIM really sought a revolution in Indian attitudes. ABC's Ron Miller laid vivid hold of life on the Pine Ridge Reservation itself by "getting inside the Indians and looking at what was happening through their eyes." But, on balance, journalists on the scene did not fully comprehend the subtleties or historical nuances of tribal government. Reporters covering Wounded Knee complained that their more precise accounts often were reduced and distorted by heavy editing. After seventy-one days, the siege ended from weariness—not because the story was fully aired or understood. The press could have unveiled a political complaint to be discussed sensibly and thoroughly; instead, it was caught up in the daily drama of quoting accessible sources and finding attractive visuals.

Maybe the principle of fairness can operate only before and after a spectacle of this kind, when the aggrieved knock on doors more gently. If that is true, owners of news businesses in the Wounded Knee region carry an obligation to develop substantial and balanced coverage of the oppression of Native Americans over the long term, even though such coverage may threaten some of their established interests. Often reporters sensitive to injustice receive little support and thus have no choice but to break stories of injustice when they fit into traditional canons of newsworthiness.[39]

This regrettable weakness in Native American coverage did not end with Wounded Knee. A decade later, 100 miles east of the Grand Canyon, the federal government began the largest program of forced relocation since the internment of Japanese Americans during World War II. Thousands of Navajos were taken from a million acres awarded to the neighboring Hopi tribe. The Navajo–Hopi turmoil is the biggest story in Indian affairs for a century and "a still-evolving issue of national significance." But, Jerry Kammer complained, major newspapers have hurried past "the way some tourists hurry across the reservations en route to the Grand Canyon. They have regarded the dispute and its people as little more than material for colorful features."[40] Violence is a likely possibility even for years after the resettlement is completed—given the sacred burial grounds involved, disputes over oil and minerals, Navajo defiance, and so forth. Periodically, banners emblazoned with "WK 73" (Wounded Knee 1973) appear to remind everyone that a battle to the death may be at hand with authorities.

If federal marshals sent to evict Navajos do battle with an unlikely guerrilla force of AIM members, Navajo veterans of Vietnam, and grandmothers in calico skirts, the press will descend like Tom Wolfe's fruit flies, just as they did at Wounded Knee. They would feast on the violence of a tragedy that was spawned by competing tribes, compounded by the federal government, and neglected by the national press.[41]

Mainstream journalism seems unable to grasp Native American culture. In May 1993, journalists from around the world descended on Littlewater, New Mexico, a small Navajo town on a 25,000-square-mile reservation, the largest in the United States. An unknown disease had killed six Navajos initially and then spread to thirty-nine people in eleven states and left twenty-six dead (including Hispanics, Hopi Indians, African-Americans, and Anglos). "A front-page headline in *USA Today* called the illness 'Navajo flu,' the *Arizona Republic* labeled it the 'Navajo epidemic,' and *NBC News* referred to it as the 'Navajo disease.' "[42] That headline stuck, said one man burying his wife, because "people think we live in tepees and our homes are dirty." Navajos chased journalists away from funerals of victims, with the president of the Navajo nation complaining that they "violated many of our customs and taboos. . . . In Navajo tradition, the four days after a burial are especially sacred. That was blasted apart by journalists aggressively pursuing a story. They were disrespectful, disruptive, and upsetting to the whole idea of harmony." The mystery illness was later identified as a noncontagious strain of hantavirus, a deadly disease carried by the deer mouse.[43] Some journalists had used offensive labels like "witchcraft," and photographers had taken pictures of sacred objects. A tribal resolution criticized sensational news coverage for inspiring "discriminatory attitudes and activities against Navajo people."

And the beat goes on. Because of this historic pattern of failure, observers predict that the confrontations now will move to the state and county levels. For example, seventy-two Wisconsin counties have formed an association to resolve the costly and complex jurisdictional disputes between the Oneida Indians and local governments over fishing rights, timber, minerals and water, property taxes, welfare, and education. Jumbled federal policies, many of them as old as the U.S. Constitution, fan the disputes rather than clarify them. Increasingly, local journalists face the same contentious issues of social justice brought to a head on the national level at Wounded Knee. Native American journalists themselves are leading the way. More than 400 belong to a thriving Native American Journalists Association, and their news stories meet all the tests of excellent journalism.[44]

Perhaps other media can redeem press failure here. In 1993, HBO produced an excellent documentary entitled *Paha Sapa: The Struggle for the Black Hills*, which described vividly Native American beliefs and legends, the "Sacred Hogs" of the Black Hills, and the meaning of the tribal name *Lakota* ("people together"). Dennis Banks has had roles in the movies *War Party*, *The Last of the Mohicans*, and *Thunderbolt*. He released a music video in 1995, *Still Strong*, featuring his original work as well as traditional Native American songs. Banks' video autobiography, *The Longest Walk*, was released in 1997.[45] Russell Means has recorded two musical albums, *The Radical* and the *Electric Warrior*, on his own label, The American Indian Music Company. His autobiography, *Where White Men Fear to Tread*, introduces Wounded Knee to young people and children. In 2001, Means founded TREATY, a total-immersion school for Ogalala Sioux children (K–third grade) based on the Sioux language, culture, and modes of learning. In addition, Means uses the Internet to reach audiences not available to him through the traditional news outlets.[46] In trying to press the contractual claims of the Ft. Laramie Treaty of 1868, Russell Means said recently: "I feel a sadness for the white man. He has no roots. No foundations." That challenge must extend to the journalist on assignment: Why am I covering this story? For whose agenda? To what purpose?

NOTES

1. Charles Beard, "*St. Louis Post-Dispatch* Symposium on Freedom of the Press," 1938. Quoted in William L. Rivers, Wilbur Schramm, and Clifford Christians, *Responsibility in Mass Communication*, 3d ed. (New York: Harper and Row, 1980), p. 47.
2. Commission on the Freedom of the Press, *A Free and Responsible Press* (Chicago: University of Chicago Press, 1947), pp. 26–27.
3. For further development of the issues, see Clifford Christians, "Reporting and the Oppressed," in *Responsible Journalism*, Deni T. Elliot, ed. (Beverly Hills, CA: Sage Publications, 1986).
4. Lee C. Bollinger, "Diversity Is Essential," *Newsweek*, 27 January 2003, p. 32.
5. Armstrong Williams, "But Not at This Cost," *Newsweek*, 27 January 2003, p. 33.
6. www.CNN.com/2003/LAW/06/23/scotus.affirmativeaction, 6/23/2003.
7. www.CNN.com/2003/LAW/06/23/scotus.affirmativeaction, 6/23/2003.
8. Curt Levey, "No Comfort for Colleges," *The Chronicle of Higher Education*, 18 July 2003, p. B11.
9. Martin Michaelson, "The Rulings Are More Subtle Than the Headlines," *The Chronicle of Higher Education*, 18 July 2003, p. B12.
10. For a summary of ten such myths, see S. Plous, ed., *Understanding Prejudice and Discrimination* (New York: McGraw Hill, 2003), pp. 206–212.
11. The authoritative and comprehensive book on convergence and ethics is Michael Bugeja's *Living Ethics: Across Media Platforms* (New York: Oxford University Press, 2007).
12. For elaboration of the ethical framework, see Clifford Christians and Leon Hammond, "Social Justice and a Community Information Utility," *Communication* 9 (June 1986): 127–149.
13. Judith Miller, "Globalization Widens Rich-Poor Gap, U.N. Report Says," *The New York Times*, 13 July 1999, p. A8.
14. Conversations reported by Associated Press writer George Esper, "Death and Deceit," *Champaign-Urbana* (Illinois) *News-Gazette*, 14 January 1990, p. A9.
15. Miller, *The New York Times*, 13 July 1999, p. A8.
16. Gary Chapman, "Addressing a New Issue E-Mail for ALL," *The Los Angeles Times*, 26 May 1997, pp. D1, D5; Mark Werschaver, "Reconceptualizing the Digital Divide," *First Monday*, 26 July 2002, pp. 1–17.
17. For DiCicco and Clinton quotations, see Associated Press, 11 July 1999.

18. "Guide Rule! Inside the Amazing World Cup Victory," *Newsweek*, 19 July 1999, p. 50.

19. Ibid., p. 51.

20. Associated Press, "On the Top of the World," *News Gazette*, 11 July 1999, p. D1.

21. "Golden Rule Inside the Amazing World Cup Victory," p. 50.

22. Associated Press, "Pace Hasn't Slowed a Bit for Energized U.S. Women," *The News Gazette*, 12 July 1999, p. C3.

23. Associated Press, "Team Still Taking Bite Out of Big Apple," *News Gazette*, 14 July 1999, p. C5.

24. Associated Press, "Nike Looks to Cash in on Chastain," *News Gazette*, 14 July 1999, p. C5.

25. "That Shirt's Coming Off," SportsIllustrated.com, http://sportsillustrated.cnn.com/soccer.us.news0714.2003, 7/14/2003.

26. Skip Bayless, "Babes? Chicks? How About Great Athletes?" *Chicago Tribune*, 9 July 1999, sec. 4, pp. 1, 5.

27. Bonnie Erbe, "Nothing Wrong with the 'Babe' Factor." 16 July 1999, bonnieerbe@compuserve.com.

28. Jane O'Reilly, "The Pale Males of Pundity," *Media Studies Journal* (Winter/Spring 1993): 125–133.

29. Barbara Luebke, "No More Content Analyses," *Newspaper Research Journal* 13 (Winter/Spring 1992): 1–2.

30. For other monitoring projects, see "Media Report to Women," published by Communication Research Associates since 1972 (www.mediareporttowomen.com). FAIR, another national media watchdog, keeps a continually updated online directory of media stories dealing with sexism (www.fair.org/index.php?page=7&issue_area_id=13).

31. For a comprehensive review of the issues and challenges, see "The Media and Women Without Apology," a special 250-page issue of the *Media Studies Journal* (Winter/Spring 1993).

32. Zechariah Chafee, Jr., "Why I Like America" (commencement address at Colby College, Waterville, Maine, 21 May 1944).

33. Neil Hickey, "Only the Sensational Stuff Got on the Air," *TV Guide*, 8 December 1973, p. 34. For details on which this case and commentary are based, see the other three articles in Hickey's series: "Was the Truth Buried at Wounded Knee?" 1 December, pp. 7–12; "Cameras Over Here!" 15 December, pp. 43–49; "Our Media Blitz Is Here to Stay," 22 December, pp. 21–23.

34. Hickey, *TV Guide*, 8 December 1973, p. 34.

35. Arnold Marquis, "Those 'Brave Boys in Blue' at Wounded Knee," *Columbia Journalism Review* 13 (May/June 1974): 26–27; and Joel D. Weisman, "About That 'Ambush' at Wounded Knee," *Columbia Journalism Review* 14 (September/October 1975): 28–31. For background, see Mario Gonzalez and Elizabeth Cook-Lynn, *The Politics of Hallowed Ground: Wounded Knee and the Struggle for Indian Sovereignty* (Urbana: University of Illinois Press, 1998).

36. For a historical overview of photography, see Joanna C. Scherer, "You Can't Believe Your Eyes: Inaccuracies in Photographs of North American Indians," *Studies in the Anthropology of Visual Communication* 2:2 (Fall 1975): 67–79. For an analysis of Native Americans in the twentieth-century press, see Mary Ann Weston, *Native Americans in the News* (Westport, CT: Greenwood, 1996).

37. Daniel Wiseman, "Indians Will Erect Own Monument Over Defeat of 'Murderer' Custer," *Casper* (Wyoming) *Star-Tribune*, 23 June 1988, p. A1.

38. "Statement of Russell Means, Lakota Nation," *Akwesasne Notes* (Summer 1989): 12.

39. For a description of the ongoing struggle of the press with Indian tribal governments over First Amendment freedoms and reporting positive news from the reservation, see Karen Lincoln Michel, "Repression of the Reservation," *Columbia Journalism Review* (November/December 1998): 48–52.

40. For details on this story and the quotations, see Jerry Kammer, "The Navajos, the Hopis, and the U.S. Press," *Columbia Journalism Review* 24 (July/August 1986): 41–44.

41. Ibid.

42. For details and quotations, see Bob M. Gassaway, "Press Virus Strikes Navajos: Journalists Invade Another Culture, Stumble over Traditions," *Quill* 81:9 (November/December 1993): 24–25.

43. Leslie Linthicum, "Of Mice and Mistrust," *Albuquerque Journal*, 19 December 1993, pp. 1E–2E.

44. For a study of four tribal newspapers between 1995 and 1999, see Patty Leow and Kelly Mella, "Black Ink and the New Red Power: Native American Newspapers and Tribal Sovereignty," *Journalism and Communication Monographs* 7:3 (Autumn 2005): 111–133.

45. See the website maintained for Dennis Banks, www.alphalink.com/~rez/dennis.html.

46. See Russell Means' website, www.russellmeans.com/int.html.

CHAPTER FIVE

Invasion of Privacy

The right of individuals to protect their privacy has long been cherished in Western culture. Samuel Warren and Louis D. Brandeis gave this concept legal formulation in their famous essay "The Right to Privacy" in the December 1890 *Harvard Law Review*. Thirty-eight years later, Brandeis still maintained his concern: "The makers of our Constitution undertook to secure conditions favorable to the pursuit of happiness. . . . They conferred, as against the Government, the right to be let alone—the most comprehensive of rights and the right most valued by civilized man."[1] Since that time, the protection of personal privacy has received increasing legal attention and has grown in legal complexity. Although the word *privacy* does not appear in the Constitution, its defenders base its credence on the first eight amendments and the Fourteenth Amendment, which guarantee due process of law and protection against unreasonable intrusion.

The many laws safeguarding privacy now vary considerably among states and jurisdictions. Yet the general parameters can be defined as proscriptions "against deep intrusions on human dignity by those in possession of economic or governmental power."[2] Privacy cases within this broad framework generally are classified in four separate, though not mutually exclusive, categories: (1) intrusion on seclusion or solitude, (2) public disclosure of embarrassing private affairs, (3) publicity that places individuals in a false light, and (4) appropriation of an individual's name or likeness for commercial advantage.

However, for all of privacy's technical gains in case law and tort law, legal definitions are an inadequate foundation for the news business. Merely following the letter of the law certainly is not sufficient—presuming that the law can even be determined reasonably. There are several reasons why establishing an ethics of privacy that goes beyond the law is important in the gathering and distribution of news.

First, the law that conscientiously seeks to protect individual privacy excludes public officials. Brandeis himself believed strongly in keeping the national business open. Sunlight for him was the great disinfectant. And while he condemned intrusion in personal matters, he insisted on the exposure of all secrets bearing on public concern. In general, the courts have upheld that political personalities cease to be purely private persons, as well as that First Amendment values take precedence over privacy considerations. Court decisions have given the media extraordinary latitude in reporting on public persons. The U.S. Supreme Court in a 1964 opinion (*New York Times v. Sullivan*) concluded that even vilifying falsehoods relating to official conduct are protected unless made with actual malice or reckless disregard of the facts. The Court was profoundly concerned in its judgment not to impair what they considered the press's indispensable service to democratic life. In 1971, the Court applied its 1964 opinion to an individual caught up in a public issue—a Mr. Rosenbloom, who was arrested for distributing obscene books. Subsequent opinions have created some uncertainties, although continually reaffirming broad media protection against defamation suits. Thus, even while adhering to the law, the press has a nearly boundless freedom to treat elected officials unethically.

Second, the press has been given great latitude in defining newsworthiness. People who are catapulted into the public eye by events generally are classified with elected officials under privacy law. In broadly construing the Warren and Brandeis public-interest exemption to privacy, the courts have ruled material as newsworthy because a newspaper or station carries the story. In nearly all important cases, the U.S. courts have accepted the media's definition. But is not the meaning of newsworthiness susceptible to trendy shifts in news values and very dependent on presumed tastes and needs? Clearly, additional determinants are needed to distinguish gossip and voyeurism from information necessary to the democratic decision-making process.

Third, legal efforts beg many questions about the relationship between self and society. Democratic political theory since the sixteenth century has debated that connection and shifted over time from a libertarian emphasis on the individual to a twentieth-century version that is much more collectivistic in tone. Within these broad patterns, several narrower arguments have prevailed. Thomas Jefferson acquiesced to the will of the majority, whereas John Stuart Mill insisted that individuals must be free to pursue their own good in their own way. Two of the greatest minds ever to focus on American democracy, Alexis de Tocqueville and John Dewey, both centered their analysis of this matter on a viable public life. Likewise, Walter Lippmann worried about national prosperity in his *Public Opinion* and *The Public Philosophy*. Together these authors and others have identified an enduring intellectual problem that typically must be reduced and narrowed in order for legal conclusions to be drawn. Professor Thomas Emerson's summary is commonly accepted:

> The concept of a right to privacy attempts to draw a line between the individual and the collective, between self and society. It seeks to assure the individual a zone in which to be an individual, not a member of the community. In that zone he can think his own thoughts, have his own secrets, live his own life, reveal only what he wants to the outside world. The right of privacy, in short, establishes an area excluded from the collective life, not governed by the rules of collective living.[3]

Shortcuts and easy answers arise from boxing off these two dimensions. Glib appeals to "the public's right to know" are a common way to cheapen the richness of the private–public relationship. Therefore, sensitive journalists who personally struggle with these issues in terms of real people put more demands on themselves than on considering what is technically legal. They realize that ethically sound conclusions can emerge only when various privacy situations are faced in all their complexities. The cases that follow illustrate some of those intricacies and suggest ways of dealing with them responsibly. The first case deals with the press's challenge to report effectively on the major post–September 11 attack on privacy, the USA PATRIOT Act. The privacy situations in cases 20 through 22 involve cyberspace, small-town gossip, and a tragic drowning accident. They represent typical dilemmas involving both elected officials and persons who became newsworthy by events beyond their control. The massive amounts of data available through blogs complicates the protection of privacy to an unprecedented degree.

Woven through the commentary are three moral principles that undergird an ethics of privacy for newspeople. The first principle promotes decency and basic fairness as nonnegotiable. Even though the law does not explicitly rule out falsehood, innuendo, recklessness, and exaggeration, human decency and basic fairness obviously do. The second moral principle proposes "redeeming social value" as a criterion for selecting which private information is worthy of disclosure. This guideline eliminates all appeals to prurient interests as devoid of newsworthiness. Third, the dignity of persons ought not be maligned in the name of press privilege. Whatever serves ordinary people best must take priority over some cause or slogan.

At a minimum, this chapter suggests, private information in news accounts must pass the test of these three principles to be ethically justified, although the commentaries introduce the subtleties involved. Clearly, privacy matters cannot be treated sanctimoniously by ethicists. They are among the most painful that humane reporters encounter. Often they surface among those journalists with a heart in a recounting of battles lost.

19 The Controversial PATRIOT Act

Six weeks after 11 September 2001, President George W. Bush signed the USA PATRIOT (Uniting and Strengthening America by Providing Appropriate Tools Required to Intercept and Obstruct Terrorism) Act into law. Written quickly and pushed through Congress in record time, the bill "shifted the Department of Justice's goal from prosecuting terrorists to preventing terrorism."[4] Then–Attorney General John Ashcroft declared that the act provides cautionary measures that preserve freedom by providing the means to stop terrorist activity even before it begins. "It's a fundamental and unprecedented shift," says Viet Dinh of the Georgetown University Law Center, "We are fighting guerrilla warfare on steroids, an attempt [by terrorists] to destabilize and defeat the Western order."[5]

Among its controversial provisions dealing with privacy are the following:

- It grants the FBI access to records maintained by businesses—ranging from medical, financial, library, and purchase records—if law enforcement agents certify that the request is connected to a foreign intelligence investigation or is intended to protect against clandestine intelligence activities or international terrorism.
- It permits law enforcement to conduct unannounced "sneak and peek" searches that the target is notified of only at a later date.
- It activates SEVIS (Student Exchange Visitor Information System), which was first legislated in 1996. The records of international students must be kept up-to-date and made available because such students are considered a potential source of espionage and terrorism.

Supporters insist that the USA PATRIOT Act is an essential tool for investigating terrorists who have targeted this country. For its advocates, the act only amends existing federal laws, that is, the federal criminal code and the Foreign Intelligence Surveillance Act. Rather than introduce new laws, its purpose is said to be threefold: (1) apply existing federal law and law enforcement to terrorism investigations, (2) allow intelligence-gathering and law-enforcement agencies to share information, and (3) enable the use of modern techniques and business practices to gather information. As U.S. Attorney Jan Paul Miller puts it:

> Before September 11, 2001, two FBI agents could be working in the same office, investigating the same person for terrorist activities and they wouldn't be allowed to talk with each other. Before September 11, 2001, a federal law enforcement officer could apply for a wiretap for a drug dealer's telephone, but he couldn't for a terrorist. Our office could be investigating someone who was planning to blow up a building. I could talk to his co-conspirators or to Al-Qaida, if we knew where they were and could get a hold of them. But I could not walk down the hall and talk to the FBI if they were investigating the same person. It was that kind of disconnect that was one of the things that led to 9/11.[6]

From this perspective, the provisions of the PATRIOT Act are measured responses that enable law enforcement to keep up with post–September 11 threats while still preserving our civil rights.

To its critics, the PATRIOT Act is a vague, overbroad law of questionable constitutional validity enacted in a climate of fear. While the information-sharing provisions are valuable, it establishes a secret information-gathering process that does not require a showing of probable cause to obtain confidential records—only that the records are relevant to an investigation. As lawyer Steven Beckett argues, "That's a drastic change in the privacy rights in our country."[7] In addition, critics say the law opens the door to broader uses of information. It expands the definition of domestic terrorism so significantly that it could be used against anti-abortion protesters, environmentalists, AIDS activists, or other movements with a history of robust activism. In fact, according to Section 501 of a proposed revision of the PATRIOT Act, any persons can be taken off the street and brought to a secret military tribunal if their activity has suspicious intent.[8] Using the bill inappropriately to prosecute standard criminal suits "guts the Fourth Amendment."[9]

continued

One year after 9/11, the federal government held 762 immigrants, many for months, without charges or counsel. Not one of them was prosecuted for terrorism. Attorney General John Ashcroft refused to disclose information on how the government used library, business, computer, and other records of individuals. In one example that made the news, Jose Padilla, a U.S. citizen, was arrested after returning from a trip to Pakistan. He was held in a military jail and refused an attorney until a judge ordered the government to allow him counsel.

Major provisions of the act were set to expire in December 2005. The House passed a bill that would have made most of the provisions permanent, but the Senate was wary. Democratic Senator Russ Feingold, who had issued the lone vote against the act in 2001, rallied 40 other Democrats and four Republicans to filibuster its renewal.[10] The legislators wanted to extend debate to address the protection of civil liberties. By March 2006, the House and Senate reached a compromise that made most of the act's provisions permanent while adding some safeguards. A vocal minority voted against the bill, convinced that the legislation was still seriously flawed.[11] The PATRIOT Act still faces challenges in the courts. In September 2007, a federal judge ruled that the revised legislation is unconstitutional because it allows the government to secretly obtain a range of personal records, in violation of the First Amendment and the separation of powers doctrine.[12]   ■

Clearly, the news media should be vitally involved in promoting awareness of these issues. But, rather than playing a substantial role in educating the public about the legislation's pros and cons, the media's record has been mixed.

In a study of the news media's role in the passage of the legislation, researchers at the University of Washington have concluded that the media largely mimicked the Bush administration.[13] They have documented that President Bush and the Attorney General engaged in a pattern of strategic public communications with the goal of pressuring Congress to adopt the proposed legislation. Their overall purpose was to engender confidence among citizens that the administration had an effective strategy for countering terrorism. The researchers' findings indicate that communications from the Bush administration "were echoed by the press, and created an environment in which Congress had little choice but to pass the USA PATRIOT Act with remarkable speed."[14]

Project Censored, an annual Sonoma State University study run by several hundred faculty and students, names "Homeland Security Threatens Civil Liberty" as their number-two censored story of 2002–2003. (Project Censored scrutinizes the media to find the most important, yet little reported, stories of the year.) Although coverage increased in the Fall of 2003 as the Attorney General went on tour, Project Censored illustrates that many of the act's dangers have been largely ignored by the mainstream press—except on its op-ed pages.[15]

However, the press has been responsive to specific agencies and to individual voices. The American Civil Liberties Union (ACLU) and the American Library Association adamantly oppose the loss of civil liberties and are frequently cited. The Center for Public Integrity leaked Justice Department proposals for tightening the PATRIOT Act and continues to update the press on their status. The National Association of Foreign Student Advisors has concluded that the United

States will no longer be the destination of choice for international students, and higher education will lose 15 to 30 percent of its future graduate students to Australia, Canada, and the United Kingdom. Some of these unintended consequences make it into the news. A former *New York Times* reporter has started the Transactional Records Access Clearinghouse, a gigantic database that obtains information through the Freedom of Information Act; the organization sued John Ashcroft to release terrorism data.[16] *The Herald News* of Paterson, New Jersey, became very active in the fight to gain information about the hundreds of Arab immigrants detained in their city. Although "the government's obsessive secrecy made it hard to report this story," the paper was able to expose the plight of detainees in a community with large Palestinian and Muslim populations.[17]

In addition to news about the act's implementation and consequences, and beyond legal analyses of it, the press ought to be reporting on this legislation in ethical terms. Understanding the moral dimensions of privacy provides the public with a foundation for coming to grips with the law and politics of the act. Privacy is a moral good because privacy is a precondition for developing a unique sense of self. Violating it therefore violates human dignity. Privacy is a moral good in a political sense also, in that respecting privacy distinguishes democratic from totalitarian societies. As persons, we need privacy, both for our own dignity and for our social relationships with others. Healthy human existence is impossible without it. Educating the public on the ethics of privacy accomplishes the long-term goal of taking the PATRIOT Act out of political disputes and legal wrangling and focusing on the central substantive issues instead.

---

20 Bloggers' Code of Ethics?

The weblog has arrived. Those communicating via this computer-mediated technology call themselves "bloggers," and the greater virtual space in which millions of blogs exist is called the "blogosphere."[18] The mainstream media have been integrating blogs into their channel mix, and now this medium is a recognized source of news, political commentary, religion, entertainment, and advertising.

Is a code of blogging ethics necessary or even possible? Martin Kuhn believes that there should be and supports the two attempts to date to create such a code. Rebecca Flood proposed one in 2002 in *The Weblog Handbook*, and Jonathon Dube, founder of Cyberjournalist.net, another in 2003 (www.cyberjournalist.net/news/000215.php). Both are explicitly tied to online journalism, and Kuhn argues for a broader code that is helpful to political blogs but is also credible to bloggers more generally. He surveyed the field of computer-mediated communication (blogethics 2004.blogspot.com) and created a system of moral imperatives.[19]

Proposed Code of Blogging Ethics
Promote interactivity
- Post to your blog on a regular basis.
- Visit and post on other blogs.
- Respect blog etiquette.
- Attempt to be entertaining, interesting, and/or relevant.

continued

Promote
- Do not restrict access to your blog.
- Do not self-censor by removing posts or comments once they are published.
- Allow and encourage comments on your blog.

Strive for factual truth
- Never intentionally deceive others.
- Be accountable for what you post.

Be as transparent as possible
- Reveal your identity as much as possible.
- Reveal your personal affiliations and conflicts of interest.
- Cite and link to all sources referenced in each post.

Promote the "human" element in blogging
- Minimize harm to others when posting information.
- Promote community by linking to other blogs and keeping a blogroll.
- Build relationships by responding to e-mails and comments regularly.

When the ethical principles of blogging are debated, some stories from blogging and politics are typically used as examples pro and con.

Matthew Drudge is a talk radio host and Internet journalist. His *Drudge Report* on the Web is financed by advertising. The *Drudge Report* was the first to break the news in 1998 of the Clinton–Lewinsky scandal. By 2002, his website had reached the one-billion-page view mark.

On U.S. election day (2 November 2004), several blogs ran exit poll numbers throughout the day that erroneously predicted an easy victory for John Kerry. "Many of the sites posting exit poll information stressed the provisional nature of incomplete polls. For example, the poll numbers on Wonkette.com came with the disclaimer: 'All with grains of salt. Huge tablespoons of salt.' "[20] But most simply reported the data, trusting website users to interpret them accurately. "Many sites displaying poll numbers experienced surges in visitors: Slate.com traffic increased from 153,000 visitors on November 1 to 412,000 on election day. Wonkette.com increased to 200,000 from 6000, and the *Drudge Report* drew nearly 700,000 visitors according to Nielsen/NetRatings."[21] During the 2004 campaign, stories often moved from blogs to the mainstream media. As Alex Jones of Harvard's Joan Shorenstein Center on the Press put it, "Things start on the fringes of the blogosphere, become the buzz, and then move to cable."[22] Blogging proved to be valuable on the whole, but running the early exit polls distinguished this medium sharply from the traditional news outlets, where verification of data is considered essential to their credibility. ■

Using this background and other cases of blogging and politics, what ethical principles ought to be included in a weblog code of ethics? Assume for the sake of discussion that Kuhn is right and codes are both credible and possible. Is he correct that the two primary principles are truth and human dignity? Truthtelling means for him "factual truth." Never intentionally deceive. Cite all relevant links to your sources. Do not erase posts, and encourage comments and reaction that help to keep your information valid. Promoting human dignity is especially important for him in a technology that tends to be anonymous and lacking in accountability. Adapting human dignity to blogging, he recommends two major principles ("Be as transparent as possible," and "Promote the human element"), each with three guidelines for implementation.[23]

Jane Singer also makes truth a primary principle in blogging ethics.[24] She observes that the codes of journalism ethics around the world include truth as a central norm. Therefore, for bloggers who concentrate on the same areas as journalists (i.e., politics, policy, and civic information), a similar standard is reasonable. She notes that people who use blogs see them as quite credible, but think of truth differently than those in mainstream news. Blogs are considered a source of open information without spin and censorship. Blogs are understood to be independent and designed for people who prefer to trust their own judgment rather than accept the narrow agenda and constraints of the usual sources.

> Bloggers do not see truth as resting on the decisions of one autonomous individual or groups of individuals within a news organization or anywhere else. Instead, bloggers see truth as emerging from shared, collective knowledge, from an electronically enabled marketplace of ideas. . . . The bloggers' truth is created collectively rather than hierarchically. Truth, in this view, is the result of discourse rather than a prerequisite to it.[25]

Kuhn admits that bloggers generally resist rules established by others. Jeff Jarvis, former columnist and editor and now blogger, is typical:

> What I have a problem with is the idea that one person presumes to come up with an ethical code for an entire culture. This is complex and can't be handled in a single code. It's as complex as human character.[26]

While bloggers are not professionals connected through associations and business networks, Kuhn believes that the code he proposes can be adopted personally and made transparent in one's weblog practices. Also, A-list bloggers are key resources for both citizens and journalists, and if they actively use and promote codes, it will enhance influence and credibility.

21 A Prostitute on Page 12

Cindy Herbig was a model teenager. A high school student and the only daughter of a prominent family in Missoula, Montana, she had won a scholarship to Radcliffe. Then, on 17 January 1979, she was murdered in downtown Washington, D.C.[27]

The *Missoulian*, a daily newspaper with a circulation of 32,000, carried a page-one story the following day—a tragedy for the community and grief to her family. The sordid details of Cindy's life in Washington were not part of that first local obituary. Indeed, Managing Editor Ron Deckert knew little until his paper was contacted by *The Washington Post*, which

continued

was developing the story to its dramatic hilt: promising, talented teenager turned prostitute stabbed on the streets, presumably in the course of plying her trade.

Cindy's transition from gifted musician to streetwalker was first manifest in an uneasy adjustment to the pressures of Ivy League competition and urban Northeastern impersonality. By Thanksgiving 1976, she was out of college and back in Missoula, but soon discontent and unable to find interesting work. Six months later, she met a recruiter in a Missoula bar, traveled with him to Washington, and entered the seedy world of Fifteenth and K Streets NW. The pimp was known to police, though he was never arrested. In December 1977, Cindy was convicted of solicitation for prostitution.

All this became clear when a *Post* reporter called the *Missoulian* on Monday, January 22, the day of Cindy's funeral, to get information from the published obituary. In return for the help, the *Post* writer agreed to dictate his story over the phone on Tuesday night.

Cindy's parents, Hal and Lois Herbig, first caught wind of the *Post*'s intentions late Monday when they also were called by a Washington reporter. They were appalled by this encroachment on their privacy and the senselessness of publicizing their daughter's problems. Family friend and Missoula attorney Jack Mudd agreed to help the Herbigs squelch the story. On Tuesday morning, Mudd called the *Post* to request a kill. The family had suffered enough, Mudd argued. Further publicity would endanger the parents' health. At least the story should be softened, Mudd contended. The *Post* declined.

Meanwhile, Mudd learned that the *Missoulian* planned to use the story in Wednesday morning's edition. Mudd appealed to Deckert, even making vague references to a resulting suicide if the story were printed locally. Deckert told Mudd that a decision to publish would have to wait until the *Post* called to dictate its story later that evening. Deckert hoped the *Post* would not go for the jugular on this one. However, he was disappointed when the story came in at about 9:00 P.M. The *Post*'s lead read: "In the 21 years of Cynthia Herbig's life, she received honors and accolades at a Montana high school, mastered the cello, won a scholarship to Radcliffe College, and finally, came to Washington to work as a $50-a-trick prostitute."

Other parts of the story also bothered Deckert. For example, the fifth paragraph read: "Herbig used to talk freely about her work, telling an acquaintance at a party here recently, 'I'm a prostitute.'" After nineteen paragraphs describing Cindy's musical gifts and general modesty, the story flipped abruptly into details of her bizarre other life. The *Post* had actually interviewed prostitutes near Cindy's corner and summarized their comments in the twentieth paragraph:

> Several women . . . described her as a bright young woman whose dress was "conservative" and whose manner with customers was "very sweet." "She charged the going rate of $50," they said. A police officer who knew Herbig said he once remarked to her that "she didn't seem like the type to be working out on the street. . . . She responded with a giggle," he said.

Finally, Deckert came to the last paragraph—the chilling quotation from Cindy herself, as recalled by an unidentified male acquaintance: "'You see, you didn't believe that I worked the street, and now you know that I'm a pro,' said Herbig."

Deckert finished reading the copy and knew that his paper would have to print the story. It had news value, after all, since much of Cindy's death was still a mystery in Missoula. Deckert also believed that her story would serve as a warning to other Missoula teenagers. The pimp who had recruited her in a bar was still doing business, along with thousands like him. Perhaps Cindy's story would prevent a similar tragedy. Finally, Deckert knew that the story certainly would be distributed nationally and around the region through *The Washington Post/Los Angeles Times* News Service; if he printed nothing, his community would question how often he suppressed other information and on what basis.

In eleven years of journalism, Deckert had never faced a quandary this intense. Local citizens were sure to protest, and in a town of 30,000, it might be hard to find many friends. He decided to run an edited version of the *Post* story on page twelve, with other local news. The *Post* headline ("A Life of Promise that Took a Strange, and Fatal, Turn") would be dropped in favor of something more sensitive: "Cindy Herbig 'Shouldn't Be Dead,' Friend Says." Deckert also killed the *Post*'s fifth paragraph, added four original paragraphs from a telephone interview with a Washington detective, deleted the report of Cindy's giggle, and dropped the *Post*'s last paragraph, including the boast, "I'm a pro." Finally, Deckert put the best light on a minor detail near the end of the story. The *Post* had noted that Cindy kept "a book of regular customers, men she thought she could trust." Deckert's version had Washington police indicating that Cindy's "book of regular customers" was "a way for her to avoid the dangers of working the street when she could."

Deckert called Mudd at 11 P.M. Tuesday to say that the story would run. Mudd voiced a final plea to hold the story until he could prepare the family.

The Herbigs and much of Missoula were shocked at the intrusion. Businesses pulled their advertisements, and the *Missoulian*'s law firm dropped the paper as a client. An advertiser boycott was threatened, though it did not materialize. More than 150 letters appeared in the paper in two weeks, most of them bristling with outrage. "The *Missoulian* has shown the public once more what a tasteless rag it can be and is," wrote one reader. "Whether the story is fact or fiction, it should not have been printed in her hometown newspaper for friends and relatives to read. . . . The *Missoulian*, in my opinion, isn't fit for use in 'the little boys' room.' " At least 200 readers canceled their subscriptions.

Yet Deckert's final embarrassment would come from his own staff. Editorial page editor Sam Reynolds, two days after the story, wrote his own letter, headed "A personal note," which began: "It was with shame that I read the story about Cindy Herbig—shame for the newspaper profession, shame for once to be a part of it, shame above all for inflicting additional hurt where hurt already had visited more than enough." Reynolds reviewed for readers the agony of the *Missoulian* decision, then blasted the *Post* story as "blatant sensationalism—the worst of journalism—and my sensation is disgust." Reynolds also was not happy (though he did not say so in print) that Deckert had edited his signed column to soften the mortar shells falling on his own position.

In the aftermath, businesses that had pulled advertising returned to the paper, Hal and Lois Herbig were given the privilege of a last printed letter on the subject, and the *Missoulian*'s publisher admitted that the paper could have handled the story better if it had honored Mudd's request to postpone publication for a day. But Deckert insisted in a later interview that if he had that day to live over again, his decision probably would be the same. Under deadline pressure, journalists do the best they can to get the news out, even news that hurts.   ■

The clash between the outrage of the Herbigs' supporters and Ron Deckert's news judgment arises from the disagreement about whether news value for the community is more important than the privacy of those personally involved. Deckert's utilitarian framework, in effect, argued that the benefit for the many outweighed the bite to the few. But, if one applied the agape principle, what would be considered morally appropriate behavior? Agape is particularly suitable because it has a strong view of personhood. And in order to understand the need for a private inner self in its deepest sense, it requires a sophisticated understanding of the human psyche.

Certainly the agapic mind would eliminate the "fallen angel" story as a totally unwarranted intrusion. Why should victims of circumstance endure punishment through a sensational account? The pimp-in-Missoula angle received only eight words in Deckert's edited version of *The Washington Post* release. Most of the gory details about the stab wounds were included: the number, size, and location on the body. The small-town, rural-virgin-off-to-Ivy-League-and-big-city slant framed the account. All of that was an indecent, sensational, obdurate invasion of privacy. Although Deckert did nothing illegal, his willingness to follow the timing and reporting framework of *The Washington Post* was irresponsible.

However, the opposite extreme—reporting nothing—would also be irresponsible. Agape would suggest that the *Missoulian* had a social responsibility to advance citizen understanding, to investigate pimps and police in Missoula, and to get that local story and take whatever additional time might be necessary to do so. There were public dimensions to the case; it was not solely a matter of innocent victims of tragedy. A compassionate story would have inspired readers to confront the community's problem with unwelcome pimps in local bars and would have given the police a public forum in which to fulfill their role effectively. In the process of developing the larger context, Cindy could have conceivably been mentioned by name, if doing so had been materially relevant to the bar-pimp focus and if it could possibly have been judged as a healing story by the Herbigs. But that substantive flavor contrasts sharply with the streetwalking-prostitute tone that actually was published.

The argument from the perspective of agape can be summarized in this fashion: Protecting privacy is a moral good. Being able to control information about ourselves is essential to our personhood. However, while being a precondition for maintaining a unique self-consciousness, privacy cannot be an absolute because we are cultural beings with responsibilities in the social and political arenas. We are individual beings; therefore, we need privacy. We are social beings; therefore, we need public information about each other. Since we are personal, eliminating privacy would eliminate human existence as we know it; since we are social, elevating privacy to absolute status would likewise render human existence impossible.[28]

22 Dead Body Photo

John Harte was the only photographer working on Sunday, July 28, at the Bakersfield *Californian*. After some routine assignments, he heard on the police scanner about a drowning at a lake twenty-five miles northeast of Bakersfield. When he arrived on the scene, divers were still searching for the body of five-year-old Edward Romero, who had drowned while swimming with his brothers.

The divers finally brought up the dead boy, and the sheriff kept onlookers at bay while the family and officials gathered around the open body bag. The television crew did not film that moment, but Harte ducked under the sheriff's arms and shot eight quick frames with his motor-driven camera.[29]

The *Californian* had a policy of not running pictures of dead bodies. So Managing Editor Robert Bentley was called into the office on Sunday evening for a decision. Concluding that the picture would remind readers to be careful when kids are swimming, Bentley gave his approval. On Monday, Harte transmitted the picture over the Associated Press wire "after a 20-minute argument with an editor who was furious we ran the picture . . . and accused [Harte] of seeking glory and an AP award."[30]

Readers bombarded the 80,000 circulation daily with 400 phone calls, 500 letters, and 80 cancellations. The *Californian* even received a bomb threat, forcing evacuation of the building for ninety minutes.

Distraught by the intensity of the reaction, Bentley sent around a newsroom memo admitting that "a serious error of editorial judgment was made. . . . We make mistakes—and this clearly was a big one." He concluded that their most important lesson was "the stark validation of what readers—and former readers—are saying not just locally but across the country: that the news media are seriously out of touch with their audiences."[31]

For photographer John Harte, Bentley's contrition was "disappointing to me and many of my coworkers." And editorial page editor Ed Clendaniel of the *Walla Walla* (Washington) *Union Bulletin* was not apologetic either about running it in his paper, even though it was out of context. "First, the foremost duty of any paper is to report the news," he argued. "One of the hard facts of life is that the world is filled with tragic moments as well as happy moments. . . . Second, we believe the photograph does more to promote water safety than 10,000 words could ever hope to accomplish."

Later Bentley entered Harte's photo in the Pulitzer Prize competition. "I really don't see any contradiction," he explained. "I think the photograph should never have been published. . . . But the Pulitzer Prize is given for journalistic and technical excellence. It is not given for reader approval." ■

Michael J. Ogden, executive director of the *Providence Journal-Bulletin*, condemns photographs that capitalize on human grief:

> I can understand the printing of an auto accident picture as an object lesson. What I can't understand is the printing of sobbing wives, mothers, children. . . . What is the value of showing a mother who has just lost her child in a fire? Is this supposed to have a restraining effect on arsonists? I am sure that those who don't hesitate to print such pictures will use the pious pretense of quoting Charles A. Dana's famous dictum that "whatever the Divine Providence permitted to occur I was not too proud to print." Which is as peachy a shibboleth to permit pandering as I can imagine.[32]

But Ogden is a rare editor. Every day in newspapers and on television, photographs and film footage emphasize grief and tragedy. Though Harte's photo did not win the Pulitzer, in fact, professional awards are regularly given to grisly pictures regardless of whether they pander to morbid tastes.

Defending photos of this type usually centers on newsworthiness. The broken-hearted father whose child was just run over, a shocked eight-year-old boy watching his teenage brother gunned down by police, the would-be suicide on a bridge—all pitiful scenes that communicate something of human tragedy and are therefore to be considered news. Photojournalists sum up a news event in a manner the mind can hold, capturing that portrayal "rich in meaning because it is a trigger image of all the emotions aroused by the subject."[33] Harte in this case acted as an undaunted professional, fulfilling his role as reporter on everyday affairs—including the unpleasantries. From the photographer's perspective, to capture the newsworthy moment is an important self-discipline. Photographers are trained not to panic but to bring forth the truth as events dictate. They are schooled to be visual historians and not freelance medics or family counselors.

On what grounds, however, can the photographer's behavior be condoned in the Bakersfield drowning? The principals at the scene tried to prevent him from intruding, though, it should be granted, the authorities' judgment is not always correct. The warning-bell thesis was generally used by the picture's proponents, asserting that the photo could make other parents more safety conscious. However, this utilitarian appeal to possible consequences has no factual basis.[34] Perhaps in the name of reporting news, the photojournalist in this case was actually caught in those opportunistic professional values that build circulation by playing on the human penchant for morbidity.

No overarching purpose emerges that can ameliorate the direct invasion of privacy and insensitivity for these innocent victims of tragedy. In all jurisdictions, the reporting of events of public concern involves no legal issue of privacy invasion. But it is here that the photographer should consider the moral guideline that suffering individuals are entitled to dignity and respect, despite the fact that events may have made them part of the news.

Photojournalism is an extremely significant window on our humanity and inhumanity. In pursuing its mission, the ethical conflict typically revolves around the need for honest visual information and for respecting a person's privacy. Bob Greene of *The Chicago Tribune* is exaggerating only slightly in calling the Harte picture "pornography." "Because of journalistic factors they could not control," he wrote, "at the most terrible moment of their lives," the Romeros were exposed to the entire country.[35] The older brother's hysteria for not watching his little brother closely enough is presented without compassion before an audience who had no right to become a participant in this traumatizing event for a suffering family. And even those who find the photo acceptable are upset by the context: The *Californian* printing the photo right next to a headline about teen killings by a satanic cult.[36]

Figure 5.1

Source: The Bakersfield Californian, *29 July 1985, p. 1. Photo by John Harte. Reprinted by permission.*

NOTES

1. *Olmstead v. United States*, 277 U.S. 438, 478 (1928). Brandeis dissenting.
2. *Briscoe v. Reader's Digest Association*, 4 Cal. 3d 529, 93 Cal. Reptr. 866, 869 (1971).
3. Thomas I. Emerson, *The System of Free Expression* (New York: Vintage Books, 1970), p. 545.
4. Tony Carnes, "Curbing Big Brother: Christians Urge Ashcroft to Respect Freedom in Surveillance Law," *Christianity Today,* September 2003, p. 27.

5. Ibid.

6. Jodi Heckel, "Patriot Act Debated at UI College of Law," *News Gazette*, 16 September 2003, p. B1.

7. Ibid., p. B2.

8. Eric Lichtblau, "In a Reversal, Ashcroft Lifts Secrecy of Data," *The New York Times*, 17 September 2003, www.nytimes.com.2003/05/17/national/11pape.html.

9. Ryan Singel, "A Chilly Response to Patriot II," *Wired*, 12 February 2003, www.wired.com/news/politics/0,1283,57636,00.html.

10. Sheryl Gay Stolberg, "Once-Lone Foe of Patriot Act Has Company," *The New York Times*, 19 December 2005.

11. Sheryl Gay Stolberg, "Senate Passes Legislation to Renew Patriot Act," *The New York Times*, 3 March 2006.

12. Richard B. Schmitt, "Patriot Act Has Setback in Court," *The Los Angeles Times*, 7 September 2007.

13. Erica S. Graham et al., "Follow the Leader: The Bush Administration, News Media, and Passage of the U.S.A. Patriot Act," paper presented at the Association for Education in Journalism and Mass Communication conference, Kansas City, Missouri, July 2003. The research included a content analysis of fifteen leading newspapers from around the country and the nightly evening newscasts of ABC, NBC, and CBS for a total of 230 texts (pp. 12–13).

14. Ibid., p. 2.

15. "#2 Homeland Security Threatens Civil Liberty." Article available at www.projectcensored.org/publications/2004/2.html.

16. Michael Scherer, "Keeping TRAC: A Tool for Mining Federal Data," *Columbia Journalism Review* (March/April 2003): 10.

17. Hilary Burke, "A Question of Security: Blanket Security is Not the Answer," *Columbia Journalism Review* (November/December 2002): 80.

18. For details on this case and theoretical background, see Martin Kuhn, "Interactivity and Prioritizing the Human: A Code of Blogging Ethics," *Journal of Mass Media Ethics* 22:1 (2007): 18–36. Also see David D. Perlmutter and Mary Schoen, " 'If I Break a Rule, What Do I Do, Fire Myself?' Ethics Codes of Independent Blogs," *Journal of Mass Media Ethics* 22:1 (2007): 37–48.

19. Kuhn, ibid., pp. 27–30.

20. Matt Carlson, "Blogs and Journalistic Authority," *Journalism Studies* 8:2 (April 2007): 264–279.

21. Ibid., p. 269.

22. David Usborne, "Bloggers Rewrite Political Opinion," *Seattle Post-Intelligencer*, November 2, 2004, p. B9.

23. Kuhn, "Interactivity and Prioritizing the Human," pp. 33–34.

24. Jane B. Singer, "Contested Autonomy," *Journalism Studies* 8:1 (February 2007): 79–95.

25. Ibid., p. 85.

26. Quoted in Kuhn, "Interactivity and Prioritizing the Human," p. 25.

27. Details in Jack Hart and Janis Johnson, "Fire Storm in Missoula," *Quill* 67 (May 1979): 19–24.

28. For further background on the ethics of privacy, see Louis Hodges, "The Journalist and Privacy," *Social Responsibility: Journalism, Law, and Medicine*, Vol. 9 (Lexington, VA: Washington and Lee Monograph, 1983), pp. 5–19.

29. "Graphic Excess," *Washington Journalism Review* 8:1 (January 1986): 10–11. In 1994, a court case alleging that John Harte interfered with a rescue operation of a drowned boy

in a local canal (*California v. John Harte*) was dismissed by a judge [see News Photographer (January 1995): 16].

30. For the quotations and details in this case, unless otherwise noted, see "Grief Photo Reaction Stuns Paper," *News Photographer* (March 1986): 16–22.

31. Ron F. Smith, *Groping for Ethics in Journalism*, 4th ed. (Ames: Iowa State University Press, 1999), pp. 211–213.

32. John Hohenberg, *The News Media: A Journalist Looks at His Profession* (New York: Holt, Rinehart and Winston, 1968), p. 212.

33. Harold Evans, *Pictures on a Page* (Belmont, CA: Wadsworth, 1978), p. 5.

34. Obviously beneficent results sometimes follow. As in Stanley Foreman's *Boston Herald-American* photos of a baby and woman falling from a broken fire escape, better safety standards and tighter inspection can be initiated after tragedies.

35. Bob Greene, "News Business and Right to Privacy Can Be at Odds," 1985–1986 Report of the SPJ-SDX Ethics Committee, p. 15.

36. This case study also appears in Paul Martin Lester's *Photojournalism: An Ethical Approach*, Chap. 14. He takes, primarily, the approach that Harte's photo fell under a categorical imperative to report what happened in as powerful a manner as possible.

Persuasion in Advertising

Sunday, February 3, 2008. It is Super Bowl XLII Sunday. 97.5 million people watched the average minute of the game, which brings it "precariously close" to matching the most widely watched network television program of all time: the final episode of *M*A*S*H*, watched by 106 million twenty-five years earlier.[1] We're purportedly the "post-television age."[2]

At a moment in time when "the death of the thirty-second spot" is almost a forgone conclusion, fifty-two unique brands made the decision that paying $2.7–3 million for a thirty-second spot was a sound strategic decision.[3] According to the executive vice president and director of strategic planning at McCann Erickson, the Super Bowl is "less about the relevance of a message but more about the entertainment quotient. [Marketers] aren't selling a product; they are creating brand buzz."[4] Brands purchased eighty-four ads for a total of thirty-six minutes of advertising time.

Live polling results told us the most popular ad was the Budweiser Horse/Dalmatian, and the most buzzed about ad was Justin Timberlake for Pepsi. The most played-back commercial was "Walt Disney—Chronicles of Narnia Prince Caspian," and the most viewed commercial was "Victoria's Secret—Woman Holding Football."[5] And, if you just happened to miss the broadcast, don't worry. The commercials are available online, even on your cell phone.

Granted, the Super Bowl is a football *and* an advertising extravaganza. But let's think about what we know about advertising by looking closely at this event. First, we recognize that advertising is an economic power in the United States, and globally. Total advertising expenditures in the United States were $150 billion in 2006.[6] These expenditures alone stand as testimonial to its value as a strategic marketing tool.

Historian Daniel Pope noted in his book, *Modern American Advertising*:

> For advertising to play a large part in market strategy, consumers had to be willing to accept this kind of self-interested persuasion as a tolerable substitute or complement to more objective product information.[7]

That is, in order for advertising to *work* as a business tool, it had to *work* as a vehicle of social communication. It had to "fit" into the culture. One look at the Super Bowl—its polling of commercial popularity, post-game buzz about advertising, podcasts, watercooler conversation—and we see advertising as a part of our culture, indeed, as a part of our everyday lives.

Amid trade press conversations about return on investment, metrics, tracking studies, and so on, it is easy to lose track of advertising's role as anything other than a business tool. Some contemporary scholars, while not suggesting that advertising fails to provide information or has no influence on consumer choices, invite us to examine what they view to be advertising's more critical role, that of social communication. Rick Pollay speaks of what he calls the unintended social consequences of advertising, the "social byproducts of exhortations to 'buy products.'"[8] Canadian scholars Leiss, Kline, Jhally, and Botterill suggest:

> The least important aspect of advertising's significance for modern society is its role in influencing specific consumer choices—whether wise or unwise—about purchasing products. . . . advertising's transmittal of details about product characteristics is a trivial sidelight.[9]

It is from this perspective of advertising as a vehicle of social communication that most critical questioning occurs.

Building on these scholars' observations, we can glimpse fertile ground for ethical debate. Historically, the dialogue underlying these perspectives has been stated overly simplistically in terms of the mirror/shaper debate. Advertisers and their advocates view advertising as a mirror, passively reflecting society. By contrast, critics view advertising as a shaper, a powerful, *selective* reinforcer of social values.

As we approach any ethical decision making situation, it is valuable to pause and reflect upon the ideological web in which the institution of advertising, its processes, practices, practitioners, creations, and audiences are grounded. Chief among these are:

- **We live in a capitalist economic system** in which there is no imposed central plan. Instead, individuals and firms decide what to do based on their own best interests. Thus, when we say, "that corporation is only in it for the money," we do well to recognize the principles of our economic system.

- **We live in a consumer culture**, a culture preoccupied with things and with the act of acquiring those things. Consumption is both a concrete institution (we have an infinite number of tools to make it easier for us to buy and reward us for buying) and a guiding myth.[10] In an article entitled, "Why the U.S. Will Always Be Rich," columnist David Brooks described consumer culture this way:

> The most obvious feature of the land of abundance is that people work feverishly hard and cram their lives insane fully. That's because there are candies all

around, looking up and pleading to you "taste me, taste me, taste me." People in this realm live in a perpetual aspirational state.[11]

- **We live in a media culture.** It is becoming increasingly difficult and perhaps impossible to separate media and culture in any meaningful way. A blogger recently gave a succinct description of media culture when he wrote:

  > Mass media has done such a good job at embedding their copyright into culture that it has become culture itself. The watercooler effect is what happens when media becomes the bits of communication—it's what lets us share our values and interests, determine common ground, etc. Conversations swirl around TV characters, brands, and movie quotes. I remember two kids in college deciding to only express themselves through Monty Python quotes in conversation. They felt that every question or comment necessary was already present in the movie.[12]

  In this context, the question of advertising as mirror or shaper is rendered moot; advertising is at once *defined* by and *defining* culture.

- **Our media culture is image-based.** Individuals actively, perhaps sometimes unconsciously, work to construct identities that are both fluid and multiple and frequently grounded in consumption. Images are powerful and ideological because they speak in a different grammar; truth and falsity no longer apply. Take, for instance, an image of a young man spraying a particular cologne and then having lots of women try to get close to him. If the image were to be articulated in words—you'll put on this body spray and the young women literally will stampede to get near you—we would laugh, and yet when we see an image suggesting exactly that, we often accept it uncritically.

- **Technology strengthens and amplifies these ideological threads.** What this has meant for advertising is expanding media options, cluttered media, and indeed, a commercially cluttered media culture. It means fragmented and multitasking audiences, increasingly said to be taking control of their media usage (hence, in 2006, we each were person of the year in *Time* magazine and *Advertising Age's* advertising agency of the year). Yet audiences that now more than ever before indicate the desire to escape from advertising are at the same time interacting with a wonder world of interactive activities on corporate websites, creating ads for manufacturers, and "making friends" with brands on social networking sites.

Finally, adding to this already complex mixture, marketers, recognizing that their "targets" view sources of communication as indistinguishable, have adopted a strategy of integration in an attempt to *guarantee* that advertising messages in fact *are* indistinguishable from other messages. Thus, the definition of advertising is fluid. Just as we might ask, "Is TV still TV when you view it on your cellphone?" so might we ask, "Is advertising still advertising when you *produce* the television program?" "Is product placement advertising, public relations, or entertainment?"

The chapters in this section ask you to confront a number of ethical dimensions that you may not have considered. Some invite you to look at institutional values and practices; others take a more practical focus. We look at two related dynamics inherent in our work and in our culture: the increasing infringement of advertising/promotional speech into public and private spaces; and the commodification of aspects of culture never intended to be marketed as commodities. We ask: What complexities arise when advertising talks not in words, but in images? We examine the implications of a media system that is supported by advertising, motivated by profit, and is increasingly concentrated in the hands of a few large corporations. Finally, we invite you to look at the values and principles that guide our profession. The ethical dilemmas are complex, intriguing, and well worth reflection.

NOTES

1. http://adage.com/superbowl08/article?article_id=124852
2. Frank Cappo, *The Future of Advertising: New Media, New Clients, New Consumers in the Post-Television Age*, (New York: McGraw-Hill, 2003).
3. www.nielsenmedia.com/nc/portal/site/Public/menuitem.55dc65b4a7d5adff3f65936147a062a0/?vgnextoid=697760772bfe7110VgnVCM100000ac0a260aRCRD
4. www.financialweek.com/apps/pbcs.dll/artikkel?Dato=20080201&Kategori=REG&Lopenr=740338958&Ref=AR
5. Ibid.
6. http://www.tns-mi.com/news/03132007.htm.
7. Daniel Pope, *The Making of Modern Advertising*, (New York: Basic Books, 1983).
8. Richard W. Pollay, "The Distorted Mirror: Reflections on the Unintended Consequences of Advertising, *Journal of Marketing*, 50 (April 1986), 19.
9. William Leiss, Stephen Kline, Sut Jhally, Jacqueline Botterill, *Social Communication in Advertising: Consumption in the Mediated Marketplace*, (New York: Routledge, 2005), pp. 18, 20.
10. Lawrence B. Glickman, "Born to Shop? Consumer History and American History" in *Consumer Society in American History: A Reader* (Ithaca, NY: Cornell University Press, 1999), pp. 1–14.
11. query.nytimes.com/gst/fullpage.html?res=9F03E0DA133AF93AA35755C0A9649C8B63
12. www.zephoria.org/thoughts/archives/2005/09/29/when_media_beco.html

The Commercialization of Everyday Life

Promotional communication permeates and blends with our cultural environment, punctuating our television watching, saturating our magazines and newspapers, and popping up in our Internet surfing, movies, and video games. In short, advertising has become an accepted part of everyday life. . . . [A]t the individual level the discourse through and about objects sidles up to us everywhere, beckoning, teasing, haranguing, instructing, cajoling, and informing our daily interactions with each other in most settings. . . . The symbolic attributes of goods, as well as the characters, situations, imagery, and jokes of advertising discourse, are now fully integrated into our cultural repertoire.[1]

Advertising is a major player in the global economy. It is estimated that worldwide advertising expenditures in 2007 will be approximately $460 billion; $163 billion will be spent in the United States.[2] An indispensable business tool, advertising, at the same time, is an integral part of our media culture. It is the commercial foundation that supports most media, and a considerable portion of media content *is* advertising.

Today, the supply of all media is exploding. Technological innovation accelerates both the development of new media—digital, interactive, mobile—and the transformation of "traditional" media. We can create, send, receive, and store audiovisual data at home and away, almost wherever we might be in the world, and much to delight of marketers (and others), technology also makes it possible to track and sort much of our activity as media users.[3]

In this world increasingly "cluttered" with media, we find those media, both old and new, increasingly "cluttered" with advertising messages. The average nonprogram time on the four primary networks *fell* to sixteen minutes and twenty-nine seconds.[4] The September 2007 fashion issue of *Vogue* weighed 4.9 pounds and had 727 advertising pages.[5] National advertisers including Coca-Cola and the National Basketball Association have "set up shop" in Second Life, a computer-generated, three-dimensional virtual world, complete with its own monetary system. CNET and Reuters have opened virtual bureaus in Second Life as well, though some advertisers remain less than impressed with the "population."[6] Brands on social-networking sites such as MySpace and Facebook garner "friends" with the best of them.

A study examining how Americans incorporate media into the "fabric of our everyday lives" found that adept at multitasking and immersed in a profusion of media, "we spend the equivalent of 94 percent of our waking day with media . . . more time with media than with any other waking activity."[7] In this chaos, depending on who you're talking to and how they define advertising, each of us is exposed to anywhere from 4000 to 20,000 messages a day.[8] Simply getting consumers' attention is both difficult and urgent. Yet, a writer in *Advertising Age*, commenting on the "clutter problem," noted:

> Like a fly repeatedly bouncing off a closed window, the ad industry is trying to fix the problem by doing more of the same. That is, by creating more ads. What that absurdly clichéd mission statement of "cutting through the clutter" has really yielded is an industry that shotgun blasts commercial messages into sexy new places as quick as it can identify them, whether it's emerging digital platforms or nooks and crannies in an increasingly buyable physical world—dry-cleaning bags, coffee cups, door hangers and even houses. Yes, clutter is leading to more clutter.[9]

Advertisers use buzz and word-of-mouth marketing, seeking "trendsetters . . . and subtly pushing them into talking about their brand to their friends and admirers."[10]

Guerrilla marketing techniques use "unusual and unpredictable tactics"—elevator button advertising, ad walkers, jeans hanging from parking meters and power lines—to get maximum attention using minimal resources. Media and audiences are fragmented. Technology makes niche targeting and even microtargeting possible, however, a media culture cluttered with commercial messages almost guarantees exposure to unintended audiences.

The blurring of editorial, entertainment, and advertising content further contributes to an increasingly commercialized landscape. One certainly can argue that in the context of integrated marketing communication, advertising, public relations, and promotional messages are *by design* virtually indistinguishable in persuasive intent, if not in form. Critics point to such phenomena as Tropicana Field (home of the Tampa Bay Devil Rays), *The M&M's Brand Counting Book* ("Pour out the candies. Get Ready. Get Set. This counting book is the tastiest yet."),[11] and corporate sponsorships of charity events as evidence of a creeping infringement of commercial logic into the public and private arenas.

All this occurs at the same time that consumers express discomfort, dismay, and occasionally something bordering on outrage with hypercommercialization.

> Americans have a very strange notion of freedom. Americans seem to think that if you're free from government, you're free, which overlooks the fact that there can be other opponents of freedom. Like corporations who have immense power within our cultural space and that censor other voices. I think we have to now think about not only what the government shouldn't do but about what any other large-scale organization should not be allowed to do, which is monopolize means of communication, means of cultural production, which is what corporations do at the present time.[12]

It is something of a paradox that even as 70 percent of Americans say they would be interested in products that would help them avoid advertising, marketers are finding increasing success in engaging consumers through websites that provide interactive opportunities and promotions in which consumers are asked to create ads for brands.[13]

Such is our media culture.

Another dimension of our commercialized landscape, more subtle perhaps, and for that very reason, some critics argue, more insidious, is the commodification of everyday life. In a 1989 PBS documentary, *Consuming Images*, Bill Moyers argues that "advertising" has become the primary mode of public address.[14] That is to say, a commercial logic is increasingly finding its way into institutions, ideas, and processes never intended to be traded as marketable commodities. Quite simply, we think about more things as if they were products.

Today, political candidates—not unlike toothpaste, cereal, and automobiles—market themselves as brands.[15] It is not unusual for infertile couples to "advertise" in college newspapers for egg donors, sometimes offering to pay top price for a donor with the desired qualities. In one *New York Times* ad, the Genetics & IVF Institute indicated that the company's "diverse donor pool includes doctoral donors with advanced degrees and numerous other donors with special accomplishments and talents."[16] Educational institutions routinely "package" their courses into specialized curricula—for example, advanced-degree executive programs on a satellite campus—deliverable commodities that can be exchanged for a profit on the market.[17]

In "Reality TV as Advertainment," Deery writes about the distinction between what is public and viewable and what is private and closed to outside viewing. She notes that reality programming, in breaking down that distinction, has turned privacy, and indeed, an individual's "reality," into a commodity. The interior is exteriorized; this is accomplished by and for money.[18] Some have argued that even anti-corporate activism and resistance to commodification has itself become a commodity, something you can "buy into" to distinguish yourself from others.[19]

The interjection of a decidedly corporate ethos into our everyday lives has come about casually, yet consistently, overwhelming the public sphere in sometimes obvious and sometimes not so readily obvious ways. The commercial imperative has come to seem natural and so has remained largely unexamined and unquestioned.

The four cases in this chapter focus on these dimensions of commercialization in our modern media culture. "Is That a Guerilla I See?" explores the ethical dimensions of how marketing messages are presented and where they are presented. "Selling Students as a 'Captive Audience' " raises questions about the commercialization of the education experience and asks whether or not advertisers have a social responsibility to maintain the classroom as a "safe harbor" from commercial messages despite the desirability of the "captive audience" within those classrooms. "DTC Advertising: Prescription Drugs as Consumer Products" examines the controversies that arise when the logic of the marketplace enters into the time-honored doctor–patient relationship. In the last case, "Shopping to Save the World," we probe the complex ethical dimensions of cause-related marketing—corporate logic entering the arena of social welfare in the guise of social responsibility.

23 Is That a Guerrilla I See?

At the end of the day, we need to have spreadsheets and impressions and photos documenting the [guerrilla marketing] event. Clients like GE and Citibank aren't looking for middle of the night guys in ski masks when budgets are hitting six and seven figures. It is a discipline like any other.[20]

There was a time when we recognized advertising when we saw it—in the pages of our magazines and newspapers, a familiar presence as we watched television or listened to our favorite radio station, and recently, even as we glanced at the "third screen" on our cell phone or Blackberry. Today, amid cluttered media in a world cluttered with media, marketers, out of necessity, are creating ever-more-inventive ways to get our attention. Guerrilla marketing (sometimes, in its varied permutations identified as viral, stealth, buzz, NBDB—never been done before—advertising, ambient, or "nontraditional marketing") is designed to get consumers "seeing things that they aren't used to seeing, creating something that lives in the context of what they do but that is out of context with what they are used to."[21] Guerrilla marketing, today a recognized part of the marketing mix, might be cleverly disguised, or something in-your-face, but it is always in aggressive pursuit of sales.

A number of books and websites offer cases, marketing coaches, and guerrilla marketing toolkits (see, for example, www.gmarketing.com). Relatively small, local advertisers seeking to promote products and services on a minimal budget are advised to undertake relatively innocuous activities: sponsor a Little League team, join a civic club, or offer services as a public speaker.[22] Not all guerrilla efforts, however, are so conventional. Let's look at a sampling of efforts.

Unconventional Messages in Unconventional Places

- Mothers Against Drunk Driving (MADD) sponsored a series of posters in restaurant and bar restrooms. The posters, depicting images of a car on the road, were smashed and crinkled against towel dispensers and urinal corners to recreate the appearance of a car accident.[23]
- In New Zealand, the television program *Ugly Betty* was promoted with stand-alone mall displays that were later covered with oversized brown paper bags (to give the effect of putting a bag over Betty's head), leaving only the sitcom's name, time, and channel visible.[24]
- In Toronto, the Daily Bread Food Bank kicked off its fall food drive by placing empty refrigerators (doors could open but for safety couldn't latch shut) at five locations in the financial district to serve as a stark reminder that many can't afford to stock home groceries.[25]

Marketers like the "stickiness" of guerrilla efforts, that is, "an environment in which a well-embedded ad can resonate with members on a personal level by infiltrating everyday interactions. It 'sticks' by not appearing to be an ad, in effect slipping under consumers' well-tuned ad radar."[26]

Taking Guerrilla a Bit Farther

- Sony Ericsson's "Fake Tourist" effort for its new camera phone in 2002 remains one of the best-known guerrilla efforts. Sixty actors wandered the streets of Seattle and New York City asking others to take pictures of them using their camera phones. This effort aroused considerable debate about forthrightness in nontraditional marketing.[27]
- The Federal Trade Commission (FTC) and the Competition Bureau of Canada created a website for Eggplant Extract Fat Foe fat blocker. "Lose up to ten pounds a week with no sweat, no starvation." The site looked legitimate, even as it promised, you could "eat . . . gooey chocolate desserts . . . and watch the pounds melt away." When users responded, they were sent to another page, which explained that the ad had been a fake and went on to warn about diet ripoffs.[28]

Too Sticky? Some Efforts Do More Harm Than Good

- John Mackey, co-founder and CEO of Whole Foods Market, Inc., posted messages under a false identity on Yahoo Finance stock forums for eight years. Using the pseudonym Rahodeb, an anagram of his wife's name, Deborah, Mackey "routinely cheered Whole Foods' financial results, trumpeted his personal gains on the stock, and bashed Wild Oats," which Whole Foods was trying to acquire. At one point, Rahodeb noted that "Oats has no value and no future." The postings came to light in documents filed with the FTC, which sought to block the acquisition.[29]
- In 2002, Acclaim Entertainment offered to ring in the introduction of its new racing-themed video game, *Burnout 2: Point of Impact*, by paying for all speeding tickets in Great Britain on the day of its release. Naturally, the Department of Transportation opposed the tactic with the argument that Acclaim was encouraging citizens to break the law.[30]
- In March 2007, guerrilla marketing company Interference placed magnetic signs promoting Turner Broadcasting Systems' Cartoon Network's *Aqua Teen Hunger Force* in ten cities, including Boston. Citizens of that city mistook the signs for terrorist devices. The devices triggered repeated bomb scares around the city and prompted closure of bridges and a portion of the Charles River. Turner Broadcasting compensated Boston-area authorities $2 million to compensate for the marketing stunt.[31]   ■

Guerrilla marketing tactics are an intriguing ethical area. At one end, we see private enterprise at its most inventive, working, sometimes ingeniously, to reach potential customers and sell them something. At the other end, we have practices that some have labeled deceptive, intrusive, and offensive. At times, relatively small firms attempt to joust with the "gorilla" marketers (i.e., large firms) in the great spirit of commercial self-interest, yet Turner Broadcasting and Sony—certainly "gorillas" by any standards—are apparently guerrilla marketers as well. And in today's digital world, video of a guerrilla event can go straight to YouTube and around the globe in a matter of minutes, for better or worse.

One can, of course, contend that if these practices truly offend individuals, the marketers will be punished by failing to achieve their sales goals. But the guerrilla marketing Web pages and newsletters abound with success stories. Even if Sony's ploys made some uncomfortable, sales of the telephone/camera in the promotional cities were 54 percent higher than anywhere else. In any number of cases, the signals that sellers are receiving from the feedback mechanism of the market (sales) is that they must be doing something right, resting on familiar—and comforting—utilitarian soil.

But sometimes the number of "votes in the economic marketplace" doesn't tell the whole story. Let's look at the *Aqua Teen Hunger Force* incident. Certainly no one would recommend or applaud anything approaching this debacle. Indeed, it served as a cautionary tale for many marketers inclined to "push the envelope." Hanging electronic devices under bridges is simply not something you do in a post-9/11 world. Still, in the competitive marketing world, one columnist in the *Boston Globe* pointed out the irony of the situation when he wrote:

> The bottom line, as the corporate types like to measure these things, is that Turner Broadcasting's guerrilla marketing assault on Boston was a fabulous success. Suddenly a no name cartoon about a talking box of French fries is the talk of the town from coast to coast. . . . Bottom line, in a world where you get famous by being infamous . . . the ratings get a big bump at the Cartoon Network.[32]

Acting in its own interest and that of its client, and celebrating the creativity that is a hallmark of those who succeed in the advertising profession, it appears that the public interest never entered into the Interference decision-making process. The device apparently was easily identified by those "in the target market," who readily critiqued the city, firefighters, and police for their "overreaction" and found humor in the fact that:

> The first five minutes of last night's news wasn't even so much about the day's events as it was explaining what Adult Swim is. . . . The problem at its heart is that something like Adult Swim talks to an underground counterculture, it talks to the people who aren't really a part of mainstream society, people who are reporting on it don't understand why it exists. . . . [33]

The company's indiscriminate use of public bridges and overpasses as a "medium" certainly raises questions of social responsibility. Overlooking for now the thoughtless creation of the device, the danger to public safety that ensued, and the exertion of time and effort by city officials and first-responders (would that we could overlook that), was the "greatest good for the greatest number" achieved when thousands had virtually no choice but to see a message that may or may not have been of interest to them and that very likely wasn't intended to be targeted to or understood by the majority of them in the first place?

The potential strategies and tactics for guerrilla marketing, as we have seen in the small sample discussed here, are bounded only by marketing imagination.

And certainly, at least on the surface, many efforts seem harmless, even socially responsible; who can argue with sponsoring a Little League team? But even here, at the most benign level, we encounter the classic question of means and ends, where it could be contended that the only reason to (say) join a civic club, give public speeches, or sponsor a Little League team is ultimately to reap marketing outcomes. This, of course, resonates with one of the essential themes of the market system—private gains ultimately will result in public good.

At the other end of the continuum, we find a Whole Foods CEO posting criticism of a competitor under a false identity, Acclaim Entertainment's offer to subsidize speeding tickets, and of course, Turner Broadcasting's light boards. In these instances, even the most forgiving might say, "This goes too far!"

Where, then, is the ethical counterground? The introduction of laws or regulations would enforce a Kantian absolutism but clearly would thwart legitimate business strategies and tactics in pursuit of the hallowed marketing driver of self-interest and the profit motive. Social responsibility? Perhaps, combined with a search for Aristotle's middle ground to avoid excesses.

One thing is certain. In our increasingly commercially driven culture, we will see more and more efforts to sell to us, not only through traditional advertising but also clearly through more creative tactics as well. To what end? Communication scholar Stuart Ewen warns:

> The main thing these [guerrilla tactics] "add" to our lives is an intensified sense of distrust of and alienation from others. This grows out of the suspicion that any human interaction, any product used or opinion expressed may be a commercially staged event designed to get us to buy, think, or behave in certain ways.[34]

Guerrilla marketing seems, on reflection, well named. The traditional definition of the adjective involves tactics of "sudden acts of harassment," the military version made infamous in Vietnam and, now, in occupied Iraq. The commercial version is benign, of course, but challenges the working relationship between a company with something to sell and an individual who may—or may not—be interested, even as it adds yet another degree of commercialism to an already highly commercialized culture.

24 Selling Students as a "Captive Audience"?

Indeed, almost anywhere one finds children, there are attempts to market to them, whether it's at doctors' offices or nature centers. The jewel in the marketers' crown of commercial infiltration has been the nation's public schools.[35]

Jane Hamilton, president of the school board in a Midwestern community of 40,000, was "doing her homework" for what was sure to be a long meeting. Tonight, the board was to decide if the school system would sign a contract with Channel One. There was no

continued

shortage of opinions on the matter, and they were *strongly held* opinions. Jane wasn't sure *where* she stood on the matter; she decided to go through her notes one more time.

Channel One had been started by Chris Whittle in 1990, sold to Primedia in 1994, and had just been purchased by Alloy Media and Marketing, self-proclaimed to be "one of the largest and most successful marketers and merchandisers to the youth market."[36] Channel One currently reaches more than 6 million students in 11,000 middle schools and high schools, and according to its promotion to advertisers, Channel One news is the "No. 1 highest rated TV show for teens in America."[37]

The company would lease the school one color television set for every twenty-three students in grades 6–12, two videocassette recorder/players, and a satellite dish with free installation. In exchange, the school would agree to show Channel One programming in its entirety on approximately 90 percent of school days, in at least 80 percent of the classrooms, and appoint a staff person to report any problems to the company within twenty-four hours.

The Channel One programming is a daily twelve-minute program. Ten minutes consist of "current events and feature material" (recent political, economic, and social/cultural stories, as well as sports, weather, features, and profiles) delivered by young, able reporters (CNN's Anderson Cooper got his start at Channel One). This is followed by two minutes of advertising. Though Channel One has strict guidelines for selection of these "corporate sponsorships" in order to guarantee their appropriateness, those two minutes have plagued Channel One since its inception.

What the Critics Are Saying

Existing evidence suggests that the program generally has been well received by many teachers and students currently using the system. However, it is opposed by both the national teachers' unions (National Education Association and American Federation of Teachers), the National PTA, and the National Association of State Boards of Education. The legislature in New York banned Channel One from New York State schools.[38] And there is no shortage of activist groups who are extremely adamant in their opposition. Commercial Alert, an activist organization whose mission is "to keep the commercial culture in its proper sphere," noted:

> Channel One was built on a reprehensible business model: force feed advertisements to kids held captive. The idea was to hijack the classroom to show children commercials wrapped around fluff programming.[39]

According to Commercial Alert and a number of other activist groups, even if the advertising were selected responsibly, Channel One is unacceptable; schools are not intended for "mandatory viewing of commercial promotions."[40]

The strength of the anti-commercialism mind-set held by those opposing Channel One coupled with the existence of a number of other venues through which marketers can reach teens led a writer in *Advertising Age* to suggest that perhaps the program was "an idea whose time has come and gone." ". . . [A]dvertising on the channel," he concluded, "seems like asking for trouble."[41] In fact, it was rumored that Primedia had been poised to close the operation before it was purchased by Alloy Media and Marketing. That company is in the business of helping companies reach teens, has published several *Gossip Girl* books with "decidedly adult" content, and is a coproducer of a television program, *Gossip Girl*, on the CW Network.[42] One reviewer in *Advertising Age* wrote of that series:

> Now here comes *Gossip Girl*, which transplants teen angst to Manhattan's tony Upper East Side, where privileged underage kids can slurp martinis at a ritzy hotel bar, smoke weed in Central Park or have sex in mom's townhouse.[43]

Alloy's involvement was sure to create more questions.

What the Advocates Are Saying

The prime rationale for signing up with Channel One had always been that the schools were able to acquire valuable equipment that they might not otherwise be able to afford. Debra Kaufman, writing in *Television Week*, notes that "Channel One intends to stay on the leading edge of all new digital platforms and plans to unveil new technology in classrooms in the fall [2007]"[44]—the equipment would be even better.

In addition to programming, Channel One provides support material teachers can use to develop classroom discussions, and teachers always receive the program the night before so that they can review it before class.

In response to the contention that the Channel One programming is "fluff," Kaufman points out that Channel One has won two prestigious George Foster Peabody Awards (in 1993 and 2004), along with "dozens of other awards." Its website won a Webby Award for the youth category in 2005. All indications are that Channel One is serious about creating a broad-based news organization. NBC has just signed on to produce the Web's daily newscast, and Channel One plans to introduce a 24/7 broadband news channel for teens and has partnerships with Cingular and Verizon. Judy Harris, president and CEO of Channel One, notes that the primary emphasis is on finding ways to engage young people in current events. "In using our airwaves," she said, "we believe we can inspire change."[45]

A study of seventh and eighth grade students who were exposed to Channel One published in *Pediatrics* found that students remembered more ads than news stories but a higher percentage of the news stories than the ads, those who were more receptive to the programming learned more from it, a media-literacy lesson given before the programming was shown to help with news story recall and increased advertising skepticism, and students with higher political efficacy were more likely to consider the program useful. The study confirmed that Channel One had the potential for positive effects as well as the likelihood of persuasion by advertisers and cultivation of materialism. The authors noted:

> Positive and protective effects such as current-affairs knowledge, political efficacy, and skepticism toward advertisers were enhanced by media-literacy training. These results suggest that schools that wish to use commercial programming such as Channel One should include in-service training for teachers on media-literacy education and should require that media literacy be taught with specific reference to the programming.

continued

They concluded:

> Whether schools should use commercial programs such as Channel One at all remains a question of ethics that empirical data such as these cannot resolve.[46]

Jane mulled over her notes. There appeared to be positive effects, particularly if the programming was combined with media literacy. But what about the educator groups that denounced it? Teachers were the ones who would have to incorporate it into their classrooms. Still, the school certainly couldn't afford the equipment without the program. And it wasn't like it would be the only commercial presence in the school. There was the Pepsi sign on the scoreboard, of course, and Jane was aware that teachers had welcomed any number of sponsored "educational" materials from reputable companies such as Nike, Kelloggs, McDonald's, and Procter & Gamble. Pizza Hut was offering its product as incentive to students for work well done, and the football team was looking for a corporate sponsor for team uniforms. More and more schools seem to be "going commercial," she thought; she'd even heard of a company in Massachusetts, BusRadio, that put commercial radio on school buses as a "behavioral tool" bus drivers could use to calm children.[47]

The commercialization of schools seems inevitable; the idea of a commercial-free school seems idealistic. And the school sure could use that equipment.   ∎

One way of examining the ethical dimensions of this complex issue is to consider the matter of consequences. We might ask, for example, if it would make any difference to Channel One's critics if it consistently accomplished the educational goals of the program—"to spark debate and discussion among teens, and also discussion between young people and their parents and educators, on the important issues affecting young people in America."[48] Almost certainly not, because their objections seem to be based on the assumption that the practice of "requiring" students to watch commercial messages in schools is simply wrong, *regardless of its potentially positive outcomes*. So the critics weren't even willing to discuss the quality of the programming. As one critic noted on his website:

> Because classroom advertising is compulsory under the [Channel One] contract, every constitutional mandate that makes school attendance mandatory also mandates commercials.[49]

Students would be a captive audience; they'll certainly pay more attention to the ads (and the news content, one might guess) than in the distraction-laden television-viewing environment. Wasn't that what advertisers wanted? But the teachers were there, gatekeepers to guarantee the rationality of the viewing situation, weren't they?

Jane, on the other hand, seems very much a consequentialist. For her, the dominant factor is apparently the opportunity to acquire the equipment, which her financially strapped school would not otherwise be able to purchase. Technology is changing so rapidly; we access information in so many ways. The equipment is a powerful lure. (At least one study has shown that Channel One is disproportionately shown in schools located in low-income communities.[50]) It seems, then, that quality of content is a secondary consideration to Jane as well. One can only guess how the discussion might be altered if either side were to be open to a definition of "doing what's best for the students" that included content beyond the existence of advertising. No one thought to ask the students for their viewpoint.

Then too, neither the critics nor the proponents seem willing to engage in the issue of funding for the schools. Juliet Schor, in her book, *Born to Buy*, an exploration of the commercialization of childhood, writes:

> The main impetus for commercialization is the chronic under-funding of schools. As budgets tighten, officials become more receptive to selling access to their students. Debates about exclusive soda contracts, Channel One, corporate sponsorships, and naming rights have all focused on challenges to funding, with proponents of the deals stressing the monies they anticipate.[51]

Jane seems to be thinking that the school *does* need the equipment, so the consequences (i.e., getting the equipment) triumph over idealism (i.e., the school as a commercial-free environment).

There is also the somewhat unformulated rationale of "ads have been in the school in one form or another for a long time," and "everybody seems to be doing it," apparently suggesting in the first case that no harm seems to have been done by other commercial incursions in the classrooms and in the second that others are doing it, so it can't be all that bad. Daily newspapers belong in the classroom, and they carry ads. Students sell advertising for the yearbook and the student newspaper.

Basically, then, the only consequence Jane deems important is the acquisition of the equipment. The critics, on the other hand, may see this as important, but not worth the tradeoff of offering students as a captive and highly sought-after "market" for a particularly compelling form of commercial persuasion.

One fact seems unassailably clear—Channel One brings what many consider to be the most powerful audio and visual symbol package available to advertisers—the television commercial—into the classroom and, as in the case of normal television programming, as part of a larger package of news and entertainment designed to attract and keep the attention of an audience. Channel One, then, remains at the center of critics' concerns over what they fear to be the rampant commercialization of schools. It formalizes an institutional relationship between the educational experience, media, and advertising that seemingly is very different from simply buying the team uniforms or selling advertising in the school newspaper.

25 DTC Advertising: Prescription Drugs as Consumer Products?

All we have to do is look back at the Vioxx situation to learn the dangers of direct-to-consumer [pharmaceutical] ads.[52]

Dear Member of Congress: Direct-to-consumer advertising of prescription drugs should be prohibited. The ads are not educational, and do not promote public health. They increase the cost of drugs and the number of unnecessary prescriptions, which is expensive to tax-payers, and can be harmful or deadly to patients.[53]

We are concerned that [DTC] restrictions could have the perverse and unintended effect of chilling the communication of truthful, accurate and useful information about the bene-fits and risks of available drug products to health-care practitioners and patients, which would be contrary to the public health.[54]

These comments, from a Senator in favor of a suspension of direct-to-consumer (DTC) advertising, a consumer advocacy group, and an officer of the Pharmaceutical Research and Manufacturers Association, respectively, illustrate the wide range of opinions on DTC pharmaceutical advertising. Indeed, DTC advertising has been beset by controversy since the Food and Drug Administration (FDA) lifted the ban on DTC broadcast advertising in 1997, but the level of public discourse on the topic escalated in intensity and scope fol-lowing the "Vioxx situation" in 2004. At that time, pharmaceutical giant Merck pulled its widely advertised blockbuster drug, a painkiller, Vioxx, from the market following studies showing that the drug sharply increased the risk of heart attacks and strokes. Pfizer's Cele-brex, like Vioxx, a cox-2 inhibitor, remained on the market, but the company stopped ad-vertising in 2005, resuming two years later. The ensuing furor set the stage for lawsuits against Merck, harsh criticism of the FDA, increasing concern over drug safety issues, and calls for the FDA to place limits on DTC advertising, especially for new drugs.

The bill that ultimately passed in 2007 was considered by the advertising and media in-dustries to be a "significant victory." The bill gives the FDA the authority to fine marketers for misleading DTC ads and boosts the number of people at the FDA who will review ads, but it does not include the harshest restrictions that had been proposed by the House and Senate earlier: a ban on advertising a new drug for the first two or three years and a special logo and warning indicating that all the side effects may not have been found.[55]

Still, as a headline in *Forbes* heralded, "Direct-to-Consumer Drug Ads [are] Booming Despite Criticism."[56] Total DTC drug spending increased more than 300 percent between 1997 and 2007, when expenditures were estimated at $4.8 billion.[57] According to the *New England Journal of Medicine*, spending on DTC advertising increased by 330 percent be-tween 1996 and 2005.[58] The United States and New Zealand are currently the only coun-tries in the world to allow DTC advertising, although apparently the European Union and Canada are considering allowing it.[59]

Let's consider a summary of the positions taken by advocates and detractors. *Supporters* suggest DTC advertising is good because:

- It educates consumers about common yet serious conditions such as hypertension, diabetes, elevated cholesterol levels, and depression that often go undiagnosed and untreated. Increased awareness brings patients into doctors' offices seeking help.[60]
- It helps to avert underuse of medicines among individuals requiring them for the on-going treatment of chronic conditions.[61]

- Patients become more involved in their health care. Advertising frequently encourages them to seek more information from their physicians, websites, or medical sites. A study published in *Drug Week* found that the number one action taken after seeing a DTC ad is information seeking, not rushing to doctors to request a prescription.[62]
- The pharmaceutical industry makes its living from drug prescriptions. At the same time, millions of Americans are living longer lives, given the correct prescription to fill their health needs.

Detractors suggest DTC advertising is not a good because:

- Advertising is overtly persuasive in intent, so it is ill-suited to educate. Studies have found that DTC ads tend to include more emotional than informational content, frequently rely on images, and rarely mention lifestyle changes as an alternative to medication.[63]
- Consumers do not understand the technicalities, are confused into believing that inconsequential changes are major breakthroughs, and develop unrealistic expectations about drug performance.[64]
- It contributes to consumers' increased anxiety, self-diagnosis, and requests to doctors for particular drugs. In research among physicians who had patients request a specific prescription brand in the previous six months, responses to patient requests were almost equally split between acceptance and refusal to prescribe.[65] However, it has been suggested that DTC advertising results in some overuse of prescription drugs.[66]

There can be no doubt that more and more DTC pharmaceutical advertising will be directed toward us, although there are indications that the media mix will change. The Fifth Annual Cegedim Dendrite DTC Industry Check-Up survey found that pharmaceutical companies planned increased spending on more targeted online activities such as websites, search-engine marketing, and e-mail in 2007.[67] ∎

Depending on your perspective, the DTC advertising boom can be viewed as "the successful marriage of the drug companies' profit motive and their patients' interest" or as an instance of patients becoming "unwitting tools of the drug manufacturer's marketing department." At the core, these perspectives differ on the perceived rationality of consumers. *If* we assume that individuals will not be prone to developing symptoms to match those described in the advertising, *if* we assume that individuals will not be "taken in" by the uplifting images that populate many DTC ads, and *if* we assume that consumers will be diligent in discerning and assessing all the possible side effects of the promoted drug, then the relationship between profit-seeking pharmaceutical companies and health-seeking consumers may well be a fruitful one. This is particularly true if we view consumers not only as "information processors," carefully reflecting on information in the ads, but also as "information seekers," encouraged by the ads to go to websites, medical sites, or their physician. When patients and physicians *support* DTC advertising, it seems largely in utilitarian realms, with the assumption that both the patient and the doctor are being well served—the patient via the empowerment that comes with awareness and knowledge and the doctor by a patient more informed about treatment options.

When patients and physicians *object* to DTC advertising, they seem to do so from two ethical positions. The utilitarian argument suggests that, on balance, the greatest good for the greatest number is *not* being served by attempts at self-medication in these complex areas made to seem simpler largely to satisfy the demands of the techniques of modern advertising. Some adopt the Kantian position that it's just wrong in any way to apply pressure on the presumed expertise of the physician in the time-honored doctor–patient relationship. As patients, we are used to having drug companies attempt to persuade us about over-the-counter, that is, nonprescription, drugs. With prescription drugs, however, we pass through the gatekeeper of the physician, who, we expect, knows far more about the condition and the treatment than we do.

Additional ethical concerns arise more starkly in the context of the unintended consequences of DTC advertising. In "Marketing Drugs to Consumers. Prescription Drugs Are Rapidly Becoming 'Consumer Products,' "[68] Asher Meir asks the seemingly simple question: What role does consumer advertising have in the prescription drug market at all? This makes one pause, for DTC pharmaceutical advertising is a clear instance of the logic of the consumer marketplace inserting itself and indeed, some would argue, overwhelming an arena never intended to function within that logic. While many have noted the possibility that the DTC ads violate the balance of the doctor–patient relationship, we might look beyond that general observation to pose additional questions. In an article in the British medical journal *The Lancet*, Dr. Jonathan Metzl, writing in light of European Union consideration of allowing DTC advertising, notes that European doctors and patients should "take heed of the cautionary tales" of the American DTC experience. He raises a number of considerations worthy of reflection.[69]

- How do patients' requests of prescription drugs by name affect the traditional notions of medical authority, medical communication, or the doctor–patient interaction? While patients have always asked for particular treatments, do DTC ads change the ways in which physicians and patients speak and listen to each other?

- How does DTC advertising change physicians' understanding of the treatments they prescribe? Here, Metzl reminds us "that physician's beliefs about and expectations of prescription drugs are shaped by the fact that they too are members of U.S. culture and are as such subject to the same advertisements as are their patients."

- How does DTC advertising amplify or change cultural expectations about illness and health?

- In an article entitled, "Merchandising Madness: Pill, Promises, and Better Living Through Chemistry," Rubin asks whether in the process of commodifying pharmaceutical brands, is it not possible that drug companies are manufacturing and commodifying not only drugs but also diseases? He writes, "People who struggle with the very common problems of shyness, sadness, nervousness, malaise, and even suspiciousness are offered refuge under the umbrella of drug-assisted well-being."[70]

- While drugs advertised to consumers are predominantly new drugs to treat chronic conditions, concerns have arisen over the increased advertising of "lifestyle" drugs, "available only to those capable of recognizing and consummating the products' constructed marketplace value."[71] One pharmaceutical industry observer sarcastically suggests that such drugs may "one day free the world from the scourge of toenail fungus, obesity, baldness, face wrinkles and impotence."[72]

- Finally, concerns over the use of images in advertising more generally are exacerbated in DTC advertising. Metzl notes:

> For instance, television in the USA is replete with images of Levitra-invigorated men throwing footballs through tyres or women who are proficient at motherhood duties because of antidepressants. . . . The advertisements connect prescription medications with assumptions about what it means to be a normal man, woman, black person, white person, lover, worker, or a host of other abstract, protean roles in U.S. society. By doing so, the advertisements promote information not only about drugs, but also about the social contexts in which medications accrue symbolic meanings, that, one might well surmise, play out in clinical contexts.[73]

Any matters concerned with health are important and are touched with a sense of urgency. This makes it particularly noteworthy that a recent Gallup Poll found that Americans rated their image of both the health-care industry and the pharmaceutical industry negatively; each industry saw its image deteriorate more than average over the past four years.[74]

Much of the controversy swirling around the issues of DTC pharmaceutical advertising seemingly arises from a discomfort with the fit of profit motive and the inviolability of the doctor–patient relationship. This comment from former FDA commissioner David Kessler and Douglas Levy illustrates the perceived fault line:

> There is nothing wrong with pharmaceutical companies communicating directly with consumers, but they should adhere to the standards and ethics of medicine, not the standards and ethics of selling soap or some other consumer product that presents minimal risks.[75]

26 Shopping to Save the World

Cause related marketing's case has never been clearer or more compelling. More people are becoming increasingly civic-minded; supporting causes by purchasing products that promote them is a simple way to express this disposition. Simplicity is the key. That's why cause related marketing provides so much money for charitable causes; it's simply more convenient for consumers than other forms of fundraising.[76]

continued

Social responsibility has not always fit easily into a business culture where, to quote a well-known economist and Harvard business professor, Theodore Levitt, ". . . the business of business is profits . . . virtue lies in the vigorous, undiluted assertion of the corporation's profit-making function."[77] Once, corporations were hesitant to link themselves to a cause, fearing that their involvement would appear to be exploitation of the cause for commercial gain. Today, however, according to the 2007 Cone Cause Evolution Survey, 90 percent of Americans agree that "companies should support causes that are consistent with their responsible business practices." Additionally, consumers indicate that they will reward companies they view to be good citizens (e.g., by switching brands or recommending products or services to others).[78]

Corporations now undertake a variety of initiatives in the name of corporate social responsibility; spending on cause marketing is expected to reach $1.5 billion in 2008.[79] Kotler and Lee suggest that one noteworthy trend indicating this change in corporate philosophy is the transformation of corporate philanthropy from giving as an obligation to giving as a strategic business tool.[80] Indeed, in a 2007 survey reported by the Conference Research Board, a business research organization, 77 percent of the companies responding indicated that "aligning their giving with business needs . . . was the most critical factor affecting their giving."[81]

Cause-related marketing refers to corporate social initiatives that depend on consumer participation. Today, these initiatives are diverse; the degree and nature of consumer involvement vary. Consumers simply may be asked to purchase a product they might buy regularly; a percentage of sales will go to the cause. Some companies create items particularly to raise money for a cause; again, a percentage of the profits will go to the cause. In still other instances, consumers are asked to buy a symbol of their support of a cause—breast cancer's looped pink ribbon, a red-dress pin for heart disease, the Nike/Lance Armstrong "Live Strong" bracelet for cancer research—"wearable proof . . . a visible declaration of concern."[82] Extreme, fitness-based events in which charitable foundations link with corporate sponsors to provide training programs for individuals who participate in endurance events to raise money for a cause have become so commonplace that a writer in *The New York Times* identified them as "the latest trend in fitness."[83]

As Glenn noted in the statement that opened this case, corporate cause-related marketing fits comfortably, almost seamlessly in our consumer culture. Individuals routinely construct their identities and announce their allegiances and generosity: buying, charging, cooking for a cause; accessorizing with yellow bracelets, pink ribbons, red Converse sneakers; walking, running, cycling for a cause. Indeed, cause-related marketing initiatives are so much a part of our business and cultural landscape that we participate almost unconsciously. Glenn continued his statement by noting:

> . . . One day soon marketers will drop the prefix "cause-related" and see campaigns that stir the consumer's conscience as plain, simple marketing—unremarkable and barely worthy of comment.[84]

Are these cause-related marketing campaigns truly "unremarkable and barely worthy of comment"?   ∎

Cause-related marketing as a strategy raises questions about the nature of corporate philanthropy and social participation. Certainly, corporations should be commended for using their assets in positive ways to make a difference, be it locally, nationally, or globally. Without such corporate social initiatives, organizations addressing issues ranging from education and arts to environment, health, and social welfare would be hard-pressed to operate. Indeed, the long-term relationships created through corporate–nonprofit alliances provide the nonprofits with a far greater ability to engage in long-term planning than more traditional, grant-based funding may. Thus, from a utilitarian perspective, we might rationalize that any type of philanthropy is ethical because the greater good of civic action is served.

Does a corporation's motive for undertaking a cause-marketing social initiative need be totally without an expectation of reward for it to be ethically virtuous, or does the concept of "strategic giving" illustrate a golden-mean balance between pure altruism and economic return?

Let's return to Theodore Levitt's logic mentioned at the outset. Certainly, the stark position that he and others, most notably economist Milton Friedman, advocated decades ago is no longer defensible. Yet, in the article from which Levitt's observation is drawn, "The Dangers of Social Responsibility," he continues:

> . . . at bottom [a corporation's] outlook will always remain narrowly materialistic. What we have, then, is the frightening spectacle of a powerful economic functional group whose future and perception are shaped in a tight materialistic context of money and things but which imposes narrow ideas about a broad spectrum of unrelated noneconomic subjects on the mass of man and society. Even if its outlook were the purest kind of good will, that would not recommend the corporation as an arbiter of our lives.[85]

Levitt encourages us to reflect on the values and principles on which decisions regarding public welfare should be made. Are we comfortable with the insertion of a commercial imperative into this social realm? Are we comfortable with corporate decision makers, who by professional necessity are motivated primarily by the needs and objectives of the *corporation* rather than by social welfare, making decisions about the relative importance of social needs in achieving/maintaining public welfare? Certainly the realization that the decision to support one cause (let's say breast cancer) over another (AIDS) may be the result of no greater urgency than to create an image among a particular target market gives one pause.

The issue becomes even more complicated. Corporate decision makers rarely have any particular expertise in the relevant areas of public welfare. Thus a decision to form an alliance with a particular group related to a cause is simultaneously a decision to advocate a particular solution to the problem, that is, to say, "This is the way that the problem should be solved." The application of a utilitarian perspective becomes a bit more fragile.

A gift to be genuinely altruistic in nature, that is, to demonstrate other–centered love, must have benefit to the recipient as its primary motive and purpose but not necessarily its *only* motivation or purpose. Therefore, strategic giving may be regarded as ethical.

Then, too, cause-related marketing legitimizes and reinforces consumption not only as a route to social benevolence but also as an act of activism. To appeal to consumption amid concerns about exploitation and depletion of resources, environmental degradation, social inequities, escalating energy consumption, and so on might seem indefensible to many. In response to the Red campaign for the Global Fund to Fight AIDS, Tuberculosis and Malaria launched by rock star and activist Bono, a columnist in *The Chicago Tribune* asked plaintively, "Do you have to suffer and sacrifice to make the world a better place? Or can you just buy more cool stuff?"[86] Indeed, has "buying more cool stuff" replaced political activity?

Finally, consider the nonprofit organizations whose causes do not align themselves easily with corporate or business objectives. In an era of "cause clutter," charities may find themselves tempted to reposition their groups or reconstruct their cause into a more marketable commodity. The temptation to dramatize and overemotionalize need in order to attract donors may only be exacerbated in this new giving environment. Here, Mill may need to be tempered with Aristotle. A utilitarian focus may emphasize the urgency of fund-raising, the acquisition of a corporate partner, as the route to generating the greatest benefit. Yet consequences of challenges, transformation, and perhaps even the violation of values and principles supporting the cause require careful consideration at both the individual and organizational levels. A balance of emotional and logical argumentation in fund-raising appeals may be needed to avoid the extremes that would justify using any means to raise funds for worthwhile ends.

NOTES

1. William Leiss, Stephen Kline, Sut Jhally, and Jacqueline Botterill, *Social Communication in Advertising: Consumption in the Mediated Marketplace*, 3rd ed. (New York, Routledge, 2005), pp. 3, 6.
2. Heidi Dawley, "The Great Media Engine that is China," *Media Life Magazine*, 14 August 2007 (www.medialifemagazine.com/artman2/publish/Media_economy_57/The_great _media_engine_that_is_China.asp); Heidi Dawley, "Rosier Outlook for Global Ad Spending," *Media Life Magazine*, 2 July 2007 (www.medialifemagazine.com/artman2/publish/ Media_economy_57/Rosier_Outlook_for_global_ad_spending.asp)
3. Matthew P. McAllister and Joseph Turow, "New Media and the Commercial Sphere: Two Intersecting Trends, Five Categories of Concern," *Journal of Broadcasting and Electronic Media* 46:4 (2002): 505–514.
4. Toni Fitzgerald, "Ad Clutter Dips on Broadcast Nets," *Media Life*, 30 April 2007.
5. David Karr, "For the Rich, Magazines Fat on Ads," *The New York Times*, 1 October 2007, p. C1.
6. Frank Rose, "How Madison Avenue is Wasting Millions on a Deserted Second Life," *Wired*, 24 July 2007 (www.wired.com/techbiz/media/magazine/15-08/ff_sheep?currentPage=1).

7. Jim Spaeth, "A Day in the Media Life," *Media*, October 2005, p. 48.

8. Joe Mandese, "Hitting the Wall," *Media*, October 2005, p. 29.

9. Matthew Creamer, "Caught in the Clutter Crossfire: Your Brand," *Advertising Age*, 2 April 2007, p. 1

10. www.businessweek.com/magazine/content/01_31/b37430001.htm.

11. Barbara Barbieri McGrath and Roger Glass, *The M&M's Brand Counting Book* (Watertown, MA: Charlesbridge Publishers, July 2002).

12. Sut Jhally, in *The Ad and the Ego,* video documentary, Parallax Pictures, Inc., 1997.

13. Laura Petrecca, "Amateur Advertisers Get a Chance; Companies Pick Up Ads Made by Novices and Regular Old Customers," *USA Today*, 28 March 2006, p. 2B.

14. *The Public Mind: Consuming Images*, PBS documentary with Bill Moyers, 1989.

15. Ibid.

16. Genetics & IVF Institute, advertisement, "Over 40 and Thinking of Having a Baby?" *The New York Times*, 30 September 2007, p. 18S.

17. David F. Noble., "Technology and the Commodification of Higher Education," *Monthly Review*, March 2002.

18. Jane Deery, "Reality Television as Advertainment," *Popular Communication* 2:1 (2004): 1–20.

19. Nato Thompson, "The Flip Side to the Commodification of Revolution: A Critique of the Activist Scene," *Journal of Aesthetics and Protest* (www.infoshop.org/inews/article.php?story=20070831101802403). See also, Thomas Frank, "Why Johnny Can't Dissent," in *Commodify Your Dissent: Salvos from the Baffler* (New York: W. W. Norton: 1997) and Joseph Heath and Andrew Potter, *Nation of Rebels: Why Counterculture Became Consumer Culture* (New York: HarperCollins, 2004).

20. Brooke Capps, "The Reserved Ruler of In-Your-Face Marketing," *Advertising Age*, 5 March 2007, p. 12.

21. Ibid.

22. Jay Conrad Levinson, *Guerrilla Marketing*, 4th ed., *Easy and Inexpensive Strategies for Making Big Profits from Your Small Business* (Boston: Houghton Mifflin, 2007).

23. http://blog.guerrillacomm.com/.

24. Ibid.

25. Curtis Rush, "Empty Fridges Land in Strange Places to Nourish Support for Food Drive," *The Toronto Star*, 22 September 2006, p. A10.

26. Christine Harold, *Our Space: Resisting the Corporate Control of Culture* (Minneapolis, MN: University of Minnesota Press, 2007), p. viii.

27. Brooke Capps, "The Reserved Ruler of In-Your-Face Marketing," *Advertising Age*, 5 March 2007, p. 12.

28. www.wemarket4u.net/fatfoe.

29. David Kesmodel and John R. Wilke, "Whole Foods CEO used alias on Web forums; Alter ego's postings on Yahoo stock forums cited in lawsuit looking to block acquisition of Wild Oats Markets," *Wall Street Journal*, 12 July 2007, p. B-11.

30. www.entertainmentopia.com/scripts/displayGame.php?id=13.

31. Michael Learmonth, "Turner Pays in Boston," *Daily Variety*, 6 February 2007, p. 4.

32. Steve Bailey, "Laughing to the Bank," *The Boston Globe*, 2 February 2007, p. C-1.

33. Ibid.

34. www.metropolismag.com/cda/story.php?artid=2557

35. Juliet B. Schor, *Born to Buy* (New York: Scribner, 2004), p. 85.

36. www.alloymarketing.com.

37. www.channelone.com.

38. Schor, *Born to Buy*, p. 87.

39. http://commercialalert.org.

40. Ibid.

41. "Controversial Ad-Supported In-School News Network Might Be an Idea Whose Time Has Come and Gone," *Advertising Age*, 16 July 2007.

42. www.commercialexploitation.com/.

43. Brian Steinberg, "CW's New Mind Candy: 'Gossip Girl,' " *Advertising Age*, 17 September 2007.

44. Debra Kaufman, "Channel One Serious About News for Kids: Organization's Critics Don't Affect Strategy for Good Journalism," *Television Week*, 22 May 2006.

45. Ibid.

46. Erica Weintraub Austin, Yi-Chen Chen, Bruce E. Pinkleton, and Jessie Quintero Johnson, "Benefits and Costs of Channel One in a Middle School Setting and the Role of Media-Literacy Training," *Pediatrics: Official Journal of the American Academy of Pediatrics* 117:3, (March 2006): e432.

47. Derrick Z. Jackson, "Listen Up: No Radio," *The Boston Globe*, 10 June 2006.

48. www.channelone.com.

49. www.ibiblio.org/commercialfree/channelone.html.

50. See "What's on Channel One," Center for Commercial Free Public Education, www.corpwatch.org/article.php?id=888.

51. Schor, *Born to Buy*, p. 90.

52. Anna Wilde Mathews and Stephanie Kang, "Media Industry Helped Drug Firms Fight Ad Restraints," *The Wall Street Journal*, 21 September 2007.

53. www.commercialalert.org, petition to sign.

54. Ira Teinowitz, "Stage Set for Senate to Shackle DTC Advertisers," *Advertising Age*, 26 February 2007, p. 43.

55. Ira Teinowitz, "House Approves FDA Bill that Leaves Out Ad urbs," *Advertising Age*, 19 September 2007, p. 1.

56. "Direct-to-Consumer Drug Ads Booming Despite Criticism," *Forbes*, 15 August 2007 (www.forbes.com/health/feeds/hscout/2007/08/15/hscout607345.html).

57. www.nytimes.com/2008/02/07/business/media/07jarvik.html?ref=todayspaper

58. Julie M. Donohue, Marisa Cevasco, and Meredith B. Rosenthal, "A Decade of Direct-to-Consumer Advertising of Prescription Drugs," *New England Journal of Medicine* 357:7 (August 2007): 673.

59. Ibid.

60. Wendy Macias and Liza Stavchansky Lewis, "Sex, Drugs and the Evening News: DTC Pharmaceutical Drug Advertising," *Issues in American Advertising: Sex, Politics, and Viral Videos*, 2nd ed., Tom Reichert, ed. (Chicago: Copy Workshop, forthcoming).

61. Donohue, Cevasco, and Rosenthal, "A Decade of Direct-to-Consumer Advertising."

62. "Regulatory Actions; 10th Annual National Survey on Consumer Reaction to DTC Pharmaceutical Advertising Reveals #1 Action Taken After Seeing DTC Ad: Information Seeking," *Drug Week*, 1 June 2007.

63. Rita Rubin, "Analysis: Prescription Drug Ads Leave Out Risks, Alternatives; Consumers Urged to Be Skeptical," *USA Today*, 30 January 2007, p. 7D; Ira Teinowitz, "Stage Set for Senate to Shackle DTC Advertisers; Bill Would Allow Ban of Up to 2 Years and Require FDA to Pre-Clear Drug Ads," *Advertising Age*, 26 February 2007, p. 43.

64. B. Mintzes, *An Assessment of the Health System Impacts of Direct-to-Consumer Advertising of Prescription Medications*, Vol. II: *Literature Review*. Retrieved from www.chspr.ubc.ca/hpru/pdf/dtca-v2-litreview.pdf.

65. Jisu Huh and Rita Langteau, "Presumed Influence of Direct-to-Consumer (DTC) Prescription Drug Advertising on Patients," *Journal of Advertising* 36:3 (Fall 2007).
66. Donohue, Cevasco, and Rosenthal, "A Decade of Direct-to-Consumer Advertising."
67. "Cegedim Dendrite; Direct-to-Consumer (DTC) Marketing for U.S. Prescription Drugs Moves Online, Cegedim Dendrite Survey Says," *Biotech Business Week*, 30 July 2007, p. 227
68. Asher Meir, "Marketing Drugs to Consumers. Prescription Drugs are Rapidly Becoming 'Consumer Products,' " *The Jerusalem Post*, 13 April 2007, p. 17.
69. Jonathan M. Metzl, "If Direct-to-Consumer Advertisements Come to Europe: Lessons from the USA," *The Lancet* 369:9562 (February 2007–March 2007).
70. Lawrence C. Rubin, "Merchandising Madness: Pill, Promises, and Better Living Through Chemistry," *Journal of Popular Culture* 38:2 (2004): 370.
71. James F. Tracy, "Between Discourse and Being: The Commodification of Pharmaceuticals in Late Capitalism," *The Communication Review* 7:15 (2004).
72. Silverstein, quoted in Tracy, ibid.
73. Metzl, "If Direct-to-Consumer Advertisements Come to Europe."
74. The Gallup Poll, Annual Update: Americans Rate Business and Industry Sectors, 6 September 2007, (www.galluppoll.com/content/default.aspx?ci=28615&version=p), 7/10/2007.
75. Quoted in Rubin, "Analysis: Prescription Drug Ads Leave Out Risks."
76. Martin Glenn, "There's a Simple Rationale Behind Ties with Causes," *Marketing* (UK), 20 March 2003, p. 18.
77. Theodore Levitt, "The Dangers of Social Responsibility," *Harvard Business Review* (September/October 1958): 42.
78. www.coneinc.com.
79. www.causemarketingforum.com.
80. Philip Kotler and Nancy Lee, *Corporate Social Responsibility: Doing the Most Good for Your Company and Your Cause* (Hoboken, NJ: Wiley, 2005).
81. Ron Nixon, "Little Green for (Red): How Much Profit Trickles Down to the Mission?" *The New York Times*, 6 February 2008, p. C-1.
82. Rob Walker, "Live Strong Bracelet," *The New York Times Magazine*, 29 August 2004.
83. C. Sweeney, "The Latest in Fitness: Millions for Charity," *The New York Times*, 7 July 2005, p. E1.
84. Glenn, "There's a Simple Rationale."
85. Levitt, "The Dangers of Social Responsibility."
86. Nara Schoenberg, "BUY(LESS) Targets Cause-Related Marketing," *The Chicago Tribune*, 23 March 2007.

Advertising in an Image-Based Culture

In any case, it is surely no longer possible to understand the media as somehow "out-side" society or an adjunct to larger concerns.[1]

Today, it seems it is becoming increasingly difficult, and perhaps impossible, to separate the media in their varied formats and their apparently endless possibilities in any meaningful way from thoughts, behavior, relationships, values, and ideas that *are* culture. Hence we no longer talk of media *and* culture but instead of *media culture*. In this context, the question of whether advertising is a mirror, passively reflecting society and its values, or a shaper, actively constructing those social values is rendered moot. Advertising both *defines* and *is defined by* culture, and is perhaps best characterized as a zerrspiegel, a fun house mirror, reflective but rich with distortion. Consider Michael Schudson's observation in his book, *Advertising*, *The Uneasy Persuasion*:

> The picture of life that ads parade before us is familiar, scenes of life as in some sense we know it, or would like to know it.
>
> Advertising picks up and represents values already in our culture. But the values, however deep or widespread, are not the only ones people have to aspire to, and the pervasiveness of advertising makes us forget this.
>
> Advertising picks up some of the things we hold dear and represents them to us as all of what we value.[2]

Historically, advertising was once primarily informational in both its purpose and content. Advertising told consumers about product features. Our culture gradually evolved from a production-based to a consumption-based culture. Advertising became what historian Rick Pollay has identified as transformational. That is, it became focused upon consumer benefits rather than product characteristics, often trying to influence "attitudes . . . toward brands, expenditure patterns, lifestyles, techniques for achieving personal and social success, and so forth."[3] Today, our media culture increasingly is image-based. As Bill Moyers noted in *Consuming Images*, "Mass-produced images fill our everyday world and our innermost lives, shape our private thoughts and our public mind."[4] The implications are nothing short of phenomenal, for images challenge our traditional ways of deciding whether an argument is true or false. A short discussion by Neil Postman, drawn from the Moyers' documentary, serves to illustrate:

> We have recognized, reputable ways of judging the truth or falsity of statements. We have means, to use a phrase from Bertram Russell, defenses against the seduction of eloquence. But, we know more or less how to do that, how to analyze what people say, how to measure the truth or falsity of something.
>
> Now let's take a McDonald's commercial. We see a young father taking his six-year-old daughter into McDonald's, and they're eating a cheeseburger, and they're ecstatic.
>
> Is that true or false?
>
> Is the image true or false?
>
> Well, the words don't seem to apply to that sort of thing. It just is no way to assess that in the way we assess statements, linguistic utterances.
>
> So we now build up a whole world of imagery where basically we are out of the realm of logic and perhaps into the realm of aesthetics. You either like Ronald Reagan or you don't. You either like McDonald's or you don't. But you can't talk about their truth or falsity. So we now need a different kind of defense against the seduction of eloquence.[5]

In an image-based media culture, the commodity has relinquished its importance to the brand. And, what of the advertising images? They, indeed, are the commodities in which we traffic.[6]

The cases in this chapter introduce you to some of the ethical dilemmas encountered and the questions raised with regard to our marketplace of images. "Making the Same Different" addresses the question at the heart of many branding activities: Is it appropriate to "manufacture" difference between parity products? "Stereotyping Attitude" explores the construction and perpetuation of stereotypes hidden behind strategies of humor. "We All Know Her: The Unattainable Ideal" examines advertising imagery that despite widespread criticism and sometimes legal challenges persists in the celebration of an ideal feminine beauty that is unattainable to the majority of women. "Real Beauty: Responsible Images?" looks at the Dove Campaign for Real Beauty as a social advocacy effort. "Pitching Sex Appeal" looks again at oppressive and stereotypical images, this time in Axe commercials. We are asked to consider the frequently articulated defense/casual dismissal: "You [the offended detractor] aren't in the target audience." The last case, "A Responsible Parent," explores the situation of Unilever, the parent company of the brands in the two previous cases, Dove and Axe. Is the contradiction evident in the identities created for those two brands defensible?

27 Making the Same Different: Branding

It got me thinking about the premium bottled-water category, and what a challenge it must be to break through with a new brand. This is the one category in which the product itself is an internationally recognized commodity that is colorless, tasteless, and (hopefully) odorless. It is a brand category that only mad dogs and marketers would venture to enter.[7]

continued

Bottled water has become the indispensable prop in our lives and our culture. It starts the day in lunch boxes; it goes to every meeting, lecture hall, and soccer match; it's in our cubicles at work; in the cup holder of the treadmill at the gym; and it's rattling around half-finished on the floor of every minivan in America.[8]

Why Do People Drink Bottled Water?

"It's better for you."
Is it?

- Big-city tap water is not allowed to contain fecal coliform bacteria and must be tested for these pathogens 100 times or more a month. Bottled-water plants face no such regulation from the Food and Drug Administration (FDA) and are required to test just once weekly.[9]
- The vast majority of the country's 55,000 municipal water systems are subject to—and every three months must pass—more rigorous quality standards than water bottlers.[10]
- According to CNN, Fiji brand water ran an ad with the copy, "The Label Says Fiji Because It's Not Bottled in Cleveland." A resulting analysis of Fiji water, commissioned in retaliation by Cleveland officials, found 6.3 micrograms of arsenic per liter in Fiji water as compared with none in Cleveland local tap water. (Fiji subsequently reported that its own analyses identified fewer than 2 micrograms per liter.)

"It tastes better."
Does it?

- In May 2001, *Good Morning America* conducted an informal blind taste test among its crew members. The results indicated that New York City's tap water, achieving 45 percent of the vote, outperformed Poland Springs (24 percent), O-2 (19 percent), and Evian (12 percent) by merit of its taste.
- In the same year, a Yorkshire study found that 60 percent of the 2800 people surveyed could not differentiate between their local tap water and the bottled varieties (Scientific American).
- More recently, and arguably a more pointed example of social commentary, an episode of *Penn & Teller: Bullshit* conducted its own experiment. The show, a documetary-style television series on Showtime, which prides itself on identifying and exposing popular sociopolitical misconceptions, aired an episode called "Bottled Water" in March 2003. The episode introduces an actor posing as a "water steward" at a fancy restaurant, offering a menu of fake bottled waters for unsuspecting diners. As each table orders its waters, commenting on the unique freshness of one or the sweetness of the next, the screen juxtaposes images of the wine steward filling each and every bottle with water from the garden hose.

If evidence suggests that bottled water is neither better for you nor better tasting than tap water, why are we, as consumers, only too happy to spend between $1 and $40 per bottle for a resource that costs us less than 1 cent per gallon from the tap? The answer, as you've likely guessed, has to do with marketing, branding, and the construction of image. Aquafina, Pepsi's contribution to the bottled-water industry and America's best-selling brand, and the water we pour from our tap have something in common: their source. Both

Aquafina and Dasani, ranked first and second, respectively, in the industry, start with water from public sources (tap water) and "refine" it using the same reverse-osmosis techniques to which the water already has been subjected. The Environmental Protection Agency's standards for safe drinking water require that. "So imagine the corporate euphoria back in 1994 when the brain trust at PepsiCo became certain that consumers would buy just plain water for approximately the same price as Pepsi."[11]

Advertisers for the bottled-water industry face a challenge that parallels that of any number of industries selling parity products: How do we make the same seem different? Our consideration, of course, is whether it is right to imply differences where, for all intents and purposes, there are none.

"Aquafina. Purity Guaranteed."

"Dasani. Make Your Mouth Water."

"Evian. Live Young."

If these slogans are familiar, then copywriters somewhere are patting themselves on the back for a job well done. They've differentiated each of their brands from the competition. In short, they developed brand equity. Some companies, for example, Nestle Waters, have the even greater challenge of distinguishing numerous brands within the same corporation; Deer Park, Zephyrhills, Poland Springs, Perrier, and San Pellegrino are all Nestle waters, branded strategically to establish individual identities within consumers' minds. As you also may have guessed (or experienced), these brand identities correspond with the prices that consumers are willing to pay for them.

In a market of virtually indistinguishable products, our job as advertisers is to create the illusion of a difference where there may or may not be one. What are the ramifications of this process? In terms of bottled water a major consideration is the argument that advertising efforts for bottled water detract from the appeal of tap water. Remember, the taste and quality for many consumers are identical (not to mention more affordable). Additionally, groups such as Corporate Accountability International argue the inherent contradiction in emphasizing the health benefits of a product whose bottling and distribution endanger the environment.[12]

A writer in *The New York Times* noted: politicians are banning the bottles, and restaurateurs are wiping them off their menus, calling attention to the ecological costs of moving millions of bottles around the world and around the United States—not to mention disposing of all those containers.[13]

Still, bottled water sales were an estimated $16 billion in 2007; we drink a billion bottles of water a week.[14]   ∎

Let's consider more generally the dilemmas characteristic of nearly all parity product advertising. According to marketing scholar David Aaker, the creation of differentiated brands is a distinguishing characteristic of modern marketing. He notes:

Unique brand associations have been established using product attributes, names, packages, distribution strategies, and advertising. The idea has been to move beyond commodities to branded products—to reduce the primacy of price upon the purchase decision, and accentuate the bases of differentiation.[15]

In the process of constructing a brand, then, we are responsible for every detail that affects consumers' perceptions, from the font to the graphics in the packaging, from the copy to the placement of ads, and even in the careful distribution of a product. In so doing, we create the perception of a product that is truly superior when we know as well as its manufacturers know that it is, in essence, interchangeable with most other products in its category. The ethical question we must ask ourselves is a fundamental one: Regardless of whether it *can* be done, is it wrong to imply differences where, functionally, there are none?

In answering this question, we might start by noting that we are all creatures of symbolic meaning and are, therefore, not ill-served by communications that suggest more than they may ultimately deliver. We may in fact feel more "comfortable" with one virtually identical brand over another—such as Dasani over tap water because of the symbolic content that makes a difference for us. So, we could contend that this is an ethical issue without a constituency: If customers in fact want to perceive their brand choices as different, for whatever reason, so be it.

In justifying our efforts, we also might argue that the consumers are aware of the parity in many of their choices. But can we be sure? Would it make a difference if people knew that certain brands were virtually identical in performance? Perhaps. But if knowledge of the parity nature of some products *would* make a difference in purchasing decisions, then the comfortable utilitarian justification of the greatest good for the greatest number is weakened.

What other justifications for making the same different are available to us? Certainly the conviction that moral duty is owed specifically to the client ("It is my job to establish a difference."), or, more generally to advertising as a communication form ("That's the way the game is played.") is an option. And, perhaps, there could be an expanded vision of utilitarianism—in this context to contend that—beyond purchase consequences—the greatest good for the greatest number is served through allowing individuals freedom of choice, including the freedom to choose to pay more for a functionally identical product if it suits their particular needs.

Certainly making the same different is legal. Adopting a viewpoint that what is good is what is legal, we might choose to continue business as usual. However, if we recognize that what is legal is not necessarily what is good for the public, then what?

28 Stereotyping Attitude

We never single out any one group to poke fun at. We poke fun at everybody, from women, to flight attendants, to baggage handlers, to football coaches, to Irish Americans, to snow skiers. There's really no group we haven't teased."[16]

Abercrombie & Fitch was founded in 1892 as a small New York City outdoors store, and over the years counted among its patrons Amelia Earhart, Teddy Roosevelt, Katharine Hepburn, and Cole Porter. The Limited, which purchased the store in 1988, set about changing the store's image into the casual, lifestyle brand the store retains today. During that process, Abercrombie & Fitch earned something of a reputation for its risqué promotions and catalogues. Morley Safer opened a 2004 *60 Minutes* segment with the observation that "the image of Abercrombie is now party-loving jocks and barenaked ladies living fantasy lives."[17] Though the company continues to nurture this risqué image—recently customers were met at the store's entrance by shirtless males—its stores have become something of a wardrobe mecca for the teenage segment.

The statement that opened this case was made by Hampton Carney, an Abercrombie & Fitch spokesperson in response to protests of the company's "attitude" T-shirts.

Let's consider these examples of Abercrombie verbiage on women's T-shirts:

Muck Fe

Who Needs Brains When You Have These?

Give Me Something to Scream About

I Had a Nightmare I Was a Brunette

All Men Like Tig Old Bitties

What are the implications and ramifications of these messages? In October 2005, the Women and Girls' Foundation of Southwest Pennsylvania organized a national "girlcott" in response to this particular line of T-shirts. This action was reminiscent of a similar protest staged three years earlier in response to a line of Abercrombie T-shirts that "poked fun" at Asian-Americans using caricatured faces with slanted eyes, and conical rice-paddy hats and slogans such as these:

Wong Brothers Laundry Service—2 Wongs Can Make It White

Abercrombie and Fitch Buddha Bash—Get Your Buddha on the Floor

You Love Long Time

Eat In—Wok Out

Both protests resulted in removal of certain T-shirts from Abercrombie & Fitch stores, but the official statements released by the company reflected neither remorse, nor acknowledgment of any wrongdoing. Indicating surprise at the reactions, Carney said, "We personally thought Asians would love this T-shirt." He deflected fault when he took a rather "aren't you overreacting?" response. "We poke fun at everybody;" it's as though a bully who assaults the whole class is somehow less culpable than one who singles out individual members.[18]   ∎

In November 2004, Abercrombie agreed to pay $50 million to settle a class-action lawsuit brought by nine former employees who claimed to have been fired or hidden because they didn't fit the "Abercrombie look" enough to work with the public. The settlement applies to women, African Americans, Asian Americans, and Latinos.[19] Given this, one might question the soundness of the decision to produce the T-shirts from a purely business perspective.

But, let's consider for a moment that Abercrombie's assertion is correct, that the T-shirts are, in fact, attempts at humor and not intentionally offensive. Who benefits from this humor? Stereotypes, used even in jest, perpetuate existing power structures and systems of oppression. By portraying girls and women as little more than a collection of body parts or as enthusiastically incompetent (as in "You Better Make More Than I Can Spend"), these T-shirts contribute to a climate in which women are not taken seriously, and perhaps more destructive, women and girls do not take themselves seriously. Today, when women account for over 55 percent of students in American undergraduate programs, should these messages not seem a bit out of place?

Abercrombie's racially stereotyped T-shirts should raise the same questions (as should any advertising that relies on stereotypes, particularly offensive stereotypes, for effectiveness). One Asian American protester noted of the T-shirts:

> It's really misleading as to what Asian people are. . . . The stereotypes they depict are more than a century old. You're seeing laundry service. You're seeing basically an entire religion and philosophy being trivialized.[20]

A journalist for Asian-focused magazine *Monolid* asked more pointedly: "who benefits, who gets empowerment, from these kinds of images? It denigrates Asian men."[21]

Who indeed? In other words, "but it's funny" is a weak argument to offer in exchange for ethical decision making. Similarly, creating humor for one group at the expense of another (or, in this case, several others) hardly seems sound ethical strategy.

Let's examine this "equal opportunity offensiveness" defense by looking at Abercrombie's T-shirt line for men. If women are objectified and Asian Americans are stereotyped as launderers and caricatures, what does Abercrombie have to say about its mainstream target, white men? The company does, after all, purportedly "poke fun at everybody?" Let's take a look:

> My Lucky Number is 3. Bring a Friend.
>
> Freshmen. I Get Older, They Stay The Same Age.
>
> I'll Make You a Star of the Walk of Shame.
>
> I'd Do Me.

Not surprisingly. These messages, like most advertising images in America, reinforce particular notions of masculinity and femininity. They celebrate masculine sexual prowess and trivialize the role of women as interchangeable parts in the masculine pursuit. T-shirts don't "poke fun" at men as Carney suggested, but rather serve to elevate their status as the group in control.

What then are ethical dimensions here? Starting with a traditional marketing defense of utilitarianism, the obvious retort is: "But people buy these shirts." This could be viewed as at least indirect approval of the advertising message. A Kantian approach might flounder on the question of whether *all* mass media representations are not likely to be offensive to at least some, thus essentially precluding the very essence of advertising as a communication form which relies on stereotypes for quick communication.

One might ask: do cultural icons and trendsetters like Abercrombie & Fitch have an obligation to society to create and disseminate more socially responsible messages? While Abercrombie & Fitch defends its efforts as being appropriate for the intended target audience of college-age students, the fact remains that younger consumers are hopelessly devoted to the brand. Jennifer Black, a retail and apparel analyst, postulates that Abercrombie "owns the most powerful stable of brands targeting the teen customer."[22] Are the ads, in this case T-shirts, appropriate for a *targeted* audience?

The difference between a billboard and a T-shirt that reads "Muck Fe" is negligible. In either case, the message comes across loud and clear to whomever the message reaches.

---

29 We All Know Her: The Unattainable Ideal

It's like the frog in the water: If you slowly turn up the heat, it doesn't know it's being boiled to death. After a while, a size 0 starts to seem normal, not cadaverous.[23]

As advertisers, we are responsible for the creation of the estimated thousands of ads to which the average American is exposed daily. Yet, for all our pride in "pushing the envelope" and "cutting-edge" creativity and innovation, the images we produce and distribute are strikingly and alarmingly similar. This is especially obvious in the portrayals of women and girls. The world of advertising is populated by women who no longer resemble even their iconic predecessors, much less the average American women to whom they represent an ideal. In fact, in a culture of Botox, plastic surgery, and digital re-touching, this ideal not only may be lofty, but also is likely to be distinctly unattainable for most women, unattainable in any number of ways. She is most likely young; a *The New York Times* writer recently noted, we are in the midst of a trend toward "the rebranding of aging from biological inevitability to outmoded lifestyle option."[24] She is almost inevitably white, particularly on the runway. "Weird," a fashion designer said looking at photos of potential models, "They're all the same."[25] "The same" meant pale, thin, with dirty blonde hair. Of all the features of the ideal, it is her downsizing that most consistently has been the target of concern, and at times, outrage.

"When the models themselves were famous, designers would gladly alter a dress to fit the girl. But when the models are generically interchangeable, it's easier to find a girl who fits the dress," reads one *Vogue* article.[26] These "interchangeable" girls comprise the nameless faces of the advertising world. We pack our advertisements with their emaciated,

continued

vacant imagery, so ubiquitous now that it takes on the semblance of normalcy. They are an entire society, narrowly constructed to represent our notions of perfection—in silence—on the runway and in our advertisements. In repeatedly casting women (and in many cases, girls) who meet an ever-shrinking standard of beauty, we reinforce practices and mindsets that are damaging to those who look to the ideal for a suggestion of what it is to "be beautiful," and are dangerous to the models.

- In August 2006, Luisel Ramos, a young Uruguayan model, collapsed on the runway and died of heart failure, assumed to have been the result of anorexia nervosa.[27]
- Six months later, her sister Eliana, also a model, died of a heart attack associated with malnutrition.[28]
- In November 2006, Ana Carolina Reston, a Brazilian model weighing eighty-eight pounds, at five feet, eight inches, died of complications of anorexia.[29]

The ensuing "ultraskinny-model uproar" began an industry-wide conversation.

- One month after the death of Luisel Ramos, Spain adopted a body mass index (BMI) minimum of 18 for its runway models at the 2006 Fashion Week in Madrid. Thirty percent of the women who participated in the previous year's event were turned away as a result of the new standard[30]
- Also in 2006, India's health minister objected to the presence of "waif-like" models on its catwalks, and Israeli retailers opted to exclude "overly thin" models from their ads.[31]
- In 2007, encouraged by the positive feedback to its "Campaign for Real Beauty," Unilever banned size zero models from its advertisements. The company said it wished to take into account "the possible negative health effects that could occur should people pursue unhealthy or excessive slimness."[32]

The Council of Fashion Designers of America also issued guidelines; Anna Bulik, director of the University of North Carolina eating-disorders program, criticized the document as "an anemic response."[33] A recent article entitled "The Vanishing Point," focused on the downsizing of male models ("chicken-chested, hollow-cheeked, and undernourished"), but commented about female models, noting: " . . . it's safe to say that they [female models] remain as waiflike as ever."[34]

If the women of fashion are pushing their physical limits to the point of death in order to maintain a standard that the public simultaneously spurns and reveres (think Nicole Richie), why do the fashion and advertising industries perpetuate the standard?   ∎

In addition to the fashion industry in general, many of the critiques are directed toward advertisers. So, what is the advertising industry to do? One might find the issue easy to dismiss as an offense residing within the fashion industry. Still, is it not our industry that takes the remote model and repackages her for mass-distribution? Walking down the street, would Kate Moss have the same effect on women if advertising had not elevated her to the "Face of Calvin Klein?"

Another perspective often offered in defense of advertising—and the media as a whole—argues that our messages are merely the reflections of existing cultural beliefs and values. The images we see in advertising then are not surprising in a culture that celebrates beauty and its frequent companion, youth, almost to the point of obsession; our role as the "mirror" (as opposed to the "shaper") is, in essence, benign. If, on the other hand, we acknowledge that the efficacy of our work as advertisers relies at least in part on our ability to shape attitudes in a direction favorable to our client, then might we not also assume some degree of responsibility for the standards that we transmit and so, reinforce?

The appeal of an advertised good lies in the perception that it has the ability to enhance an existence. To convey that potential, advertisers draw from a narrow pool of images that appear exceptional when juxtaposed with an average American's life. They choose to use thin models because they assume that they will be regarded by their target audience as attractive either directly (e.g., choose our diet plan and look like this) or indirectly (e.g., Sarah Jessica Parker uses this product and she's an appealing celebrity). Given the ambiguity of advertising effects, they would generally receive no clear confirmation that these assumptions were in fact correct, so these advertisers are probably choosing to conform to an unwritten group norm—the assumption that slim is better than not slim. And, in so doing, advertising perpetuates a standard that exists only within the borders of the ads themselves. Advertisers are responsible for the creation of that standard, so are they likewise responsible for the consequences associated with promoting an unattainable ideal?

Of course, none of this would be an issue if women demonstrably resisted the "waif look" and punished advertisers who promoted it. They could send their message directly by protest to the advertisers or indirectly by withdrawing patronage, ideally telling the advertiser why they've done so.

On a collective and an individual level, advertisers have available to them a number of ways to confront this ethical dilemma. They may opt to do one of the following:

1. "Pass the buck" to another industry, ultimately maintaining the status quo of the current advertising industry.
2. Blame society for its own superficial standards, prompting society to shift its values before advertising can reflect them more realistically.
3. Maintain the standards but publicize the unnatural and/or unhealthy circumstances surrounding the marketing of these ideal women. This option also allows advertisers to continue down their current path but introduces a disconnect between the coveted images in advertising and the reality of their attainability.
4. Accept responsibility for perpetuating unhealthy practices and thought patterns, thereby paving the way for a new set of standards. The danger in this option is, of course, that any individual actor in an industry comprised of individual actors renders himself or herself vulnerable to professional criticism, public opposition, and societal resistance.

If we agree that this is an issue in which we justifiably may be viewed to play a role, do we have a responsibility to make a change? And will a society—even one that acknowledges a problem—ultimately be receptive to that change? Where might *you* stand?

30 Real Beauty: Responsible Images?

The Dove campaign lambasts traditional women's toiletries marketing for promoting unreal images of beauty.[35]

As if women's "reality" depended on their body shape or size. This campaign is a new shade of lipstick on the same old pig.[36]

In 2004, Dove, a company that had long viewed the "everyday woman" as its core user, launched one of the most talked-about campaigns in years—The Dove Campaign for Real Beauty.[37] According to the company, the global campaign was designed to "challenge today's one dimensional and restrictive view of beauty by showing how beauty can come in many different shapes and sizes."[38] It was a risky strategy. Instead of the superthin models that are the sine qua non of the fashion and cosmetics industries, Dove used "ordinary" women. Six women of varying sizes and ethnicities wearing nothing but their white cotton underwear and sporting a good deal of attitude appeared in billboards and print ads for Dove firming products. Here, then, were real women, unadorned and unretouched, not pouting, not provocatively posed; these women were not objects, but instead, they were laughing and having fun.

The shock value was enormous, and the campaign generated mounds of publicity. Initial reactions were wide-ranging. A male staff reporter from *The Chicago Sun-Times* wrote, "Really, the only time I want to see a thigh that big is in a bucket with breadcrumbs."[39] Others pointed out the irony of telling women to be happy with who they are while selling them firming products. Skeptics doubted the longevity of the strategy, ominously forecasting boredom and the danger of becoming "the brand for fat girls."[40] Dove claimed to have received a flood of e-mails saying, "Yes. Yes." "Thank you." And sales for firming products skyrocketed, growing by 700 percent after the campaign.[41]

The Dove Campaign for Real Beauty was a social advocacy effort that aimed "to change the status quo and offer in its place a broader, healthier, and more democratic view of beauty."[42] Toward this end, the company established a website (www.campaignforrealbeauty.com) with a discussion board and an opportunity to vote: gray or gorgeous? wrinkled or wonderful? oversized or outstanding? The Dove Fund for Self-Esteem includes a number of programs all over the world. Dove expanded the campaign to younger girls via the Uniquely Me! Program with the Girl Scouts. The company endowed the Program for Aesthetics and Well-Being at Harvard to explore representations of women in popular culture and the effects of those representations.

The Campaign for Real Beauty won the 2006 Best of Silver Anvil Award from the Public Relations Society of America. In presenting the award, Dave M. Imre noted, "This campaign effectively challenged hundreds of thousands of men and women worldwide to rethink their ideas of what beauty really is."[43]   ■

The Dove Campaign for Real Beauty (which now has produced two viral videos, *Evolution* and *Onslaught*, and has launched a Pro-Age line featuring Annie Leibovitz photos of "grandmothers in the buff," which garnered publicity when it was rejected by television networks[44]) is not without its critics. Perhaps a victim of its own publicity, detractors scrutinize the motivation for the campaign as well as the ads themselves. A sampling of their concerns:

- Can a business, which exists solely to make money, sincerely promote social change, or is it simply coopting a broader social agenda as a business strategy?
- If beauty is inherent in the person, why use the product?
- Can you sell a beauty product without playing on women's insecurities?
- Real cannot be understood except in context of what it stands in opposition to, that is, the ideal, and so it serves as subtle reinforcement of the very beauty myth it seeks to negate.[45]

More recently, underlying corporate (Unilever) contradictions began to surface. One writer asked, "Can a company that owns and markets both Axe and Dove be considered sincere in either effort?"[46] Advocates stand firm in their support, suggesting that women get genuine benefit from the images regardless of the motivation.

What do you think?

1. Is the Campaign for Real Beauty simply a selling strategy, coopting social advocacy for the purpose of increased sales?
2. Is the campaign a sincere social advocacy effort?
3. It is possible for the campaign to be both social advocacy and marketing?

Are our expectations for Dove too high? Linda Scott once wrote that she thought for many, feminist thought remained chained to anti-market prejudice. She ponders, as we might:

> How is one to act as a feminist while working for an ad agency? . . . Today's feminism is so unbendingly negative in its approach to market activity that steps taken to present positive imagery in ads . . . are sweepingly dismissed.[47]

31 Pitching Sex Appeal

It's a simple sales pitch, really: Hey, dude, spray Axe deodorant all over your body, and you will become irresistible to beautiful young women. But what Russell Taylor, the Axe vice-president, proposed doing with that straightforward idea was ambitious. He wanted to turn it into a truly global marketing message, one that would work in all seventy-five countries where Unilever sells Axe. The solution that came back from advertising agency BBH was to invent a new phrase that guys would hear as an international expression of lust— a female wolf whistle heard 'round the world.

continued

The moment of truth came on February 27, 2006, at a high-pressure meeting in a spacious conference room at BBH's London offices. . . . a woman's sexy voice snarled out of a loudspeaker: "Bom Chicka Wah Wah." She made a sound like an electric guitar from a 1970's funk band. Taylor laughed out loud. He was sold.[48]

Axe, originally launched as Lynx in France in 1983, was introduced to the United States in 2002 as a body deodorant, a new category in men's grooming. Givhan, writing in *The Washington Post*, playfully describes it as "cologne with stink-prevention properties."[49] The brand spent more than $100 million advertising in the first two years—not talking about sweat or odor but about "the Axe effect": "Wear Axe, get the girls. Not just one girl, but many, many girls."[50] And tell the story with outlandish, provocative, sexual images and innuendo.[51]

Mintel, a marketing research firm, identifies the advertising as "having an absurdist bent . . . featuring hundreds of semi-clothed women clawing their way to men using Axe body spray."[52] *Adweek*'s advertising critic, Barbara Lippert, described it as "dead-on for its target, because it takes into account age compression (fourteen-year-olds who want to act twenty-one) and today's post-everything but still sex-saturated, *Desperate Housewives*–driven pop culture."[53] The spots shown in the United States are playful in comparison with those appearing in other countries.[54]

The campaign didn't stop with advertising. Street teams handed out thong underwear with the Axe e-mail address to young men on college campuses and slipped thongs into laundromat machines in the hope that young men would find them. Axe also sponsored singles' parties.

Initially, the target had to be educated about how to use the product, but competitors such as Tag and Old Spice Red Zone emerged, the category became familiar, and the Axe line now includes Axe Body Spray, Axe Dry, Axe Shower Gel, and Axe Deodorant. The advertising has continued to use quirky, somewhat more sexualized images. The spots arising in the "Bom Chicka Wah Wah" campaign are illustrative of these changes:

> The premise is simple. A woman is placed into an ordinary, everyday situation (i.e., a dinner party, a classroom, or a dentist office). A man walks into the room, presumably wearing the company's product. The woman immediately stops what she is doing and makes an utter fool of herself by undulating sensually and loudly singing "Bom Chicka Wah Wah" to the man. The phrase "Bom Chicka Wah Wah" is a reference to the cheesy music used in pornographic videos, and is colloquially used to imply an impending sexual encounter.[55]

Now, we get to the heart of the controversy surrounding Axe: " . . . the woman . . . makes an utter fool of herself." Let's listen in on some of the conversation:

- . . . I can't find it in me to laugh when women are shown basically as pieces of meat or as willing to drop everything to get their hands on some random man simply because he's wearing Axe.[56]
- . . . Those Axe commercials have got to take the Blue Ribbon for the "Greatest objectification of Women in U.S. Advertising."[57]
- Oh good grief! The Axe ads are fun. They're obviously outrageous and can't possibly reflect reality.[58]

- I've always taken the Axe ads as satirical. . . . Commercials for men's grooming products have long sold 'em with sex, and the notion that if men just use the advertised product they'll be irresistable [sic] to women. Axe's way-over-the-top portrayal of women literally pouncing on Axe-Using Dudes strikes me as parody. And I'm OK with that, because of course satire and parody are just a way of saying the original idea is ridiculous.[59]

Axe uses ethnographic research to "understand the Axe man and his life in the mating game, who he's about, why he does it, what gets him excited, what are his fears," and as a result, the "slightly shocking brand identity is unmistakable." Anita Larson, a spokeswoman for Unilever, claims that the campaign is a spoof, not meant to be taken literally. Axe regularly tests it campaigns with both men and women, and "they have shared that they see these ads as very clever and very funny."[60] Still, the brand was aware that it was walking a fine line; in the initial marketing efforts, Unilever hired a consultant to police their efforts. "Unilever didn't think the advertising would offend eighteen- to twenty-four-year-olds, but the company worried about what other people would say."[61]

And apparently boys like the advertising; pitching sex appeal has reinvigorated the category, and sales have soared. Axe body sprays, the brand's best-sellers, sold $85 million in the year ending March 31, 2007.   ∎

What do you think? At the broadest of levels, one might ask: Why would advertisers allow *any* ads that might offend? The advertiser might contend that if the ads were truly objectionable, the brand would be punished by failing to meet its sales goals. If people didn't buy the product, the company would do something different. Clearly, that is not the case here. Axe ads are effective, though many *do* see them as sexist, degrading to women (and maybe to men as well), hypersexualized, and inappropriate, particularly for the young teens.

The company might also respond that the approach is primarily a pragmatic one. That is, despite the fact that the brand established the category, the category is now an extremely competitive one. The company is simply "pushing the envelope" in order to get noticed among the din of the competition. The most oft-used defense is those who create the ads (and those who approve) simply feel they have a particularly acute grasp on their potential audience's likes, dislikes, values, and aspirations. Thus, while some may find the images and the premise of the ads offensive, those individuals are not likely to be in the target market, which again, by all indications, likes them for the humor and parody. And what of the increasingly common defense of "parody"? Because an execution is labeled "absurdist" or "over the top," does that excuse it from criticism?

Clearly, as comments indicate, many outside the target market do not find the ads objectionable and indeed, share in the humor of the approach. The advertiser might then simply argue that this is a matter of taste. Yet as a defense, is this not suspect, and perhaps even a forewarning of things to come? Doesn't this defense open the door to virtually any "crime" of offensiveness and denigration if we can simply dismiss our detractors? True, we are increasingly able to target niche groups, but does that not increase our responsibility rather than diminish it?

In an article entitled "The Taste Debate," adman Keith Reinhard notes that "taste is something we can't argue about because taste is a personal thing, very much a matter of individual choice."[62] Setting standards of taste is a task generally avoided by advertising trade organizations, so restraints would seem to have to come from either the advertiser or the media. Reinhard closes his essay with a quotation from Bill Bernbach:

> All of us who professionally use the mass media are shapers of society.
>
> We can vulgarize that society. We can brutalize it. Or we can help lift it to a higher level.[63]

Perhaps we are left with only the pull of social responsibility to lead us.

---

32 A Responsible Parent?

I am writing to urge you to end your sexist and degrading advertising for Axe grooming products. Axe advertising, which frequently occurs in media popular with children and teens, promotes the objectification and sexual humiliation of women. It is particularly disturbing that these ads continue to run at a time when Unilever is garnering praise for promoting the well-being of girls through its Dove Real Beauty campaign.

If you are serious about changing the toxic media environment that undermines girls' healthy development, you can start immediately by ending your own marketing for Axe.[64]

This letter to Patrick Cescau, Unilever's CEO, written by a consumer advocacy group, Campaign for a Commercial-Free Childhood,[65] brings to the fore an interesting dilemma of underlying corporate contradictions. Unilever, a large multinational company, is parent, as the letter suggests, to both Dove and to Axe, two companies/brands with diametrically opposed identities.

Dove's Campaign for Real Beauty is a break-the-mold, challenge-the-standards-of-beauty campaign that tells women and young girls that they are beautiful just the way they are and uses "real" women in its ads. Axe is notorious for its "naughty" ads, featuring "ultra-thin, hyper-sexualized women uncontrollably lusting after some dude wearing Axe."[66]

The contradiction has been smoldering in conversations about the Dove Campaign for Real Beauty for some time. Those who wondered whether it was possible for a profit-based company to promote social change, who questioned Dove's motivations, who viewed the campaign as one more marketing strategy and questioned Dove's altruism and sincerity frequently alluded to the Axe connection. As one woman noted:

> I still can't shake the feeling, though, that . . . Dove's appeal to righteous sisterhood is just another flavor of marketing. . . . Are we meant to believe that Unilever, the company that makes Dove, is a force for good? How to reconcile this notion with the ads for another Unilever product, Axe body spray, in which nearly every woman shown is a skinny fashion-mode-gorgeous nymphomaniac?[67]

Still, many felt that whatever the motivations, the Dove images were important, "a little ray of sanity in this anorexic world."[68]

Dove produced its second viral video, *Onslaught*. This video, criticizing advertising images, ended with the plea to: "Talk to your daughter, before the beauty industry does."[69] As the Campaign for a Commercial-Free Childhood (CCFC) said on its website, "Unilever *is* the beauty industry." And Axe was heavily invested in its new "Bom Chika Wah Wah" campaign, complete with a fictitious band wearing lingerie and stiletto heels. The contradictions could no longer be overlooked.[70] Comments in response to the video collectively reflected both the tensions of recognizing a "player" in the beauty industry warning parents about that industry, and the mixed messages of Dove and Axe. *Onslaught* parodies, frequently juxtaposing the Dove self-esteem message and an Axe commercial, proliferated—sometimes ending with the message, "Talk to your daughter before Unilever does."

"Unilever is a large global company with many brands in our portfolio, Anita Larson, a Unilever spokeswoman, said. "Each brand effort is tailored to reflect the unique interests and needs of its audience."[71]

Could you imagine a Dove woman in an Axe ad?   ∎

This case brings up an interesting dilemma, which is more and more common in a world where corporations are increasingly diversified: To what degree does the "parent" speak for its "children"? The situation here is perhaps an unusual one. In many instances, consumers are unaware of the parent company of brands they use, and given the vastly different products made sometimes by a single company, few would suspect. The two companies in this case couldn't be more vastly different in their core values and in their approaches. And perhaps it is only the fact that Dove generated so much publicity and received so many kudos that made its association with Axe a seeming "fall from grace." Certainly, each company has its own corporate identity, as does every company. They are, as the spokeswoman said, targeting different audiences. Is this merely a business problem? Or is it something more?

NOTES

1. Suzanna D. Walters, *Material Girls: Making Sense of Feminist Cultural Theory* (Berkeley: University of California Press, 1995).
2. Michael Schudson, *Advertising, The Uneasy Persuasion* (New York: Basic Books, 1987).
3. William Leiss, Stephen Kline, Sut Jhally, and Jacqueline Botterill, *Social Communication in Advertising: Consumption in the Mediated Marketplace* (New York: Routledge, 2005), p. 75.
4. *The Public Mind: Consuming Images*, PBS documentary with Bill Moyers, 1989.
5. Ibid.
6. Naomi Klein, *No Logo* (New York: Picador, 2002).
7. Barry Silverstein, "Voss: High Water," Brandchannel.com, 5 March 2007.
8. Charles Fishman, "Message in a Bottle," *Fast Company*, July 2007.

9. Bob Garfield, "The Product Is Questionable, But Aquafina's Ad Holds Water," *Advertising Age*, 9 July 2001, p. 38.

10. Sally Squires, "THE LEAN PLATE; The Bottle-versus-the-Tap Debate; Consumers Who Spent $10 Billion Last Year on Bottled Water Think It's a Better Bet. But Is It?" *The Los Angeles Times*, 17 July 2006, p. 4.

11. Garfield, "The Product Is Questionable."

12. Thinkoutsidethebottle.org (Corporate Accountability International)

13. Ian Daly, "Purification That Comes in a Bottle: Water Takes on New Responsibilities," 28 November 2007.

14. Fishman, "Message in a Bottle."

15. David A. Aaker, *Managing Brand Equity" Capitalizing on the Value of a Brand Name* (New York: Free Press, 1991), pp. 7–8.

16. Jenny Strasburg, "Abercrombie & Glitch: Asian Americans Rip Retailer for Stereotypes on T-shirts," *The San Francisco Chronicle*, 18 April 2002, p. A-1.

17. www.cbsnews.com/stories/2003/12/05/60minutes/main587099.shtml

18. Jenny Strasburg, "Abercrombie & Glitch: Asian Americans Rip Retailer for Stereotypes on T-shirts," *The San Francisco Chronicle*, 18 April 2002, p. A-1

19. www.eeoc.gov/press/11-18-04.html

20. Strasburg, "Abercrombie & Glitch."

21. Ibid.

22. Jayne O'Donnell, "Apparel sales show teens' fickleness," *USA Today*, 9 March 2007, p. 4-B.

23. Robin Givhan, fashion editor of *The Washington Post*, in Rebecca Johnson, "Walking a Thin Line," *Vogue*, April 2007, p. 384.

24. Natasha Singer, "Nice Resume. Have Your Considered Botox?" *The New York Times*, 24 January 2008, E3.

25. Rachel Dodes, "Crossing Fashion's Thin White Line," *The New York Times*, 1 February 2008, B1.

26. Rebecca Johnson, "Walking a Thin Line," *Vogue*, April 2007.

27. Rebecca Seal, "The Incredible Shrinking Woman," *The Observer*, 9 September 2007.

28. Ibid.

29. Valli Herman, "Is Skinny Going Out of Style?" *The Los Angeles Times*, 16 December 2006, p. E-1.

30. Ibid.

31. Seal, "The Incredible Shrinking Woman."

32. Unilever press release.

33. Guy Trebay, "The Vanishing Pint," *The New York Times*, 7 February 2008.

34. Ibid.

35. "Trends: The Real Thing," *Marketing Week*, 13 January 2005.

36. Louise, writing in "Media: Organ Grinder: Your Views on Whether Dove's Ad Campaigns for 'Real Beauty' Are as Clean as They Purport to Be," *The Guardian* (London), 3 April 2006.

37. www.campaignforrealbeauty.com.

38. "Trends: The Real Thing," *Marketing Week,* 13 January 2005.

39. Susanna Schrobsdorff, "Summer of Dove; Are the Women in the Company's New Ad Campaign Too Big to Sell Beauty Products, or Have Our Minds Gotten Too Small?" *Newsweek*, 3 August 2005, Newsweek Web exclusive.

40. Seth Stevenson, "When Tush Comes to Dove: These Are Not Models. They Have Paunches. And Bums. And Are Not Pouting", *The Financial Post* (Canada), 4 August 2005, www.slate.com.

41. "Trends: The Real Thing," *Marketing Week*, 13 January 2005.
42. Jeff Neff, " 'A Step Forward': In Dove Ads, Normal Is the New Beautiful," *Advertising Age*, 27 September 2004.
43. "PRSA Announces 2006 Best of Silver Anvil Award Winner: 'Dove Campaign for Real Beauty' Receives Top Honors at Annual PR Event," *Business Wire*, 9 June 2006.
44. Jack Neff, "Soft Soap," *Advertising Age*, 24 September 2007, http://adage.com/print?article-is=120640, 10/24/2007.
45. Unpublished manuscript, author unknown
46. "Hawkish on Dove," *The Toronto Star*, 23 August 2005.
47. Linda Scott, "Market Feminism: The Case for a Paradigm Shift," *Advertising and Society Review* 7:2 (2006).
48. Steve Hamm, "Children of the Web," *BusinessWeek*, 2 July 2007, www.businessweek.com/print/magazine/content/07_27/b4041401.htm?chang=gl, 10/16/2007.
49. Robin Givhan, "Strong, Man; Aimed at Guys, Axe Really Smells—Like Money," *The Washington Post*, 25 April 2005.
50. Ibid.
51. Ibid.
52. Mintel Reports, "Antiperspirants and Deodorants—US," February 2007.
53. Barbara Lippert, "Barbara Lippert's Critique: The Smell of Success," *Adweek*, 28 March 2005.
54. See the advertising and promotion section of Mintel Report for examples from a number of other countries.
55. http://bastardlogic.wordpress.com/2007/09/18/axes-bom-chicka-wah-wah-campaign/, 10/16/2007.
56. http://thehathorlegacy.info/someone-should-ax-axe/.
57. http://clicked.msnbc.msn.com/archive/2007/10/02/390718.aspx.
58. Ibid.
59. Ibid.
60. Andrew Adam Newman, "Unilever Shuns Stereotypes of Women (Unless Talking to Men)," *The New York Times*, 15 October 2007.
61. Givhan, "Strong, Man; Aimed at Guys, Axe Really Smells—Like Money."
62. www.aef.com/industry/news/data/2003/2242.
63. Ibid.
64. http://salsa.democracyinaction.org/o/621/t/734/campaign.jsp?campaign_KEY=15685.
65. www.commercialexploitation.org.
66. "Hawkish on Dove," *The Toronto Star*, 23 August 2005.
67. http://slate.com/id/2161163/, 10/14/2007.
68. "Hawkish on Dove."
69. See the *Onslaught* video at www.campaignforrealbeauty.com.
70. Few mention another of Dove's "problematic siblings," SlimFast. As the name suggests, SlimFast is a meal replacement.
71. Newman, "Unilever Shuns Stereotypes of Women (Unless Talking to Men)."

The Media Are Commercial

The media are commercial. What exactly does this mean? The casual response might be, "There are ads." And indeed, that's part of the answer. Advertising provides the financial support for most media, and for some media, is the *only* source of revenue. The ensuing trade-offs are the on-going stuff of pride (advertising helps make media available at lower cost, without possible dependence on government subsidy) and controversy. The media are also commercial in the sense that under a capitalist economic system, the media are structured so that their primary goal is profit. This can prove to be extraordinarily difficult given the normative role of the press in a democratic society. In this regard, McChesney writes:

> There is a basic conflict of interest with running a business purely for profit that has so much influence on democratic debate, culture, and the social distribution of information.[1]

How does advertising as a major funding system affect media content and the media's role in democracy?

Because of this arrangement, audiences are commodities, in a sense, products, produced and sold to advertisers. Insofar as advertisers are looking for people with resources and a willingness and opportunity to spend those resources, not all audiences are equal; some are more desirable than others. Advertisers "shop" for audiences in much the same way consumers shop for products.

As a result, media will shape their content in order to draw in the audiences advertisers want. So, for example, our media landscape until most recently was shaped by the advertising industry's p reoccupation with 18 to 34-year-olds. *Sex and the City*, American Idol, and a seemingly endless spate of reality programs, action movies, and "laddie" magazines stand as testimonial to that preoccupation.

Perhaps the most obvious outcome is the fact that advertising makes up a substantial portion of our media content. However, this arrangement between advertising and the media also gives rise to some of our most common ethical charges:

Advertising may exercise control over non-editorial content, or may attempt to do so. This is one of the most common criticisms in the area of advertising and the media; it deals with the media allegedly "selling out" to advertisers. Ronald K.L. Collins and Todd Gitlin assert in the introduction to their book, *Dictating Content*:

> Typically, we associate censorship and related problems with meddling or authoritarian government. [This book] documents that in modern America, censorship is far more likely to be imposed by advertisers and advertising-
> related pressures, and far more likely to be tolerated by our commercially supported media.[2]

Sometimes this control is explicit (e.g., a product placement written into a script, a statement that advertising will be pulled in the event of some "offense" to the advertiser); at other times, a medium might practice self-censorship, "softening" a story, or not publishing a story to avoid the possibility of a disconcerted advertiser. In 1992, the *New England Journal of Medicine* reported a study that showed that magazines that relied heavily on cigarette advertising were far less likely than others to write about the dangers of smoking. Women's magazines were found to be the worst offenders.[3]

Advertising can influence the media available. Again, the media landscape tends to be designed to attract the "haves," usually defined in terms of consumption potential. In this sense, advertisers play a powerful role in shaping the marketplace of ideas. This is a vital and on-going concern given the normative role of the press in a democracy, and is particularly troubling in face of media consolidation. The number of companies who control the majority of the media has been shrinking rapidly, placing enormous political and economic power in the hands of a few corporate giants. Even more troubling is the fact that media are often viewed, in these corporations, as having no value other than their market value. They become profit centers and not foundations of democracy. Robert McChesney articulates this point vehemently:

> Media must not be considered just another business: They are special institutions in our society. Information is the lifeblood of democracy—and when viewpoints are cut off and ideas cannot find an outlet, our democracy suffers.[4]

This profit motive can in no way be separated from the role of advertising.

The cases in this chapter examine some of the complex ethical dilemmas that arise in this area. "Marketing U.S. Latinidad" explores the processes and implications of audience targeting and construction. "Gatekeepers: Closing the Door" asks us to consider power wielded by the media in terms of advertising acceptance/rejection. "Shocking: The Case for Due Diligence" focuses on the unusual situation of shock-jock radio, asking whether advertisers have a responsibility for the content their money supports. "Blowing Up the Wall" probes the dilemma that accompanies the blurring of advertising and editorial content. A final case, "Selling the Game?" examines the ever-increasing occurrence of product placement.

33 *Marketing U.S. Latinidad*[5]

> . . . *Every consumer market is a construction of reality. This realization does not mean that the categories used to construct consumer markets have no basis in actuality. It does mean that the categories designed and the questions asked that contribute to the categories are for the benefit of advertisers and their clients, not consumers. Industry control of the basic terms by which consumers are defined not only can lead to advertising messages that are incongruent with the lived experiences of consumers, but they also can shape the manufacturing of products that are advertised, and ultimately consumed. Thus, the consumption experience is shaped as much, if not more, by advertisers and producers than by consumers.*[6]

Targeting is part of the everyday conventions of marketing practice; as advertisers, we routinely identify a group, define that group using any number of characteristics, and subsequently direct our marketing efforts toward it. Targeting is an effective and efficient approach to creating and delivering marketing messages. Stereotyping is an inherent part of this process; most anyone, even if they are not in advertising, can tell you what characterizes a boomer, a Gen-Xer, or a buppie, and "the coveted eighteen to thirty-four market" conjures up images and ideas that go well beyond age. Target marketing is so much a part of what advertisers do that we rarely give it a thought. Perhaps we should.

As the opening quotation suggests, a group's recognition as a market isn't natural or automatic; it occurs in the context of social relations.[7] That is, a market isn't just "out there" waiting to be discovered; advertisers define it into existence. Let's briefly examine the Hispanic market and how it has come to be. Before we begin, we should note that the Association of Hispanic Advertising Agencies estimated that the market's spending power in 2007 will be $928 billion; the spending is expected to top a trillion dollars in the next three years.[8]

Initially, the Latino market became a topic of conversation in the advertising trade press in the mid-1960s, identified then as untargeted, ignored, neglected, and invisible. Marketing to Hispanics primarily was local; brokers bought time on English-speaking television stations. At the time, Federal Communication Commission (FCC) rules precluded noncitizens from owning more than 20 percent of a network. Emilio Azcarraga, a Mexican TV entrepreneur with Televisa, had long been looking for a way to get Televisa programs into the United States; he began by buying television stations in San Antonio and Los Angeles in 1961 and establishing the Spanish International Network and Spanish International Communications Corporations (SIN/SICC).[9]

- By the mid-1970s, SIN owned sixteen stations.
- The network became the first U.S. network connected by satellite in 1976.
- By 1982, SIN claimed a 90 percent reach of Latino households through its 16 networks, 100 repeater stations, and over 200 cable systems.
- SIN was later sold to Hallmark and renamed Univision.

As noted earlier, in a commercial media system, audiences are commodities; that is, audiences are the products sold to advertisers. In order to develop Spanish-language broadcasting, it was essential that Latinos be identified, "called into existence" as a lucrative, untapped market. Numbers alone were not enough; the broadcasters had to convince advertisers that Latinos were consumers and that they were different enough to need separate media; that is, Latinos had to be packaged as a marketable, commercially valuable identity. In this process, Latinos, be they Cuban, Mexican, or Puerto Rican became a single "nation within a nation," with a uniquely distinct culture, ethos, and language.[10] They became identified as Spanish-speaking. Davila notes:

> "Hispanics" remain a protected segment by their mere definition as a homogeneously bounded, "culturally defined" niche. It is this definition that makes all "Latinos" part of the same undifferentiated "market"—whether they live in El Barrio or in an upscale New York high-rise, or whether they watch *Fraser* or only Mexican *novellas*, or love Ricky Martin or consider him a sellout. . . ."[11]

Davila goes on to argue that the implications of this construction go far beyond marketing. Commercial representations and recognition as a vital market have not translated into expansion of the Hispanic role in participatory democracy:

> . . . [C]ommercial representations may shape people's cultural identities as well as affect notions of belonging and cultural citizenship in public life. . . . Latinos are continually recast as authentic and marketable, but ultimately as a foreign rather than intrinsic component of U.S. society, culture, and history . . . marketing discourse is not without economic and political repercussions.[12]

Carl Kravetz, chairman of the Association of Hispanic Advertising Agencies, made a similar argument:

> . . . [W]e allowed the Hispanic advertising industry to be dragged into a Spanish vs. English debate, and . . . in order to get ourselves out of the language corner, there [are] three things we need to do: One. To move beyond defining our market in terms of English or Spanish. Two. To insist on permission to be complex. Three. To adopt a new language . . . the language of agency . . . the language of marketing . . . the language of business-building. . . . it is up to *us* to define our consumers or risk having them defined for us.[13] ∎

Targeting appears to be a valuable tool in a professional and pragmatic sense. It provides the basis of efficient communication with a group of desirable consumers, and it minimizes monetary waste as well as message delivery to individuals to whom the message might not be relevant and so might be particularly annoying. Certainly, it also can be argued that the Hispanic media created to facilitate targeting have been welcomed by many in the Hispanic community, despite that community's diversity. Those media provide not only entertainment but also information on issues important to the group and an opportunity for dialogue. In short, the Hispanic community has been given a voice, albeit a commercially driven voice.

To help clarify the issues, we might answer the following questions:

- How did a variety of people come to be identified as belonging to one group labeled *Hispanic*?
- What characteristics determine membership in that group?
- Who attributes the meanings given to these characteristics?

Now the issue becomes more complex. Hispanics were defined as such by Hispanic media entrepreneurs who subsequently assumed roles as "professional consultants" for the purpose of packaging Hispanics as a marketable audience. The market was constructed, one might say "othered," by language and identified as a nation within a nation. In being distinguished in this manner, Hispanics were marginalized as outside the mainstream, "forever needy of culturally special marketing."[14] Was the market constructed in response to the market's genuine needs or as a means to achieve a marketer-defined end? Was the Hispanic market simply constructed as an audience, a commodity, in order to ensure the viability of Spanish-language broadcast media?

If the answer to this last question were "Yes," Kant would question the morality of the process, for in its strictest sense, to "use" others in pursuit of our goals, or perhaps more clearly, in *mere* pursuit of our goals, is immoral. To show disrespect for the humanity of another human being is morally wrong. Two additional factors might be considered. One of those factors might be termed the *vulnerability* of the market. Brooks reminds us that "it is through the discourses of advertisers and their clients that the categories of consumers get established."[15] The Hispanic community was vulnerable in rather a different way than that which we might typically conceive. The community was vulnerable to stereotypical interpretations and misinterpretations by a larger community that knew very little about its cultures. To the degree that the Hispanic community lacked control of its representations, it was at a decided disadvantage. However, here again, the complicity of Hispanic professionals as brokers of understanding should be acknowledged. As Kravetz noted:

> It was the Cuban revolution that kicked off U.S. Hispanic advertising. . . . [A] number of Havana advertising men suddenly found themselves in exile and they wanted to work at what they knew best. So they began the long arduous process of convincing American advertisers that there was a vast, untapped market hidden away right under their noses. And the reason they were untapped? Because they didn't speak English and couldn't understand advertising in that language![16]

Still, he concluded that these "founders" had spawned an entire industry now some $5 billion strong.

Finally, one might call into question the persistence with which the marketing community has addressed this market as precisely that, a market. Yet, the constructed images and representations of the Hispanic market play a vital role in how individuals in that market are understood more broadly as social, economic, and political participants. Given that, is there some ethical middle ground where we recognize at one and the same time, their value as consumers *and* their value as citizens? Then too, we might ask, in our capitalist economy, is this unique to the Hispanic market?

> The truth is, however, that the oppressed are not . . . living "outside" society. They have always been "inside"—inside the structure which made them "beings for others." The solution is not to integrate them into the structure of oppression, but to transform the structure so that they can become "beings for themselves.[17]

34 Gatekeepers: Closing the Door

The marketplace of ideas, the belief that "the best way to discover truth is through robust competition of a multitude of voices," is a metaphor deeply entrenched in American culture and democracy.[18] In the introduction to this chapter, we noted that because our media system is advertising-supported, media routinely craft their content to draw audiences that advertisers find desirable. As such, entire segments of the population may be ignored; they are not participants in the marketplace of ideas.

This case explores the marketplace of ideas from another perspective, examining a medium's power to reject advertising messages (with the exception of political advertising) for whatever reason it chooses. Certainly, this has economic implications for particular advertisers, making it difficult if not impossible for them to have voice in the economic marketplace. However, if we recognize advertising as a vehicle of social communication as well as a business tool, it is quite possible that through media rejection of advertising, entire segments of the population, or particular ideas seeking to be heard via advertising messages, may be rendered voiceless. Let's look at some examples.

In 2004, NBC and CBS halted negotiations with the United Church of Christ (UCC) concerning a television spot that invited minorities to the church. The ad features two bouncers at the entrance of a church who turn away a gay couple, an African-American woman, and a Latino man but allow a young, white family to pass. The words, "Jesus didn't turn people away. Neither do we," appear on the screen, followed by the image of a church sanctuary filled with a smiling group, diverse in age, ethnicity, and sexual preference. The spot concludes with a narrator saying, "The United Church of Christ: No matter who you are or where you are on life's journey, you're welcome here."[19] According to the UCC, CBS explained its rejection of the ad with the statement:

> Because this commercial touches on the exclusion of gay couples and other minority groups by other individuals and organizations, and the fact that the executive branch has recently proposed a constitutional amendment to define marriage as a union between a man and a woman, this spot is unacceptable for broadcast on the networks.[20]

NBC merely cited the ad as "too controversial." Both NBC and CBS did, however, approve an alternate commercial from the UCC in which a girl plays the traditional hand game, "Here's the church, here's the steeple; open the doors and see all the people." Ultimately, the original ad aired on various cable channels, including ABC Family, AMC, BET, Discovery, Fox, Hallmark, Travel, TBS, and TNT.[21]

continued

Across the ocean in July 2007, the *Gay Times*, a gay lifestyle magazine published in the United Kingdom, struggled to find an outlet for its message. The magazine duplicated its cover on a series of advertisements to be displayed in stations of the "Tube," or London Underground (the equivalent of New York Metro stations). This particular cover celebrated the fortieth anniversary of the decriminalization of homosexuality, with the word "Freedom" written in bold across the center, over the image of two men in a partial embrace.

The London Underground required the *Gay Times* amend the ad, stating that one of the models was in an "unnecessary state of undress." Ironically, when juxtaposed with advertisements featuring heteronormative models the *Gay Times* ad seemed less provocative than many. *Gay Times* editor Joseph Galliano said of the ad, "We had a picture of two guys, the one in the foreground fully dressed, then behind him, craning his head on his shoulder, a guy in pants. In comparison with many ads that the London Underground run, a very tame, rather tender image."[22] Nevertheless, the *Gay Times* altered the ad; one of the models was mostly hidden, with the exception of his arms, hands in the first model's pockets. Legally, media are free to accept or reject advertising at will.

Consider a case from Georgia concerning Lamar Advertising, a prominent billboard company, and Georgia Equality, a lesbian, gay, bisexual, and transgender (LGBT) rights organization. In 2005, Georgia Equality created the "We Are Your Neighbors" campaign, pairing images of prominent community figures such as a gay firefighter with the copy, "I protect you, and I am gay. We are your neighbors," or a lesbian doctor with the copy, "I care for you, and I am a lesbian." Initially, the campaign was featured on Clear Channel billboards in the Atlanta area, but the second phase of the campaign came to a close with rejection of the ads in south Georgia by local Lamar managers. An e-mail from Lamar's president to Georgia Equality explained that although he did not necessarily object to the campaign himself, "Right or wrong, we give our local management the responsibility and authority to accept or reject ad copy."[23]

On the other end of the political spectrum lies another billboard campaign. The "God Speaks" campaign was introduced in 1998 by an anonymous donor. Black billboards featured, in white lettering, such phrases as these:

Don't Make Me Come Down There. —God

If You Think It's Hot Now, Just Keep Using My Name in Vain. —God

What Part of "Though Shalt Not . . ." Didn't You Understand? —God

Big Bang Theory, You've Got to Be Kidding. —God

The Outdoor Advertising Association of America (OAAA), a group consisting of all billboard owners and renters in the United States, adopted the series of billboards as its national public service campaign for 1999. An estimated $15 million worth of billboards (approximately 10,000) were donated to the ad campaign across the United States as a "gift to the community."[24] According to an Oklahoma City news story,[25] "Lamar Advertising says they'll keep putting them up around the metro, whenever they have space available." As of 2007, these billboards are still scattered around the country on Lamar billboard space. ∎

In this case, Lamar Advertising welcomed the "God Speaks" campaign, and it also donated the billboard space to promote it—after denying the same (paid)

billboard space to Georgia Equality. The double standard here is obvious. If the decision makers, in this case the administration of Lamar Advertising, were shaping their social contracts from behind the veil of ignorance, they would be rendered unaware of their own positions on the political and social spectrums on which our society is measured. Thus, in making their decisions, they would have to employ the principle of "justice as fairness." As self-serving individuals, they could neither condemn nor elevate any particular group's message for fear of condemning themselves.

A more familiar example of this thought process involves two people sharing one cake. If it is agreed that one person will cut the cake and the other will choose his or her piece, the cutter cannot be aware of which piece he or she will receive in the end. Thus it follows logically that the individual cutting the cake will divide it as evenly as possible, not to ensure the chooser a fair piece but to protect his or her own share. From this perspective, ethics do not necessarily arise from altruism, but from a human inclination toward self-preservation.

Realistically, we are not expected to engage in an internal, Rawlsian debate on each decision we encounter. We may, however, want to consider a turning of the tables—a situation in which we find ourselves among the less popular minority. With this in mind, we might return to the Lamar example and consider our options:

1. Would you grant access to Georgia Equality, in addition to "God Speaks," even if their message is inconsistent with your personal beliefs, to act in accordance with a notion of fairness?
2. Or would you deny access to both groups, acknowledging that each campaign may be equally controversial and/or polarizing and is thus inappropriate for your particular media channel?

These cases call our attention to an ethical dilemma that may not be viewed as such by many. After all, media have the right to reject any political advertising for any reason they choose. Common justifications for rejection include a violation of company policy, consumer protection, and belief that the ad will offend audiences. The media are not required to provide a reason for rejection. Still, legality doesn't equal ethicality. Because media *can* reject particular ads doesn't necessarily mean that they *should* reject those ads. We might ask ourselves, then: Do the media have an obligation to subject rejection decisions of advertising to strict scrutiny, recognizing the role those advertisements might play in the social marketplace as well as the economic marketplace?

35 Shocking: The Case for Due Diligence

I do not believe any client should ever have to be in the position of having to defend itself based upon its choice of media venues. Who cares what the numbers say? If the air is blue, it will stink up the message and the perception becomes the reality.[26]

continued

It all began on Wednesday, 4 April 2007, on *Imus in the Morning*, a radio program originating at CBS Radio–owned WFAN-AM in New York, syndicated to over sixty stations around the country through Westwood One and simulcast on MSNBC. Don Imus, longtime radio "shock jock," once identified by Tom Brokaw, then anchor of the *NBC Nightly News*, as a "low rent lounge act," insulted the Rutgers University women's basketball team, the Scarlet Knights, calling them "nappy-headed hos." The response was immediate and vehement. Media Matters for America, a liberal media watchdog group, posted the story on its website, complete with video clip.

- Thursday, MSNBC issued a statement trying to distance itself from Imus; the Philadelphia chapter of the NAACP called the remarks racist and unacceptable.
- Friday, the National Association of Black Journalists President Bryan Monroe indicated that "Imus needs to be fired. Today." The Rutgers president and the president of the NCAA called the remarks unconscionable. Imus apologized on his show. WFAN apologized. CBS Radio apologized.
- Saturday, Reverend Al Sharpton said, "I accept his apology, just as I want his bosses to accept his resignation."
- Monday, CBS Radio and MSNBC announced that they were suspending Imus for two weeks.
- Tuesday, advertisers began to pull their commercials.
- Wednesday, the list of advertisers canceling lengthened, and MSNBC announced that it had canceled the simulcast of Imus' program.
- Thursday, CBS announced that it had fired Imus.[27]   ■

This episode raises a particularly interesting ethical question from an advertising perspective: Do advertisers have a responsibility for the content their money is supporting? Kathleen Hall Jamieson, well-known media commentator and professor at the Annenberg School of Communication at the University of Pennsylvania, remarked that it was "interesting that [the firing] happened as late as it did. It should have happened the moment they were aware the statement had been made."[28] From Jamieson's perspective, firing Imus was a matter of professional values in response to racist and sexist remarks injurious to others. Indeed, it appears that while the decision to fire Imus may have been based on values, it wasn't until advertisers began to pull out that the decision was made. Paul Farhi, writing in *The Washington Post*, noted:

> Amid widespread media attention and expressions of dismay from prominent officials, including White House Press Secretary Dana Perino, the advertiser defections were clearly a tipping point for NBC.[29]

Let's examine this observation a bit more closely. The Imus episode sits at the intersection of two ongoing media concerns, calling our attention to the fact that our media are commercial that is, advertising-supported, and the editorial/

advertising balancing act that results. In some sense, this is a rather atypical situation; the more usual concern is advertisers' refusal to support media for drawing audiences with limited consumption potential (e.g., feminist magazine *Ms.* was unable to gather enough advertising, ceased publication and was re-launched without advertising support).[30] Still, the fact remains, few media can exist without advertising support, and this fact alone gives advertisers consider-able power to choose those who are given a voice and those who are not. In regard to the relationship between advertising and editorial content, this situation, again, is a bit out of the ordinary. While advertisers occasionally pull advertising for any number of reasons, a more frequent concern voiced in this area is the question of the blurring of lines between editorial and advertising content.

Writing in *Advertising Age*, Bill Imada, chairman and CEO of IW Group, a communication firm specializing in multicultural markets in the United States, re-counted another episode in which a program was canceled for racist and sexist comments. He wrote:

> I believe strongly that advertising agencies and media planners should listen (and watch) the programs they are supporting on air. . . . The content of pro-grams, in addition to who is listening (and watching) should be scrutinized be-fore ads are planned and duly placed. Brands that are linked to these programs may be deemed cool and hip by some consumers, but oftentimes cause pain and suffering to a whole other set of consumers.[31]

Let's examine the situation from the position of an individual advertiser, in this case, Procter & Gamble. Procter & Gamble is one of the largest consumer goods companies, one of the largest advertisers, and one of America's most rep-utable corporations. According to the company website (www.pg.com), the val-ues of the corporation are integrity, leadership, ownership, passion for winning, and trust. The company has a strong advertising and promotions policy based on honesty, intolerance of deceptive advertising or questionable promotional ac-tivity, and standards of commercial fairness. In the past, Procter & Gamble has pulled advertising from programs it did not deem "appropriate," and in 2001, the company joined in launching the Family Friendly Program Forum (FFPF), an organization of advertisers that pays seed money to networks to create fam-ily-friendly shows. In other words, Procter & Gamble clearly has taken great care in distancing itself from objectionable or offensive programming. Yet, de-spite the widely recognized impropriety, bigotry, and sexism, the company sup-ported *Imus in the Morning*. Why? When the company pulled its advertising, a spokeswoman indicated, "We have to think first about our consumers, so any-place where our advertising appears that is offensive to our consumers is not acceptable to us."[32]

One might speculate that it was a matter of concern over free speech. Opie and Anthony, fellow radio "shock jocks" supported Imus's freedom of speech, in-dicating that what he had said was no worse than the lyrics in popular rap songs.[33] Imus also identified himself as an equal-opportunity offender. Drumwright and

Murphy, writing more generally about our understanding of the First Amendment, remind us that:

> The First Amendment prohibits governments from abridging freedom of speech; it does not stand for the proposition that all speech is equally worthy and should be uttered and encouraged, or that speakers should not be condemned for the speech that they make. . . . That the government does not prosecute those who make racial slurs does not mean that racial epithets should be encouraged. . . . [s]ome misinterpret free speech law as meaning that [we] are exonerated from personal responsibility.[34]

Fran Kelly, chief executive at Arnold Worldwide, indicated that while Imus had every right to be on the air and to say what he wanted to say, "advertisers have every right to vote with their dollars."[35]

It is noteworthy as well that advertisers had been supporting Imus for years. In some respects, this remark was nothing new for Imus. *New York Times* op-ed columnist Bob Herbert wrote:

> So this hateful garbage has been going on for a long long time. There was nothing new about the tone or the intent of Mr. Imus's "nappy-headed ho" comment. As Bryan Monroe, president of the NABJ told me the other night, "It's a long pattern of behavior, and at some point somebody has to say enough is enough."

Again, why didn't Procter & Gamble and other advertisers speak up sooner? Why now? One obvious answer might be the program's ability to reach a quality audience, a large audience, two million listeners a day. The practical ability to reach this audience efficiently apparently trumped any social consequences of program content.

In fairness to the advertisers, it may be a quirk of our consumer, celebrity culture that despite Imus' known bigotry, vitriol, and racism, guests, including 2008 presidential hopefuls Barack Obama, Hillary Clinton, John McCain, Rudy Giuliani, and journalists, came regularly and apparently quite easily to chat with Imus. People listened and watched. One writer noted on Imus's firing that "somewhere in those corporate halls, there is fretting [that] Imus just cost his advertisers plenty of inconvenience ('Now where will we advertise and get such an audience?') and undesired publicity."[36]

Don Imus returned to WABC-AM in New York on December 3, 2007, "Chastened but Still Proudly Obnoxious."[37] He told his audience "I will never say anything in my lifetime that will make any of these young women at Rutgers regret or feel foolish that they accepted my apology and forgave me. . . . And no one else will say anything on my program that will make anyone think I did not deserve a second chance." He also indicated, however, that "the program is not going to change."[38] The roster of guests was familiar, including then-presidential hopefuls John McCain and Christopher Dodd. Back too were some of the long-standing advertisers.

Ah, an invitation to return once again to the original question posed here: Do advertisers have a responsibility for the content their money supports?

36 Blowing Up the Wall: Advertising and Editorial Content

In an ideal situation, reporters write the news, editors put it in the paper, and advertising sales executives manage to sell the advertising space. Today, the assembly line is not cleanly divided.[39]

Jane, the advertising sales director at a midsize, chain-owned paper, had come to the profession as an idealist—the advertising and editorial departments were separate. The integrity of the news content was paramount to maintain the readers' respect and keep circulation numbers up. But all that had changed. Jane reflected on the fact that newspapers were struggling. Declining circulation, Web and online competition, and intermedia competition for advertising dollars had led management at papers throughout the country to assert that the old business model was out of date.

Now, it seemed more than ever that collaboration between the ad sales staff and the editors and writers was the rule, not the exception. Jane's role was becoming ambiguous; sometimes she sold advertising space, but at other times she felt as though she was being asked to participate in *making* news by putting together special sections that consisted of little more than press releases from advertisers. This put a strain on her professional ethics. Even though she was on the advertising side, she believed in the integrity of the "news product"; she didn't want to "blow up the wall" between the editorial side and the business side of the paper.[40] Her position was becoming increasingly difficult.

And today, Jane's editor was watching what was going on in Memphis at *The Commercial Appeal* very closely, and so was Jane. The editor of *The Commercial Appeal* was taking steps to "monetize the content" of the paper and had issued guidelines as to how it would be accomplished. He had called it "part of the new business model that will support journalism in the future."[41] Jane had read the guidelines and found them troubling. They explained the necessity of "monetizing" this way:

> Newspapers are looking for new ways to attach ads in print and on-line to specific stories, features, and sections. This represents a marked change from past practices. No longer are there thick impenetrable walls between the newsroom, advertising, and circulation departments. Today we are in it together. In this new world of newspaper survival, we understand that our content is what makes us valuable and we want to put a meter on that.[42]

Jane was not convinced that the integrity of the news could be maintained in the environment the editor described. She became even more apprehensive when she read on:

> Deciding how best to match up specific kinds of content with specific kinds of advertising campaigns is a crucial discussion in the new world of monetized content. Some projects and publications clearly are driven by advertising objectives. Other projects and content clearly are driven by editorial objectives. Still others are powered by a mixture of advertising and editorial values and purposes. Defining and differentiating content as advertising-driven, news-driven, or a hybrid will clarify the development and execution of projects. Both departments agree to work together to resolve any misunderstandings about the scope, mission and purpose of our emerging advertising-editorial collaborations.[43]

continued

Jane took heart in the fact that fifty newsroom employees at *Commercial Appeal* had signed a petition in protest of taking money for news coverage. And certainly the comments that had been posted on the article were uniformly critical; "tantamount to bribery," one had said. Most of the comments were from readers. One wrote: "I just read the CA's monetizing content memo, and realize there is something really big missing from it: me. Nowhere in this document is there any reference to reader preferences, or what sort of news content that readers like me want to receive"[44] Weren't the readers the reason the paper existed in the first place? The editor couldn't read these comments and go on with this monetization idea, could he? The idea that she would become a part of this seemed unconscionable. How had the advertising sales staff at *Commercial Appeal* reacted? I'll have to quit my job, Jane concluded unhappily. ■

What do you think? Is there any room for compromise?

It is noteworthy that Jane's dilemma arises out of her personal and professional belief in the "integrity of the news product," and its role in democracy rather than in the possible economic consequences for her department or her paper. While she recognizes the financial crisis surrounding her, Jane believes the greatest good to the greatest number would be served by maintaining the strictest of barriers between advertising and editorial content. Implicit here is her adherence to the Society of Professional Journalists Code of Ethics which encourages journalists to "Distinguish news from advertising and shun hybrids that blur the lines between the two."[45] Inherent in this view, Jane believes the foundation of the paper will erode if content is "monetized;" the news department will likely find itself at the mercy of the advertisers, stop reporting news, and start running content that pleases advertisers. Thus, professional consequences trump Jane's concern with the economic viability of the paper.

In contrast, Jane's editor seemed to be primarily grounded in his belief that ensuring the greatest good would be served by the paper's survival, a perspective not without its merits. Jane and her editor, then, seem at an ethical impasse.

Jane may find it difficult to justify her position on utilitarian grounds given that at this point, there seems to be little apparent protest from readers about the *Commercial Appeal's* guidelines. Still, a reader's perspective underlies her professional one:

> As consumers of news, the foundation of what we believe to be credible and legitimate will become a farce, and our demand for legitimate and truthful news will be answered by a series of targeted ads.[46]

Given the depth of her concern, and her clear personal and professional belief in "right" as defined by journalistic ethics, Jane could be seen as acting on a Kantian-like ethical principle—the principle that this practice was simply wrong, regardless of clear consequences.

37 Selling the Game?

You are driving at speeds close to 200 miles an hour, trying to keep your vehicle on the roadway while also not allowing the person behind you to pass. As you approach a sharp curve, out of the corner of your eye you notice a new billboard for a soft drink. Shaking off the distraction, you move into the curve trying to stay as low in the arc as you can.[47]

You are at bat, squinting into the lights, trying to anticipate when the ninety-two-mile-an-hour sinker will cross the plate. You swing your bat anxiously, studying the fence that lies more than 380 feet ahead of you. While the pitcher throws over to first, you have time to wish you had one of the beverages advertised on the sign in the middle of the fence. "A cold one would be great just now," you think. "Maybe after this game is over." Just then, the sign changes from a beer ad to one featuring the latest tennis shoes. "What's up with that," you barely have time to mutter to yourself as the pitch sails by you for a strike.

You're hungry—really hungry—and would love a big, juicy hamburger and fries. "If only I could ask for it and someone could bring it to me," you think. "It's too risky in this construction zone for me to leave this machine somewhere to get one." But before you get much hungrier, your dream comes true. You look up to see the Burger King character jumping over machines with food for you. "The King—he is so sneaky," you hear someone yell.[48]

Just then your cell phone beeps with a new message. You lunge for it, trying not to knock over your game console as you text back: "Xbox. RU?" ■

You may be playing video games, but while doing so, you are also the target of an increasingly sophisticated arena of advertising through product placements. Nielsen indicates that by the end of 2006, about 40 percent of U.S. TV households had a games console,[49] and gamers were not just preteens—one report indicated the average gamer is now a twenty-nine-year-old man,[50] and gamers generate what is expected to be $400 million in advertising revenue worldwide by 2009. Beginning in the 1980s, game manufacturers imbedded sponsored signage within environments. Personalities added endorsements to their videos, demonstrating their use of specific brands as their video likeness played a sport. Video characters played on courts with branded banners, selected specific brands of automobiles to drive, and watched sponsored lists within games.[51] As gamers moved to active online environments, technology allowed for more variety, enabling branding images to change while the game is being played.[52]

Innovations now include "advergames" such as Burger King's Xbox King Games Innovative Campaign, a partnership with Microsoft that led to three games that put the Burger King character in three settings in which he fought obstacles to deliver food to hungry characters. The games, which were sold in Burger King outlets during the 2006 holiday season, were very successful, with a reported 2.4 million games sold in five weeks.[53] Some insiders suggest that the next step will be to introduce products such as soft drinks, clothing, or toys in video games before launching them in the marketplace.[54]

Does the advertising work? Research is just beginning. One study found that playing games with imbedded branding did develop implicit memory of the brand names, but only low levels of explicit recognition of the brands.[55] Another found that brand familiarity rose by two-thirds among gamers who had been exposed to in-game brands, and advertising recall grew by around 40 percent.[56]

It's no surprise that marketers have found another venue for imbedding brand messages into entertainment programming. Brand placement in films has been growing since the 1970s, when marketers began paying for deliberate brand placement in feature films. Bouyed by successful promotions of products there, brand placement has since spread into television programs, novels, recorded songs, plays, and now video games. It's hard to argue that anyone buying or playing a Tiger Wood golf game would be surprised to see a Nike logo on his clothing, and certainly anyone purchasing a video game at a Burger King restaurant shouldn't be surprised to see the Burger King featured as a major character.

Proponents of brand placement argue that brands are part of the reality of daily life in a consumer culture and that their presence adds to the reality of the created environment of entertainment programming. The cachet of an elite brand of automobile, liquor, cologne, or golf club has a meaning apart from the product itself, thereby creating and sustaining a symbolic reality quickly and easily. And perhaps audience members are so used to the commercial presence that they simply ignore imbedded brands.

Yet, not everyone accepts placements. Viewers have complained that some placements are too blatant—clearly resenting the intrusion of branded messages that appear out of place or out of story. Others are concerned about naive audience members who may not be aware of the duality of the entertainment–persuasion mixture and thereby may not be ready to critically assess those messages. In particular, children's and adolescent's exposure to brand placements raises ethical concerns—and the increase in game placements and in the creation of "advergames" or crossovers may heighten those concerns.

An Aristotelian analysis of this issue might consider how a balance between commercial messaging and entertainment messages can be found. For example, how might parents who purchase games for their children be made aware of the presence of advertising? The packaging might contain a disclosure statement. Or, when signing on for online access to games, such a statement might appear, offering the option to opt in or out of such exposure, particularly when the brand placements may be manipulated throughout the games (perhaps in response to information provided by players of the games). Would it be unreasonable to disclose the presence of advertisements for what may be deemed risky products, such as tobacco or alcohol?

In a capitalist culture, many do not consider brand promotion to be a vice, and yet its unannounced presence may not be a virtue either.

NOTES

1. *Free Press Beginner's Guide: What's Wrong witheMedia?* www.freepress.net.
2. Ronald K. L. Collins and Todd Gitlin, *Dictating Content*, (Washington, D.C.: The Center for the Study of Commercialism, 1992), p. 41.

3. Cited in Ronald Bettig and Jeanne Lynne Hall, *Big Media, Big Money: Cultural Texts and Political Economy*, (Lanham: Rowman & Littlefield Publishers, Inc., 2003), p. 97.

4. Free Press Beginner's Guide: Why Care About Media, www.freepress.net

5. This concept, Latinidad, is derived from Arlene Davila, *Latinos, Inc.: The Making and Marketing of a People* (Berkeley, CA: University of California Press, 2001). She defines it as "enactments, definitions and representations of Hispanic or Latino culture" (p. 17). She also clarifies the distinction between Hispanic and Latino. *Hispanic* is viewed by Latino activists as being "more politically sanitized" (p. 15). *Latino* is seen as being more politically correct; however, all agencies tend to use the official name *Hispanic*.

6. Dwight E. Brooks, "In Their Own Words: Advertisers' Construction of an African-American Consumer Market, the World War II era," *Howard Journal of Communications* 6:1–2 (October 1995): 48.

7. Roberta J. Astroff, "Spanish Gold: Stereotypes, Ideology, and the Construction of a U.S. Latino Market," *Howard Journal of Communications* 1:4 (Winter 1988–1989): 155–173.

8. Cynthia Corney, "How Do You Say 'Got Milk' en Español?" *The New York Times Magazine*, September 23, 2007.

9. The whole of this story is detailed in an excellent book by Arlene Davila, *Latinos, Inc.: The Making and Marketing of a People* (Berkeley, CA: University of California Press, 2001).

10. Ibid.

11. Ibid., p. 8.

12. Ibid., pp. 2, 4, 235.

13. Typescript of speech delivered by Carl Kravetz to the Association of Hispanic Advertising Agencies on the AHAA Latino Identity Project, September 20, 2006.

14. Davila, *Latinos, Inc.*, p. 4.

15. Brooks, "In Their Own Words," p. 34.

16. Kravetz, speech delivered to the AHAA.

17. P. Friere, *Pedagogy of the Oppressed* (New York: Seabury Press, 1970).

18. W. Wat Hopkins, "The Supreme Court Defines the Marketplace of Ideas," *Journalism and Mass Communication Quarterly*, 73:1 (Spring 1996):40.

19. Robert Marus, "Networks Reject UCC Ads, Citing Gay Controversies," *Associated Baptist Press*, 2 December 2004.

20. Alan Cooperman, "Two Networks Bar Religious Commercial: CBS, NBC Turn Down United Church of Christ's Ad Touting Its Inclusiveness," *The Washington Post*, 2 December 2004, p. A-8

21. Ibid.

22. As quoted on gaytimes.co.uk.

23. Ann Rostow, "Billboard Company Rejects Pro-Gay Ads," *Gay.com*, 1 August 2005.

24. godspeaks.com.

25. Ed Doney, "God's Billboards," Oklahoma News Channel 4 from KFOR.com, 2006.

26. Comment in response to Bill Imada, "Advertisers Do Have a Responsibility for Content," *Advertising Age*, 3 October 2007, http://adage.com/print?article_id=120902, 10/17/2007.

27. Though the chronology is readily available from individual news stories, this chronology was drawn from John Horn, "The Imus Scandal: Chronology and Aftermath," *The Los Angeles Times*, 13 April 2007.

28. Michael Klein and Michael Shaffer, "CBS Fires Imus from Radio Show," *The Philadelphia Inquirer*, 13 April 2007, www.popmatters.com/pm/news/article/33108/cbs-pulls-the-plug-on-Imus, 10/17/2007.

29. Paul Farhi, "MSNBC Drops Imus's Show; As Advertisers Pull Out Amid Backlash, CBS Director Hopes Host Will Be Fired," *The Washington Post*, 12 April 2007.

30. Gloria Steinam, "Sex, Lies, and Advertising," *Ms.*, July/August, 1990.
31. Bill Imada, msp. "Advertisers Do Have a Responsibility for Content," *Advertising Age*, 3 October 2007, http://adage.com/print?article_id=120902, 10/17/2007.
32. Jacques Steinberg, "Imus Struggling to Retain Sway as a Franchise," *The New York Times*, 11 April 2007.
33. Farhi, "MSNBC Drops Imus's Show."
34. Minette Drumwright and Patrick Murphy, "How Advertising Practitioners View Ethics," *Journal of Advertising* 33:2 (Summer 2004): 13.
35. Bill Carter and Jacques Steinberg, "Off the Air: The Light Goes Out for Don Imus," *Advertising Age*, 13 April 2007.
36. Robert Trigaux, "Advertisers Need Imus, No Matter How Crude," *The St. Petersburg Times*, 16 April 2007.
37. www.nytimes.com/2007/12/04/arts/television/04imus.html?_r=1&oref=slogin
38. Ibid.
39. Soontae An and Lori Bergen, "Advertiser Pressure on Daily Newspapers," *Journal of Advertising* 36:2 (Summer 2007): 111–121. This article provided a portion of the framework for this case.
40. "Blowing Up the Wall" is attributed to Alicia C. Shepard, "Blowing Up the Wall," *American Journalism Review* 19:10 (1997): 164–172.
41. http://poynter.org/column.asp?id=45&aid=131633.
42. http://memphisflyer.com/monetizing_memo.pdf, 10/15/2007.
43. Ibid.
44. http://smartcitymemphis.blogspot.com/2007/10/all-news-that-fit-to-rent-policy-fought.html, 10/20/2007.
45. www.spj.org/ethicscode.asp
46. Ralph J. Davila, "Ad-centric Media: Crossing the Ethical Boundaries of Advertising and Editorial Content," *PR Tactics*, September 2007, p. 27.
47. Rob Gerlsbeck. "Getting in the Game," *Marketing*, 10 September 2007, p. 9.
48. Robert Gray, "Play the Brand," *Marketing*, 25 July 2007, pp. 33–34.
49. Alasdair Reid, Lifting the Game Campaign, June 1, 25–26, www.proquest.com/, 10/7/2007.
50. Justin Townsend, "Let the Games Begin: In-Game Advertising Offers Marketers a Wide Range of Opportunities," *Mediaweek*, 19 March 2007, p. 18.
51. "A Unique Space for Direct Marketers," *Precision Marketing*, 18 May 2006. p. 16.
52. Eric Young, "EA Makes Ad Play," *The San Francisco Business Times*, 6 February 2004.
53. Beth Snyder Bulik, "In-Game Ads Win Cachet Through a Deal with EA," *Advertising Age*, 30 July 2007, p. 8.
54. "Xbox King Games Innovative Campaign," www.canneslionslive.com/titanium/win_1_1_00187.htm.
55. David Edery, "Reverse Product Placement in Virtual Worlds," *Harvard Business Review* 84:12 (December 2006): 24.
56. Moonhee Yang, David R. Roskos-Ewoldsen, Lucian Dinu, and Laura M. Arpan, "The Effectiveness of 'In-Game' Advertising," *Journal of Advertising* 4 (Winter 2006): 143–152; Gerlsbeck, "Getting in the Game," p. 9.

Advertising's Professional Culture

The professions occupy a position of great importance in America; they influence the relationships between individuals and their work and their work and society.[1] Since the late nineteenth and early twentieth centuries, advertising has undertaken efforts to attain professional stature. Earliest efforts sought primarily to distance advertising from the hucksterism so characteristic of its founders: P. T. Barnum and "snake oil" salesmen hawking patent medicines (Dr. Winslow's Soothing Syrup: "Makes 'em lay like the dead 'til mornin'").[2] Practitioners believed it essential that advertising not be viewed as "something based on inspiration, immature ideas and snappy slogans"; advertising could no longer simply rest on the cliché, "It pays to advertise," but had to demonstrate its capabilities and be accepted on its merit, not on faith.[3]

Early professionalization efforts took a number of forms:

- Formation of local clubs and national associations, which served to bring the community together, foster a sense of self-identification and recognition, and "announce" the existence of the profession to clients and the broader public.
  - Agate Club, 1894; Advertising Club of New York, 1906; League of Advertising Women of New York, 1911
  - Association of Advertising Clubs of the World, 1905; Association of National Advertisers, 1910; American Association of Advertising Agencies, 1912
- Appearance of a number of trade journals in which practitioners negotiated and renegotiated the boundaries of the profession, celebrated its victories both large and small, mourned its defeats, applauded the victors, and dissected the strategies of the losers as a cautionary tale.
  - *Printers' Ink* (1888), *Judicious Advertising* (1903), *Advertising and Selling* (1909)
- Establishment of academic programs in the field at universities.
  - Northwestern University and the University of Minnesota (1903)
  - By 1915, twenty-six universities had advertising courses for their undergraduate students

- Development of internal efforts to gain ethical control of the field; the industry's first code of ethics was the Printers' Ink Statute (1911).

- Introduction of the rationality and rhetoric of science to the practice of advertising.[4]

The success of these efforts—that is, the answer to the question, "Is advertising a profession?"—remains a point of continuing debate. The study of professions and professionalization, the process through which an occupation evolves into a profession, and the attributes that distinguish it is a dynamic one. Then, too, the term *professional* itself has acquired particular associations in everyday usage that make consensus on a definition difficult. Still, one trait seemingly serves as a foundation for virtually all definitions: the possession of a theoretical knowledge base, in some sense, a "magic circle of knowledge" that distinguishes the profession from the laity. Recognizing this, at least one scholar has suggested that advertising possesses an inherent paradox that will prevent it from ever achieving professional stature:

> The production of creative ideas is the basic work that the advertising agencies perform. Creative ideas, however, by definition resist . . . the application of any social-scientific theory in their generation. If the innovative solutions marketers need were deducible from a basic set of principles, arguably, they would not need advertising agencies to perform creative services for them.[5]

This perspective clearly emphasizes creativity ("something based on inspiration") as the core of advertising work, and it is very different from the views of early practitioners who sought stature based on their use of science.

Still, the answer to the question of advertising's professional stature is not the subject of this discussion. What is more important for our purposes is the recognition that much of "what we are" as an industry, what we think we are doing when we are "doing advertising work," what we value and what we dismiss are reflections of those early efforts to professionalize.

The cases in this chapter examine advertising's professional culture. *Professional culture* might be thought of as a shared understanding of what it means to *be* an advertising professional, that is, how we make sense of the advertising profession. Professional culture incorporates a number of dimensions, grounded in the values, attitudes, beliefs, and experiences of a profession. These dimensions are private as well as public; how our private professional culture (i.e., our internal culture) is manifest publicly is a large component of public opinion toward our profession. Additionally, each agency has an individual corporate culture as well, developed within the context/constraints of this larger professional culture. Professional culture might be thought of as:

- *What we value.* This is apparent in our *output* (i.e., our ads), *awards* we give and to whom we give them (note, for example, that most of our awards are based on creativity, not effectiveness, the notable exception being the EFFIE; indeed, we are a complicated profession!), *codes of ethics*, *behavior* (e.g., diversity), etc.

- *How we go about our work.* This includes the routines, payment processes, our relationships and interactions with clients, the developing saga of "the pitch," etc. These are readily apparent in the trade press.

- *How we think about ourselves.* Initially, advertising has sought to establish an image of rationality and continues to do so given business's emphasis on accountability and return on investment. At the same time, we work hard to create an image of glamour, youth, risk-taking, cutting-edge innovation, and creativity.

- *How others think about us.* This includes clients as well as the public. Among the general public, many find advertising to be entertaining; others find it disturbing. Those who practice advertising consistently rank low in public opinion polls based on trust and honesty.[6] An important component of our professional culture is also how our industry reacts to what the public thinks—this tells quite a lot about what we value.

The cases in this chapter are divided into three sections. The first section includes a single case, "The *American Association of Advertising Agencies (AAAA) Standards of Practice*." This case considers the role of ethical codes in defining behavior and providing guidance in day-to-day decision making. You are then invited to examine the *AAAA Standards of Practice* and evaluate its adequacy as our professional code of ethics. The second section focuses on a single advertising execution, an execution that did appear, albeit briefly. We then look at two hypothetical decision-making scenarios to probe the ethical dilemmas that might arise. The first case in the second section, "Ethical Vision: Moral Muteness and Moral Myopia," focuses on dimensions of ethical behavior and introduces constraints that might occur in certain situations in the workplace. Then, "What Does It Mean to Serve Clients Well?" explores the concept of responsibility and the relationships among advertising practitioners, clients, and the public. The two cases in the last section are at the macro level, more so than at the level of the everyday. They center on inclusion/exclusion and, in a sense, on our profession's "rules of engagement" with complex issues of diversity, looking at women and ethnic and racial groups.

THE ROLE OF CODES OF ETHICS

38 The AAAA Standards of Practice

. . . [S]uccess in business is illusory unless it is grounded in ethical business practices and those need to be . . . instilled in all the workforce from the top to the bottom.[7]

In 2005, Shona Seifert, a former Ogilvy and Mather executive, and her codefendant, Thomas Early, the former financial director at Ogilvy, were found guilty of one count of

continued

conspiracy and nine false claims in a case that captured the trade press headlines for several months. The case involved overbilling the White House Office of National Drug Control Policy, a $1 billion account, to cover a shortfall of $3 million.

Seifert was sentenced to eighteen months imprisonment, two years probation, and 400 hours of community service and was fined $125,000. Judge Richard M. Berman, in handing down the sentence, indicated that the case was essentially about the "slippage in ethics and perhaps the absence of a code of ethics." Hence, as an additional part of her sentence, Seifert was to write a code of ethics for the advertising industry.[8] Results of a poll in *Advertising Age* asking readers to comment on the adequacy of Seifert's effort, an eighteen-page "Proposed Code of Conduct for the Advertising Industry,"[9] suggested that 93 percent found the code to be inadequate. As one respondent noted:

> This document lacked any real substance, instead preferring broad, sweeping statements that said practically nothing. If I were the judge, I'd send her back to the drawing board. And this time, leave the copywriter at home.[10]

Despite the obvious irony of having a now-convicted felon write a professional code, the sentence served to draw attention to the existing code, the *AAAA Standards of Practice*, and so was a useful professional exercise.[11] As one observer noted, "Progress is made any time an industry can have positive dialogue about critical issues. In this instance, the judge's action was a bit of an oxymoron, but the end result raised the level of conversation—and that's a good thing."[12]

The industry's first effort at a professional code of ethics was the Printers' Ink Statute, adopted by the Associated Advertising Clubs of America (AACA) in 1911.[13] Quentin Schultze writes that prior to the adoption of the statute, ethics was a matter of "individual morals, not collective and professional service."[14]

> They [practitioners] were very concerned with maintaining personal standards of integrity and morality in a world that increasingly valued business success. In fact, advertising practitioners seemed disengaged with the large-scale nature of many business transactions and sought to reassert personal ethics as a means of coping with the daily pressures and demands of publishing houses and product manufacturers.[15]

The statute emerged in the context of advertising practitioners' drive to be recognized as a profession. When the AACA met in Boston in 1911 to discuss the truth movement, a newspaperman from Detroit told the group: "If you are to become a profession, you must here and now formulate a code. That code need spell but the one word, Truth, and all other worthy things shall be added unto you."[16] Thus, the Printers' Ink Statute served both an inward and an outward function: It institutionalized the collective moral standards of the profession, and it signified having done so to others.

The *AAAA Standards of Practice* were adopted in 1924 and most recently revised in September of 1990. As we consider the adequacy of the standards, it seems worthwhile to reflect once again on the role of professional codes of ethics in today's historical moment. Such reflection should begin, it seems, by considering the distinction between ethicality and legality. Cunningham defined advertising ethics this way: " . . . what is right or good in the conduct of the advertising function. It is concerned with questions of what ought to be done, not just with what legally must be done."[17] Certainly, following legal restrictions is a part of ethical behavior, but as Cunningham suggests, there is legality, and beyond that, there is ethicality. We should remind ourselves that advertising is regulated by the same laws that regulate business practices, as well as by the Federal Trade Commission (FTC) and the Food and Drug Administration (FDA), plus a host of other federal, state, and local bodies, regarding truthfulness, deception, and fairness.

Then, too, it is worth considering the matter of tastefulness of advertising content. Reinhard addresses this issue in an article entitled, "The Taste Debate: Making a Case for Decency in Advertising."[18] He begins by acknowledging that taste is not arguable or able to be regulated. He then continues, quoting a comment made by Kirk Carr of *The Wall Street Journal*:

> The fact that constructive measures are not easily crafted and that universal agreement is not likely to emerge doesn't relieve the leaders of our community from the responsibility of tackling this difficult issue [taste].[19]

Indeed, tastefulness, or the lack thereof, emerges again and again in the dialogue surrounding advertising and society. ∎

What is the role of a code of professional ethics? Harris, Pritchard, and Rabins identify possible functions of a code of ethics and of the process of its creation[20]:

- It can serve as a collective recognition by members of a profession of its responsibilities.
- It can help to create an environment in which ethical behavior is the norm.
- It can serve as a guide or reminder in specific situations.
- It can serve as an educational tool, providing a focal point for discussions in classes and professional meetings.
- It can indicate to others that the profession is seriously concerned with responsible, professional conduct.
- The process of developing and modifying a code of ethics can be valuable for a profession.

Because codes of ethics are created in response to actual or anticipated ethical conflicts, they may seem abstract when considered outside the context of everyday life. That is, they take on meaning in the "real life" application and the ethical ambiguity arising in a specific case. It is a valuable exercise to interrogate the AAAA Standards of Practice,[21] as well as codes for individual advertising agencies and agency brands, typically located on the agency website. The Vatican Pontifical Council for Social Communication also created a document, simply titled, "Ethics in Advertising," that provides a relatively balanced view of the profession and offers recommendations, though it doesn't go so far as to call those a code of ethics.[22] All AAAA member agencies must subscribe to and adhere to the *AAAA Standards of Practice*, but it is equally important to familiarize yourself with the code of ethics of the agency or company for which you work. Focus particularly on the functions of codes of ethics identified by Harris, Pritchard, and Rabins, and ask questions such as: Does it provide clear advice on the type of case you are facing? Could it support someone making the opposite choice? What general moral principles underlie the advice given? Does the professional code fit my own moral compass?[23]

Drumwright and Murphy conducted a study of advertising practitioners to discover how they think about, approach, and deal with ethical issues.[24] They found that agencies with what they identified as "talking, seeing advertising practitioners" appeared to have "developed and articulated ethical norms." It was not clear, they noted, that other agencies had done so, "at least not in a purposeful, premeditated manner."[25] This speaks strongly to the Aristotelian concept of a "good community" where balance is achieved through everyday cultivation of good habits and nurturance.

What do you think of the adequacy of the *AAAA Standards of Practice*? Practitioner-turned-educator Jelly Helm, in an article entitled, "Saving Advertising," wrote:

> In 1924 we identified our principles and wrote them up as the *AAAA Standards of Practice*. We must rejuvenate and reclarify those standards given what we now know about the state of the world and our relationship to it. The code asserts, among other things, an obligation to the public and a dedication to expressing the truth. "The Truth" is tough to pin down, but it certainly cannot include promoting ideas or products that are harmful to the health of the planet or society at large.[26]

Do you agree?

ETHICS IN THE EVERYDAY

Eroticism and fast food come together in an unlikely combination to announce the arrival of the Patty Melt Thickburger at the Hardee's restaurant chain.[27]

In 2007, Hardees Restaurants (and sister restaurant, Carl Jrs.), a subsidiary of CKE Restaurants, created and aired a "naughty TV spot" for its new patty melt sandwich served on a flat bun (see the *Media Ethics* website). The ad, appropriately identified as the "flat buns" spot, featured a young, sexy teacher in a pencil skirt gyrating to the front of a classroom, and later on top of her desk, to a rap song "celebrating flat booty," sung by the teen boys in her class. The song, aptly entitled, "I Like Flat Buns," had been created for a thirty-second radio spot that was currently running.[28]

The response from the Tennessee Education Association was as quick as it was vehement:

> How irresponsible can you get? At this very moment, there are female teachers in high school classrooms with 30+ students who are working hard to teach our children so that they can compete in today's world. It is unbelievably demeaning to every one of them to promote a television advertisement showing a young teacher gyrating on top of her desk while boys in the class rap about her body in order to sell hamburgers![29]

The ad was targeted to "young, hungry guys" who were "apt to find it appealing,"[30] and Brad Haley, the chain's marketing chief, noted that the chain had "intended [the ad] to be a humorous music video parody. . . . It was designed to be funny, not insulting."[31] The Hardees ad was canceled, and the Carl Jrs. ad was modified. Still, the sure way to make your ad a YouTube hit is to kill it, and visitors to YouTube are given the opportunity to see other Hardees/Carl Jrs. efforts: "Patty Melts for You," in which Swedish model Helena Mattson cooingly gyrates, tosses her hair, licks her lips, and then invites the viewer to join her as she bites into a patty melt sandwich, and an earlier, one can say infamous, ad for Carl Jrs. in which a very scantily clad Paris Hilton seductively soaps herself and her Bentley before biting into her sandwich.

Note: The preceding story is true. The scenarios in the following two cases are hypothetical and were created to invite you to reflect on some of the decision-making processes that *might have occurred* in the conceptualization, creation, and airing of this spot. Although there are elements of fact in the scenarios, *they did not happen* as presented here.

39 Ethical Vision: Moral Muteness and Moral Myopia[32]

Jeff was relatively new in his position as an assistant account planner on the Hardees account. Maybe that was why he felt so uncomfortable at this meeting. He and Steve, the planner on the account, had just met with the creative team to view the new executions for the Patty Melt Thickburger Sandwich—"Flat Buns" and "Patty Melts for You." The stuff was edgy, and edgy was what the client liked. Everybody was pumped. Everybody, that is, except Jeff.

Maybe, he thought, it was because he simply didn't like the product; that is, he didn't like the *idea* of the product: 1410 calories, 70 percent of the average person's daily caloric intake. What was it Andrew Puzder, the chief executive, had said when they first talked about the sandwich? "It's not a burger for tree huggers."[33] You could say that again. The rest of the world is worrying about the obesity epidemic. Is this a healthy thing to eat?

But Jeff knew it was more than that. He was uncomfortable with the executions. Sure, they were "on strategy"; they very obviously targeted the "young hungry guys" the restaurant was seeking. (Had the creative guy really winked when he said "hungry guys"?[34]) The

continued

executions were . . . what? Well, they were just too much! Okay, so sex sells, or so we say in the industry. But hamburgers? "Patty Melts for You." He thought it had been a joke, but no, they were serious. Hadn't we learned anything from the Paris Hilton escapade? To make matters worse, Jeff was mad at himself; he hadn't said *anything* about his concerns. So, it was on to the next step; later in the week, they'd meet with the client.   ■

The situation facing Jeff is a common one. Relatively new on the job, he found himself alone in his belief/recognition that something was awry with the creative executions, and he remained mute; he didn't speak up. No doubt those creating the executions felt they were "on strategy." In that sense, Jeff's colleagues were doing their jobs. But in this situation, by all appearances they were myopic to any of the possible moral consequences beyond whether or not the client would "buy into" the campaign. They knew the client to be very willing to push the envelope, to be "over the top," to be edgy, and they created advertising accordingly. Indeed, they appeared to have no concerns about the larger consequences of their executions, and may have felt that given that culture had become more tolerant, they could "go a bit farther" to get their client's product noticed. This lack of awareness or concern of social consequences is not uncommon. Research has shown that those consequences farthest away, most abstract from the individual's own environment, are least likely to be recognized. Although Jeff didn't confront the issue organizationally, he did confront it personally, which suggests that he might, in a community of reflective individuals, be comfortable to speak up.

What would you have done?

40 What Does It Mean to Serve Clients Well?

"This is the way I see it," the Hardees' marketing officer told Eric and Rob, the account planning team from the agency. "We're talking to young men—young *hungry* men. You remember when you were that age? All you cared about was food and girls. So that's what we've got here in my idea for these ads. A really big, delicious, juicy, decadent burger and a girl. What could be better?"

The client was right about the burger; there seemed to be a boom in burger sales, obesity epidemic or not.[35] And he seemed to be right about the linkage between boys, food, and girls. Brian Wansink, director of the Cornell University Food and Brand Lab, was quoted in a recent *Advertising Age* article:

> There is some correlation with manliness and appetite. There is a connection, at least in the young man's mind, of having a healthy appetite for food and having an identity that you believe is appealing to the opposite sex.[36]

The client sketched out ideas for two executions. "Flat buns," he said, "would be a play on every schoolboy's dream of falling in love with his teacher, but done twenty-first century style, you see, as a parody of a music video. And, it would go with the rap tune you guys had already created for the radio spot, wouldn't it? And then, 'Patty Melts for You'?

Well, *she* would never make it on the networks, but she could play on the website; she'd be sort of an extra treat. What do you fellas think?"

"There *was* that Paris Hilton ad for Carls," Eric reminded him. "That hadn't played too well."

"Exactly. That was a dynamite ad. It was edgy. I loved it. It shouldn't have run on the network. That was a mistake. She should have gone right on the Web. She's on YouTube, you know. And she gets a lot of hits everyday, even still today. A few feminists might have objected, but heck, they aren't in the target audience, are they? Boys absolutely loved it! They still do. And if somebody objects to the teachers, if the babe doesn't play right, we'll put her and her class on YouTube. She'll be a big hit." The client wound down enthusiastically.

Eric and Rob would have to think about this. The client certainly was right about the Paris Hilton spot. It had received a lot of critical publicity; people thought it was sexist, hypersexualized, and retrograde, and some even called it "pornographic." But the target market did like it, sales were up, and Paris, her Bentley, and her Burger were still a YouTube draw. Ads that are "banned" are always a big hit on YouTube, but it wasn't exactly a sound media strategy. And then, there was the question of social responsibility.   ■

This situation, again, is not an uncommon one, but now that the client is involved, it has new complexities. Here it becomes a matter of reflecting on what it is we think we are doing when we do advertising work. As professionals, we are bound to the service of our client. But do we not also have some social responsibility to do the greatest good possible? The client, in this situation, has had good return on his investment using images of questionable appropriateness and clearly recognizes their likelihood of offensiveness because he's planning ahead for when the executions either don't get accepted to air or create too much of a stir to keep airing. He has the YouTube escape hatch, with which he clearly is enamored.

After conducting research on advertisers' thoughts and actions with regard to ethics, Drumwright and Murphy suggested that "a paradigm shift seems to be needed regarding what it means to serve clients well. Many of [the informants interviewed] expressed a strong sense that advertising practitioners are to do the clients bidding."[37] Is the agency here in danger of "going native," of "overidentifying with the client's perspective to the point that they have lost the ability to be critical of clients and objective in assessing their behavior and advertising"?[38] Certainly it would be easier to leave the situation alone; clients aren't likely to want to be subjected to critical questioning, are they? Is it the agency's business to question the moral judgment of the client? But then, is the agency doing its job if it doesn't raise the question?

Although the client seems myopic in his lack of recognition of the social consequences of his work, Eric and Rob seem to share concerns, though both were mute in this situation. In a fast-paced, competitive, creative industry, discussion of ethical concerns frequently takes a back seat to more urgent pragmatic issues. Perhaps a conversation in the quiet of the office could help them to come up with alternative approaches. They are lucky to have a community, even if only a community of two, to talk over these types of concerns, and perhaps, to develop strategies that might better serve the client.

The advertising profession clearly possesses a strong client-centeredness, but doesn't it have obligations and indeed, loyalties, that go beyond that?

What would you suggest?

RULES OF ENGAGEMENT: INCLUSION/EXCLUSION

41 A Woman's Place Is . . .?

French Flap Reignites Gender Debate
Wild Adman's Rant Turns the Clock Back to 1960s[39]

Okay, so Neil French, then the worldwide creative director for the WPP Group, is, as a *New York Times* reporter noted, a "bombastic and controversial figure in the advertising world," a "legend" according to Matthew Creamer in *Advertising Age*.[40] Perhaps he *was* providing a "typically abrasive Neil French performance."[41] Peppering his conversation with "babe" and "bitch," French told a gathering of more than 300 advertising executives in Toronto that the reason there weren't more female creative directors in the business was that trying to balance work with family duties was "crap." "They can't put in the hours. Somebody has to look after the kids."[42] That comment, as the headline above suggests, *did* reignite a gender debate in this industry, as had an ad for "Advertising Week," New York City's annual celebration of the business earlier that year. The ad, which many referred to as "the breast ad" (see the *Media Ethics* website), simply zoomed in on female breasts (no head, of course, just breasts) clad in a black bustier, agape, but held with a tiny red ribbon and the slogan, "Advertising" (on one breast). "We all do it" (on the other breast). The ad had drawn comments both incredulous and outraged,[43] much as French's did some three months later.

Nancy Vonk, co-chief creative officer at Ogilvy & Mather Toronto, responded to French's remarks in an essay on IHaveAnIdea.org:

> What struck me so hard, as he described a group that will inevitably wimp out and "go suckle something" after their short stint in advertising, was that in his honest opinion he was voicing the inner thoughts of legions of men in the senior ranks of our business.[44]

Nancy went on to give a very concrete illustration of the destructiveness of attitudes such as that expressed by French:

> Before us was a big part of the explanation for why women aren't succeeding in advertising. If male CDs, even a little like Neil, see a female creative coming toward him with her work, and he's already convinced she's extremely limited in her ability and value, what lens is he seeing her work—her—through? Would you expect that CD to offer the same support and guidance and consideration he gives the men? Might that woman not keep herself down on the farm when her leader conveys in countless ways

she's not as good as the boys? Might she respond with a little less than her best effort when the adored leader expects little of her? Might she want to leave, not to have
babies, but because the conditions for her to succeed don't exist and the message she
can't succeed is too discouraging?[45]

And the floodgates opened. French was celebrated and vilified. Celebrated and vilified
again. Called brilliant. Called a retrograde has-been. The lack of female creative directors
had nothing to do with their gender. It was about opportunity. It was about experience. You
could make it with talent.

Two weeks after the incident, French resigned in what he suggested in an interview, was
"death by blog."[46] ∎

Advertising, almost since its earliest days, has congratulated itself on the
"welcome" it has extended to women. Initially, it was because women brought with
them "the woman's viewpoint." Here's how it was explained in a trade journal in
1914:

> Ever since women began to do things outside the preconceived limits of a so-
> called "women's sphere," no field has been opened up by them that presents
> greater assurance of success than that of advertising. Women are the purchas-
> ing agents of most American families. While the man is earning the income, the
> woman is watching the outgo. That is her business.
>
> Who more qualified, therefore, than another woman to know her process
> of thought in deciding upon a purchase? Or, who more qualified to appeal to
> her taste and tickle her fancies than one who likes the same things and sees the
> manner of living from the same side of the fence.[47]

Today, approximately 75 percent of the students enrolled in university and
college advertising programs are women; approximately 66 percent of those working in advertising are women. However, the status of women declines as we go up
the corporate ladder; the absence of women in creative positions, and particularly
in creative director positions, is especially noteworthy. It is not uncommon to see
remnants of the "women's viewpoint" even today. Bosman, for example, wrote in
The New York Times, "The dominance of men on the creative side of the business is
even more striking, considering that women commonly make up to 80 percent of
household purchasing decisions.... [S]ome experts say the gender imbalance
helps explain why some advertising is perceived in polls and focus groups as sexist."[48] Jo Foxworth's experience as an advertising woman beginning in the 1950s indicated that while the woman's viewpoint may have given women a point of entré
into the business, it ultimately constrained them in their opportunities. She noted:

> It used to burn me up for someone, for a man to say, "come in here and give us a
> woman's point of view ..." instead of the professional point of view. It always
> had to be a gender thing. They would ask you to make a phone call, ... ask you
> to do secretary's work.... I was terribly frustrated. I couldn't stand being
> treated like a non-entity or just somebody with a woman's viewpoint. I wanted
> to be treated like a professional person.[49]

Feminist historian Joan Wallach Scott reminds us that when we judge professional inclusion, we typically focus on gaining access, counting the number of individuals in a particular group who gain entry. However, more fundamental questions might be:

> How are those who cross the thresholds received? If they belong to a group different from the one already "inside," what are the terms of their incorporation? How do the new arrivals understand the place they have entered? What are the terms of identity they establish?[50]

There are indications that, for women, the "terms of incorporation" are not quite what they should be.

- "There is still [in 2003] a tremendous discrepancy in the salary levels between men and women in the advertising industry. This gap exists across the board in every job in every geographic region, in both large and small."[51]
- Women are underrepresented in awards given for achievement.
  - Only 13 of the 174 inductees in the AAF Advertising Hall of Fame are women.
  - Only 13 of the 147 inductees in the Art Directors Club of New York are women.
  - Only 5 of the 40 inductees in the One Club are women.
- A 2006 survey by the Advertising Women of New York[52] found that
  - Men working in the industry earned $16,000 more on average than women.
  - Men do not recognize what women see as their greatest strengths in the workforce, but women give credence to men's greatest strengths.
  - Men are more likely to have taken advantage of work/life balance options than women.

Why aren't there more female creative directors in advertising? Most women writing on IHaveAnIdea.org seemed to agree that it wasn't a lack of talent or a lack of knowledge. Instead, they cited an absence of women role models, limited experience ("We'll get there"), limited family-friendly policies, an "old boys' club mentality, and women starting their own companies. In short, "advertising has adopted few of the structural changes that tend to attract women executives."[53]

Nancy Vonk concluded her essay with a "call to action":

> Finally the women reading this are going to have to do better than me. I've suddenly realized that looking the other way, turning the other cheek in any situation, . . . makes me part of the problem. I'm snapping out of it awfully late, and it seems obvious we can't take this . . . and expect to see anything change. Don't be discouraged; be outraged and act accordingly.[54]

42 Diversity in Advertising: What Is It? Where Is It?

Now, here's a shot in the dark: Has it ever crossed anyone's mind that a major reason so many marketers still struggle [to connect] to our diversified consumer base is because we're less and less like them than ever before?

We talk a lot about how media savvy consumers have become but we sidestep the obvious fact that they've also gotten blacker and more Mexican, more Puerto Rican, more Chinese, more Korean, more Ethiopian, more Columbian, more Jamaican, etc. And with this have come more definitions of what's cool, what's sexy, what's beautiful, what's relevant, what's heartwarming, what's human and what ideas can and should build a brand.

How do you "think out of the box when you've hired nothing but boxes?[55]

With these words, Hadji Williams, a copywriter for thirteen years, opened up once again the dialogue on diversity or lack thereof in the advertising industry. Quite a dialogue it was. Let's think a bit about the diversity issue in the profession.

Early in 2006, the industry's minority hiring practices in New York City were called into question or, perhaps correctly, "blasted . . . as an embarrassment for a diverse city."[56] The industry had first come under scrutiny in the early 1970s. According to a report of the Commission on Human Rights in 1978, the commission then believed

> . . . that the limited minority employment was not simply the result of neutral forces, but emanated rather from discriminatory practices which have historically excluded minorities from meaningful participation in these industries.[57]

Thirty years later, apparently little had changed. And it seemed the industry was getting tired of the discussion. An editorial in *Advertising Age* subtitled, "Will We Be Reading This Same Story Again in 2036?" presented the results of a reader poll:

> Why do we—along with 93 percent of those responding to our poll—get the feeling we'll be reading something similar in another thirty years? There is something surreally Orwellian about this affair. A government agency loudly demands that an entire industry reform. The industry, on the other hand, makes public promises to meet the demands (partly in the hope it all blows over), while ignoring the realistic goals it could conceivably achieve.

Lather. Rinse Repeat[58].   ■

In his book, *Madison Avenue and the Color Line: African-Americans in the Advertising Industry,* Jason Chambers traces the history of African-Americans and, like Williams, emphasizes that increased minority hiring is more than a moral imperative or a social responsibility. "It is an economic and social necessity."[59]

Viewed in all its complexity, diversity has an impact on every aspect of the advertising profession: professional culture, production of content, content itself, the manner in which that content is placed and received, and the ways in which the profession is regulated.

Then, too, diversity, the acknowledgment and inclusion of a wide variety of peoples with differing characteristics, attributes, beliefs, values, and experiences, isn't simply about gender, race, and ethnicity. Consider, for example, primary language, spiritual practices, sexual preference, socioeconomic status, age, etc. Jonathon Feit, writing about the 2007 AAAA Media Conference Panel on "The Business Case for Diversity in Media," reported that nearly half the audience walked out of the presentation. He noted:

> Granted, the AAAA meant well by having a diversity panel. . . . But diversity has been rhetoricized ad nauseam at media and advertising industry events over the past two years, and advances are slowly being made. However, . . . two black men, one black woman, and one Hispanic woman do not a panel on "diversity" make. Diversity does not and cannot simply mean mashing together persons of color, whose experiences, while varied in their own right, far from encompass the broadest range of experiences.
>
> Where were representatives from the GLBT community, the disabled community, the Asian community, the immigrant community, the senior community, the youth community—or hey, here's an interesting one—the white community?[60]

As our lives, professional and personal, become increasingly global, diversity will continue to develop; its influence will be experienced in increasingly complex, sometimes tangled ways. In this context, it is essential that advertising professionals adopt broad interpretations of advertising's impact on diversity and diversity's impact on advertising.

Williams doesn't leave us with a call to action but instead with a simple reminder:

> To remix John Edwards, there's a different America out there. They never loved *Raymond*. They never got *Friends*, *Seinfeld*, or *Sex in the City*. They still don't get *SNL* or *The World According to Jim*. Their musical tastes aren't shaped by *Rolling Stone*, *TRL*, or even *BET*. They don't trust *FOX*. They don't shop at Banana Republic or Gap. Their ideal female isn't in the pages of *Cosmo* or *Playboy*. (And quiet as they've kept, they dismiss Dove's "real women" as an attempt to capitalize on the zeitgeist of white women's insecurities despite being propped as the standard of American beauty since Day One.) This America rarely golfs and will never drive 500 miles in a circle, much less watch others do it.
>
> (By the way: this America is not white.[61])

NOTES

1. Talcott Parsons, "The Professions and Social Structure," *Social Forces* 17 (May 1939): 457–467.
2. Vanderbilt Medical Center Patent Medicine Collection, www.mc.vanderbilt.edu/biolib/hc/nostrums/nostrums.html.

3. Stanley Resor, "What Do These Changes Mean? Do We Fully Appreciate the Nature of the Job?" Address before the meeting of the Western Council of the American Association of Advertising Agencies, Chicago, 1924. JWT Archives, Perkins Library, Duke University. Resor purchased J. Walter Thompson with a group of colleagues in 1916 and served as its president for nearly half a century. Thompson was one of the largest, if not *the* largest, advertising agency in the world at that time, and in his capacity as president, Resor played a vital leadership role in defining the professionalization efforts of the agency and of the entire field. See Peggy J. Kreshel, "The 'Culture' of J. Walter Thompson, 1915–1925," *Public Relations Review* 16:8 (Fall 1990): 80–93.

4. Kreshel, "The 'Culture' of J. Walter Thompson," p. 88–89, fn. 3.

5. Gergely Nyilasy, "Advertising and Professionalism," unpublished manuscript.

6. See, for example, Frank Newport, "Annual Update: Americans Rate Business and Industry Sectors," Gallup Poll, 6 September 2007, www.galluppoll.com/content/default.aspx?ci=28615&VERSION=P, 10/14/2007; and Giselle Abramovich, "Americans Have Skewed View of Ad Industry," *DMNews*, 25 September 2007, www.dmnews.com/cms/dm-news/research-studies/42504.html.

7. Judge Richard M. Berman, quoted in Deanna Zammit, "Seifert's Sentence: 18 Months," *Adweek*, 14 July 2005, www.adweek.com/aw/national/article_display.jsp?vnu_content_id=1000979190, 10/14/2007.

8. Ibid.

9. http://adage.com/images/random/seifertethics.pdf, 10/14/2007.

10. Matthew Creamer, "The Verdict Is In: Seifert Guilty of Shirking Sentence," *Advertising Age*, 5 September 2005.

11. www.**aaaa**.org/EWEB/upload/inside/**standards**.pdf, 10/14/2007.

12. Matthew Creamer, "The Verdict Is In: Seifert Guilty of Shirking Sentence," *Advertising Age*, 5 September 2005.

13. Quentin Schultze, "Advertising Science and Professionalism 1885–1917," dissertation, University of Illinois at Urbana–Champaign, 1978, pp. 175–176.

14. Ibid., p. 170.

15. Ibid.

16. H. J. Kenner, *The Fight for Truth in Advertising* (New York: Round Table Press, Inc., 1936), p. 18.

17. Peggy H. Cunningham, "Ethics of Advertising," in *The Advertising Business*, John Phillip Jones, ed. (Thousand Oaks, CA: Sage Publications, 1999), p. 500.

18. Keith Reinhard, "The Taste Debate: Making a Case for Decency in Advertising," *Agency*, Fall 2001, pp. 30–32.

19. Ibid., p. 31.

20. Charles E. Harris, Jr., Michael S. Pritchard, and Michael J. Rabins, *Engineering Ethics: Concepts and Cases.* (Belmont, CA: Wadsworth Publishing, 1995).

21. www.**aaaa**.org/EWEB/upload/inside/**standards**.pdf,

22. www.vatican.va/roman_curia/pontifical_councils/pccs/documents/rc_pc_pccs_doc_22021997_ethics-in-ad_en.html

23. An extremely useful site for those interested in the development and application of codes of ethics is "Codes of Ethics Online," http://ethics.iit.edu/codes/coe.html, a website created by the Center for the Study of Ethics in the Professions at the Illinois Institute of Technology. IIT was created in 1975 for the purpose of "promoting education and scholarship in the professions." In 1996, IIT received a grant from the National Science Foundation to put its collection of codes of ethics on the Web. The collection

includes codes from professional societies, corporations, governments, and academic institutions; over 850 codes are indexed on the site.

24. Minette E. Drumwright and Patrick E. Murphy, "How Advertising Practitioners View Ethics," *Journal of Advertising* 33:2, (Summer 2004): 7–24.

25. Ibid., p 18.

26. Jelly Helm, "Saving Advertising," *Émigré* 53 (2000), www.emigre.com/Editorial.php ?sect=1&id+25, 10/13/2007.

27. "New Campaigns—The World," *Campaigns* (UK), August 10, 2007, p. 29.

28. Laura Petrecca, Theresa Howard, and Bruce Horowitz, "New and Notable," *USA Today*, 24 September 2007, p. 38.

29. William Spain, "Hardees Ad Not Hot for Teacher," *MediaPost Publications*, 10 September 2007, http://publications.mediapost.com/index.cfm?fuseaction=Articles.showArticle &art_aid=67146, 10/14/2007.

30. Ibid.

31. Petrecca, Howard, and Horowitz, "New and Notable."

32. I draw these terms from Minette E. Drumwright and Patrick E. Murphy, "How Advertising Practitioners View Ethics," *Journal of Advertising* 33:2 (Summer 2004): 7–24.

33. Candy Sagon, "He Eats, She Eats, Chain Restaurants Play the Sex Card," *The Washington Post*, 7 June 2006, p. F1.

34. "Burgers Big It Up," *Irish Independent*, 6 September 2006.

35. Kate McArthur, "Cheeseburger in Paradise; Big Burger Sales Boom Despite Obesity Epidemic," *Advertising Age*, 17 July 2006, p. 4.

36. Ibid.

37. Minette E. Drumwright and Patrick E. Murphy, "How Advertising Practitioners View Ethics," *Journal of Advertising* 33:2 (Summer 2004).

38. Minette E. Drumwright and Patrick E. Murphy, "How Advertising Practitioners View Ethics," *Journal of Advertising*, 33:2 (Summer 2004) 13.

39. Matthew Creamer, "French Flap Reignites Gender Debate," *Advertising Age*, 24 October 2005.

40. Julie Bosman, "Stuck at the Edges of the Ad Game," *The New York Times*, 22 November 2005, p. C1; Creamer, "French Flap Reignites Gender Debate."

41. Creamer, "French Flap Reignites Gender Debate."

42. French, quoted in Creamer, "French Flap Reignites Gender Debate." It should be noted that accounts of exactly what French did say, that is, exactly what people *heard*, vary widely, though all are in agreement regarding the tone and general content.

43. The ad appeared in a variety of publications, mostly trade publications, and can be seen at this text's website. It ran in *Advertising Age* on 18 July 2005.

44. www.ihaveanidea.org/articles/index.php?/archives/268-Female-Like-Me.html, 10/14/2007. The entire dialogue that came about after Vonk's essay is available at this site.

45. Ibid.

46. Creamer, "French Flap Reignites Gender Debate."

47. Viscountess Rhonda, *Printers Ink*, 1914, quoted in *JWT Newsletter*, 28 February 1924, JWT Archives, J. W. Hartman Center for Sales, Advertising and Marketing History, Perkins Library, Duke University, Durham, North Carolina.

48. Bosman, "Stuck at the Edges of the Ad Game." See also Peggy Kreshel, "Interview with Liz Schroeder and Margie Goldsmith," *Advertising and Society Review* 4:4 (2003), http://muse.jhu.edu/journals/asr/v004/4.4kreshel.html, accessed, 10/14/2007.

49. Jo Foxworth in personal interview with Peggy J. Kreshel, New York City, 9 March 1999.

50. Joan Wallach Scott, *Gender and the Politics of History* (New York: Columbia Press, 1999), p. 178.
51. "AWNY to Address Gender Salary Gap," *Advertising Age*, 13 January 2003.
52. "Advertising Women of New York's National Industry-Wide Survey of Women and Men Advertising Professionals," *PRNewswire*, http://sev.prnewswire.com/advertising/20060504/NYTH02104052006-1.html, 9/13/2007.
53. Bosman, "Stuck at the Edges of the Ad Debate."
54. www.ihaveanidea.org/articles/index.php?/archives/268-Female-Like-Me.html.
55. http://ihaveanidea.org/articles/archives/295-White-Space,-White-Noise.-Americas-More-Diverse-than-ever.-So-isnt-the-ad-industry.html, 10/17/2007.
56. Lisa Sanders, "NYC to Subpoeona Ad Agency Execs in Diversity Probe," *Advertising Age*, 6 March 2006.
57. A Commission on Human Rights Analysis of Compulsory versus Voluntary Affirmative Action, "Minority Employment and the Advertising Industry in New York City," June 1978.
58. Editorial, "The Ad Industry Diversity Hiring Controversy," *Advertising Age*, 17 September 2006.
59. Jason Chambers, *Madison Avenue and the Color Line: African Americans in the Advertising Industry* (Philadelphia: University of Pennsylvania Press, 2008).
60. Jonathon Scott Feit, "Fake Friends and Lip Service: Call All GLBT Marketers and Consumers," *WITH THIS RING Magazine*. www.queersighted.com/2007/03/01/fake-friends-and-lip-service-calling-all-glbt-marketers-and-cons/, 9/18/2007.
61. http://ihaveanidea.org/articles/archives/295-White-Space,-White-Noise.-Americas-More-Diverse-than-ever.-So-isnt-the-ad-industry.html, 10/17/2007.

Persuasion and Public Relations

Much of what we know of modern business, industry, entertainment, government, even religion, has been shaped by the practice of public relations. The act of helping an organization and its public adapt to each other or to "win the cooperation of groups of people"[1] calls on practitioners to "establish and maintain mutual lines of communications"; to manage problems or issues; to help management respond to public opinion and to use change in a positive way; to "serve as an early warning system"; and to help management understand how best to "serve the public interest."[2] In other words, practitioners are asked to serve a variety of roles within the organization, including those of spokesperson, listener, planner, surveyor, and counselor.

Such a daunting task list has prompted calls for increased emphasis on ethical practice. The two largest professional organizations have adopted formal codes of ethical practice, each with something distinctive within the field of professional communication ethics: enforcement processes. The Public Relations Society of America (PRSA) and the International Association of Business Communicators have gone beyond the mere adoption of codes; they also teach, talk about, and try to enforce ethical practices. Practitioners from different industries, from health care to education, have adopted similar codes seeking to define what is "good" behavior in their settings. (See www.case.org and www.hcpra.org for examples.)

Despite these efforts, the public image of public relations practitioners remains clouded. Terms such as *spin doctor* and *flack* are all too common; phrases such as "It's just a PR stunt" and "It's all image control" come to mind too readily for the field to become complacent about its image or its role. The criticism may just reflect the general cynicism with which most institutions such as the press, big business, and government are regarded in this country. But at other times the criticism stems from the relationships between practitioners and other communicators. Organizational downsizing has meant that marketers, advertisers, and practitioners often operate within the same department—indeed, sometimes with duties divided among two or three employees. This may foster the assumption that practitioners use the same one-way flow of persuasive information that advertisers or marketers traditionally rely on in sales campaigns rather than a belief that practitioners desire to build and maintain reciprocal communication flow. The interdependence between journalists and practitioners also has been an uneasy relationship, with questions arising about how much interaction can occur between the media and other organizations before ethical standards are breached.

At times, criticisms arise from the "kill-the-messenger" syndrome when practitioners, like reporters, are held personally responsible for the actions about which they communicate. The boundary communication role between the organization and the public played by the practitioner can become a convenient point of complaint for those discontented with the actions of politicians, entertainers, or corporations. And sometimes the criticisms are well deserved, such as when practitioners choose to divert public attention from the truth or distort it or when they deliberately clutter the communication channels with confusing rhetoric or events. Ethical suspicions also result from what appears to be the ever-increasing spread of the application of public relations and persuasion campaigns into fields such as health care, litigation, and government.

The four chapters in this section cannot claim to be encyclopedic, but they seek to raise the types of questions encountered by today's practitioners and audience members. Are there fields of interest so vital to the public good that public relations should not play a persuasive role in them? Is the polishing and shaping of a public image inherently deceptive? How does one loyally serve the interests of a client or an employer and still serve the public interest? How much social responsibility should a corporation or business be required to demonstrate, and how does one best balance social responsibility with fiscal responsibility? Some of the cases that follow are drawn from actual situations; others are hypothetical cases based on a realistic understanding of these pressures. Each seeks to focus attention on the needs, pressures, contradictions, and promises of this influential profession.

NOTES

1. Philip Lesley, "Report and Recommendations: Task Force on Stature and Role of Public Relations," *Public Relations Journal* (March 1981): 32.
2. Rex F. Harlow, "Building a Public Relations Definition," *Public Relations Review* 2:4 (Winter 1976): 36.

CHAPTER TEN

Public Communication

nformation provider. Advocate. Activist: Public-relations practitioners are often called on to play multiple roles as they work with or against other stakeholders with particular viewpoints, needs, or causes. By definition, the practitioner is partisan—representing a certain group, organization, or public—with biases and loyalties apparent as he or she seeks to build or enhance critical relationships. In many settings, this partisanship raises few or no ethical questions. However, in the complex sphere of public communication in an open society, where successful or unsuccessful public relations may have an impact on political campaigns, international diplomacy, and voter confidence, the motivations, tactics, strategies, goals, and objectives of practitioners may be more questioned.

The work of this important profession is clearly informational and decidedly persuasive. And why not insist on both at the same time? Truth is never neutral, so why should the telling of truth be any less than the professional mandate of someone paid to communicate a particular perspective? In one important sense, this is a more honest mode of media work because one's biases as a communicator in a public relations setting are usually transparent. Shedding pretenses is normally the first lesson in public relations training.

Regardless of how it is categorized, the need for advocacy and information extends from PTA councils to councils of war. Dwight Eisenhower recalled in his memoirs of the D-Day invasion that soon after his arrival in London in the summer of 1942, he recognized that the Allied plan to break into Germany through France would impose immense hardship on British families and farms as American sailors and soldiers gathered in preparation. His solution was to establish early "an effective Public Relations Section of the headquarters."[1] The general went on to describe battle plans, so readers were left to wonder what role public relations played in the success of the Allied cause and in the continuation of pluralist democracy in the West. We suspect that this part of the untold story is complicated and considerable.

What we do know is that contemporary politicians and strategists rely on the information and persuasion of public relations to raise funds for campaigns, to influence decision making about legislation and policies, and to attempt to motivate what has become an inactive electorate to care about public affairs. A politician's choice of a press secretary or a campaign manager may be as avidly watched and debated as is the selection of a running mate or major policy initiative. Trade and professional organizations, labor unions, and industry groups routinely employ full-time lobbyists and send representatives to meet with policymakers and politicians in local, state, and federal offices in hopes of influencing their decisions. Indeed, the U.S. government employs thousands of public-affairs specialists, writers, photographers, and editors, even though certain provisions of federal law seemingly prohibit such appropriation of funding.[2] At times, it seems that the channels of public debate have become so overloaded with voices representing special-interest groups that there is little room left for anyone who cares to articulate the need for the general public interest.

Who should control or influence the voices in the political and public-affairs marketplace of ideas? Is the practice of journalism inherently more ethical than that of public relations because it strives more for objectivity and information? Or is public relations more honest because its practitioners admit their allegiances openly? Is there such a need to enhance the communication capability of some voices in the public forum that public relations must be employed? How far can the practice of public relations expand before it interferes with the democratic process?

The five cases in this chapter explore these questions. The first, "Mr. Ethics Sells Out," examines how journalists and public relations practitioners influence public communication. "Playing Defense on the Court[room] of Public Opinion" probes the expanding field of litigation public relations. Is the cause of rendering justice advanced when high-profile defendants or prosecutors use public relations tactics to communicate their views before trial? The third case, "Indictments Indicate Corrupt Lobbying," recounts the issues that result when money unduly influences public decision making, and "A Campaign Pioneer?" explores the practices involved in fund raising in national political campaigns. The last case, "Your Tax Dollars at Work?" questions the roles of government-sponsored persuasion campaigns in domestic and international settings.

43 Mr. Ethics Sells Out

"I can't believe you'd even consider it, Richard."

"Richard, you've always been the model reporter—Mr. Reporting Ethics. What could industry possibly offer you? You're going to become a flack!"

Richard had worked for eight years as a newswriter for a metro daily, moving from general assignment reporting to the business desk. He had enjoyed the demands and had a gift for interviewing and a fluent writing style. Editors seldom heard complaints about the accuracy of his work or the objectivity of his stances. Richard prided himself on thorough research before he interviewed or wrote.

That commitment to quality was known outside the newsroom, too. A year earlier, Richard had written a five-part series on the future of industrial and commercial development in West York. As part of the research, he had interviewed fifty local business managers and directors, read mountains of government and chamber of commerce reports, and even spent a week reporting inside the factory of the largest local manufacturer as it was retooled into a state-of-the-art technological complex. His careful work and his agreeable manner had impressed the plant manager. So, when the plant public relations officer announced his retirement, the manager approached Richard about accepting the job.

Richard was interested. The company's willingness to embrace new technology and its prospects for success were intriguing. Although he loved his job at the paper, more stable hours and more rewarding pay were tempting. He'd read the gloomy forecasts about the future of newspapers and had heard rumors of possible layoffs.[3] Richard had expected his colleagues to rib him about the move, but he was shocked at the passion of their criticism.

"I just can't see you doing this, Richard," the city hall reporter said. "The whole field of PR is about obfuscation and image control—it has nothing to do with those things you're always preaching at SPJ meetings. Apart from the few practitioners you can trust, most are on the payroll to make their companies look good, and they'll do whatever it takes to make that happen."

Another government reporter shook his head. "In my twenty-three years as a reporter, I've never had a minute to waste with a PR person. When I was coming up, we were told they were paid liars, and that's how I've always treated them. Flacks are good for free lunches and photo ops and not much else, in my opinion."

The first reporter broke in: "Think about it, Richard. You've spent eight years learning to get around the PR types to get to the truth. Now you're going to learn how to put up barriers for reporters? I don't think so."

"Barriers for reporters?" Richard said. "Listen, there is one thing I've learned by covering business. If it weren't for public relations practitioners, there wouldn't be a business section published in any paper in this country. Plenty of responsible practitioners work hard to get their stories out. Heaven knows, many of them have helped me. Without these 'flacks' as you call them, none of you could get all the stories you do."

The group was unconvinced. Richard walked away feeling a bit depressed. He had thought those old stereotypes about public relations ethics had died out, but apparently he was wrong. Were his colleagues right? Would he have to abandon journalistic ethics to successfully practice corporate public relations?   ■

For a seasoned reporter, Richard displays a surprising level of naïveté in assuming that his friends would not have stereotypical opinions of public relations practitioners. Surveys and anecdotes suggest that most journalists continue to consider themselves more ethical than public relations practitioners. Many practitioners, in turn, believe this negative attitude carries over into press coverage of public relations activities.[4] Richard's decision to leave his newspaper job and move into what appears to be a more lucrative corporate position is a natural target for the barbs of his colleagues.

Are their barbs on target? Will Richard's new position require him to adopt new standards for ethical behavior because journalistic ethics and practitioners' ethics are incompatible? Yes and no. Obviously, his communication situation will change and become in many ways more elaborate and less independent. Richard may be able to accept this lack of independence, however, if he understands how his position within the communication cycle has changed. The journalist's position as "objective outsider" is gone; the practitioner is called on to be a subjective insider. The voice of the practitioner is the official voice of the organization, not the personal expression of the individual himself or herself. The lack of a byline on most public relations writing epitomizes this change in position. Such a lack of independence is not necessarily a lack of ethics, however, as long as other values such as accuracy, fairness, and public service are still operative.

Are those concepts valued in the corporate office as they were in the newsroom? The written codes of ethics adopted by the two leading public relations professional organizations assert the centrality of at least some of the values. One of the Core Principles of the Code of Ethics of the Public Relations Society of America says that "protecting and advancing the free flow of accurate and truthful information is essential to serving the public interest and contributing to informed decision making in a democratic society." The Code of Ethics of the International Association of Business Communicators calls for professionals to "encourage the practice of honest, candid and timely communication."[5] According to these standards, Richard will retain and use his commitment to accuracy, fairness, and public service.

Richard had always understood accuracy to indicate that his writing was true and verifiable. In some ways, the corporate approval process may better ensure truthfulness than the copy-flow pattern of the newsroom because there will be more opportunity for errors to be caught. However, Richard may find some ethical tension between the truthfulness and verifiability of what is disclosed and that which is intentionally undisclosed for defensive reasons. It is in protecting this information from disclosure that Richard may face some of the issues his colleagues decried.

Fairness also may present a challenge to Richard's journalistic intuitions. Richard had always understood fairness to mean that all sides of an issue would be given an opportunity to speak. For instance, in the series that had led to this job offer, he had interviewed both those in charge of modernizing the plant and the union official worried about the potential replacement of workers with high-tech machines. He doubted whether he would be as compelled to include the negative information if he were to write a similar piece for a company publication, or if he did, he would certainly focus more on company programs for retraining workers or offering out-placement help to balance it. Although he could attempt to emphasize fairness, he anticipated times when he might instead have to rely solely on accuracy in offering the company's position or view. Of course, some of his business and general-assignment reporting had lacked complete fairness, too. It wasn't always possible for a reporter to find a responsible representative for all sides of an issue or the time under deadline pressure to pursue all sides.

Richard was determined to continue his commitment to public service, however. In many ways, he felt the new job offered him greater opportunity to work with clearly defined constituent groups and come to understand their needs and interests. The satisfaction of communicating important news to his readers in the paper would be replaced with similar satisfaction from communicating important company news to employees, shareholders, and trade organizations. In some ways, being able to adopt a partisan tone when discussing safety needs of workers, for example, or community needs that the plant and its workers could help meet would increase that satisfaction.

He also looked forward to more opportunity for personal community service. His paper's code of ethics had prevented him from joining community organizations because of a feared conflict of interest. Now he looked forward to joining groups that were actively involved in making the city a better place for its residents and to participating in programs like the Partner in Education agreement the plant had with the local vocational high school.

He even looked forward to working with the local media. The plant was a major player in the economics of the region. So, in his own way, he wanted to better communicate how its plans for the future would help boost that economy. He might even buy his colleagues a free lunch now and then, he thought, but only because it would give him an opportunity to present his company's views in a sympathetic setting. As a reporter, he had never felt compromised when a practitioner shared the company's views with him because he trusted his reportorial training to help him maintain a sense of objectivity. In turn, he trusted that reporters could keep their objectivity intact also. All in all, after thinking it through, Richard felt good about his decision to take the new job. His duties might change a bit, but his basic ethical standards did not seem to be threatened. And who knows? Maybe his behavior as a practitioner would help to change at least some of his colleagues' stereotypes about public relations.

44 Playing Defense on the Court[room] of Public Opinion?

NBA superstar Kobe Bryant was arrested on 4 July 2003 and charged on July 18 with one count of felony sexual assault. A nineteen-year-old woman had accused him of assaulting her at a Colorado resort; Bryant denied the assault charge and said the two had engaged in consensual sex.

Immediately, the story was top news in print, broadcasting, and online. LA Laker Bryant had been one of the most admired personalities in basketball. A married man and a father, his circumspect life had led to many advertising endorsements. He had been named MVP in the NBA 2002 All Star Game.

The day Colorado prosecutor Mark Hurlbert announced the charge, Bryant appeared at a news conference with his wife, Vanessa, at his side. At times tearful, he told the group: "I'm innocent. I sit here in front of you guys furious at myself, disgusted at myself for making a mistake of adultery." He spoke to his wife several times, thanking her for her support and proclaiming his love for her.[6]

About a week later, news stories reported that Bryant had bought his wife a $4 million, eight-carat pink diamond ring. On August 2, both Mr. and Mrs. Bryant attended the 2003 Teen Choice Awards in Universal City, California, where Bryant received the Favorite Male Athlete award. Bryant was shown wearing a Muhammad Ali T-shirt and a large gold cross. He and his wife wore new matching "I love Kobe" and "I love Vanessa" bracelets.

continued

While accepting the Teen Choice Award, Bryant raised a clinched fist and paraphrased a quote from the Dr. Martin Luther King, Jr., saying, "An injustice anywhere is an injustice everywhere." The allusion was to a statement Dr. King made while in jail in Birmingham, Alabama, in 1963, when Dr. King proclaimed, "Injustice anywhere is a threat to justice everywhere."[7]

The tape of the program was broadcast the same day that Bryant had to appear in court to hear the charges against him. A crowd of reporters and onlookers filled the area. Bryant was greeted with applause from those outside the courtroom as he entered and left.[8]

The day after the court appearance, Bryant and his wife visited Disneyland, where they were filmed on the amusement-park rides. Media coverage again was intense.

Reporters debated the effectiveness of what they deemed the public relations efforts of Bryant to counter the negative publicity associated with the arrest and charge. Some found the news conference, with his wife participating, to be an effective opinion-management tool. Some said attending the awards ceremony and using the altered King quote in the acceptance speech were poor choices. Others said the lightheartedness of the awards ceremony and the Disneyland visit seemed to be at odds with the gravity of the legal and social situation facing Bryant.[9]

Before the trial actually started, charges against Bryant were dismissed when the woman indicated she did not want to testify. Bryant had already signed a new seven-year, $136 million contract with the Lakers.[10] Some months later, news reports indicated that a monetary settlement had ended a civil lawsuit brought by the woman.[11] Endorsement deals with McDonald's, Spalding, Nutella, and Coca-Cola were lost,[12] resulting in what has been estimated as a loss of $4 million to $6 million of endorsement income.[13] However, by 2006, Nike released a Kobe I shoe, and sales of his jerseys were strong as Bryant continued to play outstanding basketball.[14]   ■

Should a celebrity embroiled in a legal scandal play offense or defense? The notoriety of cases involving actors, athletes, musicians, and other celebrities means that accusations against them will get high-profile coverage across news and entertainment media in ways that likely will not be true for more private persons involved in litigation. Just witness the unending media coverage of the O. J. Simpson, Robert Blake, and Michael Jackson arrests and trials. There are those celebrities who assert that they are not role models for others and that what occurs in their lives off the playing field, stage, or film should be kept from the public. However, such privacy is seldom granted and perhaps not even frequently sought under most circumstances. Granted, the scrutiny afforded celebrities in circumstances involving legal issues can be overwhelming; every public statement or appearance can be magnified by repeated media coverage. Whether one seeks it or not, media attention becomes pervasive and, all too often, invasive.

So how should celebrities facing serious legal issues approach their public communication or activities? Their access to media is far greater than that afforded most private citizens and may have unavoidable consequences when potential jurors and presiding judges are bombarded with carefully chosen and contextualized messages or when plaintiffs or their families are confronted repeatedly with painful disclosures or countercharges. In such a circumstance, is the highest duty to one's self to launch the best defense possible? What about the duty to one's family? In this case, the involvement of Mrs. Bryant in such a public manner as Kobe Bryant's press conference and public appearances may be ethically defensible as a utilitarian way of attesting to the innocence of the accused athlete, or it may have been an exploitive way of generating empathy as viewers watched the couple's interactions. The presence of Mrs. Bryant during the initial press conference and the direct apology offered to her may have been part of a healing exchange between the two, but it certainly provided an emotional backdrop for her husband's claims of innocence as well. At the awards show, Mr. Bryant's approach was different. As the recipient of the Teen Choice Award, Mr. Bryant clearly provided a role model of athleticism to those who voted for him. One might argue that there are ethical duties that accompany the acceptance of such an award and designation, and one may question the rationale behind the choice Mr. Bryant made to link his legal situation with that of Dr. King's experiences in fighting for racial equality in Alabama.

Aristotelian analysis may offer the most useful insight here. Certainly, it would be virtually impossible for a celebrity to avoid media coverage, and it would be virtually impossible for a celebrity to totally control media coverage. But a balance that magnifies dignity and justice should be sought. What were Mr. Bryant's options? He might have avoided the spotlight as much as possible, relying on his defense team or public relations spokespersons to offer his declaration of innocence to the public. He might have held the press conference, deeming it important to personally make his statement, but avoided including his wife in that setting. Mr. Bryant's framing of the situation at the news conference and the public apology to his wife may have provided him an opportunity for public humility and sorrow. The appearance at the awards ceremony and the trip to Disneyland may have been designed to demonstrate his belief in his own innocence and the continued support of his wife. Mr. Bryant and/or his defense team could have sought opportunities to appear on news and sports talk shows to present his side of the story prior to the hearings and the trial. He could have sought the advice of public relations counselors specializing in litigation public relations who may have offered insights into the most effective course for his defense. Or, in what would be another, different tactic, they could have gone on the attack against the woman who brought the accusation that led to the charges and vilified her publicly. Among these choices, consideration of others' interests, as well as those of Mr. Bryant, must be weighed heavily as decisions are made regarding public communications.

The role of assertive public relations efforts in litigation—such as news conferences, talk-show appearances, and special events—is becoming almost routine, even for noncelebrities, and both defendants and prosecutors use public relations as a tool. Many leading public relations firms have experts available to serve as counselors for attorneys and their clients in this arena. A moral judgment regarding these communication strategies should not be made without considering the legal underpinnings. Contemporary media coverage of crime and the justice system can be volatile and sometimes prejudicial, as the U.S. Supreme Court has ruled.[9] Yet public discussion and media coverage of a crime, arrest, and trial can only be abridged in certain narrow circumstances. Generally, then, arresting police officers and prosecuting and defense teams enjoy great media access. Unless barred by specific court order, from the time of the crime until completion of a case, they can address the public and media in press conferences, interviews, and speeches and thereby potentially impact public perception of a suspect and the incident.

The ethical dilemma lies in deciding when information delivery becomes trial by media. News conferences, interviews, news releases, special events: All may be employed by those hoping to alter the tone of the public debate before the trial begins and a jury is selected. Yet, by attempting to affect or alter public opinion in these ways, litigants may be undermining the judicial process. If indeed all the communication deals with only the abstract issues, the tactics may be defensible. However, typically such media contacts are more likely to be interpreted as attempts to influence potential jurors or to soften a potential judge into a sympathetic review of pretrial defense motions than as objective truthtelling. Few would argue that justice is served when judgment is rendered in radio talk-show deliberations or newspaper letters to the editor rather than in a courtroom jury box.

45 Indictments Indicate Corrupt Lobbying

The indictment and guilty plea from lobbyist Jack Abramoff in 2006 marked the apparent end of one of the most influential lobbying careers in contemporary Washington. *The Washington Post*'s Susan Schmidt, James V. Grimaldi, and R. Jeffrey Smith were awarded the 2006 Pulitzer Prize in investigative reporting for their coverage of the scandal. Their timeline detailed the following key events in the story[16]: In 1994, Jack Abramoff joined Preston Gates & Ellis, a lobbying firm, and developed a political relationship with Representative Tom Delay (R-TX). Two years later, the Mississippi Band of Choctaw Indians was solicited as a client. In 1999, Abramoff recruited Ralph Reed to organize anti-gambling campaigns in the South to help ensure less competition for the tribal casinos.

In 1997, Abramoff arranged for trips to the Marianna Islands by lawmakers and their staff members, and in 2000, Representative Delay went on a week-long trip to England and Scotland aboard a corporate jet. The next year, Abramoff changed lobbying firms. He and partner Michael Scanlon were charging extraordinary fees to their tribal clients; in one duplicitous case, Abramoff and Scanlon worked with Reed to lobby Texas to shut down a casino and then persuaded the tribe to pay them $4.2 million to lobby Congress to reopen it. A 2003 internal audit of the Louisiana Coushatta Tribe showed that the tribe spent $18 million in one year on lobbying and legal fees, most paid to Abramoff and Scanlon.

Abramoff had used charitable giving to hide some of his activities, asking clients to make donations to his charities and nonprofits rather than to his lobbying firm or to give to charities linked to important politicians.[17] He also reportedly hosted fund-raisers for lawmakers at a restaurant he owned in Washington and held other campaign events in luxury boxes at sports arenas paid for by his tribal clients.[18] In December 2005, syndicated Copley News Service columnist and Cato Institute Senior Fellow Doug Bandow admitted that the service had been paid by Abramoff to write commentaries favorable to some clients.[19]

The *Washington Post* reported in February 2004 that Abramoff and Scanlon had received at least $45 million from tribes with casinos. Abramoff resigned from his lobbying firm the next week, and Senator John McCain (R-AZ) launched an investigation of the Indian lobbying efforts. In August 2005, Abramoff and Scanlon were indicted in Florida on fraud and conspiracy charges linked to the purchase of a casino. Three months later, Scanlon pleaded guilty to conspiring to bribe a congressman and other public officials and agreed to pay back the almost $20 million he collected from tribal clients. In January 2006, Abramoff pleaded guilty to fraud, tax evasion, and conspiracy to bribe officials and agreed to cooperate with further investigations. He was sentenced to five years and ten months in prison and fined.

Others involved with Abramoff also faced indictments. An aide to Representative Robert W. Ney (R-OH) pleaded guilty to conspiring with Abramoff in May 2006, and in October following an indictment, Representative Ney pleaded guilty to conspiring to engage in multiple political actions in exchange for contributions, trips, and other items of value. Then White House aide David H. Safavian was convicted of lying and obstructing justice in June for his involvement in Abramoff's dealings. Many in Congress responded to the investigations and convictions by returning campaign contributions received from Abramoff and his partners or by donating the funds to charitable groups.[20]   ∎

While the ethical and legal lapses of Abramoff and his partners may be apparent, they are worthy of discussion. The attempted perversion of the political process through this labyrinth of fund-raising and influence illustrates the problems that arise when the values of good citizenship and truthfulness are overcome by the values of money and personal power. The willingness to exploit clients such as Native American tribes in negotiations with a powerful federal government rejects the Rawlsian call for fairness when dealing with those who have unequal social power. Similarly, the use of real or fictional charities as a cover for raising undocumented donations and influence violates Rawls' principles.

Yet, it is not only Abramoff, Scanlon, and Reed who apparently failed ethically and legally. The willingness of elected politicians and their aides to cooperate with the lobbyists is further evidence of misplaced loyalties and values. While the pressures to raise funds continue to escalate with each state or national campaign, trading one's influence and reputation for a trip, an earmark, or a contribution cannot be blamed solely on the lobbyists who may be involved. Within a democracy, the integrity of elected officials has to be regarded as too valuable to be sold—even at the high dollar amounts noted in this case.

A governmental culture that tolerates and rewards falsehood, exploitation, and corruption should face the indictment of media and public opinion. Congress passed new restrictions on lobbying in August 2007, seeking to bar lawmakers and their staffs from accepting valuable gifts, meals, or trips and imposing stiff fines and penalties on lobbyists who give them.[21] Perhaps the legal attention being paid to this arena will help to reinforce the ethics of practice as well.

The new rules also illustrate the need to reassert the values of honesty and integrity in moral rules that take the form of laws with punishments for their breach. Kant would insist that sophisticated Washington deal-making should not be above moral scrutiny. Indeed, the pursuit of government power must not violate the moral imperative of public service in an open, equitable democracy. Morally sophisticated public relations recognizes these imperatives as first-order obligations. The task of a practitioner is not to ignore moral values to advance the interest of a client—or oneself—but to help clients and constituencies acknowledge and pursue the mutual obligations to the common good.

46 A Campaign Pioneer?

Imagine overhearing this conversation:

"Bob, I'd like to invite you to attend a luncheon where the president will speak."

"The president? I'd like to, but I don't have $100,000 to donate to anyone, Bob."

"I know, Brian, but for a $2000 donation, I can guarantee that you'll receive an invitation, a good lunch, a place at the table with me and some other of the firm's employees, and a chance to establish a network with the leader of the free world."

"That sounds great. I appreciate your asking me, sir. I would be honored to attend. Will you or the firm get some kind of recognition for filling a table?"

"Well, now that you mention it, if you'll put this little four-digit code on your check and give it to me to turn in, I'll get credit for soliciting your attendance—and your money. Would you mind?"

"Not at all, Bob. I'm just excited to think about getting to hear the president. I just hope we'll get a chance to bend his ear about our views on those new trade agreements in Asia."

While this is a fictional conversation, it illustrates the reality of a campaign fund-raising strategy used by the 2004 Bush presidential campaign, a refinement of a technique successfully used in 2000 by Mr. Bush and by countless other candidates and political action committees (PACs) for many years. Using a process known as "bundling," key donors are encouraged to recruit multiple individuals to give $2000 for the campaign, and the multiple donations are then presented together at once to the candidate's campaign. (A provision within the Bipartisan Campaign Reform Act, popularly known as the McCain–Feingold Act, raised the amount an individual may legally donate to a candidate from $1000 to $2000.)[22] By using a "solicitor tracking code" on the donated checks, the key donors were granted credit for their fund-raising prowess.

Those who solicited at least $100,000, personally collected the checks, coded them, and then turned them in to the Bush campaign were hailed as "Pioneers." Those who solicited at least $200,000 were named "Rangers." Pioneers and Rangers were eligible to attend special Pioneer events with the president, to receive reports from top campaign officials, and to participate in special events at the 2004 Republican National Convention.[23] For example, in August 2003, 350 donors who had helped collect $50,000 each by June 30 were invited to a private barbecue with the president and his top political advisor on a ranch close to the Crawford, Texas, a ranch owned by President Bush.[24]

According to *The Washington Post*, many of those who registered to become Pioneers or Rangers were CEOs of major corporations, lobbyists, doctors, attorneys, or investment bankers. The *Post* said in a 14 July 2003 article, "The single factor virtually all such donors have in common is that they, their clients, their corporations, their suppliers and their subcontractors are major beneficiaries of the Bush administration's tax-cutting and deregulatory policies."[25]

By mid-July 2003, at least sixty-eight donors had become Pioneers or Rangers, soliciting about one-fourth of the $34.4 million raised by the Bush campaign in its first forty-five days.[26] The official Bush campaign website provided a full list of the Pioneers and Rangers. However, the Bush campaign reported that 80 percent of those who contributed during that period gave less than $200 each.[27]

More than 500 donors qualified as Pioneers during the Bush 2000 campaign, according to documents released in May 2003. The Associated Press reported that at least one dozen Pioneers bundled at least $300,000 for the 2000 campaign. At least nineteen of those identified as Pioneers were later appointed as ambassadors.[28]

The successful fund-raising strategy was apparent in the 2008 campaign as well. Democratic candidate Hillary Clinton set tiered goals for donors seeking to be recognized as "HillRaisers," and by April 2007, *Newsday* reported that eighty-two HillRaisers had contributed about a third of the $25.8 million garnered by the campaign during the first quarter of 2007.[29] One of her opponents, Senator Barack Obama (D-IL), introduced legislation in September 2007 that would require public disclosure of all bundlers.   ■

Certainly, there is nothing inherently unethical about politicians seeking contributions for political campaigns. In fact, representative, participative democracy will not work if politicians do not interact with constituents and supporters or raise funding to use in election campaigns. With less than half of America's potential voters participating in elections, perhaps any mechanism that increases their input or raises their interest—such as the personal solicitation strategies noted in the case—should be celebrated. And perhaps the process of bundling the donations from individual donors helps to maximize the political playing field by allowing pooled resources from many so that they can compete with the influence of those individuals or businesses who could already speak with a powerful single voice. The costs of running successful—and unsuccessful campaigns—on the state or national level are increasingly high; without active contributions, candidates without vast personal wealth would be unable to fund media purchases or personal appearances.

Recognizing those who solicit individual contributions for bundling may raise other questions, however. Consider Rawls's principle of fairness. Is the identification of donation with access or partisan position so strong that few politicians can negotiate behind the "veil of ignorance" position demanded by Rawls? If access to the political decision makers is decided primarily by donations, then those who don't or can't pay will be locked out of the political arena, and the financial stakes for those who seek influence may continue to rise. Does this suggest that organizations or causes that fail to organize and contribute will be ignored or that the amount of access will be linked to the size of the contribution made? If those with larger coffers can obtain greater access or influence, they may overwhelm the political voices of the smaller, less organized, and less financed groups or individuals. Those who criticize the influence of contributions must ponder alternatives for funding campaigns; would it be more ethical to have each campaign paid for through public monies, for example, or does that raise other issues of fairness, such as incumbency, taxation, and implied endorsements?

Does the legal activity of bundling inherently limit the political liberty of all by giving undue influence to those with greater wealth, influence, and opportunity for influencing or gaining credit for the donation choices of others? Companies or organizations are not required to be functioning democracies, nor are political candidates or campaigns compelled to seek all viewpoints on issues—indeed, such would make the need for political parties disappear—but perhaps the "wild west" of political opinions would function more democratically without the guidance of donor-herding Pioneers or the supervision of cash-raising Rangers.

47 Your Tax Dollars at Work?

You may have seen the sign when driving by highway construction or park expansions: "Your Tax Dollars at Work." Should you also expect to see some sort of disclosure when it comes to government-funded communications that may be inherently persuasive—or even propagandistic—in nature? Both domestic and international public relations campaigns financed by the U.S. government have raised that question in recent years.

Domestically, it was the Department of Education that drew attention for such a campaign. The department worked with Ketchum PR, as part of a $1 million contract with the Department of Education, to promote the Bush administration's educational policies by contracting with conservative commentator Armstrong Williams to promote the No Child Left Behind Act. Williams was paid $240,000 to promote the act in his columns and in television appearances but did not acknowledge the arrangement in the communications.[30]

The Education Department also paid for the creation and distribution of a video news release narrated by actress Karen Ryan that promoted the educational policies. [Other agencies also used this tactic. Ms. Ryan also narrated two Medicare drug plan video news releases (VNRs) promoting the Bush proposal, ending each with the tag line, "In Washington, I'm Karen Ryan reporting."] None of the VNRs disclosed the government sponsorship.

News of the unacknowledged sponsorship and the public relations campaign broke in late 2004, prompting sharp criticism of what some saw as domestic propaganda efforts from those inside public relations and the White House. Ketchum announced that it had adopted guidelines for disclosure of sponsorships. Reaction also came from the Public Relations Society of America, which sponsored an ethics summit in March and issued an advisory in April.[31] More reaction came from the Federal Communications Commission (FCC), which issued a public notice "reminding broadcast licensees, cable operators and others of requirements applicable to video news releases" and sought comment on the use of VNRs. The FCC argued that audience members were "entitled to know who seeks to persuade them with the programming offered over broadcast stations and cable systems." FCC Commissioner Michael J. Copps said the agency had gotten what he called "tens of thousands" of contacts asking the FCC to investigate the failure of broadcasters to disclose the use of government-generated VNRs. Copps stated, "In this era of huge corporate media, it has gotten just about impossible to tell the difference between news and entertainment or to differentiate between legitimate information and propaganda." FCC Commissioner Jonathan S. Adelstein, while noting the dispute between the U.S. Government Accountability Office (GAO) and the Department of Justice's Office of Legal Counsel about the appropriateness of the government-originated videos, said that the FCC would enforce its existing rules about disclosure.

Following an investigation requested by Senator Frank Lautenberg (D-NJ) and Senator Edward Kennedy (D-MA), the GAO concluded in what *The New York Times* called a "blistering report" that the campaign was "covert propaganda" that violated U.S. laws, although the Department of Justice found the practice appropriate if the information reported was factual.[32] The GAO found that the VNRs developed for the Government Office of National Drug Control Policy and the Department of Health and Human Services used techniques that made them appear to be standard news, such as using actors who posed as reporters, and were distributed without attribution on screen.[33]

It wasn't just educational issues that were prompting federally financed public relations campaigns, however. The Iraq War also prompted government-sponsored persuasion campaigns with messages constructed by U.S. public relations firms. These were aimed at international audiences, however, rather than domestic. In 2002, McCann-Erickson developed a $15 million propaganda campaign entitled, "Shared Values," on behalf of the State Department that was intended to improve the image of the United States in the Muslim world; the campaign called for print and broadcast ads, a website, and a book. However, according to reports from *The Wall Street Journal* cited on CBS, the campaign was suspended when the governments of Egypt, Lebanon, and Jordan did not want to air the spots on government-controlled channels.[34]

Yet another campaign effort soon unfolded. In 2005, the U.S. Special Operations Command awarded three five-year $100 million contracts to develop "slogans, advertisements, newspaper articles, radio spots and television programs to build support for U.S. policies overseas" to the Lincoln Group, Science Applications International Corp., and SYColeman "for media approach planning, prototype product development, commercial quality product development, product distribution and dissemination, and media effects analysis."[35] The Lincoln Group, created in 2004, was soon awarded Pentagon contracts for information warfare or psychological operations in Iraq, up to twelve government contracts that totaled more than $130 million.[36] As a part of this effort, the Lincoln Group paid Iraqi newspapers to run stories produced by the U.S. military without disclosing their source, *The Los Angeles Times* reported in November 2005. *The New York Times* reported that some twelve friendly Iraqi journalists were paid stipends of about several hundred dollars monthly.[37] The Lincoln Group also paid Sunni religious scholars in Iraq to offer advice and write reports for military commanders; the scholars were not involved in the insurgency, according to the public relations practitioners.[38] The group also distributed antiterror comics and water bottles printed with a phone number Iraqis could call to report terrorist activities and conducted research and polling, but it denied being engaged in propaganda efforts. Instead, the group told a reporter from *The Washington Post* that it engaged in "influence."[39]

continued

An inquiry by General Casey found that this practice did not violate military policy, but it raised serious concerns among many within the administration and the military about the precedent set when the goal is to establish a democratic government in Iraq. It prompted criticisms from those who questioned the value and the ethics of the campaign.[40] Following the controversy over the paid pro-U.S. articles, the contract with the Lincoln Group was not renewed.[41] However, the Lincoln Group was later awarded a two-year contract to monitor English and Arab media outlets and to produce public relations materials for U.S. forces in Iraq; according to the Associated Press, among the media to be monitored were Fox Television, *The New York Times*, and *Al-Arabiya*.[42]   ■

Governments, particularly those dependent on voting to receive power and to make decisions, must use communication strategically, and presidents and military leaders have used strategic communications domestically and internationally for years. From the Committee on Public Information in World War I to the imbedded journalist program in the Iraq War, administrative strategy has involved the control of information access and dissemination. Domestically, both the executive and the legislative branches of government have used public-information specialists and strategists to focus public opinion, build consensus, and win elections. Yet legal constraints that have been in place for decades, designed to prevent direct use of federal money for domestic propaganda campaigns in order to prevent abuse of power or subversion of the democratic process, appear to have been ignored by those intent on raising support for official policies. Negative reaction to these programs came from within the government, the media, and the citizenry. Most complaints focused on the covert nature of the government sponsorship, which suggests a corruption of the channels of communication by deceptive persuasion.

Applying virtue ethics in this situation might suggest that one investigate the motivation for the deceptions. Why not disclose the sponsorship of the domestic campaign? Was it deemed to be more persuasive and credible if the message were to be disassociated from its source, or is the audience viewed as being incapable of critical assessments when information is presented truthfully and in context? Consequential ethics might provide some justification for the lack of disclosure. Obtaining the seeming "third party" endorsement that comes from having what is thought to be an objective columnist's advocacy must have been deemed more persuasive; perhaps the deceptive nature of the VNRs and columns was seen as justifiable to obtain the perceived greater good of public support and cooperation. Yet certainly other communication alternatives or strategies, both domestically and internationally, might have allowed for dissemination of the desired message without having to use deception or subterfuge and therefore likely would have been far more effective in affecting the type of long-term education and persuasion deemed necessary to establish democracy in an emerging state or to provide support for federal policies domestically. Why risk lowering credibility when other techniques of communicating—and persuading—internal and external constituents have been both ethical and effective?

Use of the international persuasion campaign may be more easily justified as a weapon of war—or as a weapon for peacemaking. Gaining support for the new Iraqi government in hopes of restoring order and building unity within the nation is certainly a worthy goal. Historical precedents for such campaigns are easily found. However, even in that light, truthtelling is still a moral duty—again, perhaps even more so during a time of crisis and instability. Practitioners who work for governments must be willing to balance patriotic zeal with that obligation.

Certainly, the ethical issues here do not just lie with the governmental agencies that authorized and paid for the commentaries, the video releases, or the articles. The journalist or commentator who is willing to sell his or her byline and actors who are willing to masquerade as reporters bear ethical responsibility, as do the public relations practitioners who devise such campaigns. Kant certainly would suggest that the loyalties of these communicators be examined: To whom is duty owed in a democratic system? What justification must be necessary to break or bend law? Does the desire to please a government agency or a supervisor override loyalty to the citizenry?

NOTES

1. Dwight D. Eisenhower, *Crusade in Europe* (New York: Doubleday, 1948), p. 58.
2. See the 1913 Gillett Amendment [Chap. 32, §1,38 Stat. 212; Pub. L. No. 89–554, §3107,80 Stat. 416 (1966), Pub. L. No. 93–50, §305 (1973)].
3. Alison Stateman, "From Columns to Clients," *The Strategist* (Winter 2006): 6–10.
4. For example, see Jim Pritchett, "If Image Is Linked to Reputation, and Reputation to Increased Use, Shouldn't We Do Something About Ours?" *Public Relations Quarterly* (Fall 1992): 30, 34; Michael Ryan and D. L. Martinson, "Public Relations Practitioners, Public Interest and Management," *Journalism Quarterly* 62:1 (Spring 1985): 111; Jacob Shamir, Barbara Straus Reed, and Steven Connell, "Individual Differences in Ethical Values of Public Relations Practitioners," *Journalism Quarterly* 67:4 (Winter 1990): 956.
5. *Members Code of Ethics 2000.* Public Relations Society of America, www.prsa.org/Chapters/resources/ethicspdf/codeofethics.pdf, p.8.
6. Gary Tuchman and Brian Cabell, contributors, "Kobe Bryant Charged with Sexual Assault," CNN.com, 22 July 2003, www.cnn.com.
7. Janet Zimmerman, "Bryant Getting Poor Advice, PR Experts Say," *Press Enterprise*, 4 September 2003, p. A1.
8. Dan Harris, "An Unalterable Reality: Kobe Bryant Has More to Worry About Than Just the Charges," ABCNews.com, 7 August 2003, www.abcnews.com.
9. Zimmerman, "Bryant Getting Poor Advice," p. A1.
10. "Criminal Charges Dismissed in Kobe Bryant Case," City News, 1 September 2004.
11. "Suit Settlement Ends Sordid Kobe Saga," Associated Press, 3 March 2005.
12. Richard Sandomir, "Like Him or Not, Bryant the Brand Is Scoring, Too," *The New York Times*, 27 January 2006, p. D3.

13. Associated Press, 3 March 2005.

14. Sandomir, "Like Him or Not," p. D3.

15. *Irwin v. Dowd*, 366 U.S. 717 (1961); *Sheppard v. Maxwell*, 384 U.S. 333 (1966).

16. Susan Schmidt, James V. Grimaldi, and R. Jeffrey Smith, "The Abramoff Affair: Timeline," *The Washington Post*, 28 December 2005.

17. Paul Kane, "Abramoff's Web Pushed Envelope," *Roll Call*, 26 June 2006.

18. Ana Radelat, "Abramoff's Restaurant, Skyboxes Were Hot Spots for Lawmakers' Fundraisers," Gannett News Service, 13 January 2006.

19. Jeffrey H. Birnbaum, "2nd Senator to Return Abramoff Funds; Lobbyist Paid Columnist," *The Washington Post*, 17 December 2005, p. A2.

20. Darlene Superville, "Tainted Cash from Abramoff Scandal Is Steered to the Needy," Associated Press, 11 January 2006.

21. David D. Kirkpatrick, "Tougher Rules Change Game for Lobbyists," *The New York Times*, 7 August 2007, p. A1.

22. www.fec.gov/pages/brochures/.contrib.htm.

23. Thomas B. Edsall and Mike Allen, "Bush 'Bundlers' Refine Fundraising," *The Washington Post*, 14 July 2003; accessed at www.msnbc.com/news/938480.asp?OdmN17LN, 7/14/2003.

24. Will Lester, "Bush Turns to Politics as He Greets Top Fund Raisers at a Barbecue," Associated Press, 9 August 2003; accessed in Lexis–Nexis, 29 September 2003.

25. Edsall and Allen, "Bush 'Bundlers' Refine Fundraising."

26. Mike Allen, "Bush Campaign Gathers Big Donors; 68 Contributors Make Grade as 'Rangers' or 'Pioneers,' " *The Washington Post*, 16 July 2003, p. A8.

27. Julia Kalone, "President Bush's $170 Million Man," *The Atlanta Journal Constitution*, p. A6.

28. "Scope of Big-Dollar Bush Donors Revealed in Court Documents," Associated Press, 5 May 2003; accessed in Lexis–Nexis, 29 September 2003.

29. Glenn Thrush, "Banking on HillRaisers; Clinton Has Huge $30.9M in Campaign Cache after 2-Year Head Start; Edwards, Obama Lag by Millions," *Newsday*, 16 April 2007, p. A7.

30. Felicity Barringer, "Public Relations Campaign for Research Office at EPA Includes Ghostwriting Articles," *The New York Times*, 18 July 2005; accessed at nytimes.com 18 July 2005.

31. Erica Iacono, "PR Transparency—Industry Reforms in Wake of Doe Scandal Inconclusive," *PRWeek*, 17 October 2005, p. 6.

32. Robert Pear, "Buying of News by Bush's Aides is Ruled Illegal," *The New York Times*, 1 October 2005.

33. David Alexander, "When Working in Tandem with the Feds, Make VNRs—Not News," *PR News*, 17 August 2005.

34. Jarrett Murphy, "U.S. Propaganda Pitch Halted," *DBS News*, 16 January 2003.

35. Matt Kelley, "3 Groups Have Contracts for Pro-U.S. Propaganda," *USA Today*, 13 December 2005, accessed at www.usatoday.com/washington/2005-12-13-propaganda-inside-usat_s.htm; Matt Kelley, "Pentagon Rolls Out Stealth PR, *USA Today*, 15 December 2005; accessed at www.usatoday.com/news/washington/2005-12-14-pentagon-pr_xtm.

36. David S. Cloud and Jeff Gerth, "Muslim Scholars Were Paid to Aid U.S. Propaganda," *The New York Times*, 2 January 2006; Lynn Duke, "The Word at War: Propaganda? Nah, Here's the Scoop, Say the Guys Who Planted Stories in Iraqi Papers," *The Washington Post*, 26 March 2006, p. D1.

37. Jeff Gerth and Scott Shane, "U.S. Said to Pay to Plant Articles in Iraq Papers," *The New York Times*, 1 December 2005, p. A1.
38. Cloud and Gerth, "Muslim Scholars Were Paid to Aid U.S. Propaganda."
39. Duke, "The Word at War: Propaganda?"
40. Thom Shanker, "No Breach Seen in Work in Iraq on Propaganda," *The New York Times*, 22 March 2006, p. A12.
41. Griff Witte, "Lincoln Group Out of Military PR Contract," *The Washington Post*, 19 July 2006, p. D3.
42. "PR Firm That Paid Iraqi Papers Gets Deal," *AFX-Asia*, 27 September 2006.

CHAPTER ELEVEN

Telling the Truth in Organizational Settings

The pursuit of truth is common to all who seek to practice ethical communication. Yet public relations practitioners may be caught in one of the hardest arenas for truthfulness because of the special challenges arising from their liaison role. Practitioners enjoy multiple opportunities to shape information communicated to internal and external audiences. Consider the corporate website. Graphics, copy, audio, and video are carefully selected and placed. Some sites are animated to draw viewer attention; some open only after other items have been highlighted or selected. Tabs link to pages filled with targeted information about management, performance, history, values, employment, and news. Archival data may be present. All the information presents the corporations' point of view. It may be completely accurate and yet incomplete or one-sided. Just as it has always been true for those who receive information from news releases or press conferences, those who visit these sites must remember that the information gleaned there has certainly passed through the public relations gate before moving to the reporter and on to various audiences.

Is the polishing and shaping of an image in such a manner deceptive? Does it violate the truth? Perhaps not in most cases or at least no more than any gatekeeping action does. But how far can one go in polishing before one becomes guilty of overt deception? The issue is complicated by many factors. Sophisticated technologies make it increasingly simple and quick to change or shape the reality of what audiences see, hear, or experience. The rapidity of the transmission makes it difficult for time-consuming verification or investigative processes to take place adequately. Growing competition for a shrinking news hole prompts practitioners to push for the pseudodramatic rather than relying on the boring truth. Intraorganizational pressures to please or appease managers or other key constituents are rising in this era of downsizing and reengineering. As partisan group members, practitioners may find their own enthusiasm a trap. It may be much easier to tell positive news than it is to tell negative news. Enthusiasm about something may lead one to overstatement and hyperbole.

Lastly, the actual truth is almost always more than one person's story or one person's perspective. In an organizational setting, truth is often negotiated and contains components of several opinions. Practitioners operating within the multiple layers of organizations are often charged with communicating a message composed so that its original kernels of truth are well hidden. The litigious era also has prompted many attorneys to advise organizational spokespeople to hide behind a "no comment," a statement that is certainly true in and of itself but may not be truthful in its level of disclosure. The luxury of the unlimited news hole of the Internet means that multiple sides of a story may be heard, some without any attempts at objectivity or even accuracy.

The cases in this chapter will challenge you to explore the demands of truthtelling with various organizational settings, both formal and informal. The first case, "A Good Thing?" reports how the Internet and other mass media were used effectively as venues for presenting carefully crafted messages during the investigation of Martha Stewart. The second case, "Wal-Marting Across the Internet," and the third case, "Who's the Boss," examine the impact that information included in or omitted from corporate and personal blogs may have on credibility and believability. The fourth case, "This News Story Is Brought to You by . . . ," examines truthfulness and video news releases.

48 A Good Thing?

The legal struggles involving Martha Stewart's defense against a June 2003 indictment on charges of securities fraud, obstruction of justice, conspiracy, and making false statements[1] prompted use of a new tool for self-defense, a website then posted at www .marthatalks.com. Ms. Stewart had created one of the most successful brands in the country, Martha Stewart Living Omnimedia; the brand's magazines, books, newspaper columns, cable television programs, and Martha Stewart Everyday product line had become almost a $300 million business. The negative publicity resulting from the investigation and indictment placed the future of the highly successful—and highly personalized—brand in jeopardy. In response to the indictment, Ms. Stewart pleaded innocent to the charges and turned to the Web to publicly present her story.

The legal issues resulted from investigations into what had prompted Ms. Stewart's sale of almost 4000 shares of ImClone stock on 27 December 2001. The following day, the Food and Drug Administration (FDA) announced it had rejected the biotechnology corporation's application for approval of a new cancer drug, and the value of ImClone shares dropped dramatically. Ms. Stewart was known to have been close friends with ImClone CEO Sam Waksal. In June 2002, Waksal was arrested and accused of advising family members to sell shares of the corporation before the FDA announcement was made public and of trying to sell his own shares. In October 2002, Mr. Waksal pleaded guilty to securities fraud, bank fraud, conspiracy to obstruct justice, and perjury.[2]

The phone records of Ms. Stewart, her stockbroker, and CEO Waksal indicated that Ms. Stewart had returned a call from her broker, instructing him to sell the stock, and then had called Waksal, although she did not reach him.[3]

Ms. Stewart issued a few public statements denying any wrongdoing, but she appeared to be avoiding other questions from reporters and others.[4] Avoiding the press didn't seem to help; coverage of the investigation was widespread. Headlines such as "Martha's Untidy Story," "A Big House for Martha?" and "Did Martha Sweep Dirt Under the Rug?"[5] targeted her image as the impeccable home stylemaker who had celebrated the "good

continued

things" of cooking and decorating. Many print and broadcast outlets offered stories that focused not only on the legal issues of the case but also offered details on Ms. Stewart's personal and professional background, her relationship with employees, and her activities as a media executive.

Ms. Stewart seemed to follow a deliberate and controlled plan for responding publicly to the charges. The day following her indictment, a full-page advertisement in *USA Today* was used to declare her innocence,[6] and the website where "Martha talks" was opened. The site offered an "open letter" (the copy used in the advertisement) from Ms. Stewart in which she addresses her "friends and loyal supporters," telling them that "I am inno-cent and that I will fight to clear my name." She thanked them for their continuing sup-port. Another note from Ms. Stewart welcomed visitors to the site and invited them to send her e-mails of support.

Clearly, Ms. Stewart had friends and supporters. The site noted that Ms. Stewart had received more than 60,000 e-mailed notes of support through the site in the four months following the indictment. Some of the notes were reprinted by permission on the site, cat-alogued by day or month of receipt. They contained testimonials from fans about the qual-ity of her products and home-making tips and exhortations of support for her innocence. A direct e-mail link for use in contacting Ms. Stewart was featured at the site.

Other information relevant to Ms. Stewart's defense was linked to the site. One page, posted 10 June 2003, said it was "Setting the Record Straight." It corrected six of what were called "frequent errors" in media coverage of the case. Links to "Other Voices" of support also were provided on the site; for example, links to columns that appeared in *The New York Times*, *Barron's*, *The Kansas City Star*, and *The Wall Street Journal* were included.

After her indictment, Ms. Stewart stepped down as CEO of the conglomerate she created, becoming its "chief creative officer." *Newsweek* reported that Martha Stewart Living Omnimedia shares had fallen in value about 50 percent since the beginning of the investigation.[7]

Following her trial, the website was closed. Ms. Stewart was convicted and served five months in jail. However, following her release, she resumed her media career, launching a new television show and product lines. For the most part, her customers remained loyal and willing to learn about more "good things" from the style leader.[8]   ■

A desire to avoid extensive public questions during a time of business or personal crisis is understandable, even for a remarkably successful and media-savvy executive like Martha Stewart. Choosing to use a personal website (and a one-page advertisement) allows for total control of content and presentation, the type of control Ms. Stewart had advocated be exerted within one's home or en-tertainment venues for years to present the best appearance and comfort possible; there are no intervening reporters, editors, or designers. The Web offers an up-dated version of the street-corner soapbox; the speaker shouts his or her side to passersby, and those who choose to stop will hear the rhetorical discourse pro-vided. The interactivity offered by e-mail and by selected links establishes a sense of two-way communication, theoretically the hallmark of effective and ethical public relations practice. In fact, presenting evidence of 60,000 statements of support offers testimony about the goodness of one's position that may not have swayed jurors but likely reinforced the sympathies of her followers.

Use of the Potter Box for reflection on this case might prove fruitful. Consider the ethical values evident here. A concern for justice argues that innocence or guilt should be determined through careful legal considerations, not through newspaper columns, magazine covers, websites, or advocacy advertising. Perhaps Ms. Stewart's choice of controlled media, such as advertising and a personal website, was prompted by her concerns about the evenhandedness of mass-media coverage during a period when recurring corporate scandals had generated tremendous media and political attention. However, whenever controlled media are used, issues of objectivity and fairness may be raised if no opposing views are heard. On this website, all the posted messages were positive and supporting, which may not be surprising, considering who controls the site. However, visitors to this site, as is true of most others, must be critical thinkers, remembering that by selecting messages for posting or media stories for linking, the manager of the site shapes content as certainly as does an editorial-page editor for a local daily. What is posted may indeed be accurate in that it represents truthfully what was received or published, but it is still a selective truthfulness unless a representative sample of messages received or articles written about the case are posted there.

Consider loyalties. Ms. Stewart obviously has a loyalty to herself as well as to the corporation she founded and fostered. As the CEO or "chief creative officer" of a publicly traded corporation, she also has a duty to explain her actions to key stakeholders, perhaps particularly so because she is so personally identified with the brand being sold. Perhaps a more public and assertive rebuttal of the charges or more open responses during the early days of the investigation may have prevented the subsequent decline in stock value and, indeed, her indictment. She also owes loyalty to those consumers who had supported her products and media offerings and who had come to trust her advice. They, too, have an interest in knowing the truth about the charges leveled against her.

The application of philosophical principles also raises issues for discussion. Some have argued that Ms. Stewart was victimized by prosecutors or unfriendly reporters because of her gender or her economic power. While other corporate leaders had been investigated or indicted, few received the personalized, almost stylized attention that Ms. Stewart received. As the headlines indicate, obviously reporters and editors were enjoying the play against her public image. Rawls would argue that anyone approaching this story as a reporter, editor, or investigator should disregard social position and gender and treat all litigants fairly.

Yet the reverse of this rationale also should be considered. A powerful media executive such as Ms. Stewart, who has the ability to bolster great resources for use in a public defense, should not be surprised when public attention focuses intently on the case. Those who have enjoyed the benefits of the public limelight while building careers should not be surprised—nor call foul—when the light focuses on public crises or issues. Perhaps the impact of the "Martha Talks" website would have been strengthened had, indeed, Martha talked with the public, press, and investigators in an open forum before selecting this controlled medium.

49 Wal-Marting Across the Internet

Laura and Jim, traveling in an RV, wanted to park for free over night in Wal-Mart Stores parking lots as they traveled from their home to visit their three children who moved across the country from them. When the couple contacted Wal-Mart, it apparently seemed like a great opportunity for Wal-Mart to feature its stores in a family-friendly manner. In response to the request, the couple was flown to Las Vegas, where they were provided with a new RV with a "Working Families for Wal-Mart" logo on the side and sent on their way to Georgia for the "Wal-Marting Across America" tour. With their gas paid for, the couple completed the 2843-mile trip, with Laura filing a blog entry at each stop, for which she also was paid. The blog posted positive stories about the Wal-Mart employees the couple encountered.[9]

However, it was not until well into the trip that the payments and arrangements were disclosed, after questions arose within the blogosphere about whether the bloggers actually were on such a trip and if it had been were sponsored. The answers revealed that while the couple was actually traveling, a public relations agency, Edelman, had been involved in setting up the arrangement. This prompted questions about why the sponsorship information had not been disclosed earlier. In response, in one of the last blogs posted on the Walmartingacrossamerica website, Laura explained:

> Given the litigious age we live in, we decided to get permission to do so. So I called my brother, who works at Edelman and whose clients include Working Families for Wal-Mart, in order to find out if we'd be allowed to talk to the people and take pictures in Wal-Mart parking lots. . . .They didn't just give us permission. They said they would even sponsor the trip! . . . All in all, it was a perfect fit. Working Families for Wal-Mart wants to get the word out about all the good things Wal-Mart does for people. I wanted to make this trip and write about it. It just seemed to work.[10]

The explanation didn't offset criticism from some who saw this as a deceptive public relations stunt. Edelman CEO Richard Edelman apologized for the lack of disclosure in his personal blog on the agency's website.[11]

Not only was Laura's brother a public relations practitioner at the agency, but Jim actually was Jim Thresher, a staff photographer at *The Washington Post*. *BusinessWeek* online said that once this was disclosed, the *Post* asked Thresher to return the funds he received for the trip and to delete his photos from the blog.[12]

The blog was just one of the efforts Wal-Mart undertook under Edelman's guidance to foster a more positive public image. The Working Families for Wal-Mart group, BusinessWeek.com reported, was apparently also formed to counter criticism of its labor and economic policies, although its links to Wal-Mart were not disclosed.[13]

The Web offered a lively setting for posting positive and negative messages about the retailing giant from partisan groups on all sides. The website for Working Families for Wal-Mart provided news about Wal-Mart's positive contributions, likely hoping to counter the negative messages about Wal-Mart posted on sites such as WakeUpWalMart.com, launched in 2005 with funding from the United Food and Commercial Workers Union, and Wal-Mart Watch, with funding from the Service Employees International Union.[14] The Web messaging grew more intense in 2006, when the Working Families for Wal-Mart group established another website, paidcritics.com, on which it countered posts on the Wake-Up

Wal-Mart site. In turn, the Wake-Up Wal-Mart site launched a site called www.abunchof-greedyrightwingliarswhoworkforwalmart.com.

Edelman, according to *The New York Times*, also targeted conservative bloggers with information about Wal-Mart.[15] Mona Williams, a Wal-Mart spokesperson, told *The New York Times* that the corporation began working with bloggers in 2005. She explained its motivation, "As more and more Americans go to the Internet to get information from varied, credible, trusted sources, Wal-Mart is committed to participating in that online conversation."

The Web-based campaign was taken in a context of public scrutiny, but the retailer did not just rely on the Internet to stimulate a more positive image. The corporation provided generous cash and merchandise donations and work transfers for employees following Hurricane Katrina.[16] Wal-Mart also announced plans to build fifty new stores in economically challenged neighborhoods, where it would focus on helping local small businesses compete against its stores and would feature local businesses in print and radio ads and donate funds to local chambers of commerce.[17] Reaching out to other publics, Wal-Mart began underwriting National Public Radio newscasts[18] and began promoting a new environmental campaign, led by a former nun, Harriet Hentges, senior director of stakeholder engagement.[19] ■

Corporate imaging is not unethical, and speaking out on public issues is certainly legal and ethical. The Internet provides great opportunity for widespread dissemination of information but also provides an easy tool for intense scrutiny and investigation of the information. Failing to disclose sponsorship of corporate imaging raises questions about motivation and truthtelling that may distract from the original intention, and agencies or practitioners engaged in these efforts may be drawn into the questioning. Sponsoring a cross-country tour of Wal-Mart stores, with blogged entries featuring employees' stories, with disclosure that it was sponsored by the retailer, likely still would have been effective in communicating the positive stories sought and would have been more ethically justifiable. A lack of openness raises suspicions about the need for secrecy.

Similarly, sponsoring a group of satisfied customers who advocate for a corporation also would have been justifiable; General Motors found great success with its support of the Saturn customers network and its sponsorship of "Homecoming" events. Ethical behavior can be profitable behavior. But, again, failing to disclose sponsorship diverts attention from the message. What is communicated may indeed be truthful—but doubts about what is not being said may undermine the truth.

Aristotelian analysis may lend guidance here. Commercial promotion is not vice and does not have to be hidden. A complete lack of promotion or of countering critics may not be virtuous if it leads to business failure with its ensuing social impacts. The mean then may be found in truthful practice—promote even aggressively, but openly. Label advertisements as advertisements, sponsorships as sponsorships, and placements as placements. Responses to critics may be equally aggressive—but also must be truthful. Those providing public relations counsel in such cases also should remember to seek balance between their commitment to their clients and their commitment to public truthtelling.

50 Who's the Boss?

"Rahodeb" was positive about Whole Foods Market in the posts on the Yahoo message board and pessimistic about the prospects of Wild Oats Market. There is nothing too unusual about this—except for the real identity of the poster, who was CEO of Whole Foods Market, Inc., a corporation planning to merge with Wild Oats Market.[20]

"The views articulated by Rahodeb sometimes represent what I actually believed, and sometimes they didn't," Mackey said, in a quote drawn from the Whole Foods website by Reuters. "Sometimes I simply played 'devil's advocate' for the sheer fun of arguing."[21]

In February 2007, Whole Foods announced plans to buy Wild Oats Market for $565 million. The Federal Trade Commission (FTC) announced plans to investigate the merger in March and in June sued to stop the merger. The Rahodeb comments were cited by the FTC as part of the reason for the suit.

Responding to the FTC investigation of the proposed merger of the two food companies, Mackey again turned to the Internet, posting a long, assertive message in his blog on the corporate website on June 19 in order to "provide explanations of how I think the FTC, to date, has neglected to do its homework appropriately, especially given the statements made regarding prices, quality, and service levels in its complaint. I also provide a glimpse into the bullying tactics used against Whole Foods Market by this taxpayer-funded agency."[22]

Then, in July 2007, the Securities and Exchange Commission (SEC) announced an informal inquiry into the postings. Whole Foods Market announced that it would "fully cooperate with the SEC and [did] not anticipate commenting further while the inquiry is pending." Its board of directors formed a committee to conduct an internal investigation.[23] The same day, Mackey released the following statement: "I sincerely apologize to all Whole Foods Market stakeholders for my error in judgment in anonymously participating on online financial message boards. I am very sorry, and I ask our stakeholders to please forgive me."[24]

The natural and organic food retailer was founded in 1980 in Austin, Texas, and quickly grew to 197 stores in North America and the United Kingdom. Its website says that it is mission-driven: "We're highly selective about what we sell, dedicated to stringent Quality Standards, and committed to sustainable agriculture. We believe in a virtuous circle entwining the food chain, human beings and Mother Earth: each is reliant upon the others through a beautiful and delicate symbiosis." It was listed among the top 20 of *Fortune* magazine's "100 Best Companies to Work For" rankings in 2006 and 2007.[25]   ∎

The use of blogs as a medium of communication between chief executives and key stakeholders such as shareholders and customers is increasingly common. *PRWeek* reported in 2006 that at least twenty-nine Fortune 500 CEOs were blogging. Dell uses a One2One blog that features posts from a variety of employees writing to customers.[26] A 2007 survey conducted by the Public Relations Society of America (PRSA) and Dow Jones & Company of 482 PRSA and Public

Relations Student Society of America (PRSSA) members found that practitioners and students believe that blogging and other digital channels provide great opportunities for practitioners. Yet the members also indicated that the unregulated nature of blogs and social networks presents a potential for harm as well.[27]

Commercial speech is more regulated than almost any other sector of public communication, as executives of publicly traded corporations are aware. The SEC's interest in the content of anonymous postings about one's own corporation and a chief competitor—especially at a time when merger discussions may be underway—is not surprising. The blogosphere provides almost unlimited opportunity for individual expression, questions, and networking. Certainly executives must balance their desire to express personal opinions, even when it is fun to do so, with their responsibility to act as stewards of corporate resources and requirements. The ease of anonymity and pseudonymity raises ethical questions, however, that transcend regulation of commercial speech. Kant's categorical imperative may provide guidance here. Kant would assert that communications should be truthful, without compromise; thus, using a pseudonym as a cloak for what might be seen as persuasive, self-beneficial messaging likely would be regarded as lacking truthfulness. Would one want this to be a universal practice by all digital communicators, particularly those in management positions who have a financial obligation to shareholders?

Mr. Mackey's bylined postings on the corporate website, while argumentative in nature, may not have been the most strategic means of seeking approval from the federal agency, but they were issued with public acknowledgment of their source. Do members of the online community who may have read and interacted with Rahodeb not deserve the same? Because the faceless nature of the Internet itself makes it difficult to really ever know who is behind the information that is posted, there may be an equal burden on Internet users and online community members to remain skeptical about information they receive through the medium, being careful to seek authentication before repeating or relying on it for decision making.

51 "This News Story Is Brought to You By. . . ."

Seen any of these public relations messages on air lately? If so, were you told who funded their creation, wrote the scripts, and edited the video images?

- A video news story questioning the reality of global warming
- A segment about rental car insurance
- A video news story about a child-passenger safety seat
- Another that warned of the dangers of personal information being lost if a laptop were stolen

According to the Center for Media and Democracy, which has tracked video news release use by television stations, it is highly likely that if you did see the video news release

continued

(VNR), you were not informed about the sponsor—because in all these cases the "news" actually was broadcast, often verbatim, from a VNR paid for by a corporation. The center has issued two reports, "Fake TV News," and "Still Not the News" that tracked specific VNRs to see if and how they were used by broadcast stations. Writing in *O'Dwyer's PR Report*, Diane Farsette, senior researcher and coauthor of the two reports, said: "Our two reports documented 140 VNR broadcasts. In only two instances did TV stations clearly and fully disclose the source of the VNR footage to news audiences."[28] According to the PRWatch.org "Still Not the News" executive summary, "In twelve instances, television stations actively denied disclosure to their news audiences by editing out on-screen and verbal client notifications included in the original VNRs."[29] The researchers found that it was not smaller-market stations that used the VNRs without extensive editing but stations in top fifty Nielsen markets.[30]

The Radio-Television News Directors Association guidelines for the use of noneditorial video and audio call for stations to "clearly disclose the origin of information and label all material provided by corporate or other noneditorial courses."[31] PRSA issued a statement asserting that organizations that produce VNRs should clearly identify them as such and disclose who produced and who financed the work when they are distributed. Then, the PRSA says, the station has responsibility to identify the source of the footage when it is aired. But the PRSA asserted, "Excessive government regulation on the production and dissemination of such materials could have a chilling effect on open communication and work against providing the public with vital, interesting information from myriad points of view and sources."[32]

VNRs provide a worthwhile service for broadcasters, providing access to video footage of events, information, or activities that otherwise might be unavailable for coverage. Along with an edited package, a VNR also may contain additional video, a sample script, narration and voiceovers, and additional information, making it easy for a station to use the material in its entirety or through editing make the video appear as though it were local in source and origination. The total use of VNRs is unknown. The center's study analyzed only a small number of VNR airings, when considering the total number of news and information stories broadcast by seventy-seven stations, so the breadth of this issue is hard to determine. However, VNRs have been produced and distributed by practitioners for more than twenty years, so there must be some positive outcome associated with this medium. ∎

Does disclosure of the source of video or audio footage matter? While it may aid in increasing credibility, is it an ethical breach to use such material without direct attribution? Using material from a print news release in a newspaper or magazine article without direct attribution has been commonplace for years; corporations and organizations seek to make it as easy as possible for reporters to gain access not only to written materials but also to photos, graphs, tables, and streamed video. Is there an inherent difference in using an unattributed video clip than in reproducing a news article without a byline—or with a reporter's byline inserted?

Some people argue that knowing the source, writer, and editor of the VNR allows audience members to make more informed decisions about believability of the information and how the issue is being overtly or covertly framed. The interactive context of a typical newscast, the familiarity of anchors, and the routine of standup reporting may create a sense of friendliness and professionalism between the newscasters and audience members. When used during a regular broadcast, if anchors or other reporters frame the video to imply local creation, the implication is that the material has undergone the same gatekeeping processes as other news and features presented. Audience members may watch—and be persuaded—by the material without exercising critical cautions that might be aroused if it the lack of such editing were cued by having the source of the information signaled verbally or visually with a source line. However, the context of the newspaper or magazine also denotes that such gatekeeping has occurred, so audience members may be equally deceived. Thus the issues actually may be the same for print and broadcast releases. Both formats allow the creators to determine which viewpoints will be communicated.

This case provides opportunity to apply the Potter Box method for locating ethical behaviors. The definition of the situation here is important. For example, what is the source of the material? Is the original source trustworthy? Is the material available any other way? Is it possible to augment the information presented? Values pose particular issues in this case. Take, for example, the value of fairness, allowing all sides of an issue to be voiced in the public forum. Can objectivity be achievable if a VNR or a print release has only one source with one perspective, often commercial or partisan, included? What about truthfulness? Is it possible to verify the information presented in the release, or is the source so trusted that one can assume that it's truthful? These values may clash with the material values of the medium: Perhaps the low cost of using materials shot, written and edited by someone else, overrides the price of loss of editorial control or independence.

Using an unedited and unacknowledged VNR or print release may well demonstrate where the loyalties of the creator and the editors lie. Are they with the audience or with the client or employer? Is there a public-service obligation involved, as in some medical or scientific information often provided through releases? However, if the information is deemed to be in the public interest, wouldn't that value be enhanced if the source were clearly identified? From a practitioner's perspective, the question of loyalty and the value of truthtelling may seem unanswerable. Those who send releases that are clearly labeled and identified as such cannot then control how they are displayed or handled by the media editor. While a sponsor's logo might be included on screen throughout a video, such is not possible for a print release. Thus the ethical responsibility ultimately may rest with the receiver rather than the distributor.

Kant would provide some principled insight here. The categorical imperative would dictate that editors and broadcast managers should use the same standards for verification, accuracy, and objectivity with these stories and sources as with any others. Opting out of the editing and gatekeeping process simply because it is easier or more economical won't satisfy this imperative. Kant might indeed call for greater scrutiny to be brought to the editing of these materials rather than less. He also would acknowledge the public-service nature of many of these messages. The duty communicators have to share important messages with their audiences should compel them to provide the information, even if it takes effort.

NOTES

1. Peg Tyre and Daniel McGinn, "A Big House for Martha?" *Newsweek*, 16 June 2003, p. 41.
2. Associated Press, "The ImClone Scandal," *The Atlanta Journal-Constitution*, 11 June 2003, p. D4.
3. Alessandra Stanley and Constance L Hays, "Martha Stewart's To Do List May Include Image Polishing," *The New York Times*, 23 June 2002, www.nytimes.com/23MART .html?todaysheadlines.
4. Paul Cordasco, "Experts Say Stewart Must Design New Crisis Strategy," *PRWeek*, 24 June 2002, p. 5.
5. Shelley Emling, "Did Martha Sweep Dirt Under the Rug?" *The Atlanta Journal-Constitution*, 25 June 2002, pp. A1, A12.
6. Shelley Emling, "Stewart Fights Back; Newspaper Ad Calls Prosecutors' Charges Baseless," *The Atlanta Journal-Constitution*, 6 June 2003, p. B1.
7. Tyre and McGinn, "A Big House for Martha," p. 41.
8. Mark Coultan Words, "Can't Keep a Good thing Down," *The Sydney Morning Herald*, 12 July 2007, p. 6.
9. Pallavi Gogio, "Wal-Mart vs. the Blogosphere," *BusinessWeek online*, 18 October 2006, accessed 2 August 2007.
10. "The Final Word," http://walmartingacrossamerica.com; posted 12 October 2006; accessed 2 August 2007.
11. Hamilton Nolan, "Edelman Discusses Wal-Mart Incident," *PRWeek*, 18 October 2006.
12. Gogio, "Wal-Mart vs. the Blogosphere."
13. Ibid.
14. Marcus Kabel, "Wal-Mart, Critics Slam Each Other on Web," Associated Press, 18 July 2006; accessed 19 July 2006.
15. Michael Barbaro, "Wal-Mart Enlists Bloggers in Its Public Relations Campaign," *The New York Times*, 7 March 2006, p. C1; Lynda Edwards, "Retailer Critics Take War to Web," *Arkansas Democrat-Gazette*, 29 January 2006.
16. Katie Hafner and Claudia H. Deutsch, "When Good Will Is Also Good Business," *The New York Times*, 14 September 2005, www.nytimes.com.
17. Hamilton Nolan, "Wal-Mart Unveils Small-Business Strategy," *PRWeek*, 6 April 2006.
18. Jeffrey A. Dvorkin, "When NPR Crosses the Line," 25 February 2004, www.npr.org/ yourturn/ombudsman/2004/040225.html.
19. Kim Hart, "A Bid to Get Religious? Wal-Mart Hires Ex-nun," *The Washington Post*, 18 July 2006, p. D3.
20. Andrew Martin, "Whole Foods Executive Used Alias," *The New York Times*, 12 July 2007.
21. Peter Kaplan, "Whole Foods CEO Launched Anonymous Web Attacks on Rival Company," Reuters, 11 July 2007.
22. http://wholefoodsmarket.com/blogs/jm; accessed 6 August 2007.
23. http://wholefoodsmarket.com/company/pr_07-17-07a.html.
24. http://wholefoodsmarket.com/company/pr_07-17-07b.html.
25. www.wholefoodsmarket.com/company/facts.html.
26. Keith O'Brien, "Dell Launches One2One Blog," *PRWeek*, 10 July 2006.
27. "New PR Survey," *Bulldog Reporter*, 25 July 2007, www.bulldogreporter.com.
28. Diane Farsetta, "Mandated On-Screen VNR Disclosure Is Needed," *O'Dwyer's PR*

Report, April 2007, p. 12. More analysis of the ethical issues associated with the use of VNRs may be found in Louis W. Hodges, ed., "Cases and Commentaries," *Journal of Mass Media Ethics*, 20 (2005): 245–256.

29. www.prwatch.org/fakenews2/execsummary.
30. www.prwatch.org/fakenews/execsummary.
31. "RTNDA Guidelines for Use of Non-Editorial Video and Audio," Accessed at www .rtnda.org;foi/finalvnr.html; accessed 21 August 2006.
32. Public Relations Society of America, "Response to Request for Comment, FCC, Video News Releases," 24 June 2005, http://media.prsa.org/article_display.cfm?article_ id=480.

Conflicting Loyalties

Consider the following situations:

- A major corporation decides it must reduce its workforce by thousands, and its communication department is told it must release the news.
- A public relations agency decides to accept a controversial new client who may offend previously held clients.
- A consulting firm is asked to represent a political candidate with extreme views certain to arouse strong reactions.
- Beleaguered public affairs officers at a nonprofit agency are asked to explain the decisions of its executive officers to throngs of investigative reporters.

In each situation, practitioners and managers are challenged to find an ethical way to balance what may be strong personal values and loyalties with the values and interests of their various organizations.

Journalism ethicists have frequently dealt with conflicts of interest from the perspectives of news editors and reporters, warning against the lure of freebies, relationships with sources, and involvement in nonnews organizations. While these issues may have some relevance for practitioners, their professional conflicts may present a different set of challenges as well. Practitioners are expected to be partisan in their loyalties yet equitable in their actions. They are expected to represent the leadership of an organization and at the same time to serve as a boundary between that organization and its varied internal and external publics, ideally seeking to promote harmonious, beneficial relationships among them. Certainly, this may create situations in which clashing interests occur.

In an early analysis of public relations ethics, Albert J. Sullivan identified this conflict of interest as one between "partisan values" that are "highly personal and serve as a measure of the relationship between the managers of an enterprise and the men who serve as public relations counsel" and "mutual values," a concern that each group's rights and obligations are "carefully defined" and honored, with management but one of the groups considered. Sullivan said, by applying a mutual value system, "public relations may be called . . . the conscience of the institution." Partisan values involve commitment, trust, loyalty, and obedience to management. When practitioners become overly partisan, Sullivan warns, it may lead to a "my country, right or wrong" mentality, a utilitarian ethic and one-way communication flow. Mutual values, Sullivan says, ensure the honoring of each person's right to true information and a right to participate in the decisions that affect him.[1]

In such a complex professional environment, how does a practitioner emphasize mutual, rather than partisan, values within the daily workplace? What principles offer guidance toward arriving at an ethical solution?

The case studies in this chapter provide hypothetical and actual examples of ways practitioners, clients, associations, and corporations have struggled to balance conflicting loyalties and values. The pressures faced by individual practitioners as they decide which clients to represent are explored in "A New Client?" and "The Long-Distance Client." The loyalties arising from personal relationships with sources and vendors are probed in the "Friends?" cases. The pressures felt by nonprofits are seen in "The Medical Endorsement" case. The values and loyalties called on during times of human tragedy are recounted in the last case, "Tragedy at the Mine."

52 A New Client?

Bill had been with the agency for about a year and a half. He had spent sixteen months as an assistant account executive before being promoted to his current position as account executive. Now he had more responsibilities and was excited to hear that he was in line to be assigned to the new client for the agency.

But his excitement faded when he got the memo announcing the new client, Blue Valley Vineyards, a winery that had opened outside the city three years ago. He'd heard it was doing well in sales and in reputation. Now its owners were seeking an agency to plan and execute a regional campaign to enhance the winery's image as a select label and as a tourist spot.

He knew that he should be excited about the trust the agency was placing in him by assigning him to the new client as the account executive, but he was not. As the child of a recovered alcoholic, Bill was well acquainted with the dangers of alcohol abuse and was not comfortable promoting the use or reputation of any alcohol product, even a regional wine.

He talked it over with his vice president, who told him: "It's just a wine label, Bill. It's not like you're promoting vodka to children. This is a table wine, marketed and sold to adults to enhance their dining experience. These folks are responsible with their advertising and want us to be responsible with our public relations efforts. And the primary thrust of the campaign is to position their winery as a tourist site. This town could use something that would draw more tourists in."

continued

Bill spent a long evening in thought following his discussion with the vice president. He knew that he must decide if and how he could represent a client or product with which he felt conscientious disagreement. He had to reconcile long-held personal values and loyalties with the legitimate desire of his agency to serve the needs of a valuable new client, and somehow identify where he could find virtue in this situation. Bill knew that he had experienced one extreme of alcohol use; he acknowledged that his assumption that all alcohol use inevitably leads to abuse was probably another extreme.

He thought of one option in balancing his views. He could ask to have the client's campaigns divided. Bill could assume responsibility for promoting the vineyard (and the town) as a tourist site, and thereby avoid having to actually promote the wine itself as a product. Giving his full attention to what the vice president had identified as the primary thrust of the campaign should prove his loyalty to his employer and the client, he thought, while, at the same time, it would relieve him of having to promote directly the sales of a product he was not comfortable promoting. Of course, it was inevitable that increased tourism would support sales. So that probably was not the best option.

Bill wondered who would direct the campaign if he did not. Perhaps his sensitivity to the dangers of alcohol abuse would make him a better manager of the campaign than anyone else. He could use the campaign to encourage wine lovers to be responsible, smart consumers rather than abusers of alcohol. He had resented some of the promotions he'd seen other alcohol producers use and believed that he could use this campaign to balance some of their messages. The vice president had indicated that Blue Valley wanted to be positioned as a tasty social beverage and promoted in such a way that alcohol abuse was discouraged. Therefore, this theme could work.

"I'll agree to act as account executive," he told his vice president the next morning. "I know I can trust myself to plan a responsible campaign, and I trust Blue Valley to work with us in communicating a positive message about their label and the vineyard. How soon can we get started on planning?"

Bill found this solution comfortable. Was his decision a rationalization or an ethical judgment? Might he have arrived at a different position if the new client had been a brewery or a distillery rather than a winery? Or, imagine a scenario in which one of Bill's parents had died of lung cancer and his agency was asked to plan a tobacco company's sponsorship of a series of athletic events. What loyalties and values would Bill have to weigh in deciding whether he could work on such a campaign?

53 Case I: Friends?

"Hey, Jane, got a minute?"

Jane looked up from her computer screen at the door and smiled. "Of course. Come in, Tom. What brings you to the office this late in the day? Have I forgotten a deadline?"

Tom ran a small print shop several blocks from the corporate headquarters where Jane worked as communication director. He had worked with Jane on several projects during the two and a half years Jane had been at headquarters, filling in at the last minute on a couple of high-pressure deadline jobs. She had found him to be conscientious and knowledgeable. He had provided excellent advice when she purchased new desktop publishing equipment and software packages for the department last year. Jane knew that she could depend on him and his firm to do high-quality work. Moreover, she had enjoyed working with him on a personal level, too, enjoying his quick wit and quiet manner.

Tom laughed. "I've never known you to miss a deadline. It's certainly not that. No, I wanted to return this bid specification sheet I received last week."

Jane had invited five area printers to bid on the printing contract for the corporate employee magazine. The monthly four-color magazine was distributed nationally to 36,000 employees, so it was an expensive and extensive contract, offered for bid every three years.

Jane reached for the sheet. "Did you have any questions, Tom? I know it's a lengthy spec sheet, but I wanted to be thorough. I need realistic, affordable bids for this project."

"No, the spec sheet is clear—I just haven't completely finished filling it out. I guess I really wanted to talk to you about my bid. As you know, I run a small shop, and a contract this size would mean a great deal to us. You know the kind of service we can provide you, and you have plenty of samples of our printing jobs. No, I really just wanted to see if we were in the ball park. I heard you had received all the other bids already and wondered if—well, if you would give me some clue as to what I need to do to win this contract. I've helped you out as much as I could in the past and wondered if you could give me some help here.

"I'm not asking you to let me look at the other spec sheets or anything, but if you could take a look at them and then give me a feel for what I need to do to win this contract—what I could add to my proposal to give me the winning edge—I promise you won't be sorry. I'll treat you to dinner tonight, just as a gesture of appreciation." ■

Jane's first impulse was to throw Tom out of her office. But as she opened her mouth to speak, she realized that she should think the action through first. Tom had been a trustworthy friend. He must be under some real pressure if he's asking for my help, Jane thought. She knew she wasn't going to let him look at the other bids but wondered if she should give him a few hints to help him with his bid. After all, bidding for work is a ritual conducted by people who have no basis for mutual trust. It's an awkward process between friends who should be evaluated on the general quality and economy of their work, not on just a series of numbers on sheets of paper. Besides, she owed him a favor; he had helped her last year when she was in over her head on that equipment order.

"What will it hurt?" Jane asked herself. "I'll just give him some ideas about the range we're looking for. Anyway, the boss is always talking about the importance of working with local vendors. I know our money will stay here in town if we spend it with him, and this town can use all the help it can get in generating revenue."

As Jane reached for the other bids, she paused again. Memories of a college discussion about Rawls' views about fairness prompted her to question her quick decision. Was she just rationalizing so that she wouldn't have to hurt a friend's feelings? What about the other vendors who had submitted the lengthy bids? Didn't they deserve to be treated fairly? And her employer? Was it disloyal of her to allow a friendship to interfere with her job responsibilities?

Thinking quickly, she looked at Tom. "I'm sorry, Tom, but I can't help you. I think you and your shop do fine work, and I have always appreciated your help. I promise we'll consider your bid as fairly as we do the others, and I'll remind my bosses of the quality of work you always do for us when we're evaluating the pricing. I'm afraid that's all the help I can offer with the bid. Are you still interested in that dinner?"

53 Case II: The Friendly Journalist

"This is great news," Jane thought. "Imagine what this will mean for this town."

Jane had just been told that her corporation, Omega Belts, Inc., was planning a major building program, one that would expand its manufacturing capacity by almost 75 percent. With the new buildings would come new positions; perhaps as many as 2500 new employees would be hired.

Omega's CEO had encouraged Jane to release the news to area media and had indicated that while his schedule was extremely crowded, he would be available for limited media interviews about the expansion. "With news like this to share," he said, "for once I can say I'd be glad to meet with some reporters."

Jane had immediately thought of her friend Sean, the new business reporter for the local paper. She and Sean had completed college together, even taking a course in media law at the same time. They'd stayed in touch since graduation. Jane had applauded her friend's determination to succeed in print and had worked closely with her on several industry features. Sean's promotion to the business desk from work as a feature writer was one she had worked hard to obtain.

"I'll call Sean right now," she thought to herself. "I'll give her an exclusive on this story. She can interview the CEO and break the story in tomorrow morning's paper. I'll send an official release out about the expansion to everyone else tomorrow.

"That way, we'll get good play in the paper, and the CEO won't be bothered by a bunch of reporters calling. And Sean will be able to impress her new editor, too."   ∎

Is there a difference in the preferential treatment of friends in these two cases? Is there an ethical distinction between preferential treatment in financial matters as opposed to information access? Practitioners should be cautious of offering preferential treatment to friends in either case. All interested reporters should receive this breaking story at the same time and should have the opportunity to ask the CEO questions. And what if Sean asks Jane to arrange an additional five-minute interview with the CEO after the conference? Offering her friend advantages other reporters will not receive violates the Judeo-Christian "Golden Rule" treatment of others. Jane would be advised to overrule her friendship in this case and treat all involved equally.

This case also examines reportorial relationships with sources from a different perspective. What happens when the reporter and the practitioner are close allies, thereby excluding other reporters from fair access to important news? Sean, the reporter, certainly would not feel it unethical to pursue an exclusive and important story with wide reader interest. Because she did not suggest the exclusivity, her journalistic ethics are not in question. However, from almost any ethical perspective, Jane is making a bad choice by choosing to give her close friend an exclusive on this important story. She is allowing partisan loyalty to her friend to obscure her loyalties to other area media personnel and to her employer. The good news that would be of certain interest to the community and the resulting good will the corporation could reap may be lost because of negative media reaction to being scooped by the exclusive. Her later relationships with the miffed reporters could be impaired, again causing her employer potential harm. All those involved in this case will be best served if Jane seeks a fair and equitable release of the important story. Certainly, other beat reporters who know of Jane's friendship with Sean will respect her more for her fairness in this case and perhaps listen to her more readily when she next calls with good news from Omega Belts.

54 *The Medical Endorsement*

In August 1997, the American Medical Association (AMA) and the Sunbeam Corp. announced plans for a five-year alliance that would have allowed Sunbeam to use the AMA name and logo on some of its products. According to the agreement, Sunbeam was to package AMA medical information in its Health at Home product line of blood-pressure monitors, humidifiers, vaporizers, heating pads, and home air cleaners and to include the AMA seal on the package. The Sunbeam product line would be featured in the AMA consumer catalog and on its website, and a Physicians Advisor Panel was to help Sunbeam develop future products. The professional association and the corporation also would jointly sponsor blood-pressure screenings in cooperation with local retailers.[7] Reportedly, the AMA would have received large royalties from Sunbeam[8] to use for research and public-health and education campaigns.

The announcement prompted strong criticism from inside and outside the AMA. Within a few weeks, the association announced that it would ask Sunbeam to release it from the arrangement, stressing that it was the association that had erred, not the corporation. AMA Chair Thomas R. Reardon and Executive Vice President P. John Seward issued a statement that said, in part: "Our decision to approve the Sunbeam agreement in the form adopted was an error. As a result, our credibility was called into question. The AMA apologizes for creating public doubt about our motives." The executives indicated that the association would take steps to ensure no further product-endorsement deals would be contracted.[9] Subsequently, a committee was formed within the AMA to investigate how the alliance was approved,[10] and later, three executives were fired.[11]

The Sunbeam Corp. filed suit asking the federal district court in Chicago to enforce the terms of the agreement.[12] The AMA eventually paid Sunbeam nearly $10 million to settle the suit, $2 million for legal expenses and $7.9 million for damages related to the AMA's decision to withdraw from the arrangement.[13]

continued

> However, the incident did not appear to have caused lasting image problems for the AMA. Public confidence in the AMA appeared unshaken, according to results of a Louis Harris poll, which found that 83 percent of the physicians polled indicated that they believed the AMA was highly ethical, and the general public's favorable opinion rose 8 percent.[14]   ■

Professional associations such as the AMA offer important services and functions to their members and to the public at large. Certainly, they provide communication, networking, and training opportunities for their members. Frequently such groups also establish the entrance requirements and/or mechanisms for entering the profession; they also may act as a governing body of sorts, establishing standards for membership, thereby accepting a burden of responsibility to act in the public's best interest.[15] The prestige of the AMA is recognized, and often its voice is regarded as the voice of the professional community it represents. Therefore, its endorsements and its criticisms are magnified, particularly amid the debates about managed care and government health funding, where such endorsement might mean that coverage for certain items is or is not offered.

When a group such as the AMA aligns itself with a specific product—or good or service—the alignment carries tremendous significance for individuals, health-care providers, and insurers. Apparently, the top leadership of the AMA recognized that significance only after the association's announcement of its alliance with the Sunbeam Corp. drew criticism. It then was willing to go to great lengths to change the contract with the for-profit product line. One might argue that the "ethics question" was thereby solved. But the case offers an opportunity to explore the growing dual alignment of the corporate product, good, or service with the nonprofit endorsement. Should a public school system, for example, allow a pharmaceutical company to "sponsor" a biology series or an athletic-wear company to "sponsor" all the physical-education equipment? Are there ethical guidelines regarding the consequence of such implied or explicit endorsement?

Examine the issue carefully by using the Potter Box method to explore this case. Along with the AMA and Sunbeam, remember to include patients, other health-care product manufacturers, and other professional associations as key stakeholders in your considerations. What values might have been supported by such an arrangement? What might have been violated? For example, how did the agreement challenge the ideas of truthfulness and fairness? Do the values of public service and generating income clash irreconcilably here?

Deliberate on how the various philosophical principles would guide decision making here. Could utilitarianism be used to justify the alliance? While it may not be a winning argument, one could argue that the ends of persuading the public to use at-home health-care products for their own health and the lowering of their medical expenses might be seen to justify the means of selling the association's endorsement. Perhaps the end of raising additional funding for research and professional use might be seen as sufficient justification for this means of doing so; again, it is doubtful that this argument would be seen as compelling.

Would it have been justifiable from an Aristotelian perspective to supply health-care information within packages for a slight royalty fee, or would this imply an endorsement that also would be troublesome? Would this have balanced the extreme of overt commercialism with the good of providing sufficient at-use quality information?

Would Kant simply forbid any professional association from engaging in for-profit endorsements, or would his ethic allow for endorsements of only those products thoroughly researched and tested by the group? Kant certainly might take issue with the association's willingness to enter into a contractual arrangement and then quickly withdraw from it. The categorical imperative also might be used here to deny the association's involvement. It is doubtful that the general public interest would best be served by all professional associations entering into commercial-endorsement arrangements with companies in their fields of expertise and perhaps regulation.

55 The Long-Distance Client

Consider the following hypothetical scenario:

The ambassador begins: "I know this would be a first for your agency, Ms. Snyder, but we've studied your work carefully during the past few months. We have been very impressed with the creativity of your campaigns, and you were highly recommended to us by High-Tech, the firm that is working with us to update the telecommunication system in our country. They said you have deep insight into the most effective way to approach lobbying and that you were highly respected by everyone in Washington.

"Our country needs help from the United States to rebuild our economy. Passage of the Tripartner Trade Treaty would mean a new day for our businesses and government. We face many media and political contacts before the treaty will be considered by Senate committees.

"Of course, we will pay whatever your excellent service would be worth. Please tell us that you will accept our nation as your client. We need your expertise. Can we have your response by tomorrow? We will then offer all the support possible as we engage in this campaign together."

Snyder had worked for more than twelve years to position her agency as expert counselors in government affairs. Because of the nature of the work, Snyder-Holletts was not well known outside Washington, but they were regarded by those in the know as being reliable, savvy practitioners. Over the years, the small agency had represented such diverse groups as trade unions, chambers of commerce, major professional associations, and of course, High-Tech. Snyder was flattered that the ambassador had learned of her agency. She knew of a number of larger, multinational firms that would be eager to accept this very lucrative client.

However, she was hesitant about accepting. Although the current government appeared stable, its leadership had only been in power for nine months. The previous government had been extremely critical of the United States, and there certainly would be

continued

those on Capitol Hill who would remember some of the bitter rhetoric. That could make the job of selling the Tripartner Trade Treaty tough. Beyond the obvious difficulty, Snyder was not sure how she felt about the ethics of representing another government in a lobbying campaign. She knew the legalities; there would be no problem with registering her agency's activities. She just didn't know if she could or should accept this international client.

She thanked the ambassador gracefully for his kind comments and told him she would give him a definite answer tomorrow. Then she sat down and began to think.   ■

Is it ethically justifiable for practitioners to seek to persuade Congress to take action on behalf of another nation? Would such a persuasion campaign cross an ethical line about public service? Her agency had been active as a player in that system, but to this point it had always represented clients with causes that she could support or with issues that she felt at least deserved a fair hearing on Capitol Hill. She was somewhat wary of the publicity the client could bring the agency, although she knew that some agencies had represented international clients successfully. In fact, several agencies had won awards for their work with other governments during times of political crisis. The attention her small agency could receive, if the campaign were well designed and executed, could help its client list. Should political relations with the country turn harsh, however, her connection and representation could have a different impact on the agency's reputation.

She had no personal disagreement with the treaty. Increased U.S. trade could only help the people in the ambassador's country, and certainly building businesses would provide more effective help for the future than would a short-term aid bill. Increased trade would benefit the United States, too. Snyder-Holletts could incorporate such a win-win strategy in its communication plan.

After weighing a number of these arguments, Snyder decided her initial hesitation was unfounded. By acting to represent this client, she reasoned, she would not interfere with the process of government or prove disloyal to her own nation. She would follow her agency's typical campaign procedures and adhere to its usual standards of behavior, doing her best to avoid any misrepresentation or deception. The outcome of the campaign would not be harmful to the United States or its allies; in fact, it could be helpful. She would call the ambassador tomorrow and agree to represent the nation as it pressed for passage of the Tripartner Trade Treaty.

56 *Tragedy at the Mine*

It was likely lightning that ignited the 2 January 2006, explosion at the Sago Mine in Tillmansville, West Virginia, in which twelve miners were killed and another critically injured, according to a report commissioned by West Virginia Governor Joe Manchin, although the

United Mine Workers of America contest that cause.[16] The disaster was exacerbated by the spread of incorrect information both locally and nationally that mistakenly reported that the twelve miners had survived.

The search and rescue mission began around 5 P.M., nearly eleven hours after the explosion in the mine. The first body was found by rescuers at 9:10 P.M. on January 3. It took several hours more for the rest of the men to be discovered; rescuers searching the mine discovered the men about two miles inside the mine, and eleven of the group were already dead. The information was transmitted by the team using a series of five underground relay stations because their radios could not transmit through the rock. In a tragic manner, the message apparently was misunderstood and relayed over a speaker phone to the control center as "Twelve alive!"

The crisis command center was not secured, so information was not kept confidential until it was confirmed. CNN went live with the announcement. Cell phones then spread the word to the family members and friends who had gathered in the nearby Sago Baptist Church. The report to the governor said that family members were told erroneous information, such as that when the miners were rescued, they would come to the church before seeing medical providers. So family members and friends of the missing miners stayed in the church, waiting for their arrival.

However, within the hour, rescuers informed the command center that there appeared to be only one survivor. Several hours passed before the news was relayed to family members.[17] The tragic news was delivered to the church around 3 A.M. by Ben Hatfield, president of the mining company, who was escorted by state troopers. Following the announcement, the miners' families and friends left the church, some angry and yelling at the mining company and media, others crying.[18] Hatfield told reporters the next day that he had known within twenty minutes of the rescuers discovering the miners that a mistake had been made but that he did not inform the family members at that time because he did not know the extent of the deaths.

CNN corrected its story around 2:45 A.M., apparently the first medium to provide the updated information.[19] Headlines in morning dailies across the country carried the erroneous information and had to correct the stories in later editions.

The governor's commissioned report stated that rescue leaders should have been more cautious in confirming information before it leaked out. According to the report, no officials from the Mine Safety and Health Administration and the state Office of Miners' Health, Safety and Training briefed the families of the miners during the entire rescue mission. The report said, "In any rescue situation, the highest-ranking federal, state and company officials on site must be personally responsible to ensure that miners' families receive timely updates of accurate and confirmed information." Apparently, the mining company had no press officer, and its president, Ben Hatfield, was responsible for conducting the press conferences.[20]   ■

Facing such a tragedy would pose a challenge for any organization. Delivering tragic news is difficult, even more so in this instance because of the original misunderstanding. However, the communication or lack of communication in this incident by the mining and government organizations almost certainly compounded the pain for those involved and raises ethical questions.

The agape principle calls for each person involved in such a crisis to be treated with dignity and respect; the operational principle calls for each individual involved to treat others as they would want to be treated if they were in the same position. From this ethical perspective, the actions taken or not taken by the mining company and the state officials are questionable. The time lapse between receiving the accurate information and informing the families at the church is hard to justify. Loyalty to the employees and their families and friends should have compelled communication. Providing avenues for families to receive prompt updates throughout the search would have demonstrated compassion and truthfulness. Creating a secure site for reporters to receive information regularly not only would have helped ensure accurate news reporting but also may have helped to protect families and friends from the intrusion of reporters and cameras during their time of high stress and great grief.[21]

While the full extent of loss may not have been known early on, allowing jubilant but false news to circulate raises false hope and then increases suffering and anger. The call to minimize harm to others should raise questions about process and planning. Whose best interests were considered here? Why was there so little preparation for a disaster like this when mining, after all, is among the most dangerous work in the country? The ethics of caring demand an investment in planning and preparation, thereby enabling organizations and employers to respond to tragedy in a more dignified, accurate, and compassionate manner. Crisis-communication planning calls for organizations to make certain they pass along only confirmed and accurate reports. This frequently involves designating spokespersons, holding briefings, and organizing a communication center where information flow is controlled.[22] Reports of life or death never should turn out wrong for lack of the preparation required to handle crises competently, compassionately, and professionally. At Sago, a nation was praying, and families were trembling. Every piece of news carried immeasurable value—as did the lives of the miners and those who loved them. Accepting responsibility for sharing accurate information is a duty owed.

NOTES

1. Albert J. Sullivan, "Values in Public Relations," in Otto Lerbinger and Albert Sullivan, eds., *Information, Influence and Communication: A Reader in Public Relations* (New York: Basic Books, 1965), pp. 412–428. See also Kevin Stoker, "Loyalty in Public Relations: When Does It Cross the Line Between Virtue and Vice?" *Journal of Mass Media Ethics* 20 (2005): 269–287.
2. Julius A. Karash, "A Dose of Madison Avenue. Drug Companies Say Ads Help Consumers; Critics See Them as a Threat to Patients," *The Kansas City Star*, 28 March 1999, p. F1.
3. Deborah Hauss, "Pills for the People," *PRWeek*, 8 March 1999, pp. 25–29.
4. Daniel McGinn, "Viagra's Hothouse," *Newsweek*, 21 December 1998, pp. 43–46.
5. Associated Press, "Pfizer Hires Dole to Talk about Health," *The Boston Globe*, 12 December 1998, p. A3.
6. Associated Press, "Celebrity Ads Becoming Favored Prescription for Drug Companies Seeking Healthy Profits," *The Boston Globe*, 21 February 1999, p. H7.

7. U.S. Newswire, "AMA, Sunbeam Corp. Launch Innovative Consumer Education Program," press release via Comtex, 12 August 1997.

8. Steven Findlay, "AMA Reconsiders Sunbeam Deal. Company Warns It Won't Let Doctors Group Back Out," *USA Today*, 22 August 1997, p. 3A.

9. U.S. Newswire, "AMA Statement on Sunbeam Corp. Alliance," press release via Comtex, 21 August 1997.

10. "AMA Doctors Vote Against Endorsements. Investigation into the Defunct Deal with Sunbeam Also Will Be Launched," *The Minneapolis Star Tribune*, 10 December 1997, p. 10A.

11. Associated Press, "AMA Fires Three Who Made Deal to Endorse Products," *The Dallas Morning News*, 20 September 1997, p. 8A.

12. Business Wire, "Sunbeam Asks Federal Court to Enforce AMA Contract," Sunbeam Corp. Press release, 7 September 1997.

13. Reuters, "AMA to Pay Sunbeam $10 Million to Settle Suit," 1 August 1998.

14. "Louis Harris Poll Confirms Confidence in AMA After Sunbeam," U.S. Newswire release, 7 December 1997.

15. Jeanne D. Maes, Arthur Jeffery, and Tommy V. Smith, "The American Association of Advertising Agencies (4As) Standards of Practice: How Far Does This Professional Association's Code of Ethics Influence Reach?" *Journal of Business Ethics* 17:11 (August 1998): 1155–1161.

16. Ken Ward, Jr., "Sago Report Proposes Reforms: Everything That Could Go Wrong Did Go Wrong," *The Charleston* (West Virginia) *Gazette*, 20 July 2006, p. 1; Josh Cable, "Report Blames Company, MSHA for Sago Blast," *Occupational Hazards* 69:4 ( ): 14.

17. Ken Ward, Jr., "Report Criticizes Gap in Sago Rescue Info," *The Charleston* (West Virginia) *Gazette*, 25 July 2006, p. 1.

18. Frank Langfitt, "Covering the Sago Mine Disaster," *Nieman Reports* 60:2 (Summer 2006): 103ff; Randi Kaye, "Mine Disaster a Story of Private Pain Made Public," CNN.com, 6 January 2006; accessed 11 January 2006.

19. David Folkenflik, "Sago: The Anatomy of Reporting Gone Wrong," National Public Radio, 4 January 2006, www.npr.org, 8/2/2007.

20. Jeffrey A. Dvorkin, "Listeners Upset by Mine Disaster Coverage," National Public Radio, 10 January 2006, www.npr.org, 8/2/2007.

21. Gerald Baron, "The Sago Mine Tragedy: Making a Bad Story Much Worse." *Tactics*, February 2006, p. 14.

22. Ibid.

CHAPTER THIRTEEN

The Demands of Social Responsibility

Perhaps one of the overriding ethical quandaries for a public relations practitioner is defining what is meant by the term *public*. One may define publics narrowly from the perspective of the organization's and client's most critical stakeholders—those networks of interdependency and mutual benefit that demand ongoing attention, focus, and resources. Yet the tug of the greater social public also must be acknowledged. From the professional codes of ethics to the expectations that professionals will act on behalf of a greater good, this obligation is usually articulated first in codes and frequently eloquently tied to the responsibilities of citizenship. Yet the boundaries between acting in the best interest of the more narrowly defined publics and that of the larger public are not clearly marked, forcing practitioners to search for ways in which somehow to balance or meet obligations to all.

To balance these interests, practitioners and the public must weigh such issues as

1. What are the ethical considerations when the public good can be served only at great expense to the company?
2. Are time or financial constraints ever an acceptable apology for compromising ethics? In other words, how much should these constraints be considered when choosing what should be done?
3. In an increasingly pluralistic society, how does one define the general public and then decide what is best for it?

One could describe this ethical quandary as one in which Kant meets Mill. One must decide when and how duty and utilitarianism intersect or overtake one another. When does a practitioner have to decide that "the greatest good for the greatest number" becomes a categorical imperative for ethical behavior, and how does the practitioner's decision impact that of the organization or client? The mere question implies that it is possible to predict the consequences of behaviors taken on behalf of or with the discrete publics on the general social public in a timely manner so that changing or stopping behaviors could mitigate harm or expand the benefit. One also might argue that understanding the socially responsible action requires a commitment to accepting the ethics of caring as a fundamental obligation for both corporate and individual practices. Actions that honor the dignity and worth of individuals almost certainly result in socially responsible outcomes.

The cases in this chapter prompt you to consider different aspects of social responsibility from different perspectives. "Practicing Good Citizenship" illustrates how some corporations have found ways to do well by doing good. The case of the film, *Thank You for Smoking,* provides an ironic analysis of the long-term implications when individual profit outweighs social good. The last two cases look at how two organizations faced different types of crises. "Pepsi Challenged by Rumors" recounts the approach taken by a corporation needing to control rumors about product safety, and "Swept Away in the Storm" recounts the challenges the Red Cross faced in serving victims of Hurricane Katrina.

57 Practicing Good Citizenship

The headline in the *Atlanta Journal-Constitution* read, "Corporate Citizens—Many Companies Give More Than a Check to Worthy Causes."[1] The article went on to describe how Atlanta-area businesses have supported the efforts of Hands On Atlanta, an organization that coordinates volunteering in the city. From August 2005 to July 2006, the article said, more than 7700 volunteers from corporations worked on 132 different service projects.

Such involvement is not limited to the Atlanta area, nor to the corporations that call it home. For many years, U.S. corporations have moved beyond the simple donation to a charitable cause to deeper involvement. Esteemed business schools such as the Kellogg School of Management at Northwestern University have established majors in areas such as business and its social environment.[2] Some corporations and businesses adopt a single cause; others use corporate resources and encourage or pay employees as they engage in individual and group service projects locally, regionally, nationally, and internationally. And some have established benchmarks for public service as demanding and ambitious as their sales and production goals.

For several years, the "100 Best Corporate Citizens" have been recognized for their corporate responsibility efforts by a listing first published in *Business Ethics* magazine. The list is now researched, selected, and publicized by CRO, an organization for corporate responsibility officers, based on analysis of data related to socially responsible citizenship—community involvement, corporate governance, diversity, employee relations, environmentalism, human rights, and their products.[3]

The corporation ranked number one in 2007 also was first in 2006, the first time a corporation has been ranked first two years in a row. The corporation? Green Mountain Coffee Roasters, Inc., which earned the recognition through such actions as

- Establishing—and paying—a "Green Mountain Livable Wage" of $10.75 per hour minimum for all full-time employees, regardless of work location.
- Offsetting 100 percent of direct greenhouse gas emissions by purchasing carbon offsets that supported the development of the Rosebud Sioux Tribe Wind Turbine in South Dakota and a methane recapture project in Pennsylvania.

continued

- Encouraging 30.1 percent of employees to volunteer in local communities. Increasing sales of Fair Trade Certified coffees to more than 20 percent of the coffee sold.[4]

Joining Green Mountain Coffee Roasters in the top ten were Advanced Micro Devices (AMD), Nike, Motorola, Intel, IBM, Agilent Technologies, Timberland, Starbucks, and General Mills. The activities of some of these leaders?

- The 50X15 Program of AMD that seeks to make the Internet and computing available to 50 percent of the world's population by 2015.[5]
- Motorola's committing more than $21 million in Innovation Generation grants for after-school science, technology, engineering, and math education clubs and programming.[6]
- IBM's improvement of an SME Toolkit for the International Finance Corp. of the World Bank to supply free to small-business owners in developing nations.[7]

Most of the corporations recognized on the list publish a new type of annual report, one that focuses not on financial assets and liabilities, but one that describes and illustrates their commitments to social responsibility. IBM's report lists its key performance indicators in categories such as energy conservation, pollution prevision, use of landfills, and nonhazardous waste recycling, and it includes measurable goals and achievements.[8] Nike's report breaks its three corporate responsibility goals (one of which is "Let Me Play. Unleashing Potential Through Sport") into topics such as freedom of association, worker empowerment, climate change, and contributions.[9] The Motorola reports states, "Corporate responsibility means harnessing the power of our global business to benefit people. This report describes our key issues and our moves to make a substantial positive impact."[10]

The Timberland report explains its corporate commitment to citizenship this way:

What Does It Mean To 'Make It Better'?
At Timberland, we live by a simple challenge and a common commitment—"Make it better." Every day, we apply skill and passion to finding new ways to improve our products. Strengthening our relationships with stakeholders. And enhancing the communities where we live and work. "Make it better" is straightforward, practical and common sense. It is a journey and not a destination. It can be found in small measures of goodness and in revolutionary breakthroughs in product technology. It's the shoes we craft and the green spaces we restore. And at the end of the day, our hope is that, through the people and places we touch, we do our share to create a better world and a more beautiful planet."[11]   ∎

Building and sustaining mutually beneficial relationships with key publics is the foundational goal of public relations practice. These corporations offer different examples of socially responsible ways of identifying needs among key publics and work-site areas and of matching needs and resources to support solutions. In a tight, uncertain economy, it might be easier for corporations to draw back from investing in public service. In international settings, it may be especially easy to work in an insulated environment. The rewards for community relations often are indirect at best. Improving the quality of life for one's corporate neighbors never may improve the bottom line directly for the corporation or even the direct quality of life of its employees; the efforts to stem climate change by monitoring carbon emissions, for example, will not likely pay a short-term dividend.

But there may be a link between good corporate citizenship and economic benefit, providing a utilitarian rationale for these investments. Results of the 2005 GolanHarris survey of 3500 Americans indicate that consumers do notice good behavior and try to support it. "Both customers and employees report that they would 'recommend' a company for its products and services or as a place to work because of good corporate citizenship."[12] According to the survey results, the consumers would be more willing to try the products of these businesses or to welcome development of their sites in their area. The list of corporations on the "Top 100 List" certainly includes many who are also leaders in terms of profitability as well.

Organizations that choose to act for others rather than just for shareholders or employees may exemplify the best of citizenship behavior. In particular, acting on the basis of stated corporate values demonstrates an ethical commitment to living truth as well as telling truth, that ideal of Aristotelian *phronesis* of both knowing what is virtuous and how to practice it. When there is a dichotomy between corporate mission statements, goals, and values and subsequent interactions with employees, shareholders, communities, and/or consumers, such virtue and practical wisdom are lost.

Certainly, a citation on any "100 Best" listing doesn't guarantee ethical purity or consistent performance. CRC notes that corporations lose consideration when they become aware of legitimate complaints about performance. Being listed one year does not ensure that a corporation will continue on the list or hold or improve its place on the list. However, such a list does offer an essence of accountability for the citizenship responsibilities of these leading national and international firms.

Recognizing the positive efforts of corporations is also ethically worthy. In a media culture cluttered with what can be overtly negative news of corporate profiteering, identifying corporations that are financially successful and socially responsible offers moral exemplars that support continued belief in the possibilities for socially responsible capitalism. The organization that seeks to promote greater social responsibility among businesses is using its voice in the public forum to recognize excellence rather than just offering castigation or criticism.

58 Thank You for Smoking

A handsome public relations spokesperson counters the talk-show appearance of a teen dying from cancer by asking why the tobacco industry would want to kill its best customers—those who are young and could buy cigarettes for years to come. Representing

continued

the Academy of Tobacco Studies, a lobbying group supposedly devoted to researching ties between tobacco and health, Nick Naylor works to counter proposed national legislation that would have imposed a skull and crossbones symbol on all tobacco packaging.

To accomplish this, Naylor bribes the cancer-stricken cowboy whose image had become synonymous with tobacco use to drop his lawsuit with a suitcase of cash. He convinces a major Hollywood producer to promote smoking in films as a way of gaining popular support, particularly among young people. Along the way, Naylor is shown lunching weekly with representatives of the alcohol and gun industries—the "M.O.D. Squad" as they call themselves, the "Merchants of Death." Following a television debate with the sponsor of the "skull and crossbones" packaging bill, Naylor is kidnapped and is almost killed by having numerous nicotine patches placed on his body. He is saved only because he has developed enough tolerance of nicotine through his smoking habit to survive the poisoning. Any more exposure to nicotine, even by smoking one cigarette, however, will kill him.

Naylor's no-holds-barred tactics are revealed in a tell-all newspaper article written by a reporter with whom Naylor has been having an affair. In disgrace, he is then fired by the academy. But he's not done yet. Just as the kidnapping didn't kill him physically, getting fired doesn't destroy his career. He turns the table on his ex-lover and destroys her reporting career by revealing their relationship. Summoned to testify at a Senate hearing about the proposed legislation, he turns in a stellar performance in which he appeals to libertarianism in his cry against the regulation. At the end of the film, he has recovered prominence and is shown at the helm of a prosperous public relations firm about to take on other causes.

The plot of the 2006 film, *Thank You for Smoking*, directed by Jason Reitman and produced by David O. Sacks, was drawn from a novel by Christopher Buckley.[13] The film was nominated for a Golden Globe award.   ∎

The film provides a satirical—and darkly comical—look at the interplay of lobbying, public relations, health communication, and newspaper sourcing and what may occur when careerism and client loyalty come before public interest and when dangerous products are promoted without much thought about consequences. It also provides an opportunity for two levels of analysis of public relations and social responsibility.

Within the plot of the film, the Potter Box may be used as a tool in analyzing the ethics of the public relations practices depicted. The definition of the situation is easily summarized. What loyalties are felt by the public relations practitioner? Loyalty to his employer and to his "M.O.D. Squad" friends is demonstrated. His loyalty to his reporter/lover is shown to be ill-advised. What other loyalties are demonstrated through plot interaction? What about his values? He obviously values money and influence but asserts that he values personal freedom. What philosophical principles might guide his behavior? Is he relying on utilitarianism, asserting that the greater good is served by maintaining the freedom of market choice, or is this a subversion of utilitarianism because the consequences of increased tobacco use, particularly by the young, are strongly linked to ill health and high costs? Or is he applying a balancing analysis, accepting some regulation of his client's products as an effort to protect by informing but opposing any more efforts at either warning or increased regulation?

The philosophy of care and the respect for human dignity is noticeable by its absence. Throughout the film, Naylor manipulates or is himself manipulated by those seeking to maintain economic power. Neither he nor his employer cares about the real medical and financial needs of the cowboy; they offer money only as a bribe, not as a gesture of compassion. The reporter uses her sexuality to gain his trust and a huge byline.

The film itself also may be analyzed for its impact as a public relations message. Its central theme—that people should be free to make bad choices if they want to—omits much of the other issues within the debate, including the pain and suffering of others who have not chosen to smoke but who have become ill or whose loved ones have been ill, the cost of providing health care borne by those who have and who have not smoked, and the differences between the critical choice-making abilities of minors and adults. The definitions and locations of vice and virtue on an Aristotelian analysis may shift emotionally as the audience grows to sympathize with the unscrupulous lead as the "good characters" of the crusading legislator and reporter are shown to have flaws. In *Thank You for Smoking*, few emerge as worthy examples of public servants—not the politicians, the reporters, the industrialists, nor the public relations practitioners.

59 Pepsi Challenged by Rumors

The full-page ads proclaimed: "Pepsi is pleased to announce . . nothing." The ads, which Pepsi-Cola placed in newspapers across the country in June 1993, culminated a one-week rumor-control campaign conducted by the soft-drink corporation. The crisis began on 10 June 1993, when a Washington state couple claimed they had found a syringe floating inside a can of Diet Pepsi. The next day, a woman in a nearby city reported finding another needle inside a can. Within a few days, reports of needles found in cans came from states as far away as New York and Louisiana. Stories about the claims and about a Food and Drug Administration (FDA)–issued warning ran as lead stories in news outlets across the country, including the broadcast network evening news programs.

The first day, the corporation did not react to the allegations publicly, but then Pepsi responded. A crisis-management team that was formed with Pepsi CEO Craig Weatherup as its leader began by investigating the claims internally at its Seattle bottling plant. Within two days, it issued an internal advisory reporting on the security of its bottling process and continued the employee advisories throughout the crisis.

The corporation then began an aggressive media campaign, disseminating four video news releases (VNRs) by satellite to news stations across the country that showed the canning process, the initial arrest for a false claim of tampering, and a cut from a convenience store surveillance video showing a woman apparently inserting a syringe into an open can. The VNRs were seen by more than 365 million viewers on more than 300 stations.[14]

Weatherup and a company safety expert appeared on network evening newscasts and talk shows describing the safety of their bottling processes and the corporation's desire to

continued

maintain openness throughout the crisis. Weatherup was quoted on National Public Radio as saying, "We have to share everything we know, not only with the FDA, but with the American public and let them know we take this, obviously, incredibly seriously."[15] The corporation fully cooperated with the FDA and other government agencies during the investigation. In fact, Weatherup appeared with FDA Commissioner Dr. David A. Kessler on an ABC *Nightline* broadcast when the FDA announced a product recall was not needed.

The crisis ended with a June 17 press conference where the FDA called the allegations of tampering unfounded. Eventually, more than twenty suspects were arrested in connection with the claims.[16] The company's response did not end then, however. The promotion involving the announcement ads led to a July discount opportunity touted as a "Thanks America" campaign. Consequently, sales of the soft drink increased during the summer. The company's innovative use of VNRs during its crisis campaign earned it and Robert Change Productions a PRSA Silver Anvil Award in 1994 for excellence in crisis communication not involving accidents or national disasters.[17]   ■

Perhaps no situation tests the ethics or credibility of an organization like a product-tampering scare does for a manufacturer. The survival of the business depends on consumers who trust a product enough to buy and use it. Real or rumored safety hazards, however, can shake consumer and employee trust. Organizational and personal instincts may prompt a corporation to hide until the controversy passes, but a duty to public interest calls for prompt confrontation and resolution of the problems.

In this case, Pepsi had several choices about responding to the initial tampering claims and the subsequent charges. It could have chosen to avoid the media inquiries, hiding behind a "no comment on advice of our attorneys" stone wall. It could have initiated a smoke-screen campaign by ignoring the complaints and launching its discount campaign early as a diversion method. It could have appointed a less visible personality to head the crisis team to protect the CEO from media questions and public scrutiny. It could have evaded the government inquiries, hoping the controversy would die down, or tried to develop a scapegoat by blaming any product tampering on the outlets where their products were sold or on the media for creating a climate ripe for copycat claims. Each of these options might have been successful in diverting some of the attention from the claims themselves.

Instead, the corporation chose to exercise its duty to the public by opening up its processes to media and public scrutiny in an innovative and aggressive manner. Its VNR campaign invited and enabled the public to view the bottling process and law-enforcement actions for itself. Leaders in management served as representatives and advocates for all employees publicly; CEO Weatherup's willingness to be interviewed live on CNN, ABC, and PBS was evidence that the corporation was not afraid of scrutiny. Cooperating with government investigators also reinforced the company's claim in the safety of its products. Pepsi successfully calmed a communication crisis in this case. Certainly, the safety of its bottling procedures provided a strong defense against the false claims, but its open communication campaign helped to ensure that its defenses had credibility with its various publics. This case demonstrates that the ethical response of truthfulness and candor can reconcile the best interests of the organization and the best interests of the general public.

60 Swept Away in a Storm

Hurricanes Katrina and Rita brought heartache, tragedy, and loss to the Gulf Coast. They also tested the ability of the Red Cross to manage response to another widespread disaster, and the efforts on the part of America's leading charitable organization were commendable—although not without some problems.

The ferocity of the storms and the damage caused by them were unparalleled. Shelters were needed in twelve states, reaching from Utah to Florida.[18] The crisis relief involved more than one quarter of a million Red Cross relief workers. In all, about $1.5 billion was distributed to more than four million people, and shelter was provided for almost half a million survivors.[19] The huge effort was supported by a flood of gifts as well. Almost $2.3 billion was raised for Katrina relief,[20] although for the first time in its history, the agency had to borrow funds to cover disaster relief—some $340 million to cover its costs.[21] The Red Cross did not have a central national financial management system, making it hard to coordinate aid and then to audit how it was used. Even accepting gifts was difficult—the online donation system was not capable of handling the volume of posted donations.[22]

It may have been the widespread nature of the relief effort that was the greatest challenge—the hurricane, the collapse of the levees, and then the second hurricane; residents driven from their homes at different times; the disparate responses from federal, local, and state governments. It's not surprising that the Red Cross encountered problems distributing supplies, coordinating logistics, using volunteers, and reaching minorities, as an internal 2006 report noted. No disaster-wide shelter database was available, so it was difficult to keep track of the conditions and needs at each shelter. Some who needed help didn't receive it, at least not in a timely or regular manner. Others who perhaps did not need help took advantage of the crisis. Allegations of some fraud were investigated, and at least forty-nine people eventually were indicted.[23] Perhaps the storm swept away some personal ethics with the fury of its rain and wind.

Despite its heroic response efforts, the Red Cross was criticized[24] not only by those in Louisiana and other Gulf states but even by the British Red Cross and the International Committee of the Red Cross.[25] To address these concerns, the Red Cross added a link on its website for anyone wishing to report fraud, waste, or abuse (www.redccross.org/contactus) and developed a code of conduct that included a ban on anyone seeking financial advantage or gain as a result of their affiliation with the American Red Cross.

The criticism may have prompted management changes within the agency, according to *The Chronicle of Philanthropy*. Marsha J. Evans, chief executive, resigned in December 2005. In April 2007, the agency named Mark W. Everson to the position. Everson had served as Commissioner of the Internal Revenue Service. In April 2007, Congress passed legislation that reduced the Red Cross board from fifty to a maximum of twenty members by 2012, hoping to streamline decision making and oversight. The expectations for the role

continued

of the agency also shifted. The Red Cross would no longer have responsibility for coordinating shelter, food, and first aid to disaster victims under the country's National Response Plan. Instead, the Federal Emergency Management Agency would be in charge. The agency also would prepare disaster-response scenarios in conjunction with other emergency officials rather than having to prepare to cope with all types of disasters alone.[26]

But the Red Cross was not willing to give up on its humanitarian mission. Determined to apply the lessons learned through Katrina and Rita, the Red Cross took steps to improve and to prepare for future disasters. *The Atlanta Journal-Constitution* reported that the Red Cross spent $80 million to move supplies and food closer to vulnerable coastal areas and tripled its warehouse space around the country. One million debit cards have been prepared so that they can be activated quickly to be ready to be distributed to victims. Telephone service has been expanded to handle greater call volume. Greater ethnic, racial, and age diversity within its volunteer base has been sought.[27]   ■

Disasters are *agape* moments. Measuring an agency's efficiency and precision in such a time is an awkward—perhaps irrelevant—calculation. In situations so dire, ethical decisions always must be other-centered, with care of the suffering afforded the highest priority. The care should not be parceled according to a victim's status, nor offered mechanically or without compassion. Empathy, effort, and sacrifice all rush help to those in need, hoping that those who are involved will act virtuously. Yet nothing goes perfectly, and fatigue may take physical, fiscal, and emotional tolls.

Hurricane Katrina was a real "worst-case scenario" that pushed agencies and leaders at every level. Many appeared unprepared, overwhelmed, and entangled in bureaucracy. However, heroic efforts saved lives and provided hope. Despite some problems, the Red Cross was there helping, coordinating, and providing disaster relief during and after Katrina. Had the thousands of volunteers not been willing to help, what would have happened? The agency was there—a known and trusted organization around and through which contributors, volunteers, residents, and officials could rally and respond.

In a disaster of this magnitude, ethical questions are everywhere. Who gets help? What is the best way to provide help when systems are overstretched and overstressed? How much effort should go into monitoring help and auditing quality when time and quantity are insufficient? The Red Cross, one hopes, operates above the indecision, mismanagement, and selfishness that the breakdown of civil order invites. The Red Cross is the symbol of life and help. How do symbol and reality maintain integrity in such conditions?

Following the disaster, the organization held itself accountable, conducting an internal investigation that it made public. It cooperated with legal officials to identify and pursue those who had abused the privilege of helping others. The Red Cross demonstrated its commitment to truthtelling, even when the truth was somewhat painful or embarrassing, and then demonstrated a willingness to change as necessary to improve.

This case provides several key areas for discussion, both from an organizational perspective and from an individual perspective. What are the ethical obligations of a social-service organization that depends on volunteers and donors? How and when might such an organization admit its shortcomings without losing public trust? How should it weigh its obligations during times of great crisis? How is the greater good served? When working with volunteers, how may an agency best ensure that its volunteers will act honestly and be dedicated to public service? The ethical issues associated with verifying need also should be explored. How does one treat a suffering victim "as one would want to be treated" and still ensure accountability?

This case does not just demonstrate issues faced by the American Red Cross, but it also demonstrates the ethical issues faced by anyone interested in volunteering or donating to disaster relief. What questions should be asked or what knowledge should be obtained by the donor or volunteer before funds, supplies, time, or work is given? What standards of ethical behavior should a volunteer bring with him or her?

Ultimately, the virtues of action must be judged after the fact. Other-centeredness is inherently action-based. Agencies such as the Red Cross have been exemplars for decades because they are willing to take the risk of serving—and not even storms like Katrina and Rita could sweep away their commitment.

NOTES

1. Laura Raines, "Corporate Citizens: Many Companies Give More Than a Check to Worthy Causes," *The Atlanta Journal-Constitution*, 20 August 2006, pp. G1, 3.
2. Ed Finkel, "Doing Well By Doing Good. New Kellogg BASE Major Explores the Social Context of Business," *Kellogg World*, Winter 2002, www.kellogg.northwetern.edu/kwo/win02/indepth/doingwell.htm.
3. "!00 Best Corporate Citizens 2007," www.thecro.com/?q=be_100best.
4. www.greenmountaincoffee.com/.
5. www.amd.com/us-en/assets/content_type/Downloadable.
6. www.motorola.com/motldoc/6/6801_MotDoc.pdf.
7. www.ibm.com/ibm/responsiblity/performance.shtml.
8. Ibid.
9. www.nike.com/nikebiz/nikeresponsibility/#.
10. www.motorola.com/motldoc/6/6801_MotDoc.pdf.
11. www.timberland.com/investorRelations/index.jsp?to=csrreport.
12. Golin Harris, "Doing Well by Doing Good 2005: The Trajectory of Corporate Citizenship in American Business," www.golinharris.com.
13. Fox Searchlight Pictures (www.foxsearchlight.com/index.php)
14. Adam Shell, "VNRs Are the Right Thing, Uh Huh!" *Public Relations Journal* (August 1993): 6.
15. "Evidence Indicates Pepsi Tampering Allegations Unfounded," on *All Things Considered*, National Public Radio, 17 June 1993.
16. Keith Elliot Greenberg, "Pepsi's Big Scare," *Public Relations Journal* (August 1993): 6–7, 13.

17. Eugene Marlow, "Sophisticated 'News' Videos Gain Wide Acceptance," *Public Relations Journal* (August/September 1994): 17–21, 25.

18. "Facts at a Glance: American Red Cross Response to Hurricane Katrina," *PR Newswire*, 5 September 2005.

19. David Crary, "Red Cross Completes Candidly Self-Critical Report of Its Response to Katrina," Associated Press, 27 June 2006.

20. Ben Gose, "Ready or Not?" *The Chronicle of Philanthropy* 19:19 (26 July 2007): 25.

21. Jacqueline L. Salmon and Elizabeth Williamson, "Red Cross Borrowing Funds for Storm Aid," *The Washington Post*, 28 October 2005, p. A1.

22. Crary, "Red Cross Completes Candidly Self-Critical Report."

23. Erica Iacono, "Katrina Fraud Prompts Red Cross Comms Probe," *PRWeek*, 3 April 2006, p. 1; "Dozens Indicted in Alleged Katrina Scam," CNN.com, 28 December 2005.

24. David Crary, "Despite Huge Katrina Relief Operation, Red Cross Draws Criticism," Associated Press, 28 September 2005.

25. Jacqueline L. Salmon, "Counterparts Excoriate Red Cross Katrina Effort," *The Washington Post*, 5 April 2006, p. A14.

26. Gose, "Ready or Not," p. 25.

27. Mark Bixler and Bill Hendrick, "Red Cross Beefs Up for Hurricanes," *The Atlanta Journal-Constitution*, 1 June 2006, p. 1A.

PART FOUR

Entertainment

When the question came before the Hutchins Commission on Freedom of the Press regarding whether the film industry was part of "the press," the first reaction of several of the assembled scholars was "rubbish." In their eyes, movies were diversionary, escapist, and silly. What claim could one make to count movies as part of the modern media?

Fortunately, a more farsighted view prevailed. Motion pictures are part of the culture and need to be looked at carefully. The commission invited Will Hays, then chief of the Motion Picture Producers and Distributors of America (later the Motion Picture Association of America—MPAA), to present the case for industrial self-regulation. Eventually, the Hollywood model of codes and intraindustry regulations was adopted by the commission as the best way of expressing social responsibility in a democratic society.

On the importance of entertainment media and their responsibility to the public, the commission displayed wisdom in its landmark 1947 report. News and consumer information are vital to democratic life, but clearly, entertainment occupies most of the broadcast spectrum and cinema screen and a healthy share of the printed page as well. From these media we receive symbolic clues concerning what we should believe and how we should act. Entertainment, for all its recreational value, does much to educate and socialize us.

Should entertainment programs be subject to ethical reasoning? Robert Redfield, distinguished anthropologist and one of the Hutchins commissioners, urged that the direction of all our social productivity be toward a "new integrity" of idea and institution, a creative order wherein symbols and practices make "coherent sense when we state them and when we comply with them," leading to a "model society that will command the confidence of other free peoples everywhere."[1] Redfield, no dreamy chauvinist, was arguing for the interdependency of social institutions (such as the media) and social beliefs (such as the sanctity of life). Yes, he would argue, the entertainment media must be put to the test of ethical reasoning.

Redfield's intuitions were a preface to ethical theorizing in the 1980s, when narrative discourse and narrative communities became important concepts in the work of Duke University ethicist Stanley Hauerwas. Hauerwas argued that culture is built around stories that distinguish good from evil, hero from villain, success from failure. Because of the importance of story, a community that wants to live responsibly among other communities is obliged to set its compass on truthful narratives, without which a social ethic becomes detached intellectualism.

We organize the study of ethics around key questions: the relation of personal and social ethics, the meaning and status of the individual in relation to the community, freedom versus equality, the interrelation of love and justice. These are crucial categories for the analysis of a community's social ethics. The form and substance of a community are narrative-dependent, and therefore, what counts as "social ethics" is a correlative of the content of that narrative. Good and just societies require a narrative that helps them to know the truth about existence and fight the constant temptation to self-deception.[2]

Hauerwas begins his appeal for narrative ethics with a long analysis of the novel *Watership Down*, a rabbit story with a profound political message, a fictional narrative that helps us to develop our own. Constructing journalistic narratives, public relations messages, advertisements, and entertainment programs involves process, hierarchy, imagination, constraint, profits, and power. Our aim is to examine the moral dimension and press toward justified solutions.

George Gerbner underscored the importance of this examination in his lecture at the fortieth anniversary of one of the country's premier communications research institutions: "I think of communications as the great story-telling process that guides our relationships to each other and the world." Later, he warned that "children are born into a home in which a handful of distant corporations tell most of the stories to most of the people and their families most of the time."[3] His point was to urge a more careful study of the field, entertainment primarily, and its cultural and moral foundations.

The emphasis on narrative and authenticity gathered momentum in the 1990s as philosophers and essayists as different as Richard Rorty and Wendell Berry began to explore how communities form, how people connect with each other, how suspicion and distrust replace generosity as a first impulse.

Between the undefined "public" and the private individual, Berry writes, is the community, formed by a mutuality of interests and ennobled by "virtues of trust, goodwill, forbearance, self-restraint, compassion, and forgiveness." But, he adds, electronic media by nature "blur and finally destroy all distinctions between public and community." Television, for example, "is the greatest disrespecter and exploiter of sexuality that the world has ever seen."[4] Our narratives have gone crazy, self-destructive, and antihuman.

And from the time of Redfield's concerns to the late "naughties," we can do no better than cite Stephen Carter's book, wherein he urges us all to do better at (1) discerning right from wrong, (2) acting on that discernment even at personal cost, and (3) saying openly that we are acting on moral principle. He titled his book *Integrity*.[5]

The terrorist attacks on 11 September 2001 provided the most gripping real-time news coverage ever to appear on TV screens. Those images and the new global realities following that frightful day have had an impact on entertainment as well. Movies scheduled for release were postponed, reworked, and reconsidered. How much fright could the public endure? How much bitterness and hate could the world endure?

The following chapters raise only a few of the questions and suggest some ways of approaching answers. Violence is a pressing concern; its threat to social order is immediate and dramatic. Nearly 500 people in America die every week from gunshot wounds, many self-inflicted or tragically accidental. Many of these deaths are the result of a momentary act of passion among friends and relatives.

Media violence, some argue, is the same threat one step removed and a hundred times more potent. Television violence sets the stage for social maladjustment, argues Purdue University researcher Glenn Sparks, especially among children.[6] While researchers debate the audience impact, ethicists ask how much media violence is tolerable, even though only one person might be affected or none.

And what about problems generated by big media's huge financial stake? Fortunes and careers ride on fractions of rating points. So many in the entertainment industry doubt that ethical reasoning has any word to speak at all—money alone counts.[7]

Other problems in entertainment programs are less overt than violence or greed: the stereotyping and typecasting of racial groups, age groups, geographic groups, and communities of faith; or the bias expressed by the omission of substantive narratives about our society's small cultures; the offense created by our no-punches-pulled video and Internet explorations of sexual experience and crime; or the monotony of canned laughter and endless reruns.[8] It becomes clearer, as we proceed, that every level of the entertainment industry—producer, actor, writer, and viewer—closely encounters decisions of an ethical kind and requires a thoughtful response.

NOTES

1. Robert Redfield, "Race and Human Nature," *Half a Century—Onward* (New York: Foreign Missions Conference of North America, 1944), p. 186.
2. Stanley Hauerwas, *A Community of Character* (Notre Dame, IN: University of Notre Dame Press, 1981), pp. 9–10.
3. George Gerbner, "Telling Stories: The State, Problems, and Tasks of the Art," Fortieth Anniversary Program Highlights, Institute of Communications Research, University of Illinois at Urbana–Champaign.
4. Wendell Berry, *Sex, Economy, Freedom and Community* (New York: Pantheon, 1993), p. 124.
5. Stephen L. Carter, *Integrity* (New York: Basic, 1996), p. 7.
6. Glenn G. Sparks, "Developmental Differences in Children's Reports of Fear Induced by the Mass Media," *Child Study Journal* 16 (1986): 55–66.

7. See Clifford Christians and Kim B. Rotzoll, "Ethical Issues in the Film Industry," in Bruce A. Austin, ed., *Current Research in Film: Audiences, Economics, and Law*, vol. 2 (Norwood, NJ: Ablex, 1986), pp. 225–237.

8. For balanced accounts, see Richard Winter, *Still Bored in a Culture of Entertainment* (Downers Grove, IL: Intervarsity Press, 2003); and William D. Romanowski, *Eyes Wide Open*, rev. ed. (Grand Rapids, MI: Brazos, 2007).

CHAPTER FOURTEEN

Violence

Media reformers gather to television and filmic violence like sugar ants to jelly. It's their cause, their concern—and the rest of us may quickly dismiss them. At least until the tragedy at Columbine High School in the Spring of 1999. That day was so bizarre and brutal, everyone asked: "Why would teenagers plan and plot to kill their classmates and then themselves?"

News coverage of that terrible scene seemed like a surreal drama, yet the images were all too real. Had we—the American people—developed this culture of violence? Had entertainment violence made real-life violence less spectacular, more commonplace?

Three months after Littleton, two teenagers in Los Angeles stabbed and killed one boy's mother. They claimed their attack was inspired by the film *Scream*. Again we asked: "Is this *us*? Are we so vulnerable, or naive, or hardened that a B horror film can snap our sense of humanity and turn homes into slaughter-houses?"

Violence is inevitable in any drama, even in comedy and melodrama, such as when Spiderman fights the treacherous, spunky Green Goblin. But the irrepressible increase in real violent crime, much of it perpetrated by juveniles, often has been linked to video games and the Internet. What a juvenile sees, it is argued, too easily becomes what a juvenile does. Because society cannot endure the anarchy of criminal rule, it must move to eliminate the causes.

Confronting the censors of violence are combat-hardened libertarians who insist that all speech be protected. Violent programming may or may not breed violent behavior, they contend, but curtailment of speech surely heralds a retreat from democracy into feudalism, a return to the medieval monastery where utterances were controlled and political choices programmed. Such a fate, they claim, is worse than all others, and avoiding it is worth the risk of too much latitude.

Much of the current debate over violence in entertainment takes up the arguments of the last national inquiry, the controversial Meese Commission and its outspoken opponents. Organized in 1985 by Attorney General Edwin Meese, the commission was charged to "determine the nature, extent, and impact on society of pornography in the United States" and to recommend to the Attorney General how pornography "can be contained, consistent with constitutional guarantees."[1]

The commission's research included content analysis, participant observation, case studies, interviewing, and experimental studies. Its findings supported the cultivation hypothesis advanced by George Gerbner and others and at points suggested an even more direct link between pornography and the acting out of sex crimes by certain persons. The commission's ninety-two recommendations were nearly all in support of tougher enforcement of existing obscenity laws, with even stricter measures against child pornography. The rationale for control and enforcement was a widely shared conclusion that viewing and reading sexually violent material tends to create an incentive for violent sex crimes and to develop a socially destructive linkage of sex and violence in the minds of persons who may, under some conditions, act out their new attitudes.

From the first commission hearing, opponents issued charges of comstockery (a pejorative term recalling Anthony Comstock's anti-obscenity crusades of the 1880s). The American Civil Liberties Union (ACLU) published a "Summary and Critique" of the commission, entertainment professionals organized to protest the commission's implied call to curtail cinematic art, journalists trailed the commission and reported on the bizarre nature of some of its testimony, and columnists pointed to "dark lunacy" and "potential danger" underlying the commission's report. Much of the opposition can be summarized around five claims:

1. Artistic freedom and aesthetic integrity demand a laissez-faire approach. Government has no business policing writers and directors.
2. No direct effects can be documented or proved. Indirect effects are the consequence of living one's life in a world of mediated messages and cannot be made the basis of criminal prosecutions.
3. Violence is a social and historical problem, not the result of violent television shows or films. To think otherwise is to blame John Wayne for the Vietnam War.
4. Worry over media violence is really our fear of changing social institutions. To suppress television and film is to forcibly maintain traditional notions of family, friendship, and marriage in an era when these social arrangements are undergoing radical change.
5. Boundaries between news and entertainment programming are fluid. Television news-magazine shows are so hungry for material that anything visual (even if it must be staged for replay) is turned into a major "investigation." All the free-marketplace arguments that traditional news has enjoyed must now be applied equally to entertainment programs. The public has a right to know.

These objections seem less important in the face of enduring questions concerning the causes and cures of real violence. One author has suggested that media violence be treated like obscenity, which would remove its First Amendment protection in some cases.[2] Ethicist Sissela Bok compares the attraction of modern media violence to the Roman gladiatorial contests, wondering why civilized peoples permit uncivilizing entertainment.[3] The Clinton administration called for better industry self-control and clearer prosocial messages for the nurture of youth. Here and there, a producer and a network executive toned down the violence to show respect for the most recent shooting victims. The Michigan state senate passed a bill to require warnings on tickets and ads where a performer's music also carries such warnings. Small gestures, cautious solutions.

The cases in this chapter struggle constantly with the impulse to freedom and the moral boundaries of liberty. The first case raises the effects argument: Hear violent lyrics, do violent deeds; show a violent program, commit a violent crime. No matter that the violence is sometimes directed toward the self and sometimes to others.

But what would stories tell if all violence were expunged on moral claims? The second case insists that violence has its purposes. It cannot be read out of human experience, and it should not be so tempered in entertainment that we fail to deal with reality and history. The third case—which was part of the first edition of this book and remains here as one of the classics—wonders if media producers are oblivious to the violence they contribute to the culture. The final case, "Comics for Big Kids," looks at the persistence of violence in media entertainment.

Frustrated by the visual carnage in popular video games like "Mortal Kombat" and "Night Trap," Senator Joseph Lieberman once called for Congress to ban them. "We're talking about video games that glorify violence and teach children to enjoy inflicting the most gruesome forms of cruelty imaginable," he said. But in the same breath, Lieberman acknowledged that such games were constitutionally protected.[4] A bill to ban violent video games would face a long and politically powerful tradition of artistic liberty for entertainment programmers. In the face of such constitutional obstacles, the ethical arguments take a primary place.

61 Hear It, Feel It, Do It

Friday evening in October. John McCollum, nineteen years old, is alone in the house. An Ozzy Osbourne fan, he cranks up the family stereo—loud, intense, reverberating. Side one: "Blizzard of Oz." The first song, "I Don't Know," celebrates in the manner of heavy metal the chaos and confusion of human life. The second song, "Crazy Train," points to insanity as the inevitable result of our inability to explain life's contradictions. The third, "Goodbye to Romance," advocates cutting ties to the past as the only way to personal freedom. The last song is "Suicide Solution." That tune's lyrics convey a nihilism—a giving up on life—that even drug-induced addictions cannot solve. What's the solution to such bleakness? Ozzy points explicitly to the last and only act of the will available to a depressed soul who has lost every reason to maintain life. Then, masked in a twenty-eight-second instrumental break, and heard at one and a half times the normal rate of speech, are lyrics which, prima facie, advocate immediate self-inflicted death via gunshot.

John McCollum turns off the family stereo, walks to his bedroom, and puts another Osbourne album, "Speak of the Devil," on his personal stereo. Volume up, headphones on, he lies on the bed. Nearby, a handgun, .22 caliber. Music. The cool small muzzle against his right temple. Volume up. A muffled pop.

continued

McCollum's body was discovered the next morning. He was still wearing headphones, and the stereo's needle was riding around and around the center of the album. He had had problems with alcohol abuse that complicated other serious emotional problems, but in their suit against Osbourne and CBS Records, the McCollum family claimed that these lyrics had a cumulative impact on a susceptible listener; that the impact was antisocial in its emphasis on despair, Satan worship, and suicide; and that the record company had sought to cultivate Osbourne's "madman" image in press releases and sales promotions and to profit from it. The music was a proximate cause in McCollum's death, the suit alleged, because CBS negligently disseminated Osbourne's albums to the public and thereby "aided, advised or encouraged McCollum to commit suicide." The beat and the words had created in John McCollum "an uncontrollable impulse" to kill himself, a consequence entirely foreseeable and therefore intentional, the suit contended. Death, his family insisted, was brought on by pressures and forces hidden in the grooves and ridges of a plastic disc, made and sold by an industry that does not care.[5]   ■

Can media inspire violent crimes? A celebrated murder case in 1977 confronted the nation with a Florida teenager who shot his neighbor, an eighty-two-year-old woman, took $415 from her home, and went on a spree to Disney World with friends. Ronny Zamora's defense attorney proposed that his client was the victim of "involuntary television intoxication." A person who is drugged or becomes intoxicated without his knowledge is not legally responsible for actions while under the influence. Ronny had seen up to 50,000 television murders in his fifteen years, and he could not determine whether he was on a television program or committing a crime when he shot the victim, the attorney claimed. The jury decided otherwise, however, and Zamora was convicted. But similar cases keep coming to the courts.

Can violent media inspire self-destruction, and if so, who is responsible? The argument that linked repeated listening to rock albums to John McCollum's suicide is similar to the argument in the celebrated *Born Innocent* case that occurred a decade earlier. In September 1974, NBC sent to its affiliates a program starring Linda Blair as a girl whose innocence is shattered through her experience in a girls' reformatory. Because the drama would include violent scenes possibly objectionable to some viewers, NBC ran a warning at the start of the program: " 'Born Innocent' deals in a realistic and forthright manner with the confinement of juvenile offenders and its effects on their lives and personalities. We suggest you consider whether the program should be viewed by young people or others in your family who might be disturbed by it." As a portent of the show's later troubles, fifteen sponsors withdrew shortly before the broadcast.

Born Innocent did, in fact, raise objections from viewers. Hundreds of calls and letters were received by NBC affiliates across the nation, 700 in New York alone. Only a few callers, notably social workers familiar with reformatories, applauded the network for its realistic portrayal of a pervasive problem. Particularly troublesome was one scene in which Blair was raped by four female inmates using a plumber's helper for penetration. The character was shown naked from the waist up.

The program and its forthright realism would have been largely academic but for a real-life rape three days later. On Baker Beach near San Francisco, nine-year-old Olivia Niemi was attacked by three girls and a boy, ages nine, twelve, thirteen, and fifteen, who raped her with a beer bottle in a fashion similar to the attack on television. Olivia's mother filed suit for $11 million against NBC and the owners of KRON-TV, charging that NBC was guilty of negligence in broadcasting the program during family viewing hours (8 P.M. on the West Coast). One of the assailants had in fact referred to the television show when she was arrested.

The link between dramatic and real violence might not be strictly causal, but the network had not taken adequate precaution against the program's potential effects on young viewers. The case was strengthened by the absence of any similar type of rape in the casebooks of juvenile authorities. If Olivia's attackers had perpetrated a first-of-its-kind rape, their teacher and proximate cause was the television network that had prestaged the event.

NBC declined to argue the facts. Instead, defense attorney Floyd Abrams contended that the First Amendment protected his client from damages from alleged effects of a media program. California Superior Court Judge John Ertola agreed. In September 1976, he ruled in favor of NBC without calling a jury, claiming, "The State of California is not about to begin using negligence as a vehicle to freeze the creative arts."

But the California Court of Appeals overturned the ruling. Niemi had a right to a jury trial on questions of fact, the appellate panel contended.

Before the case was argued, NBC urged the U.S. Supreme Court to quash the trial. At stake, the network claimed, were basic constitutional rights. On behalf of NBC, the American Library Association filed an amicus brief suggesting that the Appeals Court ruling might lead to lawsuits against libraries by victims of crimes suggested in books. The Writers Guild of America wrote of the "chilling effect" on popular drama that a trial on the facts could have. For Niemi, the California Medical Association filed a friend-of-the-court brief. The Supreme Court declined to intervene.

Each side geared up for the coming courtroom battle. NBC would argue that a warning had been given before the drama, that the four attackers had previous juvenile records, and that some testimony suggested that none of them had seen the televised rape. Causal explanations for the crime other than the television show rested on stronger psychological evidence. One of the attackers, for example, had been molested by her father. In theory, NBC insisted, the plaintiff's case would shift accountability for criminal acts away from the persons responsible and toward the producers of televised drama.[6]

Niemi's attorney would argue that the rape scene in *Born Innocent* ignored NBC's own production code and the National Association of Broadcasters' code that proscribed graphic depictions of violence at that time. The rape scene, in fact, had been abridged in telecasts after the first showing. No one should be absolved of civil liability because of the First Amendment, the plaintiff said.

Commercial television networks would be hard pressed to justify graphic violence based on Kant's imperative. No reasonable person could will that such portrayals become standard television fare because reasonable people do not, by definition, seek to promote gratuitous suffering. There should be little argument here. People who delight in causing or feeling pain are pathologically disturbed or criminally insane. Reasonable people may not choose to avoid all suffering (e.g., running into a fire to rescue a child), but suffering without purpose (e.g., merely running into a fire or pushing someone else in) is irrational by any common definition. Likewise, a constant media diet of violence and pain is irrational, assuming even a remote connection between what one views and how one behaves.[7]

Notice how close Kant (the doer of duty) and Jeremy Bentham (the calculator of pleasure) are on this issue. Bentham, the father of modern utilitarianism, wrote: "Nature has placed mankind under the governance of two sovereign masters, pain and pleasure. It is for them alone to point out what we ought to do, as well as to determine what we shall do."[8] Kant's appeal to rational duty would have little prescriptive value if people were unclear about whether to seek pleasure or pain. Let us assume that the history of human civilization is not remiss here: Avoiding gratuitous violence is the normal response of a rational person.

But "Suicide Solution" is only one song, and *Born Innocent* is only one program, and the rape scene is only one sequence in that one program. This is hardly a trend and certainly not an unrelieved diet of mayhem and bloodletting.

Yet, to describe the problem in this way is to miss the point of even the utilitarian response. Hans Jonas, a modern utilitarian, has argued that the consequences of a nuclear holocaust are so incalculable that we must set our goals specifically at eliminating even its possibility.[9] (Notice an underlying Kantian-style commitment to the reasonableness of human survival.) A similar argument warrants eliminating graphic violence on television. If the possibility of increased real violence or loss of sensitivity to violence exists, and the means to avoid the possibility are available and not onerous, then reasonable people will take those means—and ought to, violence being hurtful.

What means are available for avoiding graphic violence on television? Certainly, viewers can choose not to watch, which is the preferred solution of the networks because it imposes no direct obligations on them. Let the buyer beware!

On the other hand, the state could impose limits on television violence in the same way it regulates cigarette and liquor commercials. (Is there any objection to banning the advertising of unsafe medicines?)

Or again, the television industry—in this case NBC—could set its own limits based on steady evidence that television violence at least creates a culture of suspicion and fear[10] and in fidelity to the belief that violence is never inherently justified. But this would require rebuilding Rome, according to syndicated columnist Suzanne Fields. She argues that media violence, unlike the violence in classical literature, occurs in an "ethical vacuum." What's the point of most television violence? There is none. Even Hansel and Gretel do better than that, Fields claims.[11]

In 1993, the nation's four broadcast networks (ABC, CBS, NBC, and Fox) agreed to provide television viewers with warnings preceding shows that contain violent material. This concession was announced one day before congressional hearings on new technologies to let parents block out violent shows. The agreement was a step toward industry self-regulation and responsibility. Peggy Charren of Action for Children's Television called it a "benign solution, inadequate to the problem."[12] That was the same reaction of Lois Salisbury, executive director of Children Now, when the television industry announced its new rating system, the first of its kind for television programming, in December 1996.[13]

Important distinctions separate the McCollum case and the *Born Innocent* incident. First, John did not take his handgun onto the street to apply the "solution" to any passersby. Grievous as its consequences were to his family, the harm done was self-inflicted. Second, the message blamed for inspiring McCollum's violence was offered in an easily repeatable format, unlike the 1974 television show. Whereas Olivia's attackers could have been influenced by a single viewing, McCollum had occasion for a total environment of Osbourne's music, as loud and as often as he chose to listen. Third, the Osbourne persona created by marketers and PR writers—with his cooperation—corresponded to his music's destructive themes. Neither Linda Blair nor NBC suffers under a reputation aligned with shower-room violence. Finally, NBC issued a warning as part of its message; CBS Records did not.

Is moral blame less heavy if no one other than the self is directly harmed in a violent act? In quantitative terms, yes. Given the choice of a terrorist blowing up an airliner in the sky or that same person blowing herself up on the ground, we would reasonably opt for the latter. But the McCollum case involves the suicide of a young man who had a history of emotional and behavioral problems. For these individuals, we bear obligations to offer aid, not a prompt to self-destruct. Suicide is no solution to life's turmoils, and promoting it in music, film, or word is perpetrating a lie. Osbourne did not hand the gun to John McCollum, but his music is distributed in a format that carries no alternative point of view. No voice is heard after "Suicide Solution" arguing that self-destruction is morally wrong. McCollum heard only the most errant element of a many-sided ethical issue.

Is artistic integrity in jeopardy if we attach moral blame to a mere message? Roxanne Bradshaw of the National Education Association, commenting on violence in media, said: "We're not interested in censorship. We're interested in re-educating ourselves and our children about electronic media."[14] No moral theory would excuse media managers and artists from helping in the task Bradshaw describes. The more vulnerable the viewer or listener, the greater is the obligation to talk, to help interpret, and to channel responses toward beneficent ends.

California courts excused both CBS and NBC from liability in these two court proceedings; the First Amendment would not tolerate damages sought by these aggrieved plaintiffs. But our mutual human responsibility to seek each other's best interests and to help each other avoid meaningless hurt and harm—a responsibility expressed in both Judeo-Christian and Kantian ethics—knows no constitutional boundaries. NBC need not graphically show the tools and techniques of sexual abuse. CBS Records has no moral right to profit from the genius of an artist who would be foolish and wrong to practice what he preaches. Nonetheless, if the corporation chooses to exercise legal rights to such expression, fair warnings—if not outright disclaimers—would put record buyers on notice. People closest to troubled, vulnerable users of such media could then make more informed choices. In the present case, our objective is to prevent the lie of Osbourne's music from becoming John McCollum's final tune, or worse, that another confused teenager shoots schoolmates for the experience of just being bad.

62 Violence-Centered

Oliver Stone surprised the movie world in 2006 with a film about two New York Port Authority officers buried in the rubble of the World Trade Center for thirteen and twenty-one hours on 11 September 2001. Sargent John McLoughlin, a twenty-three-year veteran, and first-year officer Will Jimeno survived the towers' collapse and ultimately were lifted back to safety in one of the least likely but most heroic rescue efforts in modern times. Stone told their story in *World Trade Center* much as they told it to him, straight up and without an explicit political agenda. The result was a film about two returned-to-life cops and the meaning of their rescue for the rest of us.

Violence happens throughout this film. After all, 2769 people died that day. Extraordinary violence took those lives—the violence of terrorism, jet fuel burning, crushing concrete, and the eerie violence of bafflement, incredulity, failure to communicate, reckless courage, and the violence that chips away at hope when the chance of rescue seems so remote. No story of that day could be told without violence. 9/11 and violence are related terms.

Director Stone had the good fortune of casting two leading actors—Nicolas Cage and Michael Pena—who successfully conveyed the human sensitivities of McLoughlin and Jimeno, both above ground and near death underground. *World Trade Center* was not a documentary, but a narrative of resurrection on a day of pain and grief. Stone let the story tell itself, granted with the panache of camera angle, lighting, sound, and one dramatic dolly-up sequence that set the New York rescue in its global context. *Newsweek* noted the movie's celebration of the "ties that bind us, the bonds that keep us going, the goodness that stands as a rebuke to the horror of that day."[15] *Rolling Stone*, in an up-beat review, called the film a "salute to heroes who could have easily walked away"[16]—a reference to the rescue work of David Karnes and Jason Thomas, who saw the violence as a call to extraordinary action and whose unblinking approach to the violence, their climb into the rubble, saved McLoughlin and Jimeno from the pit of hell. ∎

Our first thought is that violence is bad. Road rage is the bad side of freedom to travel on highways. Hurting someone is the bad side of relationship building. Assault with a deadly weapon is the bad side of an argument. To avoid these calamities—to find alternatives to this violence—is the path we celebrate as morally good. But not all violence is bad. Some violence is necessary to prevent worse violence. Police use force to apprehend criminals. Sports teams use violence to entertain. Some violence is unavoidable or accidental. Nature kills skiers in an avalanche, but we do not hold nature guilty of a moral lapse. Humans make mistakes, and people are hurt. Sometimes we must simply say, what a tragedy, but no one is to blame. Some violence is humorous, as kids' cartoons have demonstrated since Mickey Mouse. Even Hallmark TV tear-jerkers depend on violence to create drama and dilemma. Without violence, where's the story?

Yet violence that causes hurt for its own sake is morally condemned, along with violence done with such little sense of empathy as to contribute to the "banality of evil" that Hannah Arendt observed at the trial of Adolph Eichmann, one of the most violent persons of the twentieth century. Arendt was "struck by a manifest shallowness . . . that made it impossible to trace the incontestable evil of his [Eichmann's] deeds to any deeper level of roots or motives. . . . There was no sign in him of firm ideological convictions or of specific evil motives. . . . Except for an extraordinary diligence in looking out for his personal advancement, he had no motives at all."[17] Eichmann's violence is morally without excuse. No appeal to "following orders" or "I didn't know" mitigates the moral judgment.

The violence of *World Trade Center* is anything but banal, pointless, or overwrought. The movie portrays the violence of Islamic jihadists taking the lives of ordinary (noncombatant) Americans, along with many citizens from around the globe, and their own lives, in a cause they regarded as holy war. That violence is portrayed in *World Trade Center* in brief sequences of blood-soaked victims fleeing the building, a man down on the sidewalk, the gasping horror of the jumpers who chose gravity as their doom instead of fire, and the ominous street shadow of a low-flying airplane just before impact.

Most of *World Trade Center*'s violence focuses on the small team of Port Authority policemen who entered the Trade Center that morning. The most troubling portrayal is the death of Officer Dominick Pezzulo, who survived the first tower's fall only to die while trying to free Jimeno from the rubble. Was Pezzulo committing suicide in his last moments or firing his revolver into the darkness to attract the attention of rescuers? We do not know and cannot know. Pezzulo dies violently on screen, as it really happened.

Clearly, *World Trade Center* brackets the violence of the jihadists themselves, offering no comment and focusing no attention. The violence of *World Trade Center* is violence suffered, not perpetrated. McLoughlin's firemen are victims. We watch their fight for breath and hope against all odds.

Virtue ethics from the ancient world assumed violence to be part of human experience and celebrated courage as the proper human response. Moreover, the Golden Mean established moral limits on violence: It must be used proportionate to its need and only when other means of achieving a just result have been exhausted. These limits and conditions were brought into a coherent theory of "just war" by Augustine in the third century. The Christian tradition from which he speaks has challenged "just war" with claims that only radical pacifism follows the example set by Jesus. Yet "just war theory" remains the most widely accepted set of moral boundaries on violence, in no small measure owing to Reinhold Niebuhr's insistence that "Christian realism" accounts for the obvious need to meet immoral violence (e.g., the Nazi war and extermination machine) with measured violence.

Utility does not forsake all violence, and the "veil of ignorance" could achieve a choice for violence if conditions warranted. The Kantian imperative never imposes defenselessness, and the *Qur'an* famously permits war under certain bounded conditions.

The violence of *World Trade Center* is defensive. Only an airliner's shadow points to unjustified violence, and that judgment is so nearly universal that Stone need not underline it. Even within Al-Queda, the attack on the towers is considered ill-advised, if not wrong per se.[18] The gripping violence of *World Trade Center* is captured in scenes of people caught in events where escape is the rational and self-reflexive response, but they choose against it for the sake of trapped victims needing rescue. This we call courage.

Some viewers claim that even this violence is presented too soon after the real disaster and dishonors the dead by making a film (and lots of profit) while survivors and families still grieve. A morally attuned filmmaker must listen to these concerns. Five years is not five months, but wounds heal at different speeds, and some never do. Certainly, the world is morally richer for careful films depicting the Nazi Holocaust (although survivors are still with us) and the more recent Rwandan genocide. Pearl Harbor and D-Day took the lives of thousands, but filmmakers have yet to exhaust public fascination with that terror. Stone could have waited another five years, yet with the support of many New Yorkers, he had sufficient moral allowance to move forward without blame.

Viewers of *World Trade Center* are not without choice as well. No one mandates movie patrons to see this film. Even the mysterious corescuer, the Marine identified only as Sergeant Thomas, when he finally emerged from obscurity, indicated that he had not seen the movie. "I'm not ready," Jason Thomas told the press. "I don't want to relive everything."[19] By all accounts, the courage this man displayed on 9/11 warrants a society's gratitude, no matter his reluctance to see himself portrayed. Thomas's choice to pass on the film is a choice open to everyone.

Most who see *World Trade Center* will be stunned, but not morally offended, by its violence. The cringing we do watching this movie reminds us that our rough, belligerent, morally flawed social universe sometimes requires heights of moral action when one's deep commitments to human care weigh the danger for the sake of the other. Violence that leads to courage has purpose and benefit, although we would choose, if we could, to smother the violence before its sparks burst into flame.

63 The Storyteller

In oral cultures, "storyteller" might connote the village historian or tribal sage, the person responsible for interpreting the outside world to kindred with lesser vision, the personal repository of a culture's myth and wisdom. With perhaps the same idea in mind, scriptwriters Richard Levinson and William Link, creators of the police drama *Columbo*, gave the title *The Storyteller* to their introspective drama about the crisis of conscience faced by a television scriptwriter whose work, aired one evening on network television, portrayed several acts of arson. In the story, the show is seen by a youth who immediately after viewing leaves his home to try to burn down his school. The youth dies of smoke inhalation in the fire.[20]

Levinson and Link broke into television writing just as the industry came face to face with questions of the influence of televised violence on the real world. The many studies, essays, and investigations following the Kennedy assassinations, however inconclusive, at least established the intuition that television can be a factor in why real people do some things and do not do other things. Not that violence was new to popular drama. Levinson and Link grew up on Dashiell Hammett, Zane Grey, and the squeaky door of Dr. Frankenstein's laboratory, and they "survived not only intact but also enriched." But the next decades brought a new fascination with the "actual moment of slaughter," slow-motion carnage, and the chilling spectacle of audiences cheering the cinematic bloodlust. Whose was the moral burden?

The purpose of "The Storyteller" was, in Levinson and Link's words, to "analyze our own feelings and attitudes, not only about the violence issue, but also about the responsibilities, if any, of those of us who enter so many homes and minds each night of the week." To the consternation of some viewers, the drama did not follow predictable television endings. Instead of taking a point of view and suggesting answers to their dilemma, Levinson and Link were satisfied to "explore the problem . . . to present the audience with the incredible tangle of pros and cons involved." Yet their sense of moral accountability comes through when the mother of the dead boy asks the writer, "You come into people's homes, the homes of people you don't even know. Do you think about that every time you sit down at your typewriter?" The village sage never faced a question like that.   ∎

This kind of self-reflection is a big step toward responsible media; it stretches the mind and draws out the issues, even if it reaches no conclusions.

Perhaps it falls to agencies such as the Screen Actors Guild (SAG) to coalesce opinion and reach positions on these matters. Its members and board formally passed an antiviolence resolution that read:

> While various studies do not lead to absolute conclusions, there is reasonable cause to believe that imitation of violent acts seen on television is a potential danger and examples of this phenomenon are well documented. There is reasonable cause to believe that the excessive violence viewed on television can also increase aggressive behavior patterns and that repetitive viewing of violence leads to greater acceptance of violence as a norm of societal mores. . . . What is disturbing in television programming is the emphasis on violence and the degree of violence portrayed. . . . The extent and degree of violence in television programming is excessive. . . . Degrees of violence can be lowered in entertainment just as we hope to reduce such excess in our society. . . . We challenge those who are responsible for the programs aired to make the effort—and for the sake of all—the sooner the better.[21]

Someone might object to these sentiments, of course. The statement assumes that a reasonable cause connects media violence with real behavior. This, someone might argue, is the same kind of speculative social science that makes up the rhetoric of media watchdog groups.

And another objection: The SAG statement purports to recommend change "for the sake of all," a clear appeal to the utilitarian principle of the greatest good for the greatest number. But that principle can never demonstrate the difference between too much and appropriate violence. Would the SAG statement suggest that violence is appropriate if and only if no one in real life is physically harmed in any way? Unlikely. Everything from eating bacon to brewing moonshine has some inherent risk. And such a prescription would be too late to help the victims anyhow. Would the SAG statement preclude violence that harms a significant number in a significant way? Impossible. Who could calculate such an application? Ergo, the SAG statement and all others like it are mere rhetorical flourishes and soapbox oratory. The only workable principle is to give writers and producers a free hand in the scripts they develop. True art is achieved only in the context of free expression. Artificial or arbitrary constraints will keep television drama forever immature. Even the SAG recognized the whimsy of its statement. Since Kathleen Nolan's retirement from leadership, the SAG has not voiced an opinion on violence in drama.

If art requires freedom, is it also morally accountable? Is art good because it is free, or is it good when it captures in poignant and resonant ways a slice of the human search for meaning? The latter principle avoids the easy pairing of art and freedom that excuses so much nonsense, and it brings art squarely into the moral domain. Art and ethics are not mutually exclusive categories. In times past, the violence of art was mitigated by the social context of its production and display. Medieval art is among the most graphic and horrific of all visual forms: beheadings, impalings, the skinning alive of various criminals. But, in context, this art has purpose beyond market revenue. The same events portrayed on television for commercial ends would invoke the moral rage that Levinson and Link understood so well. Context and purpose are morally loaded terms. It should be possible, then, to conceive a policy for the portrayal of television violence that will remain true to the aspirations of creative talent without violating the genuine moral claims of actors, viewers, and others drawn into the process after major decisions have already been made.

Does the Golden Mean provide a basis for responsible violence? Appropriate violence must steer away from portraying humans as mere beasts or as unrealistically angelic. Can specific policies be drawn from such an appeal to principle? Whereas such policy statements often turn into dead letters uniformly ignored, on occasion, intelligent manifestos, conscientiously promoted, have aroused attention and changed opinions.

64 Comics for Big Kids

Flesh Gordon carries on its cover an M for "mature readers," whether as a marketing device or as a warning is hard to say. The story line begins on Planet Porno, where Flesh has destroyed a "sinister ray" aimed at Earth by Emperor Wang. Flesh saves Earth from slavery to Wang with the help of his companions, the beautiful Dale Ardor and the bearded Dr. Flexi Jerkoff. The reader of this simplistic tale should expect plenty of old double-entendres to compensate for the colorless pages.

Ernie Evil, on the other hand, is full of color. Lots of red, as in blood. Lots of pale green, as in slime, rot, and poison. Plenty of white and black, and always a beautiful woman about to have her brains blown away. As Mary, the gorgeous brunette, says in one frame, "Think I'm gonna be sick." That seems to be Ernie's big appeal—the sicker you feel reading his tale, the more successful is the book.

Heavy Metal is a series of panels featuring sex, technology, and death, with a few devils for motive power and a few drinks for the orgy's afterglow. The graphic novel *Mark of the Devil* is a richly textured tale of all the above, plus danger, pain, extraordinarily proportioned breasts, fearsome creatures shorn of human sympathy, and lots of Ur-passion. It's a novel that could send your night dreams into neverland, wherever that is for you.

The comics these days seem more and more pitched for ages higher than seven. Certainly, no hint of childhood mars the dark and lascivious worlds of these books. Some are artless; some are well drawn and doubtless literary as the comic world judges writing merit. All are escapist, elemental, and sinister. ∎

Violence dominates the comics. Researcher John DiFazio has analyzed the comic book treatment of fourteen American values and found that "peaceful resolution of conflict" was one of the values least often portrayed.[22] Our own quick review of a comic rack revealed plot resolutions involving a woman blowing herself up with a shotgun while trying to save an infant from a monster, the crashing of a boulder on the cranium of a muscle-bound cyclops, and the introduction of a new Dream Team called Justice League of America, just to prove, it seems, that nationalism survives as the last moral stand. So vicious are modern comics that one can almost hear Frederick Wertham, author of the classic 1954 *Seduction of the Innocent*, uttering "I told you so" to the numerous critics who disparaged his work.[23]

Such unrestrained violence was not always the rule in children's literature. Note, for example, the ethic of restraint that characterized the popular Nancy Drew detective series, according to James Lones:

> There was an abundance of violence in the Nancy Drew series, but it was controlled violence. Clubbings, wrecks, assault and battery were common. Attacks fell indiscriminately on many types of characters with Nancy often the target. Despite this violence no one was murdered. Criminals who assaulted their victims did not go beyond beatings. In a decade [the 1930s] when sensational real-life kidnappings stirred the population, these fictionalized kidnappings ended happily and no victim of abduction was killed. Guns were used but were either fired as warnings, and not directly at persons, or used as clubs.[24]

More recent commentary on the comic book industry is as troubling as Wertham's case studies. Joe Queenan of *The New York Times Magazine* wrote:

> Over the last decade, comics have forsaken campy repartee and outlandishly byzantine plots for a steady diet of remorseless violence. "Green Arrow" depicts a woman whose eyes have been plucked out by vultures. In "Spider-Man," seven men are ripped to pieces by a wolf. The back pages of "Wolverine" show the hero puffing on a cigarette as blood drips from his lips. . . . "Black Orchid" begins with a woman being tied up and set on fire, then moves on to child abuse, a mutant fed live rats, and a jailed hybrid—half woman, half plant—who avoids rape only because her jailers find her too repulsive.[25]

The comic industry grosses more than $300 million a year, with DC Comics and Marvel in the distant lead, followed by Archie Comic Publications and then about 200 minor-league hopefuls, many of them willing to go beyond the editorial boundaries (broad as they are) still observed by the market leaders. One distributor explained: "Our readers are teenage boys [with] lots of repressed anger. [They are] going through puberty [and they] like to see characters act out their aggressions."

As a shortcut to moral analysis, some might close the case by waving the banner of First Amendment freedom. But, even among legal theorists, First Amendment freedom weighs in primarily with political speech as a means to democratic process, not with comic book speech as a means to personal entertainment happiness.[26] The issues most salient to freedom of speech today are campaign financing and workplace safety, not graphic novels or comic strips. Associate Justice Stephen Breyer calls the First Amendment a tool of "active liberty," not a cure for limitless expression.[27] First Amendment enthusiasts may ring the bell, but the heart of this controversy must be settled in moral, not legal, terms.

A reasonable argument can be made that older readers are capable of discerning reality from fantasy. The older a reader is, the more credibly he or she will process imaginative stories. On this basis, the two-dimensional static violence of comic books may qualify for broader license than the violence in films' so much more emotionally engaging dynamic images. Give greater freedom to media of lesser evocative power, one might say.

Finally, however, the avid reader of adult comics, like the fan of almost any media challenging common values, must face the matter of loyalties. Do the imaginative dimensions stimulated or satisfied by violent or sexually oriented material help or hurt a reader's capacity to be a responsible member of primary social groups: friends, family, community? Perhaps the moral test is whether you can freely talk about the content of your entertainment reading. Can this part of your life be shared with people who depend on you?

Certainly we do not share every notion of conscience with everyone else. Such a surrender of privacy is often taken as a sign of mental or emotional need today. Yet this is also true—we ought to live a singular (not dual) life of moral accountability to self and others. You are free to show masks, but you cannot do so with integrity. Your presentation to others ought to be the same self you know yourself to be. Loyalties depend on such integrity, and in the Potter Box analysis, loyalties keep us linked to the moral lives of others as an anchor to our own.

Stay loyal by choosing comic book entertainment about which you can speak openly to those you admire and respect.

---

65 *Grand Theft Youth*

In the early morning hours of 7 June 2003, policeman Arnold Strickland stopped a young man named Devin Moore on suspicion of auto theft. Strickland took Moore to the Fayette, Alabama, police station for booking. All went according to plan until, suddenly, Moore grabbed Strickland's .40 caliber gun and shot Officer Strickland twice, killing him. Moore proceeded to kill Officer James Crump and dispatcher Ace Mealer, whom he shot five times. Then Moore took a set of car keys, left the building, and rode away in a police cruiser.[28]

Once in custody for murder, Devin Moore told police, "Life is like a video game. Everybody's got to die sometime." After further investigation, it became clear that Moore played the popular video game *Grand Theft Auto* (GTA) on a daily basis for months prior to killing Strickland, Crump, and Mealer. As a result, in 2005, the families of Officer Strickland and dispatcher Mealer sued the game's maker, claiming that the game acted as "a murder simulator" that "trained" Moore. They supported this claim by insisting that Moore acted out a scenario directly from *Grand Theft Auto*.[29]

A similar incident occurred on 25 June 2003, when William Buckner, age sixteen, and his stepbrother Joshua, age thirteen, shot at vehicles passing on Interstate 40 in Tennessee. The Buckner brothers killed a Canadian man and wounded a nineteen-year-old woman from Virginia.[30] Like Devin Moore, the boys played *Grand Theft Auto* regularly. Once in police custody, William and Joshua told authorities that after playing the game, they took rifles from their home, and just like they did in the video game, they decided to randomly shoot at tractor trailers.[31] In October 2003, the families of the victims filed a $246 million law suit against the maker of *Grand Theft Auto* alleging that the game inspired the shootings.[32]

Despite the lawsuits and controversy, *Grand Theft Auto* is an extraordinarily popular game for understandable reasons. Many players rave about the incredible graphics, excitement, game-play freedom, and addicting nature of the game. The many versions of the game (most notably *Vice City* and *San Andreas*) sold more than 35 million copies by March 2006. With global sales close to $2 billion, it is one of the most successful video and computer game series.[33]

But why are there so many lawsuits over *Grand Theft Auto* when the video game industry is full of shoot-em-up products? Similarly, why are there so many critics of *Grand Theft Auto* when nobody is forced to play it? Opponents contend that even in an increasingly violent industry, the game stands out as being exceedingly savage. Drug dealers are beaten with bats; pedestrians are run over by cars; individuals are killed by bazookas, knives, and chainsaws; and sexual violence towards women is rewarded.[34]

As a result of this over-the-top violence, many family groups and politicians strongly criticize *Grand Theft Auto*. Connecticut Senator and former vice-presidential nominee Joseph Lieberman called the game "horrendous."[35] He described it by saying, "The player

continued

[of GTA] is rewarded for attacking a woman, pushing her to the ground, kicking her repeatedly and then ultimately killing her, shooting her over and over again."[36]

The controversy over *Grand Theft Auto* escalated during the summer of 2005 when
computer programmer Patrick Wildenborg posted a notice on his website explaining how
users could unlock a hidden element of the *San Andreas* game that allowed players to engage in a pornographic minigame involving simulated sex acts.[37] Initially, the makers of
Grand Theft Auto refused to acknowledge that they hid the code in the game. However,
public outcry became so strong that large retailers such as Wal-Mart stopped selling
the game, and politicians began calling for investigations.[38] For example, on 14 July 2005,
New York Senator and former First Lady Hillary Clinton said, "The disturbing material in
Grand Theft Auto and other games like it is stealing the innocence of our children, and it's
making the difficult job of being a parent even harder."[39] Eventually, the maker of *Grand
Theft Auto* released an updated version without the hidden code.[40] However, by this
point, well over one million individuals had downloaded Wildenbord's code to unlock the
explicit material.[41]   ∎

Even after the controversy in the summer of 2005 cooled, opponents continued to charge that *Grand Theft Auto* is a "virtual reality murder simulator."[42] Moreover, critics insist that even though nobody is forced to purchase or use the game,
it affects individuals like Steve Strickland, who insists that it caused the murder of
his brother. Others criticize the game because it makes police the bad guys, violent
criminals the good guys, and vicious abuses of human life a glorified end. In addition, Stanford-trained psychologist Dr. Craig A. Anderson notes that violent
video game research is quite consistent in finding that these products are "significantly associated with" increased aggressive behavior and thoughts.[43]

Is *Grand Theft Auto* really as dangerous to society as some claim? After all,
millions of gamers enjoy playing the game without going on shooting rampages.
Are threats of Federal Trade Commission investigations, introduction of legislation to limit the reach of such games, and public boycotts really necessary? Violent
video game producers insist that it is part of their right of free speech to create
these products. Advocates such as attorney Paul Smith point to a litany of court
cases where judges struck down as unconstitutional restrictions on minors' access
to violent games.[44] Producers maintain that nobody is forced to buy, play, or watch
these games. The person who is offended or upset by the content can choose to
avoid the game.

Those in support of games such as *Grand Theft Auto* also insist that ample
moral guidance is provided through the industry-wide ratings system. The Electronic Software Ratings Board (ESRB) rates games as EC (Early Childhood), E
(Everyone), E10+ (Everyone 10 and older), T (Teen, those 13 and older), M (Mature, those 17 and older), and AO (Adults Only, those 18 and older).[45]

However, critics contend these ratings are loosely observed and enforced.
For example, one study found that 42 percent of the time, boys as young as nine
succeeded in purchasing video games rated Mature—games that should not be

sold to those under age seventeen. Moreover, critics point to the case of *Grand Theft Auto*, where its producers hid content from the rating board, allowing the game to receive a M (Mature) rating when it should have received a rating of AO (Adults Only).[46] Given the strong opinions on both sides, is there a real-world solution to this case? From a pragmatic point of view, with the incredible popularity of these games, the large financial incentives to create these products, and the judicial concerns over protecting free speech, there is little chance that those hoping to control violent video games through government regulation will get their way. Instead, the real-world solution to those concerned about *Grand Theft Auto* is more likely found in parents who take an active role in their children's lives by playing video games together and closely monitoring purchases.

What would the Potter Box suggest? The values taught through violent video games are antithetical to those necessary for society to flourish. Moreover, *Grand Theft Auto* teaches behaviors that disrespect human life, degrade women, and glorify lawlessness. Finally, *Grand Theft Auto* seems to tell its players that any loyalties to society and those who protect our way of life should be disrespected. In light of the moral hazard present in these violent video games, perhaps *Grand Theft Auto* is stealing our moral compass and needs to be pulled over. But turning on the flasher will require that players themselves—certainly the millions who are past parental oversight—come to awareness that misdirected recreation at best steals hours from better, more satisfying play and at worst ventilates a bipolar morality. "Play at your worst and live at your best" can work only if the self enjoys two lives, a feat no ethical system recognizes. Good play tests moral boundaries and sometimes flaunts them, but radical identification with violent, socially destructive behavior cannot build a stable moral center. The Potter Box (i.e., moral accountability) has no escape tab: "Out to play, be back in an hour."

NOTES

1. United States Department of Justice. *Attorney General's Commission on Pornography: Final Report* (1986), p. 1957.
2. Kevin Saunders, *Violence as Obscenity* (Durham, NC: Duke University Press, 1996).
3. Sissela Bok, *Mayhem: Violence as Public Entertainment* (Addison-Wesley, 1998), p. 15ff.
4. Joseph Lieberman quoted in the *Daily Herald*, 2 December 1993, sec. 1, p. 11.
5. *McCollum v. CBS*, 15 Med. L. Rptr. 2001.
6. Material on *Born Innocent* was drawn from "TV Wins a Crucial Case," *Time*, 21 August 1978, p. 85; T. Schwartz et al., "TV on Trial Again," *Newsweek*, 14 August 1978, pp. 41–42; "NBC's First Amendment Rape Case," *Esquire*, 23 May 1978, pp. 12–13; "Back to Court for 'Born Innocent,' " *Broadcasting*, 1 May 1978, pp. 37–38; "Judge Restricts 'Born Innocent' Case to First Amendment Issue," *Broadcasting*, 7 August 1978, pp. 31–32; Karl E. Meyer, "Television's Trying Times," *Saturday Review*, 16 September 1978, pp. 19–20; *The New York Times*, 18 September 1978; *The Wall Street Journal*, 25 April 1978.
7. If media-effects research finally eliminates any connection, and even the possibility of connection, between viewing habits and behavior, then real harm is eliminated as a factor, and arguments to curtail media programming for any reason fall away. But the weight of our society's beliefs leans heavily toward a connection, the contours of which are the substance of effects researchers' debates.

8. Jeremy Bentham, *An Introduction to the Principles of Morals and Legislation*, eds. J. H. Burns and H. L. A. Hart (London: Athlone Press, 1970), p. 11.

9. Hans Jonas, *The Imperative of Responsibility* (Chicago: University of Chicago Press, 1984).

10. The many writings of George Gerbner and Larry Gross are just the tip of the iceberg supporting this contention.

11. Suzanne Fields, "The Trouble Is That TV Violence Occurs in a Moral Vacuum," *Daily Herald*, 6 July 1993, sec. 1, p. 8.

12. *Daily Herald*, 30 June 1993, sec. 1, p. 14.

13. Quoted in "TV Industry's Rating Plan Faces a Tough Audience," *The Chicago Tribune*, 19 December 1996, p. 1.

14. *Media and Values* (Fall 1985): 9.

15. David Ansen, "Natural Born Heroes," *Newsweek*, 7 August 2006, p. 53.

16. Peter Travers, "Heart from a Stone," *Rolling Stone*, 24 August 2006, p. 107.

17. Hannah Arendt, *Eichmann in Jerusalem* (New York: Penguin, 1994), pp. 235–236. Quoted in *Moral Leadership*, ed. Deborah Rhode (San Francisco: Jossey-Bass, 2006), p. 27.

18. So reported in a CNN documentary, *In the Footsteps of Bin Laden*, 23 August 2006.

19. Wendy Koch, "Quick to Save Lives, But Not to Take Credit," *USA Today*, 25 August 2006, p. 3A.

20. Richard Levinson and William Link, "A Crisis of Conscience," *TV Guide*, 3 December 1977, p. 6.

21. "SAG Position Re Excessive Violence on TV," minutes of the Special Meeting of the Executive Committee of the Screen Actors Guild, 29 November 1976, p. 9919.

22. DiFazio's study is cited in Alexis S. Tan and Kermit Joseph Scruggs, "Does Exposure to Comic Book Violence Lead to Aggression in Children?" *Journalism Quarterly* 57 (Winter 1980): 579–583.

23. Frederick Wertham, *Seduction of the Innocent* (New York: Rinehart, 1954).

24. James P. Lones, "Nancy Drew, WASP Super Girl of the 1930s," *Journal of Popular Culture* 6 (Spring 1973): 712.

25. Joe Queenan, "Drawing on the Dark Side," *The New York Times Magazine*, 30 April 1989.

26. Cass Sunstein, *Radicals in Robes* (New York: Basic Books, 2005), p. 229.

27. Stephen Breyer, *Active Liberty* (New York: Knopf, 2005), p. 55.

28. www.cbsnews.com/stories/2005/03/04/60minutes/main678261.shtml.

29. www.cbsnews.com/stories/2005/03/04/60minutes/main078261.shtml.

30. "Boys Charged in Death of Canadian Post Bail," *The Ottawa Citizen*, 2 August 2003, Saturday Final Edition, p. A10.

31. Matthew Wi, "Gamemaker Sued over Highway Shootings," *The San Francisco Chronicle*, 23 October 2003, Thursday Final Edition, p. B3.

32. Ibid.

33. www.cbsnews.com/stories/2005/03/04/60minutes/main678261.shtml.

34. www.msnbc.msn.com/id/6399463/.

35. www.forbes.com/technology/sciences/newswire/2004/01/25/rtr1226141.html.

36. Ibid.

37. Seth Schiesel, "Los Angeles Sues Video Game Makers," *The New York Times*, 28 January 2006, Late Edition Final, p. B8.

38. Ibid.; Allie Shah and Patrice Relerford, "A Story of Sex, Lies and Video games: 'San Andreas' Sparks Latest Fracas in Battle over Cultural Boundaries," *Star Tribune* (Minneapolis, MN), 23 July 2005, p. 1A.

39. www.clinton.senate.gov/news/statements/details.cfm?id=240603.

40. Julian Borger, "Video Game Maker Sued over Sex Scenes: Los Angeles Wants Firm to Surrender Profits; City Acts over Explicit Content Buried in Code," *The Guardian* (London), 30 January 2006, p. 16.

41. Hiawatha Bray, "Sex Scene Stirs Up a Fuss Over Grand Theft," *The Boston Globe*, 9 July 2005, p. C1.

42. www.suntimes.com/news/nation/72320.CSC-NWS-donaldson26.article.

43. www.apa.org/science/psa/sb-anderson.html.

44. www.esrb.org/ratings/ratings_guide.jsp.

45. http://Lieberman.senate.gov/newsroom/release.cfm?id=249371; www.esrb.org; Shah and Relerford, "A Story of Sex, Lies, and Video Games," p. A1.

46. Schiesel, "Los Angeles Sues Video Game Makers," p. B8.

CHAPTER FIFTEEN

Profits, Wealth, and Public Trust

Entertainment media in America are 90 percent business and 10 percent public service. Or are these figures too weighted toward public service? Gerry Spence, the well-known trial attorney, insists that "ratings are what television is about, not freedom, not truth. If American television could sell lies and falsehoods more profitably, we would never hear another word of truth."[1] Only the most unrepentant idealist would argue that social responsibility is a major consideration in most entertainment media decisions. If social benefits show up in the product, all well and good, but woe to the producer, director, editor, or recording executive whose product shows a financial loss, whatever the social gain. The profit motive is the most compelling concern in entertainment industry decisions; some observers insist it is the only concern.

As earlier parts of this book have indicated, the bottom line of profit and loss affects media of all types, but entertainment media feel the impact most directly. A major survey of executives in the motion picture industry confirmed that here was a media system operating on essentially amoral criteria. A vice president of a major production and distribution company commented: "There are no ethical decisions in the movie business. In a word, the profit motive renders ethics irrelevant. The only counterbalance is that certain individuals—and precious few at that—live their personal and professional lives according to some reasonably high standard."[2]

The first case in this chapter, "Copyright Wars," raises two concerns simultaneously: the moral infringements of pirated material and the morality of copyright laws that effectively disenfranchise vast populations from mainstream culture. "Deep Trouble for Harry" looks as the cost to actress Linda Lovelace of profits she never saw. Then "Super Strip" points to an example of fairness that carries a note of human care when legal contracts did not require it. And the last case jumps a couple of Superman generations to the story of Christopher Reeves. Our guest writer, Christopher Smit (an expert on disability and communication) asks: Did Reeves understand the plight of disabled people, or lend his considerable prestige and charisma to a mission that the disabled may find morally unacceptable?

66 Copyright Wars

Your favorite DVD will cost $18 to $60 depending on its packaging. Your CD, a little less and a download, less still, if you have an Internet connection. That's the price of enjoying someone else's creativity. It's a price clearly pegged to the salary of a typical $10-an-hour worker who twice a month will spend a half-day's wage on take-home entertainment. The marketing system provides enough incentive to fuel the dreams of every garage band, and for the very talented, well, they land the big prize—more money than one person can spend. Consumers are happy, too, with unlimited use and reuse of the plastic they own, constrained only by the contract embedded in the small print, usually for home-use only.

Yet, in every major city around the world, you can buy counterfeits (unauthorized look-alikes that violate copyright) of nearly everything from Colgate toothpaste to computer software to this week's Hollywood releases. Chinese counterfeits are especially threatening to U.S. markets. Nearly two-thirds of all pirated goods seized at U.S. borders come from China. Numerous shops in Beijing, and especially at the Silk Street market, sell DVDs for under $2. When Chinese President Hu Jintao visited the United States in 2006, his country's counterfeits were a major talking point. Not only is international law at stake but also the profits to be realized from China's immense market. U.S. entertainment giants have no way to tap that huge Chinese market unless the cost of counterfeiting exceeds the cost of copyright compliance. New Chinese legal initiatives are beginning to make that correction.   ■

The U.S. Constitution, Article 1, Section 8, grants Congress the power to "promote the Progress of Science and useful Arts" by laws that protect intellectual property through a process we call "copyright." Anyone can use this law to protect a creative, original expression, saving its value for their own discretionary exploitation. The copyright process is among the simplest our government has ever devised. Enforcing your copyright gets complicated, but many creators do it successfully.

The heart of this protection is the exclusive right of the creator to determine the distribution of his or her work. And the phenomenal success of this protection is the most vibrant film, TV, book, writing, singing, acting, drawing, sculpting, dancing, composing (etc.) industries in the world—and one can easily surmise in the entire history of the world. This is the American dream: the opportunity to make something new and capitalize on it. Without copyright protection, the superaffluent stars of Hollywood, Vegas, and New York would be working day jobs at Wal-Mart.

But the system suffers one gaping blind spot. No, it's not the cheap-shot easiness of breaking the law here and there, copying a friend's CD or photocopying a high-priced textbook. The system still works despite these violations. Copyright's blindspot is the immense difference in economies between the affluent West and Middle East—and everywhere else.

Copyright, including international copyright, legally forecloses vast populations from enjoying the culture products marketed for profit by Western standards. When you earn the equivalent of $1.50 a day, you're not going to hear

Tchaikovsky's Concerto No. 1 on that $24 Van Cliburn CD or pay $75 to get a back-row seat to hear him play it.

Federico Mayor makes the case clearly in his turn-of-the-century review of the developing world:

> Creation and innovation are certainly favored by adequate rights protection. But too much protection works against the interests of rights-holders and users. Over-restrictive intellectual property rights lead to secure incomes [and] monopolies without benefiting public interest in any way.[4]

This kind of appeal does not cut the cake for Louis Vuitton and four other international designers who recently hired the law firm of Baker & McKenzie to prosecute Beijing's counterfeiters. They want pirating stopped, and China seems to be making new efforts. A six-person team of intellectual property rights investigators was added to the police arm of China's Ministry of Public Security. Bounty hunters can earn up to $37,000 for a tip-off that exposes an underground DVD operation. An exhibition at Beijing's Military Museum of the Chinese People's Revolution now features intellectual property protection—a symbolic nod, at least, to China's commitment to link hands with other nations promoting the "Useful Arts."[5]

Mayor, however, thinks that better policing is not the long-term answer. He insists that we "broaden the notion of public domain and bring down the norms and standards currently used so as to offer free competition, free circulation of ideas, and creativity in all cultures." He advocates the idea of "copyleft," where authors reduce their control to "moral rights," a British common-law term that denotes the right of an author to keep his or her work intact, its meaning and character as he or she created and intended it.[6] In Mayor's view, the world's poor still would be required to pay for material, but the cost of access to world creativity would be proportionate to their ability to pay.

The problem of a fair return on creative material and increased access to lower gross national product cultures should not present moral theory with insurmountable problems. No moral theory coaches us to eliminate all private interests, and none legitimizes a purely free and viciously competitive marketplace. America's founders recognized the limits to property protection when they put a clock on intellectual property protection. Unfortunately, that clock has been reset by corporate reluctance to give up control. The Bono Amendment to the U.S. Copyright Act of 1976 was inspired by Disney's horror at Mickey Mouse going into the public domain. Mayor, speaking for the developing world, would urge us to resist those efforts to hold property for yet another twenty years of profit and control. He urges a shorter period of protected use before a work is legally open to all.

Mayor advises that we readjust our mean between profit and public good, that creators enjoy distribution rights and find their market but not to the point where only criminals and the wealthy have access to literature and art. A Golden Mean of equitable copyright might include adjusting a creator and distributor's profit to local economies or providing "public copies" for communal use through agencies designed to serve the needs of the economic underclass.

At the same time, there is no moral justification for the widespread illegal copying of protected material among collegiate Americans, whose pocket change exceeds the weekly wages of most of the world's workers by many times. Only greed inspires the easy use of technology to usurp the real claims of copyright.

---

67 Deep Trouble for Harry

By any definition, *Deep Throat* is a pornographic film. Released at the crest of the sexual revolution, the film tells the story of a frustrated young woman (played by Linda Lovelace) who cannot "hear bells" during orgasm, no matter who is the partner. She consults a psychiatrist (played by Harry Reems), who diagnoses her problem as freakish: She has a clitoris in her throat. The promiscuous doctor then joins a long line of other bell ringers who gratify themselves on, according to *The New York Times*, "virtuoso talent for fellatio."[7]

Neither Reems nor Lovelace had great acting talent, and neither found fortune in this film that grossed $600 million. Reems had done bit parts in the National Shakespeare Company and other theaters when director Jerry Gerard invited him to join the production crew of this new "white-coater," a porn genre specializing in portraying flaky doctors. Reems was paid $100 for two scenes, then waived all editing, marketing, and distribution rights to the movie. Two years later, Reems was indicted as part of an alleged nationwide conspiracy to profit from the interstate commerce of an obscene movie. He became the first performer to be prosecuted on federal charges for artistic work—a dubious honor. Reems was convicted in Memphis, but on appeal, the government declined to retry the case (following the Supreme Court's 1974 *Miller* decision).

Deep Throat made Lovelace a sex queen. Her starring role helped produce the most successful porn film ever made to that time. The same film typecast her and essentially ended her career, but not before silicone injections enlarged her breasts and tainted blood gave her hepatitis. Wrote Lovelace, "I was a robot who did what I had to do to survive." Her first husband earned $1250 for Linda's role in *Deep Throat*; she never saw a penny.

Lovelace quit her movie career, remarried, and moved to Long Island, where she began to build a new identity, helping at her children's elementary school and giving lectures on the social and personal effects of pornography.

A liver transplant brought on, she insisted, by the silicon injections she took to entertain men lengthened her life, but not her happiness. She divorced again, moved to Denver, where she worked for minimum wage, and died in 2002 at the age of fifty-three from injuries sustained in an auto accident. In the last year of her life, she finally saw the entire movie from start to finish. Still trying to shake her star status, she remarked about the film, "What's the big deal?" ■

Civil libertarians point out that twenty-three states banned this movie at some point during the ten years after its release. In one important legal battle in Texas, a nuisance abatement strategy was turned back by the federal appeals court and the U.S. Supreme Court as a dangerous movement toward prior restraint.

Whether the film deserved suppression at all is both a legal and moral problem. In a customs case in Massachusetts concerning the confiscation of a film print, the court heard an expert witness say that *Deep Throat* "puts forth an idea of greater liberation with regard to human sexuality and to the expression of it" that would help "many women" overcome particular sexual fears. Yet, to argue that *Deep Throat*'s blatant appeal to lasciviousness has redeeming social benefits that warrant First Amendment protection is really to nullify common definitions of obscenity. Only a First Amendment absolutist can effectively maintain that this film should be freely allowed to find its audience. Only the true believer in laissez-faire popular culture would want marketeers of this film to be let loose on the populace at large.

In its much maligned *Final Report*, the Attorney General's Commission on Pornography created five broad categories of material around which to organize its ninety-two recommendations. The first two categories—sexually violent material and nonviolent materials depicting degradation, domination, subordination, or humiliation—were deemed harmful by most of the commission. Class IV, nudity, was an innocuous category that included both classical art and toddlers bouncing around in naked innocence. Class V ("the special horror of child pornography") was so blatantly exploitative that commissioners urged the strongest measures to disrupt and prosecute this market. But the third category (nonviolent and nondegrading materials) was the most controversial.[8] It included portrayals of consensual and equal vaginal intercourse and oral–genital activity or "two couples simultaneously engaging in the same activity." The commission could not cite any film titles that fit this category, so perhaps *Deep Throat* was, in their minds, an example of Class II. Yet many people would claim that *Deep Throat* and other nonviolent pornographic films are mere entertainment that hurt no one (in a demonstrably causal fashion) and attracted no one other than interested, paying customers. As long as unsupervised children are not permitted to rent the video, the market logic goes, let adults choose *Deep Throat* if they wish. And obviously many wish.

But the free-market argument would pass no muster with Linda Lovelace Marchiano. She was the Agent Orange victim of pornographic profiteering, her body devastated by the chemicals that made her sexy and the trauma that made her desperate.[9]

And the free-market argument also must face the fact that this movie was a financial boon for organized crime. On a $25,000 investment, the Colombo crime family made well over $50 million on *Deep Throat*, with some of the profits being directed to Caribbean drug-smuggling operations.[10]

A principled market cannot exploit (in this case, it was a form of slavery) and abuse its artisans, and it cannot tolerate siphoning wealth into criminal empire building. The porn-film business, with *Deep Throat* a shaded example, is too regularly guilty of each count to warrant our waving a free-market flag in its defense. Freedom, Kant argued, is in the pursuit of right reason. Freedom, Reinhold Niebuhr and his compatriots would urge, is in overcoming greed and prurience through a movement of love guarded by justice. Exploring sexuality in film is inherently a good goal, but this porn film was a heist on humanity. No market potency can justify destroying a life.

A real white-coater who sat on the attorney general's commission, Park Elliott Dietz of the University of Virginia, stated, as the work concluded:

> As a government body, we studiously avoided making judgments on behalf of the government about the morality of particular sexual acts between consenting adults or their depiction in pornography. This avoidance, however, should not be mistaken for the absence of moral sentiment among the Commissioners. I, for one, have no hesitation in condemning nearly every specimen of pornography that we have examined in the course of our deliberations as tasteless, offensive, lewd, and indecent. . . . It has been nearly two centuries since Phillipe Pinel struck the chains from the mentally ill and more than a century since Abraham Lincoln struck the chains from America's black slaves. With this statement I ask you, America, to strike the chains from America's women and children, to free them from the bond of pornography, to free them from the bonds of sexual abuse, to free them from the bonds of inner torment that entrap the second-class citizen in an otherwise free nation.[11]

68 Super Strip

Jerry Siegel and Joe Shuster were high school students in Cleveland, Ohio, when they came upon the idea of a cartoon figure who, born in a distant galaxy, would escape to earth as a baby, grow up in an orphanage, and as an adult, impervious to gravity and mightier than a locomotive, would aid the forces of justice in their battle against evil.

Siegel actually conceived the idea. His buddy Shuster liked to draw. So the two fledgling cartoonists set out to sell their story. Five years of pounding on doors finally won them a contract with Detective Comics, and the first "Superman" strip appeared in 1938. Siegel and Shuster were paid $10 a page for their work, about $15 a week per man.[12]

The contract favored the company. The more popular Superman became, the clearer was Siegel and Shuster's loss. Finally, they brought suit against Detective and were awarded some money, but still they had no rights to their hero. When the legal dust settled, Detective fired Siegel and Shuster, and the two creators were left to watch others get rich and famous off their idea. More lawsuits proved futile. With legal routes exhausted, the men defied the advice of their attorneys and went public with their story.

Their tale was one of sadness and struggle. Neither man had received any money from Superman sales since 1948, though profits from the Man of Steel were in the multimillions. Shuster now was legally blind, living in Queens with a brother who supported him. Siegel was ill and lived with his wife in a tiny apartment in Los Angeles, where he worked as a government clerk typist for $7000 a year. The men appealed to Superman's current copyright owner "out of a sense of moral obligation," said Shuster. The National Cartoonists Society and Cartoonists Guild lent their full backing to Siegel and Shuster's moral claim.

The appeal brought results. Warner Communications, which owned movie rights to Superman, claimed "no legal obligation," but "there is a moral obligation on our part." Two

continued

days before Christmas, Siegel and Shuster signed a contract with Warner: They would each receive $20,000 yearly for life, and their heirs also would be helped. The creators' names would appear on all Superman productions. At the signing, a Warner executive commended the two cartoonists. The contract, he said, was "in recognition of their past services and out of concern for their present circumstances."   ■

The money awarded Siegel and Shuster presented no threat to the profits of Warner Communications. The sum of $40,000 a year may be less than the company spends in processing receipts from Superman sales. But, as a gesture neither required by law nor essential to public relations, it represents an application of the Judeo-Christian ethic of other-mindedness.

Consider the dynamics of the award. Siegel and Shuster had sold their idea under the duress of the Depression and at a time in their youth when neither could be expected to negotiate a contract with business savvy. Events had changed dramatically since then. One had become disabled, the other ill; both were living on a bare-bones income. Exhausted by fruitless legal efforts, they nonetheless persisted in a moral claim for some relief.

Warner could have called their appeal a nuisance. Business is business, after all. Investors who cash in stock certificates, for example, never qualify for *ex post facto* profits. Farmers who sell a corn crop in November may not appeal for extra payment when the bushel price rises in January. Buyers and sellers each assume part of the risk, and each understands that one could emerge from the deal a clear winner. Because the terms are understood, the bargain is fair.

But contracts are not independent from the economic milieu in which they are made. Were they selling a cartoon character today instead of in 1938, Siegel and Shuster might negotiate for a compensation clause should their idea become a bonanza. Indeed, they could have insisted that direct successors to their character, should Superman ever die (inconceivable until he met his fate in 1992 saving the world from Doomsday), be part of their legacy also. (It seems now that four new Supermen will vie for the honor.) The economic climate of the late 1930s was not ripe for such risk-reducing appendices.

So the recognition awarded Siegel and Shuster was for the cartoonists a humanitarian gesture of life-sustaining aid, whereas to Warner it represented no loss to shareholders and no risk to corporate solvency. Perhaps a thorough application of "others as ourselves" or Rawls's ethic of undifferentiated negotiators would have resulted in larger awards or royalties for Siegel and Shuster or a cost-of-living adjustment in their $20,000 annual amount or life insurance policies to establish an estate for each man. Maybe so. It may be argued that Warner hemmed and hawed until it was expedient for it to make a gesture, quite apart from what was fair for the two penniless cartoonists. But the award, such as it was, points to a residual sense of group solidarity and caring, a dissonant but hopeful interlude in the normally amoral entertainment business.

69 Superman Walks Again

On 27 May 1995, actor Christopher Reeve fell off his horse during an equestrian event, breaking his first two cervical vertebrae. Although his spinal cord was not completely severed in the accident, Reeve would never walk again and would spend the remainder of his life in a wheelchair. Or would he? Only six months after his accident, still in rehabilitation at the Kessler Institute in New Jersey, Reeve appeared on ABC's *20/20* to report on his progress. And soon after, in January of 1996, he began what would become a personal campaign to increase funding and awareness for spinal cord injury research. In May of that year, while lobbying in Washington, D.C., Reeve declared that he would walk again in seven years.

Reeve had become a celebrity years before his accident with his film portrayal of Superman in 1978, a hero whose strength and patriotism had loomed large in the imagination of American culture since 1933, when the first Superman comic book was published. In essence, Reeve was Superman to his fans. Consequently, in an odd fusion of fantasy and reality, Reeve's seemingly brisk transition from private recovery to public advocacy carried on the "super-man" traits he had cultivated years before his accident. The heroism he depicted on screen began to be projected onto his efforts to "cure" himself and others of the debilitating effects of paraplegia. As one reporter for *The San Francisco Chronicle* put it, "The man who once played Superman [has become] a superhero in his own life."[13]

Perhaps the most heroic and controversial act of this new "super-man" was his involvement in a Nuveen Super Bowl commercial in 2000.[14] The $4 million, sixty-second advertisement encouraged investors to see their future as more than pragmatic financial decisions but rather as key components to important advancements in medical discovery. Through a lofty visual display, a Nuveen representative is shown discussing how investments have led to great progress in the fight to cure AIDS and cancer. At this point in the commercial, Reeve (through computer-generated imagery) is shown walking to the podium to present an award for "remarkable breakthroughs in spinal cord injuries." Reeve is joined on stage by other formerly disabled individuals, all of whom appear to be cured through research funded by Nuveen clients.

The commercial drew mixed reactions. Many viewers were inspired by this triumphant message of hope. Reeve himself considered the advertisement a "motivating vision of something that can actually happen."[15] Other reactions landed somewhere in the realm of confusion and anger. Many spinal cord injury clinics were bombarded with inquiries from people with disabilities about how to obtain the remedy that cured Reeve.[16] Disgruntled disability advocates interpreted the advertisement as Reeve blatantly denying the reality of his own physical condition.

National and international press coverage of the advertisement was primarily positive. However, many reporters asked Reeve to defend his participation in the commercial. On 31 January 2000, Reeve appeared on *Good Morning America* to answer the critics who found the advertisement distasteful. Reeve told Diane Sawyer that "the biggest problem . . .is people who have been in a chair for a very long time. . . . [I]n order to survive psychologically they have had to accept, 'Okay, I'm going to spend my life in a chair.' So I get shots from some of them, you know, that—that I don't know what I'm talking about. Well, I'm certainly not an expert, but I have access to the experts and they're not going to lie."[17] Instead of settling the matter, Reeve's interview fueled more debate on how to properly respond to physical disability.   ∎

Even a cursory glance at Reeve's postinjury interviews shows that he never intended to accept a life with a disability.[18] He saw his condition as temporary, something curable through future developments in spinal cord injury research. Reeve had raised what many considered false hope and others took as suggesting that "people in chairs" should fight to get up and walk. What values played in his advertisement and in responses to it?

The Nuveen advertisement evoked an argument regarding the value of the human body. What is the body, and what should the body be? Reeve's agenda, as illustrated in the commercial, values able-bodiedness as the preferred condition of life. In his interview with Diane Sawyer, he seems to criticize an acceptance of physical disability, seeing such tolerance as a hindrance to a person's assumed desire to be "normal" and ambulatory.

The disability rights movement disagrees. This movement is a community of politically motivated people with disabilities that since the 1960s has been fighting for a new and empowered value of the disabled body in the United States. Unlike Reeve's advocacy, the work being done by these people challenges culture to see disability not as something to be overcome but as something to be embraced as a contributor to personal and communal identity. Sum Linton, a leader in the disability rights movement, has attested to this in her statement: "We have found one another and found a voice to express not despair at our fate but outrage at our social positioning. Our symptoms, though sometimes painful, scary, unpleasant, or difficult to manage, are nevertheless part of the dailiness of life."[19]

Linton's comments offer a moral critique of Reeve and his digitally manipulated walk—namely that it forced viewers to place a higher value on people with disabilities who fight for a cure than on those who fight to eliminate stigma. The advertisement is a potentially devaluing text, one that classifies people according to their physical (in)capabilities. Rather than allowing a sort of disability contentment, the advertisement seems to say that living with a disability is ultimately a negative experience. Such a critique employs loyalties to the larger disabled community. Linton, who is a person with a disability herself, works fiercely for the disabled community when she writes or speaks.

Reeve's actions were motivated by loyalties as well, specifically to people who shared his condition. Such a loyalty is expressed clearly in his book, *Nothing Is Impossible: Reflections on a New Life* (2002). In the book, Reeve lays out a research program that, if implemented and funded by the U.S. government, would benefit all who "suffer" from the effects of spinal cord injury. Such loyalties are apparent in the Nuveen commercial as well.

So why the disconnect between Reeve as a person with a disability and the disability rights community? Why couldn't Reeve team up with the disability community in his efforts? The answer is that Reeve's advocacy for a cure illustrates his longing for an able body and his discontent with his disabled body. A person with such a view could not work cooperatively with a community whose identity is rooted in disability and whose goal is to integrate the disabled body within the normative cultural experience.

Western media always has overvalued the healthy body, often promoting impossible ideals of perfection and wholeness. DaVinci's *David* speaks volumes about ideal shape. On the contrary, media have depicted the disabled body as a symbol of deviance from the norm, as something to be dealt with and cured.[20] Think, for example, about most of the villains in the James Bond films—many are physically disfigured or disabled, the symbolism of which connects to their "evil" intentions. One could speculate that because Reeve played such a prominent role in Western media, both as an actor and as a celebrity, idealized characterizations of the body were unintentionally impressed on him by the press and his fans. Needing to remain in the good graces of the media to gain public support for his agenda, it could be argued that Reeve's devaluing of the disabled body was a product of necessity.

However, Reeve missed an opportunity to help people with spinal cord injuries see value in their disabled conditions. In other words, rather than force these folks to see their bodies as being broken and in need of a cure, Reeve, through his celebrity status, instead might have used the media to portray himself as a person living a meaningful life, even with a disability. In walking again in the Nuveen advertisement, Reeve rejected such a possibility and consequently declared that being disabled was a state of being no one should want or accept.

NOTES

1. Gerry Spence, *From Freedom to Slavery* (New York: St. Martin's Griffin, 1995), p. 177.
2. See Clifford Christians and Kim B. Rotzoll, "Ethical Issues in the Film Industry," in *Current Research in Film: Audiences, Economics, and Law*, vol. 2, ed. Bruce A. Austin (Norwood, NJ: Ablex, 1986), pp. 225–237.
3. "Whose Values Run Hollywood?" *USA Weekend*, 23–25 October 1992, p. 8.
4. Federico Mayor, *The World Ahead: Our Future in the Making* (New York: UNESCO, 2001), pp. 300–301.
5. "China Grows More Aggressive in Thwarting Counterfeits," *USA Today*, 21 April 2006, p. 4B.
6. Ibid.
7. Quotation and background material from Edward de Grazia and Roger K. Newman, *Banned Films: Movies, Censors, and the First Amendment* (New York: R. R. Bowker, 1982).
8. United States Attorney General's Commission on Pornography (1986). The report is summarized in Michael J. McManus, "Introduction" to *Final Report of the Attorney General's Commission on Pornography* (Nashville: Rutledge Hill Press, 1986), pp. xix–xxi.
9. Linda Lovelace has written (with Mike McGrady) on her experience in prostitution and pornography, her victimization, terror, and exploitation in *Ordeal* (New York: Bell Publishing, 1980).
10. McManus, "Introduction" to *Final Report*, p. 295.
11. Ibid., pp. 491–492.
12. Material in this case is from *The New York Times*, 22 November, 10 and 24 December 1975.
13. Patricia Holt, "Reeve Is 'Superman' for Real," *The San Francisco Chronicle*, 11 May 1998, p. D1.

14. This commercial may be viewed at www.youtube.com/watch?v=OFYSUPIZmeg.

15. John Williams, "Christopher Reeve's Super Bowl Ad Scored a Touchdown," *BusinessWeek Online*, 11 February 2000.

16. Robert McRuer, "Critical Investments: AIDS, Christopher Reeve, and Queer/Disability Studies," *Journal of Medical Humanities* 22:3–4 (Winter 2002): 221–237, 228.

17. Diane Sawyer and Christopher Reeve, "Two-Part Interview," *Good Morning America*, ABC News, 31 January to 1 February 2000; transcript accessed at www.more.abcnews .com, 11/30/2006.

18. For a complete archive of his public speeches and interviews, go to www.chrisreeve-homepage.com.

19. Simi Linton, *Claiming Disability: Knowledge and Identity* (New York: New York University Press, 1998), p. 4.

20. For more on depictions of disability in the media, see Paul K. Longmore, "Screening Stereotypes: Images of Disabled People," in Christopher Smit and Anthony Enns, eds., *Screening Disability: Essays on Cinema and Disability* (Lanham, MD: University Press of America 2001), pp. 1–19.

Media Scope and Depth

For every medium there is a scale; we may call it an "aesthetic scale." On one end are the serious artists and producers, careful about the integrity of their craft and insistent that their labors give audiences a better insight into meaningful human life. On the other end are writers and producers who want to provide the most popular product possible. They care little if lofty artistic visions are part of their work; theirs is the task of attracting the largest possible share of the audience—because if they do not, competitors will. Success is measured by best-seller lists and Nielsen ratings.

The pull of the media's commercial base inevitably may lead to television programs, movies, and books that trivialize human dilemmas or escape entirely from them. Perhaps forces resisting such trends are too weak to activate much of a counterthrust. Yet only the cynic will claim that money is really all that matters in popular culture, and only a misty idealist will assert that money does not matter at all.

Between the demands of art and the marketplace are a host of moral questions that media practitioners face every day: Must art be compromised when it passes from one medium to another? Are stereotyped characters fair to real people? How far should commercial concerns dictate cultural products? What is a fair portrayal of a religious or ethnic character on television?

In the first case in this chapter, "Reel History," the story of the Nixon presidency is retold with glaring historical boldness. Against this background, we have to ask what is truth if it fails to make emotional sense? In the second case we examine one of our most current vogues, reality television, with a particular look at *Paradise Hotel*, a program supposedly about love but more about anti-love, jealousy, fickleness, and young exhilaration gone sour. Did these contestants know what they were getting into? The third case, "Tragedy Lite," wonders if some human trauma goes too deep for fictionalized accounts of it. The fourth case ponders whether classic stories remade and remixed devalue the originals and obscure their authors' contributions.

Long before television, Justice Louis Brandeis wrote: "Triviality destroys at once robustness of thought and delicacy of feeling. No enthusiasm can flourish, no generous impulse can survive under its blighting influence."[1] Ought we to wink at mass-mediated entertainment—its romance and simplicity—or is the

291

beast really more fearsome than mad Dr. Frankenstein imagined? These cases raise the question and spotlight the moral issues.

70 Reel History

It was the most famous "nothing" in American history.

On 17 June 1972, five men broke into Democratic National Committee Headquarters at the Watergate office building in Washington, D.C. What at first appeared to be a second-rate burglary turned into one of the most devastating political scandals of all time. Suspicion grew that President Richard Nixon knew of or even approved the break-in. When it was discovered that Nixon secretly taped conversations in his office, the special prosecutor in charge of the Watergate investigation demanded that the President hand over his tapes. After months of legal haggling, the President relinquished some of the tapes, including one of a 20 June 1972 conversation between him and top aide Bob Haldeman. Right in the middle of the tape, prosecutors discovered 18½ minutes of nothing—a blank space that interrupted the Nixon–Haldeman discussion about what to do concerning Watergate. Prosecutors quickly suspected that the tapes had been tampered with.

What was said during the missing 18½ minutes has been a topic of speculation ever since. No one really knows what was said—until now. In his three-plus hour docudrama *Nixon*, writer and director Oliver Stone reveals that the tampered tapes contained a Nixon confession that he planned and supervised "Track II," a 1960 assassination plot against Cuban President Fidel Castro. Apparently, Nixon explained to Haldeman that the mission involved a cooperative effort between the CIA and the Mafia, but the election of John Kennedy thwarted the plan. The film hints at some connection between Nixon's work on Track II and the Kennedy assassination.

Critics of *Nixon* were livid, while fans cheered Stone's portraiture. Gene Siskel and Roger Ebert gave it an "epic thumbs up, way up,"[2] and other reviewers crowned it "brilliant," "intriguing," and "extraordinary."[3] Anthony Hopkins and Joan Allen (playing Richard and Pat Nixon, respectively) were rewarded with Best Actor and Best Actress nominations.

Others were less impressed, however. Howard Rosenberg blasted the film on ethical and aesthetic grounds,[4] whereas most critics launched their response against Stone's alleged cavalier handling of the historical record. Foremost among the complaints was the Castro assassination story line, but Track II was not the only bit of scriptwriting that had film critics and Nixon scholars scratching their heads. Among the other surprising "revelations":

- Nixon secretly met with right-wing fanatics in the Texas desert. They promised to deliver the White House in 1964 if Nixon would run, and again in 1968, even if political victory meant the elimination of certain Kennedys along the way.
- These same extremists threatened to bring Nixon down in 1972 when they perceived he had become soft on the far-right agenda.
- Nixon was a heavy drinker, often inebriated in the presence of aides, albeit sober in public and with visiting dignitaries.
- Nixon lost the 1960 television debate to Kennedy because Kennedy divulged the Cuban invasion plans while Nixon, as vice president, could not discuss them.
- Nixon and wife Pat came close to divorce several times.

When Oliver Stone was publicly chided for such historical revisionism, he produced a screenplay annotated with hundreds of footnotes from over 100 sources, an introduction containing twelve articles defending the accuracy of his film, and a 200-page bibliography of Watergate documents and tapes.[5]   ■

What does it mean for a docudrama to "tell the truth"? Clearly, many historically questionable details and events were included in *Nixon* for the purpose of dramatic impact. Some events, such as a scene in which Nixon aide John Dean and burglar E. Howard Hunt meet on a bridge, definitely did not occur.[6] Other events, such as Nixon's involvement in the alleged Castro plot, or the meeting between Nixon and extremists in the Texas desert, are highly unlikely.[7] But, as Stone said, this type of loose commitment to historical accuracy has always been part of the genre.[8] One critic ruefully pointed out that an artistic retelling of history can be traced back at least as far as Shakespeare.[9] Stone is right when he reminds his critics that all observers of history, including filmmakers and professional historians, view the past through their own agendas and biographies.[10] What is important, Stone insists, is that storytellers get the "deeper truth" right.[11]

Los Angeles Times media critic David Shaw remarked that one of the worst examples of the dangers of docudrama was the CBS production of *The Atlanta Child Murders*, the story of convicted child killer Wayne Williams (implicated in twenty-three homicides, convicted of two). The obvious slant of *Child Murders* portrayed Williams as the victim of circumstantial evidence. CBS did precede the two-part show with an advisory that the program "is not a documentary but a drama based on certain facts. . . . Some of the events and characters are fictionalized for dramatic purposes." Viewers were left to their own knowledge of the case to sort out the factual from the fictionalized scenes. Shaw called this kind of television product the "bastardization and confusion of fact and fiction."[12]

Professor Gregory Payne was a consultant to NBC during the making of *Kent State*, a docudrama of the 4 May 1970 National Guard shootings of four university students. Although he is a proponent of the docudrama genre, Payne has meticulously described the fictionalized interactions of guardsmen and students in *Kent State*. For example, the burning of the ROTC building at Kent State on May 2 has never been definitively explained, and only last-minute insistence by consultants and actors kept those ambiguities intact. Payne observes that whatever were NBC's exaggerations (such as building much of the drama around Allison Krause's romance), they were nothing compared with the distortions of James Michener's book *Kent State: What Happened and Why*.

At a conference in Boston, actor Rick Allen, who played guardsman Wesley in *Kent State*, noted that his portrayal of being overcome with tear gas and retreating from the line of march was pure fiction intended to humanize the "bad guys" and, in addition, to win a couple of seconds of additional on-camera time (valuable for a young actor). Allen was troubled that history was being written for thousands of viewers on the basis of a director's urging his people to ad-lib.

In 1988, the plight of surrogate mother Mary Beth Whitehead put a spotlight on the womb-for-hire business and its legality. Whose child was Baby M? Her natural mother's or William and Elizabeth Stern's, who held the contract? (William was the natural father through artificial insemination.) ABC would help the nation decide with a four-hour, $6 million docudrama. Since neither the Whiteheads nor the Sterns would cooperate, ABC used court transcripts, published accounts, and psychiatric evaluations made public with court records. Of course, the obligatory disclaimer preceding the telecast notes that "certain scenes and dialogue are interpretive of this material."[13]

In 1644, John Milton was confident that truth would emerge in a free marketplace of ideas. Though falsehood might grapple for a while, human rationality eventually would make the distinctions, since the universe could not end on a lie. In 1985, psychiatrist M. Scott Peck began to forge a new vocabulary based on clinical observations that in some people, deception becomes truth and leads to the grim realities that destroy their lives.[14] Perhaps human rationality is not as powerful as the great liberal democrats believed. And if not, is truthtelling all the more a moral imperative, as fragile of understanding as we are?

Is the docudrama genre a powerful vehicle for reviving our culture's important stories or a cheap distortion based on television's insatiable need for new material?

In favor of docudrama: How many students would know or care about Kent State's Allison, Jeff, Sandy, and Bill were it not for the efforts of NBC, albeit profit-tinged, to give new life to that fateful spring weekend in northeast Ohio? Few, we suspect. How many dry eyes and stoic hearts walked out of theaters after *Mississippi Burning* (a film about three murdered civil rights workers that fictionalized the FBI investigation), unmoved by the suffering and careless about the future of racial justice? Journalist Bill Minor covered the Freedom Summer of 1964 and won the Elijah Lovejoy Award for "most courageous weekly editor in the nation" after his exposure of Klan activity in Mississippi. He defended *Mississippi Burning* as "a powerful portrayal." For viewers who depend on film for stories not experienced firsthand, the movie "got the spirit right."[15]

If a film recreates the texture of an event such that participants can affirm the veracity of context and struggle, is that not sufficient? History is more than mere facts, and no story corresponds exactly to events. Perhaps the docudrama is our best vehicle for keeping at bay those who claim the Holocaust, for example, never occurred. Yet audiences can do amazing things with a story. One high school audience admitted to believing, after seeing Stone's version of the 1960s, that Lyndon Johnson had conspired to murder John Kennedy. When confronted with that reaction, Oliver Stone replied: "I am not responsible for the interpretation that an audience takes away. Sometimes it [the film] is misinterpreted."[16] But in this case, apparently, no one is saying.

The crucial variable is the judgment of the subject. If a docudrama wins the approval of those closest to the real-life drama, viewers are ensured that a truthful perspective on events survives the dramatic process. If the subject cannot recognize his or her struggle for all the romantic clichés and garbled characterizations, we rightly worry that rampant revisionism threatens to obscure and distort the meaning of the past. Morally sensitive producers of docudrama will incorporate fictional elements without padding history or violating the pain of those whose stories they tell.

---

71 They Call It Paradise

Summer season 2003. Networks are struggling for viewers. How to get the right ages, the right consumers, inside to watch television instead of outside under the sun or on the beach? Fox Television answers with a beach and a pool and sun on the screen, populated by tanned young adults, bikinis, kissing contests, faded-gray shots of bedroom snuggling, and the "tension" of each contestant trying to ingratiate himself or herself to the others so as not to be forced to "leave paradise, *forever!*"

Paradise Hotel began its run in July. Each week a new player was added from among thousands of viewers applying to get on the show. Newcomers had to prove their sexuality to the group at the hotel, who coaxed libidinous data from each wannabe before voting admittance. And each week someone at the hotel had to leave, usually amid tears and bravado mixed to hide the shame of exclusion. Host Amanda Byram kept her sturdy demeanor throughout, as if she were den mother to these eleven young twenty-somethings assembled at a resort in Acapulco to do nothing but drink, play, and touch. Five couples shared rooms, but one person was always left out, cast into the black room, as it were. Cameras and microphones recorded the smooching, the primping, the push-ups, the sipping, and mostly the gossiping, as this "lords of the pool" group sorted out their all-important relationships and defended the one part of their person that this unscripted reality show sought to exploit—sexuality. Indeed, at the start of each episode, Byram admonished her troop—these ripped and supple postteens were promised no money and given no incentive other than to prove their cool—you either hook up or pack up. ■

Reality television uses no scripts. The setup generates the story, but the ending is unpredictable. Stars are not so different from viewers, and in the genius of the creators of *Paradise*, viewers become stars each week. Of course, some sort of fuel must propel whatever happens, and that fuel is normally sex or wealth or both. For viewers, there's the mystique of a relationship built on the flimsiest basis: Will it take? For contestants, there's a short moment of fame, and for some, the hope of a casting director's call.

Contestants on *Paradise*, however, were not promised money and were not likely to break into professional acting. The incentive, then? Simply that eleven cuties get a free sandy-beach, big-king-bed vacation together. The setting called to mind the omnipresent cameras of *The Truman Show*, but in this case, all eleven allowed their hormones to rage and their pettiness and sobbing to become entertainment for millions. Kant, frankly, could not approve. That might be a minuscule worry to producers of this show, if only advertisers did approve. The persons on this show were means to an end, pure and simple. Though each player chose freely to come, the normal progression, visible any week, was elation

("What a cool place") to disillusionment. The sulky twenty-one-year-old waitress from St. Paul, Charla, remarked, "They call it paradise, but it's not."

Reality television as a genre must face up to Kant's claim that each person should be valued, no one should be treated as fodder for another's exploitation. To violate this principle is more than "dissing" an eighteenth-century philosopher. It is, rather, to put human relationships in jeopardy. As the *The Hartford Courant* editorialized: "America's ravenous appetite for 'unscripted' reality shows reflects a cultural emptiness in an era of over-stimulation." Jane Eisner, columnist for *The Philadelphia Inquirer*, added: "We chase after money, good health and educational status, thinking they bring happiness; we deride marriage and faith, not believing they bring happiness; we waste our time watching dumb entertainment. . . . " And producer Aaron Spelling cogently testified, "The reality trend makes me puke."[17]

Paradise Hotel is an opera of raging hormones played by emotionally vulnerable young adults led to believe that sun, surf, and sex represent the ultimate human environment. The ethic of duty and human care imagines that people, to prosper and mature, must discover the resilience to endure trouble with hopefulness, to plot a course that contributes to others, and to satisfy the appetite for happiness indirectly, in vocation and service, or in strong, long-term relationships. *Paradise Hotel* undermines our best wisdom about happiness with its visceral, short-lived, superficial unreality. Paradise it's not.

72 Tragedy Lite

When Roberto Benigni, the director, writer, and star of the 1998 film *Life Is Beautiful*, jumped up on his chair in his excitement to get his Oscars for Best Actor and Best Foreign Language Film, many people were thrilled with both his over-the-top acceptance speech and the film itself, a comic "fable" about the Holocaust. Others, however, including some concentration camp survivors, were far less pleased. Even at its initial screening, the film provoked widely differing reactions; some critics found it to be a uniquely uplifting triumph, whereas others were disgusted and greatly disturbed by it.

The first half of the film is the charming but conventional story of Guido, an Italian Jew, who falls in love and courts Dora, finally carrying her off, in true romantic style, on a white horse. In the second half of the film, however, the tone changes drastically when, in the midst of planning for a birthday party, Guido and his four-year-old son Joshua are taken away to a Nazi concentration camp. What makes the film unique, and also the cause of the controversy surrounding it, is that director Roberto Benigni presents even this second part of the film as a semicomic fable. We enter the world of one of the greatest horrors of the last century, but we find ourselves laughing and being uplifted. Benigni elicits these responses through a brilliant conceit: Guido must protect his son from the terrible reality around them by pretending that, as a surprise birthday present, they have come to the camp to participate in a game.

Guido begins by telling his son that they have joined an elaborate contest in which they compete with the other prisoners for the prize of a real tank. One of the best examples of the comic potential of this situation occurs when they first get to the camp. A German officer enters their barracks, and although Guido does not speak German, he offers to translate the camp instructions into Italian so that Joshua will only hear his invented rules for the "game." While the guard lists rules in German, Guido translates, "You'll lose points for three things: One, if you cry. Two, if you want to see your mommy. Three, if you're hungry and you want a snack. . . . Don't ask for any lollipops. You won't get any. We eat them all."

Amazingly enough, Guido is able to pull off this major deception; this feat is partly possible because Benigni's camp has almost no violence or terror. Benigni does hint at those aspects of the concentration camps that he assumes his audience will recognize: The child's grandfather is sent to the showers, and the boy himself ignores the call for all the children to go take a shower and thus survives. Late in the film, however, there is one scene in which Guido is carrying the sleeping Joshua back to bed, and he stumbles upon a staggering mound of corpses in the mist. He backs away, and shortly after this, we see the chaos of the Germans leaving as the Allies enter the area to liberate it. Guido tells Joshua to hide for the last time, but he himself is caught by a guard and killed off-screen. Joshua has survived the Holocaust having never even realized he was experiencing anything but a game. A voiceover representing Joshua as an adult says, "This is the sacrifice my father made. This was the gift he gave to me," even as the young Joshua is reunited with his mother gleefully shouting that they have won the game.   ■

The controversy is seen in the extremes of the reactions of the reviewers. Some proclaimed it a masterpiece, but other critics wrote scathing opinions. The most notable of these have come from Jewish Holocaust survivors, who fear that such an easy-viewing version of the death camps may have too great an influence on younger viewers who likely never have seen more explicit narratives or documentaries. Some concentration camp survivors, however, greatly appreciated the film and felt that it showed respect for those who died in the camps.

Criticisms of the film generally focused around three separate but related issues. First, people condemned the complete lack of violence, terror, and the horrifying reality of the death camps. The film's camp was a sanitized version of the real thing. Children were not immediately taken from parents. Nazi officers did not shoot or even hit the deportees. Second, a number of critics argued that using the Holocaust for a comic fairy tale is always wrong because humor is completely out of place in such an event. And finally, others were offended that Benigni seemed to be presenting the message that love and imagination were all it took to overcome the horrors of concentration camps.

All three criticisms relate to the question of what ethical obligation a writer/director has in using a historical event that caused great pain to the survivors and the relatives of the millions of victims. Are all events fair game for comedy? Benigni, in response to the criticisms about his glossy presentation of a death camp, claimed that he never wanted to make a historically accurate Holocaust film and that he purposely referred only obliquely to some of the worst terrors. In a later interview with Graham Fuller, he said, "Historically the movie may have its inaccuracies. But it's a story about love, not a documentary. There's no explicit violence because it's not my style."[18]

The problem with the first argument that life in concentration camps can only be portrayed with detailed historical accuracy is that films will always distort and fail to recreate what many have called "indescribable." If filmmakers are not allowed to even attempt their own versions of horrific events, with the awareness that their films have to be palatable to a general audience if they wish them to be seen, we will have few, if any, Holocaust films for viewing by the general public. Film representations do educate and provoke controversies that then allow for further education. If artists do not feel the freedom to use the Holocaust story, the memory of it will fade, particularly for those people who do not have the stories of survivors as part of their family inheritance. So a demand for strict historical accuracy or true-to-life details would seem counterproductive in the end. But what about changing a horrifically tragic event into a comic, life-affirming tale?

The problem in recreating a painful, terrifying period of time in which survivors and relatives are still affected by the presentation is not only related to the filmmaker's historical accuracy or attention to detail but also to the message that accompanies the story. To present a fairly comic, sanitized death camp is to use our collective memories of what these camps were really like. This is problematic for both younger viewers who may not have many other visual memories of this period and for those for whom the actual memories contrast so greatly with this picture. If you combine this picture with a message that evil can be survived and transcended through love and imagination, you add to the feeling that you are not only using our sense of the "worst" moments a person can go through but also that you are using them to give a message of hope or survival that seems at odds with the experiences of most of those who actually lived in these camps. The picture may just be a fable, but it is a fable that is using our memories of a real event. One Holocaust survivor, Daniel Vogelmann, reports of his own father's return from Auschwitz without his child (whom Vogelmann sardonically notes was evidently not able to save his child with a clever story).[19] He contrasts Benigni's comic and triumphant view of life with his father's; he was able to proclaim that life was beautiful, but only with pain in his voice. For Vogelmann and others, the problem seems to be not merely the combination of humor and a death camp but also a sense of a too easy and glib response to the evils his father had experienced.

At the same time, Benigni was clearly aware of the risk he was taking in making a comedy about the Holocaust. One can certainly appreciate his ability to create a fable that in the end supports the values of courage, sacrifice, love, and compassion that were opposed by the Nazis. Individual moments in the film show great restraint and concern that his depiction of the camps not show any disrespect to the victims of Nazi violence. He has made a Holocaust film that can be seen by children—and this feat is both a triumph and a terror.

In fact, life is beautiful, tragic, hopeful, and desperate. An artist's vision of life may be outrageous but morally justifiable if those closest to the event depicted can affirm that they recognize the reality described and if some, at least, affirm the interpretation presented. Benigni polarized his audience but did not sacrifice his moral warrant. His "take," not universally applauded, is nonetheless a defensible effort to redeem a complex tragedy, the memory of which we keep alive in order never to repeat.

73 The League of Literary Makeovers

Director Stephen Norrington and 20th Century Fox released their summer would-be hit, *The League of Extraordinary Gentlemen*, in mid-July 2003. The cast was anchored by Sean Connery playing adventurer Allan Quartermain of *King Solomon's Mines*. Around him was an ensemble of literary figures: Jules Verne's Captain Nemo, Dorian Gray, Tom Sawyer (grown up as a secret agent), the great change-agent Dr. Hyde, and the bloodthirsty Dracula. Together the League weaves a tale of daring and international peacekeeping, acting under orders of a mysterious British boss, "M."

Reviewers called *The League* a long bore, tacky, far-fetched, and bogus. The action was quirky, and the setting, 1899, more than a century removed from its primary audience. So bad was the script and sketchy the plot that the film was gone from most theaters by the end of the month. Something about the mix of characters stretched fiction past credibility. The film bombed. ∎

Makeovers are a rage: new hair, different wardrobe, total color overhauls. Since continuity is the conservative approach to identity, youth and midlifers alike turn to the makeover as a star might move to a new constellation. The more radical the change, the more newsworthy and attention grabbing it is. Director Norrington became the makeover artist for fictional heroes whose personas had become passé. Of course, his ideas sprang from a comic book series, but he took the literary makeover to a new level.

The film failed, but what of the idea itself? Should Tom Sawyer, an American literary icon, be made over into a comic superhero?

The integrity of Mark Twain's genius presents one consideration. He gave us youthful Tom to help us laugh at ourselves, our less-than-perfect institutions, our prejudices. Tom Sawyer with Huck Finn was Twain's gift to the ages. An author cannot control the life of his fictional characters any more than Davy Crockett could control the persona made of him. Perhaps Twain therefore is obliged only to do his best work, offer it to readers, and then watch how his character adapts over time. Finally, in *The League*'s version, Tom Sawyer is hardly recognizable. Apart from Twain's market power, the film could have called its character Tom Smith. Nothing lost.

What about the viewer, especially the young viewer? Before a youngster can read a good novel, he or she may see a poor film. What happens to a young viewer who sees *The League* before trekking through Twain's book?

A culture requires change and constant renovation but also stability and shared heritage. Cultural stories are verbal and personal among preliterates but mediated in the postindustrial West. Yet we need stories, too—points of contact between each other and others from a different time. Literary classics help to fill that need. The integrity of those classics helps us to move toward a changing future with a common cultural base to anchor our past. Chances are the children of America will hear about Abe Lincoln for a very long time to come. Likewise, the tales of Robin Hood and Captain Ahab give us enduring icons of what we want to become and avoid. Should classic literary characters such as Nemo and Sawyer be preserved from fanciful makeovers? Romeo and Juliet have been updated, but still within the conflicting passions that led to their original tragedy. Shakespeare still sells despite the modern versions of his most famous characters.

Kant's categorical imperative is built on the foundation of a common human nature and universal sense of logic and reason. In a word, continuity is at the heart of Kant's ethic. We do not insist that Twain's Sawyer cannot be fashioned and formed to fit a new generation of readers, but we prefer a recognizable Sawyer, a Sawyer reflective of Twain's creation. For the sake of a culture that has quite enough change but precious little stability, we beg 20th Century Fox to let Tom remain a mischievous youth. When we need a secret agent to fill a part in a B-action film, there are plenty of writers capable of dreaming up a newcomer. Let the literary classics remain for all of us a repository of tales that we hold in common. It makes sense to do so, and it reminds us that people in our national past were not so different from people today.

NOTES

1. Louis Brandeis, with Samuel Warren, "The Right to Privacy," *Harvard Law Review* 4:15 (December 1890): 196.
2. Quoted in Howard Rosenberg, "Critics' View of 'Nixon': A Dirty Trick on History," *The Los Angeles Times*, 22 December 1995, p. F41.
3. Walter Goodman, "With Fact in Service to Drama," *The New York Times*, 3 January 1996, p. C9.
4. Rosenberg, "Critics' View of 'Nixon,' " p. C9.
5. Eric Hamburg, ed., *Nixon: An Oliver Stone Film* (New York: Hyperion, 1995).
6. Stephen J. Rivele and Christopher Wilkinson, "Critic's Ploy to Review 'Nixon' Is the Only Dirty Trick," *The Los Angeles Times*, 1 January 1996, p. F3.
7. Stryker McGuire and David Ansen, "Stone Nixon," *Newsweek*, 11 December 1995, pp. 68–70.
8. Hamburg, *Nixon*, p. xix.
9. Rosenberg, "Critics' View of 'Nixon,' " p. C9.
10. Hamburg, *Nixon*, p. xix.
11. Quoted in Charles W. Colson, "Demonizing Nixon Is the Least of Stone's Sins," *The Houston Chronicle*, 31 December 1995, p. 4C.
12. *TV Guide*, 20 April 1985, p. 5.
13. Tom Shales reported on and reviewed "Baby M." His column appeared in *The DuPage Daily Journal*, 20 May 1988.
14. M. Scott Peck, *People of the Lie* (New York: Simon and Shuster, 1985).
15. *Quill* (March 1989): 24–26.
16. Quoted in Richard Reeves, "Nixon Revisited," *The New York Times*, 17 December 1995, p. H41.
17. Quoted in *USA Today*, 21 February 2003, p. 15A, and 14 July 2003, p. D1.
18. Graham Fuller, "The Brave Little Film That Could," *Interview*, November 1998; accessed at www.findarticles.com/cf_dis/m1285/u11_v.28/21248649/print.jhtml.
19. Daniel Volgelmann, "Can One Write Fairy Tales About Auschwitz?" *Triangolo Ross*; accessed at www.deportati.it/film/benigni_debattito.htm.

Censorship

Censorship, one of the ugly words of the English language, speaks of the repression that democratic beliefs officially condemn. It warns of the consequences of state tyranny, church tyranny, union tyranny, corporation tyranny—the strong hand of any institution silencing the dissenting voice. *Liberty*, on the other hand, provokes cherished feelings that resonate with our deepest human longings—an elusive goal, perhaps, but worth the sacrifice required for each step in its advance.

So by our ideals we set the stage for the great paradox of democratic theory: Liberty can never be absolute; censorship can never be absent. Liberty requires constraints at every level—speech, sex, movement, health care, business, religious practice—in order for people to create an ordered society. That which we prize most must be taken in measured portions.

Few of our essential constraints partake of the spirit of Star Chamber repression in seventeenth-century England. The jailing and hanging of writers no longer occurs at the whim of a monarch. Yet many contemporary restrictions are nonetheless called "censorship." One of our fundamental questions, then, is where to draw the lines. This is the question of ethics.

At the end of World War II, the Hutchins Commission on Freedom of the Press struggled over this question as it deliberated toward a theory of press freedom that would promote social responsibility as a new and important concept in media studies. All the commission members were ardent democrats; some might even be called dreamy-eyed in their praise of democratic virtues. True liberals in the historic sense, they held free inquiry to be paramount. Yet they wrestled with the question of censorship. The chief philosopher of the commission, William Ernest Hocking of Harvard, captured the dilemma poignantly in an essay written as plans for the commission were being laid:

> Are . . . thoughts all equally worthy of protection? Are there no ideas unfit for expression, insane, obscene, destructive? Are all hypotheses on the same level, each one, however vile or silly, to be taken with the same mock reverence because some academic jackass brings it forth? Is non-censorship so great a virtue that it can denounce all censorship as lacking in human liberality?[1]

The first case in this chapter points the moral compass at one of the most popular entertainment figures in the world. We wonder if an artist can ethically assault moral values if he claims not to *really* mean it. The second case finds moral boundary lines drawn once again by force of law and moral logic, not to everyone's pleasure, to be sure. The third case focuses our attention on the most destructive impulses that we as humans feel. Mediated experience gives vent to those feelings but also may propagandize and convert too many of us for public comfort and safety. The moral outcome of our last case will depend on how you read art and what role popular art plays in sorting out human affairs.

While the reader puzzles with us over these democratic conundrums, we may be encouraged in the knowledge that to do so—to read this book and think about these questions—is testimony that we are at least on the way to answers. In too many societies, the range of permissible media is tightly defined by a powerful elite. At least we can claim the advantage of a bias toward latitude: Censorship must be justified. In these cases, we ask whether modern censors have demonstrated their case for building dikes against the flood.

74 The Voice of America

The white rapper Eminem, the blue-eyed, backwards-capped, genius of rhyme, has sold upwards of 20 million CDs, appeared in film, and runs a successful recording company. If "he didn't care," as the lyrics suggest, at least he works hard at it. *Rolling Stone* lauds his work ethic, calling him "the Voice of America," the "original gangsta," all "hip-hop swagger and hard-rock self-loathing."[2]

If Eminem is America's voice, it's a country of angry young adults, disillusioned by whatever, delighted to "dis" any cultural zone once recognized as prima facie worthy of respect, from family relationships to the president. Religion is in the "post-dis" zone—not even on the screen. At the same time, Eminem cannot be cornered; he resists stereotypes. If he hates his mother, he loves his daughter. As he projects the image of the "entertainer you love to hate," he seems increasingly popular. Although antiestablishment, he is the center of a multimillion-dollar business.

American entertainment has always celebrated the performer on the fringe, from Elvis' hips to George Carlin's "seven dirty words." Yet Eminem's robust popularity has created a new and different class of star: young, caustic, and platinum rich. In "Sing for the Moment," he celebrates the disconnectedness of youth, the inner anger that seeks a cause, but absent a cause will protest anyhow:

Walking around with his headphones blaring
    Alone in his own zone and he don't care . . .
    His thoughts are whacked,
    he's so mad he's talking back
    Talking black, brainwashed from
    rock and rap.

Eminem's high-charged "own zone" may be redefining America and the West. When those schooled by his music come of age, what will they believe? How will they live? Toward what will they aim?

Rap is not so much a message as a snapshot of emotions. Rappers and fans play dress-up in the various emotions of the "music." The overloaded anger, brutality toward women, and rejection of tradition that typify rap are like a set of new clothes, a word game that carries little more than play-at-it ferocity, if you allow the argument of fans who listen to rap but still say please and thank you and finish their homework.

Prosocial rap is a contradiction in terms. Rap aims at a culture's hypocrisies; it releases the pent-up anger of minorities long repressed by the values of moral elites. Were rap to turn prosocial, it would oppose its own opposition. Make sense? Why not?

Every moral principle holds this in common: the prize of doing well. For Kant, that prize was coherence—a life lived as life ought to be, rational and ordered, contributing capably to the "kingdom of ends." For Rawls, the prize was social fairness, a level playing field for all participants. What, then, if coherence is the enemy, and the assumption that everyone wants to play (why else work so hard for fairness?) turns out not to matter: No one shows up at the whistle.

The collective wisdom of humanity's moral imagination distinguishes between good and bad behavior, good and bad attitude, and good and bad intention. These distinctions play out differently by eras and cultures, but they always show up. Intrinsic to human nature is the embrace of good and the rejection of evil. What if that distinction is itself the target of reproach and reaction? Where does the human soul go when the very idea of an end point is sick, ugly, boring, old, and hateful?

Rap castigates and criticizes. Good entertainment, whether comedy or tragedy, must do so. But Eminem offers nothing to fill the vacuum. Rather, he admits repeatedly throughout his albums that his lyrics are not to be taken seriously. They are feelings from the angry/hopeless side of his persona, Slim Shady. If the minds of rap's listeners are indeed whacked and brainwashed, that itself is not a moral point, just an observation. The problem child in Eminem's messed-up world has nowhere to turn, not even inward. Apart from the loner's conduit to rap itself—the message through the headphones—there is nowhere to go with nothing positive to do. For America's great "problem child," problem solving is a matter of volume up.

Nihilism disguised as rhyme and artistry finally makes nonsense even of its own sense. There is no "problem child" apart from a problem an aberration from what should be. Eminem rejects every "should be" and has no right, therefore, to call anything a problem or to register anger at anyone. To do so anyway—without moral warrant—is sheer self-infatuation—the very heart of every Eminem protest. No human life can prosper as a self-absorbed pod, blinkered by headsets, streamed by contradictions, nurtured by incoherence, in love with anger and angry with love. To live in the emotional world the rapper describes is to expire as a human person, which even a rapper moving toward 40 million in CD sales would not advise.

Entertainment media must offer something worth living for. Those who claim otherwise are conning the audience. And even the best con eventually burns out. Adrenaline alone cannot sustain us. Escapist entertainment is only as good as the return to reality. No one can honestly enter the *Total Recall* world without a passage back.

"Confused" is the motto embroidered on Eminem's backwards baseball cap. That's okay, for confusion can be the forerunner and catalyst to solution. It's time for America's richest rap voice to acknowledge even his own accountability to articulate an answer. And it's time for millions of fans to ask for one.

75 Fencing the Net

Most rental stores keep adult videos on the back shelves, and porn magazines are covered or behind the counter. But it is hard to hide adult content on the Internet. With a click, anyone may go to one of over 100,000 adult sites to view or read sexually explicit messages of the sort that clandestine industries once grew fat on.

For years, federal legislators have wrung their hands about protecting public morality while honoring historical commitments to freedom of speech. The latest attempt was the Children's Internet Protection Act (CIPA). The act linked federal funding for public libraries to filtering software that would prevent children from unhealthy exposure to material beyond their maturity. Adults using library systems could ask that filters be disabled. As soon as CIPA became law in 2000, a federal suit challenged its constitutionality.

CIPA was not the first effort to curb Internet pornography. The Communications Decency Act (CDA) in 1966 was expansive and far-reaching—too far, said the United States Supreme Court. Then followed the Child Online Protection Act (COPA), which clarified some of the problematic language in the CDA, but not enough to pass muster with the High Court, which followed a long tradition (since the 1950s) that government must show a compelling interest and use the narrowest means possible to achieve that interest. In effect, any plan that restricts lawful material from adult users cannot survive, which means that any plan limiting access to children cannot at the same time limit adults. For the Internet, that was a difficult distinction.

CIPA is much less expansive. It touches only public libraries. It works like a light switch—on for adults, off for kids. Its incentive is financial. Everybody appears to get everything they want, except children, who never get everything they want. And never will. ■

So said the Supreme Court in a six-to-three decision rendered in June 2003. Protecting children is okay, said the majority, and doing so through filters on public library computers is okay. It's the least intrusive means of protecting the innocence of youth without baby-bibbing the maturity of adults. Loyalties are the key to understanding this latest, and the only successful, effort to curb the spread of Internet porn.[3]

Loyalty to the Constitution's First Amendment is, of course, the Court's first priority. Obscenity is illegal, but proving to a jury that a website or a video is obscene is so difficult today that very few prosecutors waste their time and political capital bringing such cases. The Miller standard, established in 1973, requires the state to prove that a given product hits three "prongs" before it can be judged obscene and penalties applied. Those prongs are necessarily difficult to hit and more so after more than thirty years of mostly missed shots and embarrassed prosecutors.

But the Court also recognizes the responsibility of legislators to exercise their responsible oversight of public interests, including a vaguely understood interest in raising healthy children. The alternatives all carry social costs: juvenile courts, jails, special-education programs, crimes of violence. It is not difficult for the state to show that loyalty to children requires fences to be placed around certain material that would, in the best judgment of people who know child development, contribute to delinquency or significantly impede a child's chances of emerging into the adult world intact, able to function and contribute, motivated to work, and willing to operate within the law.

Not everyone drew the lines as the Court saw them. For many, including the American Library Association (the named defendant in this action), CIPA imposed federal oversight in spaces best left to local counsel. Who better than an Ingham librarian should know what material is good and proper for children in that county? Let the local professional decide, not the Washington bureaucrat, many urged. Only at the local level could "bugs" associated with filtering software be worked out and community integrity preserved.

John Rawls' veil of ignorance offers a strategy for sorting out competing loyalties. He urges that in the "original position" where social indicators have melted away and no party to a negotiation knows what social role he or she may occupy when the deal is cut, the deal tends to favor the least powerful player and therefore achieves something close to justice. At least the result will be fair, because a deal so achieved disregards the special interests of the rich and powerful. Rawls gives weight to the interests of children in this case, even if children are not at the deal-making table. Perhaps the best the veil can do for children is to ask of adults whether childhood is better for the bargain. Few adults would insist that their own childhood would have been better served by free access to sexually explicit material. CIPA is a small infringement on the freedom of a child to read and view. The Court reflects the culture's belief that such an infringement is still better than the risks of open access to forbidden knowledge.

76 Frontal Assault

Stormfront.org began as a private dial-in bulletin board in 1990 for members of the David Duke campaign to communicate. In 1995, Stormfront was the first extremist hate-speech site posted to the Internet. It now reportedly attracts 15,000 visitors daily. Visitors are greeted by a Celtic cross surrounded by "White Pride World Wide" and "Stormfront.org"

continued

in a gothic font. Don Black, who created the site, calls Stormfront a white nationalist re-source page for "those courageous men and women fighting to preserve their White West-ern culture, ideals and freedom of speech and association—a forum for planning strategies and forming political and social groups to ensure victory."[4]

Don Black's involvement as a white nationalist began in high school as he distributed white power literature. At the age of seventeen, Black organized a chapter of the White Youth Alliance, an organization led by David Duke. Black also joined the Ku Klux Klan and climbed the ranks, becoming the grand wizard (national leader). A year after becoming grand wizard, Black and nine other white supremacists were arrested as they prepared to invade the small Caribbean island of Dominica to establish a "white state." Black served two years in prison, where he learned computer skills. On his release from prison, he said, "I am here to build the greatest white racist regime this country has ever seen."[5] He re-signed from the KKK, moved to West Palm Beach, Florida, and began using his computer knowledge to further his white nationalist agenda.

Black uses the Internet to promote his ideas worldwide. According to Black, "We pre-viously could only reach people with pamphlets and by sending tabloid papers to a limited number of people, or holding rallies with no more than a few hundred people—now we can reach potentially millions of people."[6] People from around the world access Storm-front, which offers German- and Spanish-language sections. "We have recruited people to our point of view, many people which we otherwise wouldn't have reached. Sites such as Stormfront which are interactive, provide those people who are attracted to our ideas with a forum to talk to each other and to form a virtual community," said Don Black on an *ABC News Nightline* interview.[7] The virtual community can be reached through Stormfront's White Nationalist Community Forum (www.stormfront.org/forum). According to Black, the forum exists "to provide information not available in the controlled news media and to build a community of white activists working for the survival of our people." The forum has over 17,000 members, and over 500,000 messages have been posted. Included in the message boards are sections for news, announcements, and a general section with a va-riety of topics, including white nationalism ideology and philosophy, culture and customs, poetry, science/technology/race, privacy, self-defense, health and fitness, education and home-schooling. An activism section offers topics such as events and strategy, and oppo-nents can argue against white nationalism in an opposing-view section. The international section displays discussion boards on issues of interest to white nationalists in the fol-lowing geographic areas: Britain, Canada, Australia, New Zealand, France, Ireland, Italy, Spain, Portugal, Latin America, Netherlands, Serbia, Russia, South Africa, Sweden, Nor-way, Denmark, and Finland. Another aspect of the virtual community is the white singles section, where one can "meet other white nationalists for romance or friendship." Storm-front even maintains a calendar of members' birthdays.

In addition to the forum, the site exhibits essays covering a variety of issues about white nationalism, including affirmative action, immigration, racial differences, National Socialism, Zionism, and revisionist materials that deny the Holocaust occurred. In the essay "What Is Racism?" the author claims that whites are taught to be ashamed of their race, and "Who Rules America?" decries the control of the media over society and claims that Jews are masters of the media. The article calls for white nationalists to do whatever is necessary to break Jewish control. The site posted the "Color of Crime" study that "proves" blacks are more dangerous than whites. Stormfront offers a White Nationalism FAQs section, a well-articulated statement of their philosophy. In response to the first question, "What is White Nationalism?" the answer is: "The idea that Whites may need to create a separate nation as a means of defending themselves." Stormfront also reveals a collection of racist graphics and logos.

Stormfront has special versions of the Web page for women and children. The women's page (www.women.stormfront.org) is "not a feminist page, but rather a page to celebrate and honor Aryan women." Janice, Web master of the women's page, first became curious about Stormfront after a Don Black TV interview. She visited Stormfront and felt that Stormfront was not hate speech but pride in the white race. "I get angry with this whole hate thing because it's simply not true at all," she says. She wonders why it is permissible for other cultures to celebrate their race, but when European-Americans have "white pride" it's considered hate. Janice wrote on Stormfront's women's page:

> We must remain separate to maintain our past, our roots, who we are and where we come from. I do not want to mix with other cultures. I do not want to adopt their dress, their music, or anything about them. I want to keep what is mine, what I was born with. I can learn about the others, I can eat all kinds of weird other foods, but when I wake up in the morning, I'll still be a European-American.[8]

The women's page includes a "public service announcement" urging women to boycott any foods with Jewish kosher symbols so as not to support Zionism. The site presents sample kosher symbols, Janice's correspondence to companies requesting they remove the labels, and links to other anti-Semitic sites, including Aryan Nation's. The women's version of Stormfront also displays essays of and for women in the white racialist movement.

Derek Black, Don's teenage son, is said to be the Web master of Stormfront for Kids (kids.stormfront.org). Visitors to this site see two Celtic crosses and a banner announcing "White Pride World Wide." Derek greets fellow youth with a message: "I used to be in public school. It is a shame how many white minds are wasted in that system." Now homeschooled, he says that he is no longer attacked by gangs of nonwhites and spends most of the day learning rather than tutoring slower learners. He is finally learning to take pride in himself, his family, and his people, he says.

Stormfront for Kids provides activities that include a "hit the dots game," a kaleidoscope painter, optical illusion puzzles, and sound files of white-pride songs. Youth can learn about the history of the white race, view European flags, and follow a link to the "real" history about Martin Luther King, Jr. An animated U.S. flag constantly changes into a Confederate flag, and a child can follow an anti-kosher link to the women's page. ■

The enduring popularity of Stormfront, and its apparently growing worldwide appeal, points to a festering boil in many lives—a sense of victimization—and to the daffy extremes some will go to win a feeling of security amid self-imposed fears. A racist, above all, approaches the world with tightly conceived presuppositions about trust and community. Only those who fit a preferred model are welcome to the club.

None of the moral traditions used in this study can be marshaled to support Stormfront's race bias. Kant's universal duty speaks strongly against it. Rawls' justice game could never condones it. The idea that one could "love one's neighbors" by hating them is nonsensical. Only the most twisted pragmatic logic might render momentary support, until the facts are in and the logic of race exclusion fully calculated. Morally, Stormfront and its kin are bankrupt. Should a liberal, morally sensitive people permit an organization devoted to Stormfront's aims to communicate its message and perhaps convert others to its position?

Suppression is one tactic a culture can use to rid itself of tainted philosophy. Driving up the social cost of membership will reduce the benefits of joining and eventually marginalize or eliminate the movement. But utilitarian constraints can only contain, never defeat, dangerous and faulty ideas. At the end of the day, the attraction of hate—its (albeit perverted) sense of justice, its (albeit phony) sense of security—must be surrendered to a greater idea, a more satisfying way to live and think. That transaction occurs not under compulsion but in the open air of free choice.

Stormfront offers a worldview, a frame of reference, a "moral universe" to subscribers and followers of race-based prejudice. Its commitment to racism goes deep. Its preposterous political intentions are a fool's dream. But racism will not turn to neighbor-care unless its adherents are offered a better way by word and deed. As long as Stormfront does not act on its philosophy, let its creators have their space to brandish a way of life so morally impoverished and globally isolated that other free-space messages—justice and unconditional mutual regard—will overcome it. Kant and Rawls and Judeo-Christian agape will all give space for that.

77 Rescue Us

Launched in 2004 as a vehicle for comedian Denis Leary, *Rescue Me* capitalized on America's post-September 11 deifying of New York firefighters, albeit with a twist. Billed as a "dramedy" by the FX Network, *Rescue Me* would act as a worthy NYFD complement to their already successful LAPD Emmy-winning juggernaut, *The Shield* (2002), a gritty drama exposing the dark underbelly of America's "heroes."

At Engine House 62 in the Naked City, desires trump logic, and conflicts are resolved with schoolyard justice; may the bigger asshole win. Arguably, the biggest at Engine 62 is Tommy Gavin, played by Denis Leary, a character you hate to love; a psychotic megalomaniac whose unfettered duty to self is at once both repulsive and surprisingly refreshing, an alcoholic, forty-something Irish firelighter whose phantom conversations with both Jesus Christ and Gavin's dead cousin are the least of his problems.

High on "vitamin testosterone," low on political correctness, *Rescue Me* is a virtual Plato's Retreat* for the male ego, SpikeTV on E, big fires, big attitudes, bigger breasts. In the 20 June 2006 episode entitled "Sparks," there is an exhibition for the male rape-fantasy—the fantasy of women turned on by their attackers.*

*Plato's Retreat was a famous 1980's New York night club.

The plotline from the previous episode, "Torture," acts as a precursor to this culminating rape scene. Tommy Gavin's soon-to-be ex-wife, Janet, is sleeping with Tommy's brother, NYC police detective Johnny Gavin. Tommy sees it and avenges himself with a thorough Irish beat down of his philandering brother. Always a head case, in the closing minutes of the "Sparks" episode, Tommy arrives at Janet's apartment to discuss the pending divorce proceedings, including the division of material goods. What transgresses next shocks both dedicated fans of the show and television pundits.

As the discussion between characters escalates to rage, Tommy pushes Janet onto a nearby couch, receiving several face shots and pleas of "No" in the process. Fighting through her resistance, Tommy forcibly has intercourse with her or, in the opinion of many viewers and critics, rapes her. In addition to this violent and forced sex, what shocks viewers most is the scene's resolution, as Janet succumbs to the pleasurable, albeit brutal, nature of the act and seems to enjoy it. As Tommy exits the apartment with vindication on his face, viewers are stunned. Was this shock TV at its worst? Did the FX Network just condone its anti-hero Tommy as a violent rapist? Is this appropriate and responsible TV drama?

The promotional material for *Rescue Me* includes a tagline that hints at undercurrents of NYC firefighters' needing saviors of their own with the slogan, "They save us. But who saves them?" Yet, in the aftermath of the "Sparks" episode, many viewers questioned, "Who saves us from them?"

∎

Hollywood actor Don Cheadle, in the opening reel of 2005's Oscar-nominated film *Crash* comments on the alienation and disconnect of modern Los Angeles, resonating truths about humanity at large. "It's the sense of touch," he says, pausing, "We're always behind tin, metal, and glass. I think we miss that touch so much that we crash into each other, just so we can feel something."

Rescue Me is about crashing into each other. It's about men crashing into men, men crashing into fires, but ultimately, the cluster bomb: men crashing into themselves and the reality of their personhood. The "Sparks" episode reflects crashes at several levels.

Initially, the "Sparks" debate centered on whether the sexual encounter constituted a rape or just forced (and reluctant) sex between lovers and if there is a difference. Where is the line of consent? These are situational dilemmas and questions that psychologists and psychotherapists may ponder forever. However, what is definitive in the episode is Janet's initial physical refusal, followed by her seeming enjoyment, resulting in the ambiguity as to whether the act was "forced, then consensual" or "rape." For the sake of this examination, however, the act will be referred to as rape. And the question we address is not rape as an act but television drama that includes rape as part of a rocky, unpredictable, coarse, mutually intriguing relationship.

Is rape-TV appropriate for a cable audience?

Consider the viewers. The FX Network is available on cable TV only, making its viewing a form of paid-for-entertainment much like going to the theaters, downloading a CD, or buying a book. Implied in the purchase of this entertainment is the consumer's consent to the product. In short, viewers of *Rescue Me* have not been forced to watch the episode. They do so willingly, out of pocket, and with the foreknowledge of the product's tone and script strategy. In addition, it should be noted that *Rescue Me* airs at 10 P.M., a timeslot acting as a precaution against inappropriate age viewing.

The appropriateness of any art—in relation to the viewer—depends on the viewers' sensibilities. Viewers are the final watchdogs, filtering out the inappropriate through the program choices they make every day. Viewers familiar with *Rescue Me* tones and themes should find that a rape scene—while shocking in any circumstance—remains honest to the drama, not simply exploitative or shock-fodder TV. This is not *Bum Fights* or *Girls Gone Wild*. "Sparks" is a devastating, violent, complex extension of the storyline. And if cowriter Peter Tolan were in fact the writer of a post bearing his name, he said the day after: "The idea of any woman 'enjoying' being raped is repellant and caused all of us (and the network) a great deal of concern. But again, these are seriously damaged people who are unable to express their emotions—and so expression through brutality has become expected."[9]

Other entertainments, such as *A History of Violence*, a 2005 film starring Viggo Mortensen, follow similar logic. In that highly acclaimed film, Mortensen's character initiates sex with his wife only to be violently fought off, a scene culminating in both respect and passion. In some instances, sexually violent episodes, while unsettling, act as appropriate storyline progressions.

Some argue that violence and obscenity are of one cloth and that First Amendment protections cover both. Some argue the contrary: that First Amendment protections protect neither.[10] This debate, so polarized by High Court obfuscations and so little used in courtrooms today, will not help here.

The distinction between art and life helps to free the viewer to "hate the act" but "embrace the act's depiction." Art does not equate to advocacy. Showing violence is not preaching on its behalf. Excessive modesty flies in the face of reality. The audience and producers of *Rescue Me* have together created a "misfit hero" whose edgy art draws no easy answers. In a wonderful understatement, Tolan told *The New York Times*, "What Denis likes to write . . . is never the expected thing."[11] This is also, simply and really, what a lot of TV viewers like to see. As long as people can choose (the off-switch still works) and the drama has integrity (shock with purpose, albeit controversial), the viewer and producer may engage in morally troublesome material with their own integrity intact.

NOTES

1. William Ernest Hocking, "The Meaning of Liberalism: An Essay in Definition," in *Liberal Theology: An Appraisal*, eds. David E. Roberts and Henry P. Van Dusen (New York: Charles Scribner's Sons, 1942), pp. 54–55.
2. Keleta Sanneh, "The Voice of America," *Rolling Stone*, 24 July 2003 (927), p. 64ff.

3. *United States v. American Library Association*, decided 23 June 2003. The case is available on many sites, including www.supct.law.cornell.edu/supct/html/02-361.ZS.html.
4. Statement of the Anti-Defamation League on Hate on the Internet before the Senate Committee on Commerce, Science and Transportation, 20 May 1999.
5. www.stormfront.org, 2003.
6. Kent Faulk, "White Supremacist Spreads Views on Net," *The Birmingham News*, 19 October 1997, p. 1.
7. Ted Koppel, "Hate websites and the Issue of Free Speech," *ABC News Nightline*, 13 January 1998.
8. www.women.stormfront.org/writings/abouthate.html, 2003.
9. http://forums.televisionwithoutpity.com/index.php?showtopic=3130552&st=1050p=5521508&#entry5521508. post 1064.
10. Kevin W. Saunders, *Violence as Obscenity* (Durham, NC: Duke University Press, 1996).
11. Jacques Steinberg, "He's Cornering the Market on Misfit TV Heroes," *The New York Times*, 12 June 2007, p. B1.

Index